The Margins of Empire

The Margins of Empire

Kurdish Militias in the Ottoman Tribal Zone

Janet Klein

★

STANFORD UNIVERSITY PRESS

STANFORD, CALIFORNIA

Stanford University Press
Stanford, California

Printed in the United States of America on acid-free, archival-quality paper

Library of Congress Cataloging-in-Publication Data

Klein, Janet, 1969– author.
The margins of empire : Kurdish militias in the
Ottoman tribal zone / Janet Klein.
pages cm
Includes bibliographical references and index.
ISBN 978-0-8047-7570-0 (cloth : alk. paper)
ISBN 978-1-5036-0061-4 (pbk. : alk. paper)
ISBN 978-0-8047-7775-9 (electronic)
1. Turkey—Militia—History. 2. Turkey—Armed Forces—Minorities—
History 3. Kurds—Turkey—History. 4. Kurds—Turkey—Government
relations. 5. Turkey—Ethnic relations—History. I. Title.
UA817.K55 2011
355.3'708991597056—dc22
2010043991

For my parents

Contents

Acknowledgments

Many individuals and institutions contributed to the writing of this book. First and foremost, I wish to acknowledge the Fulbright-Hays fellowship, which allowed me to travel and live abroad to conduct research in multiple archives; the MacArthur Foundation / Center for International Studies; the Mellon foundation; and the University of Akron's Faculty Research Grant, which granted me the funds necessary to conduct additional research in France and Turkey.

The administration and staff of various libraries and archives made my research smoother and more pleasant. I thank in particular the staff at the Public Record Office in London; the Archives du Ministère des Affaires Étrangères in Paris and Nantes; the Archives du Ministère de la Défense, Château de Vincennes; the Nubar Pasha Library in Paris; the Institut Kurde de Paris; the Başbakanlık Osmanlı Arşivi in Istanbul; the Library of Congress in Washington, D.C.; Princeton University Library; the University of Montana Mansfield Library; and the staff involved with OhioLink and Interlibrary Loan at the University of Akron's Bierce Library. Vera Saeedpour was a unique and thought-provoking presence at the Kurdish Library in Brooklyn.

During my time at Princeton, M. Şükrü Hanioğlu taught me the nuances of late-Ottoman history and was always extremely generous with his time in checking my translations from Ottoman to English. Hamit Bozarslan, Heath Lowry, and Negin Nabavi offered invaluable comments on an earlier draft of this work. Norman Itzkowitz helped to train me in the lessons of Ottoman history and life, and Michael Cook was always available and forever humorous and helpful in his advice to me. At New York University, Khaled Fahmy, Zach Lockman, Farhad Kazemi, and Samira Haj challenged my thinking. Rifa'at 'Ali Abou-El-Haj was more inspiring to my intellectual development than I can express in words. He taught me to be my "own guru," and for this—and for his continued love, interest, and support—I am indeed grateful. Martin van Bruinessen and

Hamit Bozarslan, who have continuously supplied support, advice, and inspiration to me, have been particularly helpful as I explored the nuances of Kurdish history. Hamit Bozarslan and Cristina Cramerotti were especially hospitable during my stay in Paris. The late Şinasi Tekin helped to refine my understanding of the Ottoman language, and Michael Chyet and Birusk Tugan did their best to teach me proper Kurmanci (Kurdish), and although I let them down on many occasions with my mistakes I am indebted to their efforts. Many friends in Princeton helped me to think about my topic in new ways, and a number of them continue to provide me with feedback, friendship, and support. In particular I think of Christine Philliou, Herro Mustafa, Baki Tezcan, Jocelyn Sharlet, İpek Yosmaoğlu, Mike Reynolds, Orit Bashkin, Mustafa Aksakal, Milen Petrov, Jessica Tiregol, Asma Sayeed, Şuhnaz Yılmaz, Noha Bakr, Ronen Raz, Berrak Burçak, and Firoozeh Kashani-Sabet, who visited Princeton and became a friend and mentor.

My colleagues in the history departments at the University of Montana and the University of Akron have been supportive, helpful, and indeed fun. Diane Rapp, in Missoula, was ever ready with administrative support and comic relief. Kym Rohrbach and Wade Wilcox have been friends, support systems, and a constant source of levity. Martha Santos has gone through the book-writing process with me and has been a wonderful friend throughout. My students at both universities have provided me with rewarding discussions that have enriched my thinking.

My friends "on the outside" have also given me valuable insights and welcome distractions. Here I think of Chandra Sriram, Stephanie Harves, Stephanie Smith-Browne, Mary Newsome, Margaret Lo, Ping Foong, Helen Hauser, Genia Kozorovitskiy, Karen Ballentine, Ritsuko Yamamoto, Audrey Welber, Melina Pastos, Helena Hoas, Ken Lockridge, Michel Valentin, Anna Lockowich, Margaret Boyer, Karin Knight, Romy LeClaire Loran, Lis Bacus, Hilda Ahmed, Jehan Mullin, Resa Whipkey, Brian Bostaph, and Alan Savoy. Sinemkhan Bedir Khan and Salah Saadallah brought history to life for me as I spent time with them in the regions my study explores. My beloved companions—my rescue dogs, Elliot and Buzzy—have warmed my lap during the many hours I was at my computer. Lastly, my parents—Daniel and Heidi Klein—to whom I dedicate this work, have always been inspiring for their ethical principles, smarts, creativity, open-mindedness, and sense of humor.

This work would not be possible without the confidence, support, and advice of Kate Wahl, my editor at Stanford University Press. I feel so fortunate to be involved with an editor of such quality and integrity. Joa Suorez has also been very helpful and generous in responses to queries about my manuscript. Tim Roberts has been an insightful, supportive, and efficient production editor, and Andrew Frisardi has been not only a thorough and careful copy editor, but extremely patient as he worked through my long and messy bibliography. Barbara Roos was a speedy, thorough, and friendly indexer. The readers of my manuscript provided insightful and invaluable comments about my work. I thank them for inspiring me to consider additional angles and to refine my thoughts. Müge Göçek's discerning eye has been particularly helpful. She has gone beyond the call of duty in suggesting additional areas of inquiry and connection and in providing ever helpful words of support. Reşat Kasaba has also long been a source of encouragement and advice. I cannot close without acknowledging the archival help that Sait Özervarlı and Kamal Soleimani provided. While all of the institutions and individuals named above have contributed to the writing of this book in various ways, any errors in fact or interpretation are entirely my own.

As is so often the case in the "tribal zone," the battles of empire are continually refought across the pages of military histories; the wars that military brokers prosecute in their shadows go largely untold.

—Lawrence Bragge, Ulrike Claas, and Paul Roscoe, "On the Edge of Empire"

The Hamidiye Light Cavalry in the Ottoman Tribal Zone

★

Early in the spring of 1891, while heavy snows still blanketed their mountainous homeland, a group of influential Kurdish chieftains departed on a lengthy journey to the capital of the Ottoman Empire, whose borderlands they inhabited. It would be the longest voyage they had ever undertaken, through which they would blaze a trail for others. Used to a level of respect and deference accorded to them by their tribesmen and clients, the pomp and ceremony with which they were received in Istanbul was, however, a new experience. Dressed in special robes adorned with gold brocade befitting an audience with the sultan and caliph of the empire, these chiefs made their formal act of submission to His Imperial Majesty. In return they received decorations and the highest of distinctions during ceremonies that were at once solemn and festive, which were held in their honor.[1] Having prepared for this moment for weeks, it was the crown jewel in their long journey. They would stay in the capital for another two months, basking in the glory of their newly accorded honors, and would return to their distant homelands changed men.

Those who monitored these events, however, were very concerned. The British military attaché to the Ottoman Empire remarked that there was "general consensus of opinion native and foreign that a very large organisation with little or no modern discipline and with very shadowy government control is not likely to give good results and might lead to unpleasant incidents."[2] Soon, protests flowed from the pens of Ottomans and foreign observers alike over the activities and indeed the existence of these special Kurdish tribal cavalry units—the Hamidiye, named after

Sultan Abdülhamid II himself. Most of these complaints surrounded the unsavory activities with which this militia came to be associated—lawlessness, violence, and land-grabbing. But a few more insightful observers began to notice how the dynamics created by this militia, and particularly its fuzzy relationship to state power, were affecting much larger processes, not only in the six eastern provinces in which they were active, but across the empire as well. In the words of one British diplomat, writing one decade after the militia was first organized,

There is no doubt that the Hamidieh movement, the appointing of tribal leaders as colonels of regiments, has had and is having a great effect in consolidating various broken factions of Kurdish tribes, and mitigating in a great measure the want of unity and tribal authority which supervened when the great "derebeys" were exterminated by the Turkish Government 50 or 60 years ago. . . . The Turks have taken great trouble to get rid of the remnants of the old ruling families in Kurdistan, but now the various Hamidieh cavalry leaders, themselves created and given rank by the Sultan, bid fair to occupy the places of the lost "derebeys," and this, too, with good arms and a certain organization supplied them by the Government. . . .

The Kurds are quick to recognize the advantages of belonging to Hamidieh regiments, such as the possession of good arms, practical immunity from all civil law, and rank given to their chiefs; but for the other side of the contract they really care nothing, and use the advantages gained for furthering their own ends and advancing the Kurdish national spirit. When the Turks find themselves in difficulties elsewhere, the Kurds will bring this home to them.3

This leads us to ask the question: under what conditions does a state empower a group that it would ultimately prefer to suppress, and when does this actually serve to undermine the state's very intentions to establish authority? How are all parties and institutions involved transformed in the process? What were the unique factors in the political geography that set the scene for this new militia? And related to all of these questions, what was special about the historical moment in which this story unfolded, or about the contingencies that coalesced to produce the dynamics that played out?4

In the late nineteenth and early twentieth centuries the Ottoman state perceived multiple threats—internal and external—in its eastern regions. Russia loomed large with its designs on eastern Anatolia. Kurdish tribes and sheikhly clans continued to act as "parallel authorities" in the region and demonstrated that the Ottoman state's attempts throughout the nineteenth century to centralize and better manage its periphery had been largely unsuccessful.5 Armenian nationalist-revolutionary activity, however, proved to be the greatest perceived threat; many in Ottoman governing circles began to see the entire Armenian population as a fifth column, one that not only challenged state authority on the domestic level but that could potentially serve as the Trojan horse that would bring the Russians in. The state took one of these "hostile" elements—Kurdish tribes—and tried to transform them from a local power that was a challenge to state authority into an arm of state authority itself in order to manage the other "threats." While the state may have succeeded in attracting the temporary loyalty of those Kurdish tribes that it organized into a tribal militia called the Hamidiye Light Cavalry, the larger impact the militia had on local and state levels moved beyond anything that its creators had ever imagined: the on-the-ground conflict over resources that had begun unfolding just prior to the militia's debut on the stage of eastern Anatolia was exacerbated, and violence increased in the region. A number of Armenian (and other Christian) peasants were uprooted and displaced along with many Muslim Kurdish peasants as well. Armenian revolutionaries were not suppressed, but instead were further antagonized and found greater raison d'être for their cause. Local officials faced more challenges in their task of maintaining peace, security, and the rule of law in their districts. Kurdish leaders, whose authority the state had been on a long campaign to diminish, were empowered as their tribal structures were unwittingly strengthened through the very process that sought to dismantle them. And while the state gained the temporary loyalty of select Kurdish chiefs, the long-term goal of binding the Kurds to the state was undermined through the very institution that sought to incorporate them. The Hamidiye organization left a lasting impact on the region and on state-society relations, and some of this impact arguably has lasted into the present day.

The Hamidiye Light Cavalry Regiments (Hamidiye Hafif Süvari Alayları) were an irregular militia composed of select Kurdish tribes, created in 1890 by Sultan Abdülhamid II (r. 1876–1909) and his trusted confidantes Şakir Pasha and the marshal (Mehmed) Zeki Pasha. The latter pasha was commander of the Fourth Army, based in the town of Erzincan, and was also related to the sultan through marriage. The Fourth Army was otherwise known as the Russian front, a vast and very important stretch of territory that extended approximately from the north of Mount Ararat all the way to the present "corner" where Iran, Iraq, and Turkey meet today, to Cizre in the southwest, to the town of Erzincan in the west. This land had rocky, steep mountains where pastoral tribes herded their flocks and cool plateaus where they grazed them in the summer. It was also agriculturally very rich in many areas, as well as symbolically fertile, as it was an extension of the ancient civilizations of Mesopotamia—the scene of important biblical events and stories. It was the "cradle of mankind," in the words of one traveler.[6] But for the Ottomans, who chose to focus less on the symbolic weight of this region than would their Turkish republican successors, this territory was mostly important for strategic reasons as the buffer between Ottoman dominions and those of empires to the east. It was the land that became the front line for many of the Ottomans' wars with their eastern neighbors, and the land where many of the battles were fought. And it was the land on which much blood was shed during the Russo-Ottoman War of 1877–78, which erupted shortly after Sultan Abdülhamid II began his reign. It was the land seen as increasingly vital to the Ottomans as they tried to prevent the deepening trend of territorial losses from striking the empire's eastern frontier, and it was the land that was giving slow rise to the expression of Armenian nationalist activities.

It was also the land that was among the most difficult for the Ottomans to control. In spite of intensive efforts in the nineteenth century to promote administrative reforms aimed at the progressive centralization of the empire with particular attention to far-flung domains like Kurdistan, the region continued to be tricky, and in some parts impossible, to govern, tax, and conscript. Locals heeded their own community heads, mainly Kurdish tribal chiefs and sheikhs, particularly in the countryside, more than they did any Ottoman governors. In many parts these notables were the true "masters" of the country, as many travelers and other foreign observers noted.7

Against the backdrop of the particular importance attached to this territory as the nineteenth century neared its close, the Hamidiye Light Cavalry was established from among these "masters" of the country, or at least from potential "masters." Although the ostensible reason provided by the sultan for the new organization and arming of select Kurdish tribes was the protection of the frontier from external aggression through the expansion of regional military forces, there were actually a number of other goals the sultan and his associates hoped to accomplish through the Hamidiye Light Cavalry. It was, in fact, a manifold mission, not only to protect the frontier, as official statements suggested, and not only to suppress Armenian activities, as some contemporary observers and later historians have argued; nor was it only to bolster the ties of Islamic unity in the empire by creating a special bond between the sultan and the Kurds, as other authors have suggested. It was a mission organized for all of these reasons, and more. Perhaps most significant, it was intended to bring the region into the Ottoman fold and to ensure, by almost any means necessary, that it remained there. The Hamidiye would serve as the channel to this end, for it offered explicit advantages to its members to act in the interests of the Ottoman state, or at least not to act against them. In an era when the security of frontiers and their transition to bordered lands was of central significance in the wider project of modern state building, this region gained new importance to the center, and the sultan decreed that all efforts should be spent to this end, in spite of the vast material, human, and international-relations costs that the Hamidiye venture would entail. These aims were to be accomplished through the arming and pampering of select Kurdish tribes, particularly their chiefs, who would now find it advantageous to turn down any offers to work for "the other side," which the central Ottoman government saw as a distinct threat.

As the project unfolded, it was clear that other visions existed for the Kurdish tribes in the minds of the sultan, Şakir Pasha, Zeki Pasha, and many of their contemporaries. Revealing a worldview not unlike that of many of their contemporaries in other parts of the globe, they also envisaged the project as a civilizing mission—a means through which the "barbaric" tribes could be transformed into peaceful agriculturalists in body and Ottoman (indeed Turkish) "citizens" in spirit.[8] The first step in this process was to settle the tribes, an undertaking that had been sporadically attempted by the Ottoman state for centuries. A few years into the enterprise, it also became apparent that through the Hamidiye venture two primary aims could be accomplished at once. The project could take advantage of trends already underway, namely the growing importance attached to land ownership and the changes in land-tenure practices that had already begun to unfold in several regions. Although the central government did not initiate the process whereby powerful local notables began to appropriate peasant holdings for themselves, the state certainly turned this development to its advantage. It did so by offering free reign to its supporters, here Hamidiye chiefs, to usurp the land of Armenian (and also Kurdish) peasants, with the long-term effect of dispossessing the Armenian element, which was increasingly viewed with suspicion. The state could then accomplish its goal of weakening the "internal enemies" in the threatened borderlands by depriving them of their means of subsistence and causing them to emigrate elsewhere so as to diminish or disperse their numbers. At the same time it provided material incentives for the Kurdish tribes to settle and remain loyal to the sultan and the empire.

The Hamidiye project continued to unfold not only for the duration of Sultan Abdülhamid II's reign but well beyond. Even when the sultan was deposed in April 1909, his special project was not dissolved by the new rulers of the empire, but rather was given a new name, the Tribal Light Cavalry Regiments (Aşiret Hafif Süvari Alayları). Although leaders in the new regime had considered shelving the scheme, they instead settled for a reorganization of the militia, even if in reality the organization remained largely the same as it had been under the sultan they had just overthrown. When the Ottomans entered the First World War, the regiments took on a new role, as they were no longer intended to repress domestic threats or stand against a vague external menace. Now faced with wartime conditions, they were deployed on several fronts, and also became identified with the mass murder and deportation of Armenians that took place during the war (known by Armenians as the Great Catastrophe). And although some of the militia's chiefs became disillusioned with the nascent Kemalist government after the war and joined the growing Kurdish nationalist movement, other Light Cavalry tribes joined the regular army in battling the Greek invasion, and were lauded for their participation in the Turkish War of Independence. It was not until after the war that this Kurdish cavalry officially ceased to exist by any name, although a version of village guards was established by Turkey, one successor state to the empire, soon after its declaration of independence. They were revived in 1984 to combat the PKK (the Kurdish acronym for Partîya Karkerên Kurdistan, or the Workers' Party of Kurdistan) in southeastern Anatolia. The Village Guards in Turkey remain active today, thus lending contemporary significance to its historical legacy.

Over the course of the three-plus decades that spanned the life of this tribal militia, the Hamidiye Light Cavalry would impact the lives of its member tribesmen, their families, neighbors, clients, and the entire region. The Hamidiye regiments would also play a part in shaping the trajectories of Ottoman politics on regional, empire-wide, and even international levels. The militia would figure prominently in the transformation of the local power structure, and indeed the very social and political organization of Kurdish society itself. It would play a significant role in transforming the economic landscape through its effects on the nature of land tenure in the region. The militia organization impacted wider state-society relations in the late-Ottoman period, and is indeed an illuminating lens through which we can view the transformation of the Ottoman state in the nation-state moment. And last, it would serve as a model and precedent for the subsequent Kurdish tribal militias created by leaders of post-Ottoman states to contend with their own internal threats.

METHODOLOGY, HISTORIOGRAPHY, AND SOURCES

The relevance of the Hamidiye to present-day events not only piqued my interest in the topic, but also shaped the process through which my inquiry was conducted. Apparently due to the sensitivity of the topic, I was denied access to all Turkish research facilities, including the Ottoman Archives, for several years. My initial research was based, therefore, primarily upon extensive research conducted at the Public Record Office in London, the

French Ministry of Foreign Affairs Archives (Archives du Ministère des Affaires Étrangères) in Paris and Nantes, the French Ministry of Defense Archives (Archives du Ministère de la Défense) at Vincennes outside Paris, and also, albeit to a lesser extent, the Kurdish Institute (l'Institut Kurde) and the Nubar Pasha Library, also both of Paris, as well as the Library of Congress in Washington, D.C. My research was additionally informed by published Ottoman materials, the Kurdish-Ottoman press, travel literature, missionary reports, and a variety of secondary sources in diverse languages. The British and French diplomatic sources on which my initial conclusions were largely based were taken with a note of caution. While extremely rich and descriptive, they nonetheless revealed the distinctly Orientalist bias of their authors, many (but not all) of whom saw the protection of the Armenians as a primary matter of interest, and whose reports on this region reflected this concern. Although this was the case, I believed that future research conducted in Ottoman archives would bear out my suggestions. Thankfully, in the summer of 2006 I was finally granted access to the Ottoman Archives of the Prime Ministry (Başbakanlık Osmanlı Arşivi). The documents I obtained from diverse wings of the Ottoman bureaucracy not only confirmed my impression that I was on the right track, but they also served to strengthen the contentions I had made. The present study is based on all of these rich and diverse sources.

The political significance that the topic of the Hamidiye continues to carry has affected not only the present work but also earlier studies that have dealt either directly or indirectly with the Hamidiye question. Four main trends become apparent when examining previous treatment of the Hamidiye, many of which may be considered nationalist approaches or trends and all of which fail to regard this institution as part of a dynamic Kurdish society with its own historical processes. The first is the Armenian (or Armenophile) approach, which seeks to locate the Hamidiye in a narrative of the Armenian Genocide of 1915, and the events leading up to that year. The militia's empowerment against Armenians is provided in these works as evidence of a long-term Ottoman policy designed to uproot and annihilate the Armenians of the empire and as part of the larger attempt to document the culpability of the central government in these tragic events by showing how the troops, under the orders of the government, participated in the deportation and extermination of the Armenians in 1915 and also during the earlier massacres of 1894–96.[9] The second approach may be called Turkish nationalist, which has generally sought, in the case of the Hamidiye in particular, to gloss over the unsavory activities with which the Kurdish tribal militia came to be associated (as this approach also dodges official activities in this regard). On occasion the Turkish-nationalist approach has also worked to employ them (and the activities of Kurds in general) to deflect responsibility from the central Ottoman government in the Armenian Genocide and earlier episodes of anti-Armenian violence by blaming them, not on an organization maintained by the state, but on an unruly bunch of tribesmen, whose thirst for revenge drove them to violence.[10] Others adopting this broader approach have also contrasted the despotic Hamidian regime with its successor, the Ottoman Committee of Union and Progress (CUP), out of which grew the leadership of the early Turkish republic.[11]

The third approach may be called Kurdish nationalist. Proponents of this approach have generally not attempted to sidestep the question of the Hamidiye's role in regional violence, instead working to emphasize the parallel between the Hamidiye and the Village Guards in order to add punch to their argument that the state has long been playing the divide-and-rule card in its war against the Kurds. This approach also emphasizes the government's support of the objectionable activities with which this present-day Kurdish tribal militia has been associated.[12]

A fourth approach can also be discerned among writers in Turkey who, contrary to those who have characterized Sultan Abdülhamid II as a reactionary despot, have gone to the other extreme, representing him as a far-sighted ruler who should be admired for his efforts to preserve the territorial and economic integrity of a country under the siege of internal and external threats. This group of scholars is also particularly focused on the sultan's dedication to strengthening and elevating the position of Islam in state and society.[13]

None of these approaches are completely devoid of truth. As the "Armenophile" writers have asserted, the Hamidiye was indeed organized by the Ottoman government in part to be employed against its Armenian element. The regiments were, moreover, involved in extensive violence against Ottoman Armenians, and were also implicated in the mass murder, deportation, and looting that took place during the First World War. As the official Turkish line suggests, the Hamidiye regiments did often act in this regard without official orders from the state, and indeed in spite of attempts by some well-meaning local officials to prevent such atrocities. As the Kurdish camp submits, the parallels between the Hamidiye regiments and the Village Guards are truly striking on certain levels, and they reveal much about the state's historical relationship with its Kurdish population. And as the "Hamidian revivalists" suggest, Sultan Abdülhamid II did envision the Hamidiye as part of his greater drive for Islamic unity. When these characterizations of the Hamidiye stand alone, however, they tell only a slice of the story and also serve to skew our notions of what the Hamidiye was and why it is important to understand past and present history, as these approaches are too narrow and too imbued with political and nationalist import to provide a broad and complex picture of this institution. Moreover, they impede our attempts to understand Kurdish society as a dynamic society with its own historical processes. In other words, in these narratives, Kurdish society is viewed only as it relates to "the other," whether that other is the non-Kurdish neighbor or the government. Or worse, Kurdish society is seen as having no historical dynamics of its own. As one writer from this school has put it, "There is no such thing as Kurdish history." All it consists of, he claims, are "various stories that recount tribal events and actions."[14]

This study aims, in part, to rethink the history of the Hamidiye organization. It does not completely discard the aforementioned depictions of the Hamidiye, but rather nuances and adds to them in an attempt to arrive at a more comprehensive understanding of this Kurdish tribal militia. However, the real (as opposed to incidental) contribution that I aim to offer readers is not simply a "better" or "more complete" history of the Hamidiye institution in and of itself, but rather, a more complex understanding of modern Ottoman state-building processes—processes whose far-reaching dynamics have not adequately been covered by scholarship to date. This seemingly peripheral militia organization was not only emblematic of, but also an important part of, the Ottoman expansion of what Giddens calls "administrative power" in its transition to a nation-state,[15] and the related process of transforming the political geography and demography of its borderlands. This path was tortuous and had far-reaching consequences for locals, for the survival of the Ottoman state itself, and indeed for its successor states. Although the dynamics unleashed by the formation of this militia were often unintended, I will demonstrate that this case study not only illuminates the specificities of the modern Ottoman state-building narrative but also shows how much the Ottoman path had in common with that followed by other (often European) states as they made similar transitions. The Ottomans and many others perceived internal threats and attempted to cope with them; local power relations and identities were significantly transformed through the state-sponsored empowerment of certain groups; and violent conflicts previously understood to be ethnic or religious were at least partially about something much larger, here the conflict over resources. The Kurdish- and Armenian-inhabited Ottoman periphery became central to these processes in the late nineteenth and early twentieth centuries.

Because one key question that lies at the heart of these processes is what happens when a state empowers a group that it would rather suppress we need to adopt a more nuanced version of the state and of state-society relations—one that recognizes how states and societies transform one another through their very interaction, how the state-society distinction is often extremely blurry, and particularly what makes states act in ways that seem counterintuitive. The work of Joel Migdal, for example, allows us "to understand the appearance of multiple sets of practices, many of which might be at odds with the image (and morality) of the state,"[16] and how the "participation of the fragments of the state in such coalitions that intersect the state-society divide" contribute to a situation in which the "'practices of the state' may directly contradict the 'idea of the state,'"[17] and indeed, I would add, the very *interests* of the state. By handing the reins of state power, in a sense, to the tribal Kurds the state wished to suppress, the Ottoman state was contradicting the idea of itself (at least insofar as it "owned" state power). And the outcomes of this grant of power also demonstrated that it was undermining its own interests and image in both the domestic and the international spheres. For those who suggest that this should be seen in light of the larger Ottoman decline (as one more of many examples of the state's inability to perceive and act on what was best for its preservation), Migdal's approach again offers some nuanced perspective: "It is not simply poorly designed policies or incompetent officials or insufficient resources that explain the failures or mixed results of state policies. States must contend with . . . groupings . . . of opposition [that] have created coalitions to strengthen their stance, and these have cut right into the structures of states themselves. The resulting coalitional struggles have taken their toll: state policy implementation and the outcomes in society have ended up quite different from the state's original blueprints."[18] This is because, as the Hamidiye project illustrates very well, the Ottoman state was not the monolithic actor that many have presumed it to be in much of the literature; rather, "the internal contradictions in the state's practices created multiple political spaces that [local] populations could occupy and exploit depending on their assessment of the advantages and disadvantages of each."[19] In other words, local Kurdish chiefs possessed a great deal of agency in the affair, and as military brokers, instead of engaging in open acts of rebellion to pursue their agendas, they were able to harness the awesome power of empire to their own advantage.[20] But the story at hand is not simply about what happens when a state empowers a group that is a threat to it, for after all, states and other dominant elites have been making all kinds of "effort-bargains" for centuries. Rather, it is the specificity of *this* effort-bargain that took place in a particular political geography at a moment of transition not only in the status and conception of that geography but also in the wider transformation of the Ottoman state to a modern nation-state. And it was not only local and empire-wide power structures that were changing, but the very nature, conception, and practice of power itself. Power and periphery intersected in a profoundly new manner in late-Ottoman Kurdistan, with many tragic short- and long-term results.

Some have argued that the location and terrain of Kurdistan have determined its relationship to the states (particularly the Ottoman state) that have incorporated and/or bordered the region. The political geography and terrain of Kurdistan have certainly been factors in these relationships, but we must be careful not to assign causal or deterministic features to this geography. As Balta points out, it is not the "inherent characteristics of physical terrain" that are of essential note, but rather how states (and I would add, locals) *respond* to that political geography.[21] This does not mean, however, that space and spatial relationships are unimportant; to the contrary, this study finds that the location of the internal threats that the Ottomans sought to overcome was, in fact, key, but it was essential in a particular moment and *became* fundamental through specific dynamics. The Kurds lived on the frontiers of empires for centuries, and then in the borderlands of these empires (Ottoman, and Safavid then Qajar Iran) for several more centuries. During the period in which the story at hand unfolded, this borderland region was in the process of becoming a *bordered* land,[22] a transformation that is indeed part of the story I tell in this book. Adelman and Aron remind us to make the distinction between "frontiers" and "borderlands," and to historicize the transition from frontier to borderland to bordered land.[23] A few Ottomanists who work on borderlands have recognized these differences and historicized this process, and they have certainly made important contributions to our understanding of Ottoman peoples in borderland regions and center-periphery relations. They have generally not, however, problematized these distinctions in a meaningful way, relying in their analyses on more mainstream notions of core-versus-periphery.[24] The internal and external threats that the Ottomans perceived and tried to quell in their militia project were not pressing earlier, when the region was indeed a frontier; they were urgent precisely during this moment when Kurdistan was one of the Ottoman territories that was changing from borderland to bordered land, a process that has been shown to be intimately connected with the transition to nation-statehood.[25] It was the goal of modern state-crafters to create and expand state spaces and to incorporate or at least neutralize the nonstate spaces it could claim, but perhaps not yet *govern*,[26] as "these stateless zones . . . played a potentially subversive role, both symbolically and practically."[27] It was in this context that the Ottoman state felt a greater need to strengthen its grip on the region—the "tribal zone," as Ferguson and Whitehead have dubbed it—and incorporate it into its modern state-building project.[28]

In this regard, the Ottomans were not alone. The nineteenth century saw states all over the world make this transition, and like others, the Ottomans employed modern state-building technologies as they sought to delimit their borders and to define and control the people inside of them. Key in making societies and the spaces they inhabited more "legible," as Scott calls the process,[29] and hence, more governable, was not only the effort to map and demark the terrain to be governed, but to map and classify the people within. This was "social gardening"—a project that strived to "shape a people and landscape" to fit the modern state-builders' "techniques of observation" and classification.[30] After all, "institutions confer identity,"[31] and the institutions of the modern state produce labels, which "stabilize the flux of social life and even create to some extent the realities to which they apply."[32] In other words, this was a process of "making up people," and in this "dynamic process . . . new names [were] uttered and forthwith new creatures corresponding to them emerge[d]."[33] Kurdishness, Armenianness, Turkishness, and Ottomanness (and indeed "tribalness") took on new meanings in this dynamic practice of constituting modern peoples, and these identities were given new relational significance on new terrain for power struggles, of which the Hamidiye project was part and parcel. As an institution, the Hamidiye conferred a new identity on its members and also reshaped relationships within individual tribes as well as the larger relationship of state to tribe. But perhaps ironically, while the conditions of threat, conflict, and outright war helped to crystallize emergent *ethnic* identities,[34] lines between state and local power (and hence, state and local identities) became more blurred. The Hamidiye project is, as such, an important study in the contradictions of modern statecraft.

One important feature of these gray areas of state building that my study of the Hamidiye venture also illuminates is the need to acknowledge not just the blur between state and society but also that between and among local Ottoman groups in the convoluted state-society nexus. It also outlines how new, and often apparently puzzling, identities emerged from the conditions of conflict. This book challenges many longstanding and widely held assumptions about identity construction and, most importantly, ethnic-communal conflict. The vast body of works on nationalism and other aspects of identity formation have demonstrated the constructedness of national and ethnic identities, emphasizing their historicity to the point where such recognition is now commonplace or even mainstream among scholars. Ottomanists (and other area-specific specialists) have followed suit and have also turned to examining these processes in interesting and enlightening studies. However, when it comes to some of the finer points of identity construction, certain gray areas remain elusive, are taken for granted, or rest unexamined or underexamined. In other words, the field has done a good job of overturning decades of scholarship that took the ethnic and communal identities of Ottoman subject peoples as sui generis by instead historicizing their construction; however, the murky areas where things are not always what they seem and where actors do not necessarily behave in ways that we expect still need attention. To put it differently, we now acknowledge that the ethnic and religious mosaic of Ottoman peoples was not a recipe for disaster, a toxic mix ready to explode, but we have difficulty in recognizing how, in the early twentieth century, some groups who claimed to be nationalist were not necessarily separatist and those elements who played the separatist card were not necessarily nationalist. In its examination of the Hamidiye and state-society relations in the post-1908 period, my book examines the complex layers of opposition that emerged when the new regime attempted to curtail the power and privilege that Hamidiye affiliates had enjoyed under the ancien régime, and it also analyzes how the new government—against its own better judgment and in face of numerous protests—reinstated the power of the group that they really wanted to suppress. Here the reader will find that the labels that various Kurdish groups assigned to themselves (along with those given to them by outsiders) were often misleading. Part of this book explores what we might make of those nonseparatist Kurdish nationalists and nonnationalist Kurdists in the context of the changing construction of power and identity in late-Ottoman Kurdistan.[35] In other words, within the larger process of "making up people," "individual persons ma[d]e choices within the classifications."[36] The nationalist identities that many today see as self-evident were instead the result of a complex set of historical contingencies within which people opted for identities that might not make sense to the perspective that sees the formation of the modern nation-state and nationalist identities as entirely linear.

The historiographical problems related to conflict and identity are much deeper than a problem of labels, though. Ottomanists rightly began to rectify longstanding Orientalist portrayals of separate and segmented societies and started to demonstrate how lines between the "hard" divisions of ethnicity and religion were softer than previously imagined. However, soon a kind of overcorrection took place, and we emerged at the other end with a somewhat romanticized image of extreme fluidity and overlap between "opposing" and "different" groups. Conflict then began to be explained largely as a result of colonial or imperial intervention, and domestic and local dynamics took a backseat to the story.[37] Of course this alteration was sorely needed, but the interest that scholars have taken in dismantling the picture whereby Muslims and Christians, for example, were "natural" enemies, has still left us scratching our heads when we want to understand the conflicts that did arise, for indeed they did. The rosier representation of mutual accord and interdependence may be much more accurate than the previous portrayal of natural discord, but it is nonetheless incomplete. Rather than airbrushing conflict out of the picture, my study aims to understand its deeper roots and to contribute to this wider discussion as well. Here I have benefited from the work of scholars who have analyzed more recent and contemporary struggles and who have addressed the economic sides of civil war and other armed conflict.[38] My book explores how conflicts over resources and the changing face of land tenure in the eastern Ottoman provinces contributed to violent conflict between Armenian Christians and Muslim Kurds, thereby historicizing the conflicts that have been otherwise noted to be "primordial." Concomitant with the state's attempt to expand its "administrative power" to better control the territories to which it laid claim, locals worked to increase their control over resources (mainly land) against the backdrop of the larger global process of the commercialization of land and the attached rise in the value of land. Kurdish chiefs who signed on as militia members became well positioned to press forth in their own agendas with state backing for other goals, and they appropriated the land and resources of their neighbors, many of whom were Armenian. Although weaker Kurdish neighbors were also at risk in this larger scheme, Armenians were in greater peril precisely because of the contingency of the various factors described above—the Russian threat to the eastern borderlands, the rise in Armenian revolutionary-nationalist activities, and the process of identity construction from above and below. As Ferguson and Whitehead put it, "'Ethnic conflict . . . is a problematic category of emergent, complex, and highly variable processes—anything but the eruption of some primitive and fixed group loyalty."[39] What started out as a conflict over resources did become ethnicized, but only because it occurred precisely during the wider moment in the Ottoman transition to nation-statehood where people were being "made up." It took place at a time when the notions of majority and minority were emerging, and where the Ottoman state along with many local Muslims (mainly Kurds)—now envisioning a new kind of majority—began to *imagine* Armenians as a group to be a minority and "a demographic and political challenge."[40] In other words, what it meant to be Armenian, Kurdish, Turkish, or Ottoman was not simply a neutral development, but these distinctions came to be loaded "with moral and political content."[41] What began as a local conflict over resources was harnessed by the state to its own ends, and over time the process combined with new nationalist ideologies and turned to one of murderous cleansing.[42] We must also overcome the temptation, as Mann notes, to view episodes of murderous cleansing as organized and premeditated. "Early events, early decisions," he writes, are too often read back from the ghastly known end result. In doing this, we may suppress the complexity and contingency of events. Though prior events may seem like a single chain of escalations, to the actors concerned they may not have been intended as such. . . . We must prove it, not use hindsight to assume it."[43] In its presentation of the Hamidiye moment, this book works to highlight these contingencies so that we might better understand the violence associated with the creation of modern ethnic and political identities while at the same time being wary of nationalist historiographies that assume a sui generis existence of these identities.

The development of ethnic and nationalist identities, and the world-view behind better classification and control of peoples and territory (what Foucault calls "governmentality") that the Ottomans sought (and that many locals resisted), also deserve our attention here.[44] Too many works on the Ottoman Empire still regard the Ottoman path to modern state-hood as unique and peculiar vis-à-vis European states, a portrayal that has been eloquently disputed by Abou-El-Haj, for one.[45] The field of Ottoman history has seen significant steps in dispelling the notion that the Ottomans (i.e., "the East") and the Europeans (i.e., "the West") were binary opposites, had different trajectories, and, concomitantly, different agencies, with "the West" as the core and the Ottomans as "the periphery," not only in economic terms but also in terms of knowledge. As such, the transformation of Ottoman identities and Ottoman modernizing projects were seen, until recently, as purely derivative—the Ottomans borrowed from Europe to catch up to Europe. I suggest that the Ottomans did not merely borrow the technologies or worldviews from European thinkers and states, or even simply pass them through their own "ideological sieve" when they did;[46] they developed many of their own ideas and corresponding projects for similar purposes. They were not merely mimicking Europe, but had their own specific reasons for developing "civilizing" and centralizing projects and had their own "needs" to meet as they, too, transitioned to modern nation-statecraft. It appears that empires and other states in the nineteenth and early twentieth centuries simultaneously found similar solutions and even justifications for their state-building ventures.[47] The "civilizing mission," which represented a driving element behind the Hamidiye project, was acted out *simultaneously* with similar projects across the globe. The Ottomans (and other "easterners") were not just on the receiving end of the European *mission civilisatrice*, but formulated their own projects in the context of (re)conquering their borderlands.[48] Indeed, as Troutt Powell has demonstrated in her study of Egypt, Ottomans at times were colonized colonizers.[49] After all, internal colonization is a process that unfolds as part of the development of modern statecraft,[50] and just as the

Ottoman state may have been the target of the European civilizing mission, in the Hamidiye example, it was a kind of "colonizer" in Kurdistan. And just as the Kurdish tribal chiefs' roles as military brokers enabled them to move beyond the receiving end of the internal Ottoman imperial mission, they also turned them into a sort of local colonizer themselves.[51] There were many layers of colonizer-colonized relationships here. I believe that the present study contributes to the larger body of recent literature on state building that not only explores the gray areas between state and society, east and west, and colonizer and colonized, but which also traces and historicizes their constructions, interactions, and impacts, and further exposes the discursive arenas in which these power plays were staged.

While this is not the place to cover the discourses of power, identity, and tradition that were developed in late-Ottoman state circles—as Deringil, for one, has already done a very good job of this for the Hamidian period[52]—I would like to draw attention to a few salient features of this discourse, and more importantly, illustrate how Hamidiye chieftains were able to perform acts of "symbolic jujitsu" in their appropriation of the state's own discourse about power, loyalty, and rebellion.[53] One helpful way to consider this dynamic is through the lens of what Scott calls the public and hidden transcripts of power. Power, as Giddens defines it, "means 'transformative capacity', the capability to intervene in a given set of events so as in some way to alter them," and power is related to "the resources that agents employ in the course of their activities in order to accomplish whatever they do." These resources are allocative and authoritative, but they "do not in any sense 'automatically' enter into the reproduction of social systems, but operate only in so far as they are drawn upon by contextually located actors in the conduct of their day-to-day lives."[54] As in any other state or society, there were many layers of power and kinds of power jockeying in the late-Ottoman period. The Great Powers aimed to influence events in the Ottoman Empire for their own strategic, political, and economic interests. The Ottoman state wanted to continue to extract surplus from its population as it had for centuries. And local groups strived for economic and authoritative control in their immediate regions. What is important to note, however, is that this was no "classic" Ottoman struggle; all of the agents involved were acting within the new set of circumstances that arose as the Ottoman state made its transition to nation-statehood, and in this it joined others around the world. What we need to discern here are the specificities of how domination and resistance played out in this changing Ottoman context. I suggest that the Hamidiye moment in the Ottoman periphery provides an extremely helpful lens through which we might view this wider process.

It is particularly interesting to watch this unfold by analyzing the discourses of power that evolved as various agents battled for control of economic and authoritative power under the changed conditions of the late nineteenth and early twentieth centuries. For Scott, key forms of domination "are institutionalized means of extracting labor, goods, and services from a subject population." What I'd like to focus on here is the point that "they embody formal assumptions about superiority and inferiority, often in elaborate ideological form, and a fair degree of ritual and 'etiquette' [that] regulates public conduct within them. . . . Although they are highly institutionalized, these forms of domination typically contain a strong element of personal rule" (and personal terror as well). And "like most large-scale structures of domination, the subordinate group has a fairly extensive offstage social existence which, in principle, affords it the opportunity to develop a shared critique of power."[55] This "offstage" existence is elaborated in what Scott calls the "hidden transcript." Precisely because it is "hidden," however, the voices of the subordinate groups are difficult for historians to discern because we often are left with mostly official records. In this study, many of my sources are certainly problematic as they include not only those documents generated by the Ottoman state but also a large number that were produced by the European consular officials who had their own agendas and prejudices that colored their analysis of the events they described. Nonetheless, while it is admittedly arduous to locate the hidden transcripts of the most subordinated groups in this story—Kurdish and Armenian peasants—we can certainly read some of these documents as "prose of counter-insurgency."[56] But what I am more interested in here is how Kurdish Hamidiye chieftains and their opposition, who increasingly published in the late-Ottoman (especially Kurdish) press, engaged with the state's "public transcript" in order to press their own agendas. All of these parties turned the state's official discourse on its head and filled pages of the press with an elaborate "performance of deference and consent";[57] and while the official discourse may have changed slightly between the Hamidian and post-1908 periods, Kurdish Hamidiye chiefs as well as their opposition were able to deftly use the "public transcript" in a ritualized performance of subordination that masked their agency in the situation. The power of the Hamidiye chiefs in particular was also closely connected to their ability to "create an intricate world of illusion,"[58] in which they exacerbated the "Armenian threat" to show how indispensable they were to the state. Even when the new regime came to power in 1908—a regime that was avowedly hostile to this most blatant of Hamidian institutions—Kurdish Hamidiye chiefs worked to manage information to their own advantage and continued to demonstrate the necessity of the state to empower them and to see their "transgressions" as minor concerns compared with the larger threats the empire faced. In recounting the story of power struggles in the late-Ottoman periphery, it is important to recognize Foucault's observation that power relations are fluid and mobile, but also to note that these struggles had to do with concrete, material benefits. This study aims to recount an important part of late-Ottoman history by connecting power, periphery, and performance. In the body and conclusion to this study I will connect the theoretical, the empirical, and the "colorful" more explicitly.

CHAPTER OUTLINE AND NARRATIVE STRUCTURE

Chapter 1, "A Manifold Mission," will describe the multifarious aims of the sultan and his appointed commander of the project, Zeki Pasha, as they set out to create and implement the Hamidiye Light Cavalry beginning in 1890. This chapter will trace these goals, underscore the context for their development, highlight the nuances in the priorities assigned to some of these objectives over others, and describe the worldview of the authors of the militia as they designed and executed their plans. Of course the architects of the Hamidiye mission could not have envisioned the extent to which the institution would contribute to the larger and more far-reaching transformations underway in Kurdish society. The remainder of the study, then, traces the interplay of state-tribe relations as they developed through the Hamidiye project, and highlights the impact of the organization on transformations in the Kurdish power structure and on political and social relations in Kurdish society and on state-society levels. Chapters 2, 3, and 4 will bring these changes to light by each focusing on a different Hamidiye pasha whose career best exemplifies the theme treated in that chapter. These figures grew to be some of the most important Kurdish chiefs in the region through this process, and of the many Hamidiye pashas that were empowered during this time, these three left such a mark that their names are still known in the Kurdish regions. Chapter 2, "The Hamidiye Under Sultan Abdülhamid II: 1890–1908," will highlight the career of Mustafa Pasha, the Hamidiye commander of the Mîran tribe of Cizre, in its analysis of the ways in which the Hamidiye organization influenced the transformation of the regional power structure in Ottoman Kurdistan during the period under review. Chapter 3, "The Tribal Light Cavalry Under the Young Turks: 1908–1914," will examine how the Hamidiye project developed under the rule of the Ottoman Committee of Union and Progress, and will draw attention to the career of İbrahim Pasha, the Hamidiye head of the Millî tribe based in Viranşehir, in order to illustrate both the changes and continuities in the Hamidiye organization and its impact on Kurdish society as its leadership changed hands. Chapter 4,

"The Hamidiye and the Agrarian Question," underscores the material basis for the theme of power in the Kurdish periphery by addressing the link between the so-called "agrarian question" that emerged in 1908 and its intimate connection with the Hamidiye Light Cavalry. The career of Hüseyin Pasha of Patnos, the Hamidiye chieftain of the large and powerful Hayderan tribe, stands out as representative of this process and of the politics surrounding the "agrarian question" when it emerged as such beginning in 1908. The final year covered in the main body of this book is 1914, the year in which the Hamidiye and the state that backed it entered a new period consumed by war, with new circumstances that prompted the state to employ the Hamidiye in real battle under wartime conditions. However, 1914 is not the end of the Hamidiye story. Although an extensive discussion of the Hamidiye after 1914 is beyond the scope of this work, it is important to draw attention to the legacy the Hamidiye has left—a legacy that continues to the present day. We may now turn to the beginning of that story.

CHAPTER ONE

A Manifold Mission

★

Officially, the Hamidiye was formed to "protect the country against foreign assaults and aggression" and to find a way to enforce conscription in
a region that contributed relatively few recruits to the Ottoman army, and
accordingly, was attached to the "just aim of increasing and multiplying
the general strength of the Ottoman forces."[1] Later scholars writing on
the Hamidiye have, however, found different motives for the creation of
this institution. Most writers concur that the regiments were formed for
various reasons, including bolstering the Ottomans' military might along
the borders, serving as a counter to Armenian revolutionary activities, and
finding means to control the Kurds and attract their loyalty. Each writer,
however, has emphasized a different aspect of these plans and has contributed valuable insights to the task of understanding what was behind
the Hamidiye enterprise.[2] When added together, nuanced, and elaborated,
their contributions can offer a much more complex appreciation for how
the Hamidiye fit into its historical moment and what its architects had in
mind as they drafted the plans for these irregular cavalry units. However,
while all of these motives may have been present throughout the history of
this tribal militia, some among them took precedence over others at certain
times. Mapping the Hamidiye and tracing the locations of these regiments
as they were raised, for example, provides small clues about some of the
roles the sultan and his advisors assigned to them. First, however, to better
understand the manifold nature of the Ottoman mission to fashion these
irregular cavalry units, it is in order at this point to present a snapshot of

the situation in southeastern Anatolia and the empire at large when the Hamidiye regiments were being planned and formed.

ON THE EVE OF 1890

In less than eight months after Sultan Abdülhamid ascended the throne in 1876, war broke out between Russia and the Ottoman Empire, and in two years left much of eastern Anatolia in ruins. The war and its aftermath only increased the sense of impending doom felt by many in the empire as they had witnessed the loss of most of their Christian territories earlier in the century, and feared that one of the last areas where Christians formed a significant part of the local population—Armenia—was about to be severed from the empire. A limited number of Armenians had offered assistance to the Russians during the Russo-Ottoman War (1877–78), and, following the war, the British had put forth a program of reform in 1879. Both were acts that Ottomans saw as further steps toward their impending loss of control over this region. The sultan considered it his personal mission to find ways to revive the empire and its people after the devastating war.[3]

Certain Kurdish groups that came together in 1879 under the leadership of the prominent Sheikh Ubeydullah and soon rose in revolt against the central government also sensed that the region was about to be lost to the Armenians or their European supporters. Fearing the implementation of reforms as outlined in Article 61 of the Treaty of Berlin, which were designed to guarantee the security of Armenians in the region against the incursions and depredations of Kurds and Circassians, Sheikh Ubeydullah built a broad-based and mighty coalition composed of leading Kurdish tribal chiefs in response to this perceived threat. He also held that neither the Ottomans nor the Iranians were capable of ever controlling the region to the extent necessary to bring about stability in the region, and believed, then, that the Kurds should control their own destiny.[4] He was initially supported by the Ottoman government in his attempts to invade Iran, as the latter saw his movement as a good counterbalance to any Armenian ascendancy in the region and perhaps also as a means to compensate territorial losses incurred during the war. However, the Ottoman government soon realized that such a powerful alliance of Kurdish chiefs and sheikhs could eventually undermine its own already weak authority in the region, and worked to suppress the movement in 1881.[5]

Armenian nationalism was also a growing force that challenged the control of the Ottoman government over eastern Anatolia. Already a palpable intellectual movement by the middle of the century, ideas of socialism and nationalism combined with attempts by Armenians to protect their peasant compatriots who were too often becoming victims of oppression by local Kurdish bandits and who were not sufficiently protected by the state. Some of them began to establish various revolutionary organizations with aims that ranged from the struggle for equality within an Ottoman framework and other reforms to outright independence. In 1880 a secret society called the Defense of the Fatherland was established in Erzurum, with the goal of procuring arms and acquiring military training. In 1882, the Ottoman government became aware of these activities when the Ottoman police seized a document of the organization, and subsequently arrested some four hundred Armenians. By 1885, small revolutionary bands were reported as appearing in districts from Eleşgirt to Dersim.[6] The next five years saw the establishment of three important revolutionary organizations: the Armenakan (est. 1885), the Henchak Party (est. 1887), and the Dashnaktsutiun (est. 1890).[7] The Armenian community had already become increasingly suspect in the eyes of the government for the backing it received from the Russians as well as the diplomatic attention it drew from European powers. These nationalist revolutionary organizations and their armed activities only strengthened the suspicions, and indeed bitterness, of many in the empire, including the sultan himself.[8]

The Ottomans' control over the region was further tested by local magnates—urban notables in cities like Diyarbekir and Van—who prevented Ottoman governors from ruling effectively, and Kurdish tribal chiefs, who were virtually independent of all authority but their own throughout much of the region. Economically, large parts of these provinces remained distant from the grasp of the central authorities, as taxes went unpaid by most of the pastoral Kurds, and as Armenian and Kurdish peasants were too squeezed by their Kurdish overlords to pay taxes to the state. Caravan trade was increasingly disrupted by brigandage, and the overall sense of security in the region, felt not only by Christians but also by the weaker Muslim elements, was in decline. Steps taken earlier in the century by Ottoman rulers toward reform and centralization did not seem to bear healthy fruit in the early years of Sultan Abdülhamid II's reign. In the years immediately preceding the formation of the Hamidiye the central government was seriously concerned with controlling tribal feuds and lawlessness.[9]

Facing challenges from all directions as he stepped into his reign, Sultan Abdülhamid II worked to combat these affronts to his authority by initiating a rigorous plan of centralization, devising carrot-and-stick policies to keep alternate sources of power balanced, promoting a program of modernization, continued from his predecessors, and elaborating a symbolic framework of loyalty to strengthen the ties of Sunni Muslims to the empire and to his person. He wished to extend the state's arm domestically, keep foreign influences at bay, and prevent further territorial losses. All of this occurred in the context of the wider global transformations involving modern statecraft, particularly the transition to the nation-state and the larger processes that accompanied this shift. The Ottoman Empire continued to be an empire, but was now "thinking" like a nation-state in many regards. Its rulers were concerned with expanding administrative power and governmentality in all of its domains, but particularly in its "nonstate" spaces or "tribal zones." To this end, the state embarked on a project of internal colonization in its borderlands, but this involved a shift in perceptions of peoplehood as well. New identities emerged in this transformation as the concern with borders—which necessarily had to be less porous than frontiers—was accompanied by a mission to define, if not create, the peoples who occupied the lands on either side of these borders, and to further control their relationships with one another and with the state. The Hamidiye Light Cavalry was created in this historical moment, from which its inspiration and implementation cannot be divorced.

MAPPING THE MILITIA

Late in 1890, plans were underway for the recruitment of tribes to establish these irregular cavalry regiments, the idea for which had been brewing in the sultan's elite circles for at least five years.[10] There were many compelling reasons for raising the tribes in this irregular military formation. First, it would bring elements that were outside the reach of central authority into the fold. Access meant control: the opportunity to learn about and thus regulate the movements and activities of a largely mobile people; the ability to collect taxes and recruits for the regular army from a people who scarcely contributed either; and the chance to introduce the sultan as a higher authority than the local chiefs. It would balance the existing powers, each a certain threat to central rule, playing one against the other and backing some over others, but ensuring that such support was clearly a gift from the sultan and could be withdrawn at any time. It could penetrate a region where the notion of "Ottomanness" was weak at best, could help "civilize" and assimilate the people who lived there, and could further the Ottoman project to extend state power, or "governmentality."[11] It would help to bolster military forces against a future Russian invasion. And lastly, it would act as a counter to the newest, and seemingly most potent, of threats—the perceived Armenian "conspiracy" and the budding Armenian revolutionary movement.[12]

As Zeki Pasha, the supreme Hamidiye commander, set out on a tour of the region to promote his new militia and to recruit tribes, he had many tribes to choose from—hundreds, in fact. What initially determined which tribes would be selected was their location and also their willingness to enroll. The Hamidiye regiments, eventually numbering sixty-four or sixty-five in all,[13] were recruited in batches, the first lot being drawn from tribes based largely in the vicinity of the Russian Caucasus and Iranian borders and around Lake Van. At a glance, it appears that the principal concern motivating the Ottomans as they recruited tribes to form this irregular cavalry was to protect the empire's eastern borders from incursions by neighboring powers. This was certainly the official reason given for the Hamidiye in its regulations and was surely a consideration in its architects' choice of locations. However, even though the Ottomans were well aware of the slow but steady movement of Russians southward with their eye on the Ottoman border regions, the central Ottoman government was also growing increasingly suspicious of Russian intrigues among the border populations in the region, both Kurds and Armenians. They knew that the Kurds were generally motivated by the desire to work with whichever power allowed them the most independence and privilege, but they viewed the Armenians as having conspiratorial designs in cahoots with the Russians. Therefore, the more pressing mission becomes clear when we consider the demographics of the region and bear in mind where the Armenian population centers as well as the budding hubs of Armenian revolutionary activity were in relation to these tribes-turned-militia.

Several authors who have commented on the Hamidiye have contended that the militia was created as part of the Ottoman government's anti-Armenian policies at the end of the nineteenth century,[14] but none of these authors has offered much evidence for this claim, aside, perhaps, from pointing to the role of the Hamidiye Kurds in the horrific massacres of Armenians that bloodied many parts of Anatolia in 1894–96.[15] Mapping the Hamidiye does, however, substantiate at least the connection between the establishment of the Hamidiye and the state's desire to establish control over what was believed to be a Russian-Armenian conspiracy as well as to suppress revolutionary activities as they intensified. It also demonstrates that while not the sole motive in this manifold mission, the suppression of Armenian nationalist-revolutionary activities was of increasing importance especially in the years immediately following the establishment of the organization.

In southeastern Anatolia at the end of the nineteenth century,[16] Armenians comprised a significant segment of the population in the "Six Provinces," although they did not form the clear majority anywhere but in the *kaza*s of Karcan, Adilcevaz, Bergiri, and Moks in the central *sancak* (subgovernorate) of Van. In fact, this was the only *sancak* in which the Armenian population reached 50 percent of the total, with the remainder of the population being mostly Kurdish. In these provinces, Armenians' numbers were spread across the region, in both rural, and especially, urban areas. Major southeastern Anatolian towns, such as Van, Bitlis, Erzurum, Arabkir, Diyarbekir, Harput, and Muş, had considerable Armenian populations. Although they were a largely urban people, they also comprised a healthy segment of the agricultural countryside, particularly in the Erzurum and Muş plains and in various regions of the Van province. There were also sizeable Armenian populations elsewhere in the Bitlis, Diyarbekir, Sivas, and Harput provinces. In the cities, Armenians pursued various professions, often concentrating in occupations dealing with trade and money lending. Many were artisans and shopkeepers as well. In the countryside, Armenians tended to be peasants who farmed small garden plots of their own or larger tracts belonging to their villages, but who were increasingly forced into sharecropping and tenancy; in this they lived a life much like their settled Kurdish neighbors.[17]

Armenians from predominantly urban centers (and even some rural areas at this point) were exposed to the latest ideas through literature delivered to them by their cosmopolitan compatriots, who would visit their hometowns after residing in the empire's capital or abroad, and also through the various missionary schools that Europeans, and especially Americans, established for their education.[18] Socialism and nationalism figured prominently in the ideas espoused by a growing segment of the literate Armenian population, and revolutionary societies, which first emerged in centers abroad, gradually proliferated throughout the towns and villages of the Armenian plateau in southeastern Anatolia. Beginning in the late 1880s and especially in the early 1890s, revolutionaries would sometimes transport their numbers, accompanied by literature and weapons, across the Iranian, and particularly Russian, frontiers into the empire.[19] Incidentally, these borders had also been serving as an escape route for villagers who, in the face of growing poverty and oppression, sought to emigrate illegally. Relatively fluid borders further allowed revolutionaries, most of whom were from Russia,[20] to cross over into the empire, carry out a raid, and duck back across the frontier so as to avoid capture by the Ottoman authorities (a tactic long employed by frontier tribes).[21] While revolutionary activity was certainly on the rise during these years, it could not, however, be considered large-scale. The heightened level of activities, coupled with the Ottomans' memory of how some Armenians behaved during the Russo-Turkish War, nonetheless produced an image of serious threat in the minds of many local Muslims and ruling circles.[22]

The major perceived menace crossing the borders that concerned the Ottomans, then, was from the Russians through their Armenian "collaborators." Particularly after 1890, revolutionaries traversed these frontiers (chiefly in the Eleşgird and Bayazid regions of the Erzurum province and the Başkale/Van regions of the Hakkari *sancak*, bordering Iran), and then hid out in certain Armenian towns and villages, especially around Lake Van and in the mountains and plains of Muş and the Sasun mountains.[23] Hence, if we were to superimpose a map of the Hamidiye regiments on a map showing the distribution of the Armenian population in the region, keeping in mind where the embryonic centers of Armenian revolutionary transit and activities were located, we would find a strong overlap between the two (see the Appendix in this book).[24] Moreover, a document from the Ottoman archives demonstrates that the regiments as initially planned were to be organized in the Bitlis and Van provinces, where the Armenian "conspiracy" (*fesad*) was greatest and where they would serve to counter that threat.[25] Although revolutionary activities were admittedly small-scale and revolutionary organizations were merely in an embryonic state in the years immediately preceding the formation of the Hamidiye, they were nonetheless a clear factor in the establishment of the tribal militia. Moreover, as the movement spread and as armed activities became more prevalent in the years following the initial recruitment for the Hamidiye, the anti-Armenian component of the Hamidiye's raison d'être was further confirmed in the eyes of its creators.

While the *post-facto* involvement of the Hamidiye regiments in anti-Armenian activities is certainly amply documented and a significant part of the story, it does not necessarily prove what the intention of the Ottoman authorities was at the time of their foundation. Even though Armenian revolutionary activities themselves were only just beginning as the Hamidiye was formed, the Armenian "conspiracy" was a strong presence in the minds of the Ottoman rulers, especially in the border regions. After the regiments were created and after revolutionary activities expanded in scope in the early 1890s (indeed, partially as a response to the creation of the regiments), the focus of the Hamidiye organization on these activities became more tuned to dealing with a concrete threat, rather than a vague "conspiracy." Additionally, even over the following years as Ottomans worked to refine their plans for the Hamidiye—doubling the number of regiments and incorporating new tribes for motives quite beyond the suppression of Armenian activities[26]—the distribution of the Hamidiye in largely Armenian regions or areas where Armenian revolutionaries were becoming increasingly active was nonetheless a striking feature of these irregular cavalry units, and must be considered as an essential factor in the larger Hamidiye venture.[27] This is why the Kurds were the tribal group most targeted to form the regiments, as they were the group who lived in and near historical Armenia—in the "Six Provinces" targeted by Europeans for reforms.

The number of Hamidiye regiments reached sixty-four or sixty-five, its maximal extent, in 1900.[28] These regiments, still largely located in areas with substantial concentrations of Armenians, were nonetheless also, albeit to a lesser extent, present in areas with few Armenian inhabitants—in various parts of the Hakkari *sancak*, for example. Although places like Hakkari may not have been Armenian population centers,[29] they were certainly locales where revolutionaries operated or which they traversed, particularly after 1890, as Dasnabedian's map illustrates.[30] However, it is also true that the Ottomans had further plans for the Hamidiye than simply acting as a force to counter Armenian revolutionary activities.

STICKS, THEN CARROTS: RAISING THE REGIMENTS

The sultan had grand plans for the Kurds. In the mosaic of peoples that was the Ottoman Empire, they would be his special element; he would be "the father of the Kurds," or *bavê Kurdan* as he was known in Kurdish.[31] The Kurds would be drawn into the fold of the Ottoman state and "civilized," and would offer their "special martial qualities" in service to their patron's domains. To show them how special they were, he even named the organization into which they were to be drafted after himself to highlight the special bond that was to develop between himself and "his" Kurds.

Although Şakir Pasha was one of the key architects of the project and continued to be involved in its implementation, Zeki Pasha was designated as the on-site commander—a post that he would enjoy for nearly two decades. Zeki Pasha, a bright and promising young officer of Circassian origin who was connected to the sultan through marriage,[32] was the perfect choice to head this venture as he was smart, energetic, extremely loyal to his patron, and familiar with the people of Kurdistan.

Zeki Pasha first had to tackle the associated problems of conscription and collection of taxes, connected because in order to achieve either aim the state had to be able to track the Kurdish tribes and induce them to surrender men and money—a feat that the Ottoman government had never been able to realize successfully. This was a mission the central government took seriously in its efforts to centralize, modernize, control, and "governmentalize" the empire's remaining domains, and it extended to Kurds beyond the Sunni tribes eyed for enrollment in the Hamidiye regiments (and even beyond the Kurdish tribes).[33] While contemporaneous with the desire to contain Armenian revolutionary activities, the mission to extend the arm of the state was a separate and broader concern.

In order to recruit the numbers projected in initial proposals for the Hamidiye, Zeki Pasha and his men needed to engage a good segment of the tribal population in the venture. Filling the registers to meet projected standards would continue to be a challenge for this Hamidiye commander. First was the task of surveying the region and determining the details of their target population. Attempts to take the census did not go over well in various parts of Kurdistan, with Kurds suspecting that the reason for the census was their impending conscription into the army. Some hid their children or lied about them, while others temporarily abandoned their homes. Some fled across the border, and still others threatened census takers with violence.[34]

In early November 1890 a dozen Kurdish chiefs were gathered and summoned first to Erzurum, then on to Erzincan, the seat of the Fourth Army Corps, before being shipped off to the capital two months later.[35] The voyage to Istanbul was meant to create the bond of loyalty between the tribes and the sultan—a very personal bond.[36] This first group of Kurdish chiefs was already wary of the government's plans for them. They had been called out by the governor of the Erzurum province to form an irregular cavalry and pursue bands of armed Armenian revolutionaries across the border into the Russian Caucasus. Recognizing this as a foolhardy plan and seeing the dangers if they were surprised by Russian border guards, the Kurds refused to respond to the governor's mandate.[37] Others, suspicious of the government's motives, declined further attempts by Zeki Pasha and his agents to man the militia as they suspected that the government planned to take them hostage once they had arrived in the capital.[38] The chiefs were not the only skeptical parties, however. As the British consul at Van reported, many of their tribesmen were "inclined to believe that their Aghas have been cajoled by the Sultan into selling them as soldiers for the Turkish Government."[39]

Nonetheless, a group was still somehow attracted or induced to join the ranks, perhaps due to the extensive "publicity campaign . . . to make the formation of the Hamidieh regiments more appealing to the tribal chieftains."[40] The campaign must have been successful, as tribal chiefs wishing to travel to the capital to see the sultan filled the headquarters of the Fourth Army and expressed their desire to enroll.[41] Leading chiefs heeded a summons to Erzurum before moving on toward official enrollment. Once at Erzincan, the next stop in the journey, the chiefs were persuaded to accept the terms of registration in the Hamidiye: They would form a cavalry totaling twenty thousand men; they would be commanded by Kurds of their own tribe of the rank up to and including squadron commander (or colonel, according to a different source), with superior officers being sent from the imperial army. The government would arm them, but they would provide their own harnessed horses, which would each be branded with a different symbol.[42] They would consent to drills for two months out of the year, during which time they would be housed and fed by the government. All this was agreed upon after the Kurds had been lavished with attention and favors during their stay in Erzincan.⁴³

By February 1891 the first lot of chiefs from three tribes set out for the capital with dozens of their tribesmen to present themselves for official ceremonies and an audience with the sultan. The voyage had been planned by the central government down to the last detail. The chiefs and their retainers would travel together to Trabzon on a boat outfitted with food and provisions for their horses, and once in Trabzon, would be fed and would make arrangements to have their animals looked after while they were in the capital. Others, like the Hayderan tribe who had many in their camp and who could not be present for the first journey, would come as the second group.⁴⁴

Right on schedule, the group passed through Trabzon in March, where one Italian consul describing their sojourn pointed to the importance the sultan must have placed on them given the reception accorded to them by civil and military officials. The consul described the group as

twelve *beys* more or less highly placed and others belonging to their entourage. They were all armed with *yatagans* and *kancar* revolvers, while the chiefs had Winchester cavalry rifles, in use in the Russian army. At the center of the group there were two armed only with lances. The *vali* [provincial governor], the military authorities, and the chief of the municipality went to greet them several miles [from the town] with a company of *nizamiye* (soldiers of the regular army) and military fanfare. Upon arriving before the commander of the place, they were placed in the quarters of the principal notables of the town. Yesterday at 16:00 they boarded the liner Diana, from the [Austrian] Lloyd, specially chartered by the government. . . . A company of *nizamiye*, headed by music, rendered them honors before their departure as did the general commander of the place and the *vali*, who climbed on board to salute them. To receive the *beys* [notables], two chamberlains had come from Constantinople: one from the sultan and the other from the *serasker* [minister of war].⁴⁵

The people of Trabzon would witness many more such processions, especially in the months to follow.

At the end of March, the first group of chiefs finally arrived at its destination. According to the *Tarik* of March 30, "the officers and privates of the new regiment formed from the nomad tribes arrived yesterday (Sunday) in the Austrian boat 'Diana' from Trebizond. His Imperial Majesty the Sultan received them from the kiosk, in the vicinity of the Palace, and sent Dervish Pasha to convey to them his greeting. He ordered them to be quartered in the 'new barracks' and their smallest wants to be attended to."⁴⁶ The Kurdish chiefs awaited the next step in their adventure.

These Kurdish chiefs, joined by others who had made a similar journey to the capital via Trabzon, were invited to ceremonies held in their honor, where they received decorations and distinctions from the sultan. For those who remained suspicious of the government's purpose in keeping them there, it would certainly take such honors to win them over. The British Colonel Chermside, who met several of these chiefs, described these men as "suspicious of the intentions of the government is [sic] natural from traditions of Asiatic History. They are afraid of detention as hostages or prisoners and feel the restraints as to their liberty as Turkish officials or officers constantly accompany them. They are mostly lodged in Barracks and dissatisfied with their food and quarters."[47]

The ceremonies that would eventually flatter and win over the chiefs commenced with their attendance of the *selâmlik* on cavalry horses and foot.[48] They awaited the completion of their uniforms and standards for the scheduled procession at the end of their visit, which was designed to parade the sultan's new brainchild before a wider audience. The display seemed to please the sultan and impress all onlookers, who, after seeing the "heroic warriors [*cengaver*]" in their military formation, felt confident that they would be able to resist even the most orderly of cavalries.[49] After some time, the uniforms and standards materialized and the Kurds were bestowed their ranks and decorations and were showered with gifts representing the highest distinctions in the empire.[50] Haci Yusuf of the Sibkan tribe was decorated and given a jeweled tobacco box by the sultan himself; Mirza Beg of the Adaman tribe was presented with an Arab horse; and Fethullah Beg of the Hasanan tribe was offered a ring. Most were decorated with the Third Class Osmaniye, the Third Class Mecidiye, or the Fourth Class Osmaniye.[51] Lastly, each regiment was given a red satin banner with the sultan's coat of arms embroidered on one side and a verse from the Qur'an on the other along with the imperial decree gilded on white silk.[52] Many were nonetheless displeased that top command posts were not assigned to the chiefs themselves.[53]

After two months' residence in the capital, the newly decorated and ranked chiefs were given a royal send-off before they headed back to Kurdistan. Embarking on the Austrian Lloyd steamer Helios on May 16, they arrived three days later in Trabzon,[54] where the British consul noticed that they were wearing different garments than when they had passed through on their way to the capital, writing that their "gaudy costumes" had been abandoned for "more sombre attires."[55] Armed with rifles and revolvers, they had been stripped not only of their traditional costumes but also of their customary lances. Revealing his prejudice, the Italian consul added: "So equipped, they no longer had the ferocious appearance they had in their barbaric costumes."[56] The next day the new recruits, representing some twenty-four tribes and subtribes in all,[57] departed for home, crossing paths with the second group of Kurdish chiefs and their retainers on their way to a similar destiny.[58]

Now decorated Ottoman officers, possessing a new status along with their new attire, the tribal chiefs returned to home, each with orders to raise hundreds of their tribesmen to form the regiments they had promised. The process of raising the regiments would continue intensely for at least a year, with new regiments being appended more sporadically over the following decade. Projected numbers fluctuated in the early years from a total of twenty thousand to eighty thousand fighters divided into from forty to one hundred regiments. Critics on all sides were rightly skeptical that such a force would ever be put together, although those closest to the sultan dared not voice such doubts.[59]

At first, the enterprise was extremely unpopular among the tribesmen as they saw no benefit for themselves in the venture since they were still responsible for paying taxes and furnishing recruits for the regular army from tribesmen not enrolled on the Hamidiye registers. With the second group of Kurds at the capital, the main cause of dissatisfaction with the enterprise stemmed from the fact that militia members would still have to pay the sheep tax as long as they were on active duty, but other members of the tribe would have to pay all taxes *and* be subject to conscription.[60] Sensing that he would go nowhere if he upheld this demand, Zeki Pasha soon revised this requirement, returning to the original proposition; hence, entire tribes who had members participating in the Hamidiye enterprise would be granted exemption from the sheep tax and conscription beyond the Hamidiye.[61] Such a measure would perhaps make membership in the Hamidiye a bit more palatable for the tribe as a whole. Later it became clear that the impunity granted to Hamidiye horsemen in any sort of animal-raiding or land-grabbing activity would draw many to apply for "membership" in this exclusive "club."

These "incentives" began to make themselves felt almost immediately after the regimented chiefs and their retainers returned from Istanbul. Reports of boasting and bragging, of threats,[62] and of new crimes committed with the guarantee that they would go unpunished were given in the months following the homecoming of the tribes. Already in November 1891 the British consul at Erzurum testified:

The formation of the new Kurdish cavalry appears so far to have but little re-straining effect on these outrages, in which many members, and even prominent officers of the new force, are accused of taking part. . . . It is said that the Kurds of the Sibkanlu tribe, who are members of the new cavalry, avail themselves of that pretext to take forage, food, etc., from the villagers of Alashgerd without payment. This system of military robbery has hitherto been the speciality of the police and regular cavalry patrols.[63]

And in early January 1892 the French consul stated that "in the vicinity of Bayazid, a Kurdish chief, a Colonel of one of the new regiments, attacked a Persian caravan and stole five loads of carpets."[64] Reports of similar crimes continued to fill pages of European consular statements and Ottoman documents.

Other "notorious" chiefs joined as a type of bargain with the authorities so that they would receive amnesty for their past crimes. Mustafa Pasha, chief of the Mîran tribe in the Cizre-Botan region, was one example. At a time when all other tribal heads approached had turned down Zeki Pasha's overtures, Mustafa Pasha responded positively and negotiated a deal with Zeki Pasha. Just a few months prior to his agreement, Mustafa Pasha had allegedly carried off hundreds of sheep belonging to a merchant from Urfa and had ignored all summons of the Mardin governor to appear before him and account for his offenses. With Zeki Pasha, however, he was able to negotiate a pardon in exchange for promising to form a Hamidiye regiment.[65]

While financial incentives and pardons would prove to be of key importance, also essential was the heightened status—an "authoritative resource," as Giddens might call it—accorded to chiefs so decorated by the state.[66] For Kurdish society, Martin van Bruinessen has observed:

> Chieftains, as tribal ideology has it, reach and maintain their position due to a combination of descent, character ("manliness," i.e. generosity and courage) and consensus of the members of the tribe. In practice, however, their position is based on political skills and the support of outside allies. One of the major functions of a chieftain is to constitute a bridge between the tribe and the outside world, in which other tribes and the state (or states) are the most important actors. The recognition of a chieftain by the state—which in the case of the emirates took the form of sumptuous robes of investiture and beautifully calligraphed deeds of confirmation, and now at the lowest level that of collusion with the regional gendarmerie commander—is the best possible prop of a [sic] his position.[67]

With official endorsement by the sultan and the badges and uniforms to make such sanction public, the chiefs began to vie with one another for command of their tribes' cavalry regiments. In February 1892 reports came in that Celalî Kurds were fighting among themselves over which of their various chiefs was to hold the leading rank in the new cavalry; seventeen men and women were killed and twenty-eight were wounded. The Hayderan tribe north of Lake Van experienced a similar feud, with the loss of six lives.[68]

Others who had turned down Zeki Pasha's initial overtures were now alerted to these benefits and rushed to join the new cavalry. But this time around they were not so easily accepted: "It is said that certain Kurdish chiefs who had not joined in thus far decided at the last moment to come to seek ranks and standards from the marshal; but the latter, reminding them of the hostility they had previously displayed, refused to listen to their pleas in order to prove to them that in order to obtain such a favor from their Master the Sultan, they had to seek, before anything else, to tear down any barrier by their trust and their submission."[69] Furthermore, possibly from the fear that somehow membership would be revoked or they would have fewer benefits if they did not raise the numbers requested by Zeki Pasha, these chiefs began to engage in sundry means of building their numbers. A "private letter" confided to the British military attaché read, "The village Kurds do not like the auxiliary cavalry regiment business at all. They say the Aghas, in rivalry of one another, have pressed them very hard, registering everything in the shape of a man even if 100 years old, and that for instance they compel a poor Kurd to sell his cow and buy a horse."[70] When the new troops were called out in summer 1892 for the flag ceremonies, one observer noted that in addition to having mostly horses of "very inferior quality," there were also "a large number of elderly men and very young boys in their ranks."[71] Even as the chiefs scrambled to put their units together with such tactics, the numbers were still not forthcoming (nor would they ever approach in reality what they were said to be on paper).[72] Instead of 500 men per regiment, tribal chiefs were lucky to muster 100 to 150 mounted men (some still fewer, indeed far fewer), and even this after stealing or borrowing horses from client or neighboring peasants or tribes.[73] Since each cavalryman had to provide his own horse, this was a huge obstacle. The French consul at Erzurum observed that

most Kurds have neither a horse nor the means to buy one. Furthermore, due to a serious error of political economy, the Sublime Porte has, for some twelve years, prohibited the export of horse breeds; this measure, which was believed to cause the race to multiply, had a diametrically opposed result, as horse breeders, no longer finding a market, have progressively abandoned this industry, so that at present, the most optimistic estimates give no more than twelve thousand horses in all of Kurdistan, a large number of which are employed in agriculture. Zeki Pasha needed to content himself with what the Kurdish chiefs are able to give him, first because he cannot obtain any more than this . . . and most importantly, because he has been the promoter of this Kurdish cavalry and he needs to raise forty to fifty complete regiments. In order to not go back on his promise he has lined up regiments which [in reality] are but a mere smokescreen.[74]

Zeki Pasha continued to campaign throughout much of the region in 1891 and 1892 in attempts to boost enrollment. And when decorations and privileges did not suffice to make the new regiment heads produce, he reverted back to the stick, holding some of them hostage in Erzurum and imprisoning some of their relatives to make them turn over the tribesmen they had promised.[75] Pressed hard, some tribal chiefs continued to wring their tribesmen and client peasants for money and horses, while others simply fled across the very borders they had been organized to patrol. The French consul reported that

the project of organizing the Kurdish cavalry has not advanced a step since the return of the chiefs to their homes, and doesn't seem to be seeing an immediate beginning of execution, or to ever see it. Various rumors are circulating to the following effect: some confirm that the future cavalrymen have refused to allow themselves to be enrolled, others say that the principal chiefs have taken refuge in Persian territory in order to not have to keep their promises. What is certain is that the Kurdish chiefs are in over their heads and find themselves currently hard-pressed to furnish even a quarter of the men they had insisted they could enroll. No sooner had they returned to their villages than they engaged in quarrels stemming from each chief's desire to encroach on his neighbor's domain in order to expand his [own] contingent. In spite of this, they have not managed to bring together a number of men even remotely close to their strongly exaggerated promises. The Ottoman government perceived a bit late that it had been duped by the Kurdish chiefs and their agents, who led them to believe it was possible to raise an imposing corps of forty to fifty thousand Kurdish cavalrymen.[76]

The execution of the plan may not have gone as smoothly, then, as Zeki Pasha had initially predicted. Nonetheless, by use of the carrot and stick, he was still able to assemble a considerable number of Hamidiye regiments, even if they were not, nor ever would be, the desired number. And to keep these new recruits, bring them into the fold of state administrative power, and train them in their new profession, he organized an additional series of ceremonies, this time held in the provinces for locals to witness.

FROM TRIBESMEN TO TROOPS AND BACK AGAIN

While the aims of the Ottoman government in forming the Hamidiye regiments were multifaceted, the methods exercised in achieving these ends were equally diverse. One means was through sheer force—arming some Kurds and threatening others with military might. Another was through the attempted inculcation of the very modern concepts of patriotism and belonging to the Ottoman territorial, political, and social entity. After trying to dispel the Kurds' initial suspicions about the government's intentions through assorted concessions granted to the tribes of those who enrolled, the government found that while it was easy to arm the Kurds and gather a number of them under the Hamidiye umbrella on paper, a much greater challenge rested in their ability to convince them to perform the state's bidding and to truly incorporate them, not just physically but "spiritually," into the Ottoman body. First to play a role in this operation would be the manufacture and issue of uniforms, and second would be the flag ceremonies surrounding the inauguration of the newly created regiments. After the first initial push to form the regiments, a series of induction ceremonies were held in the main Hamidiye centers of Diyarbekir, Van, and Erzurum, with smaller initiation processions also taking place in other towns. The regimented tribes belonging to each of these provinces reported to their respective provincial seats for ceremonies that took place in May and June 1892.

In early May, Zeki Pasha arrived in Diyarbekir accompanied by some of the sultan's aides-de-camp, a colonel, and two other high-ranking officers. After being greeted by some of Diyarbekir's most eminent civilian and military officials, the group proceeded to organize the local regiments and the inauguration took place outside the town with "due ceremony." The imperial edict explaining the aims behind the formation of these regiments, along with their obligations and privileges, "was solemnly read in their presence," and the colors designed expressly for them were presented "on behalf of the Sultan with His Majesty's gracious salutation." The Hamidiye troops were reported to have looked "very smart and soldier-like" in their new uniforms, which they wore just for the ceremonies. A few days later, Zeki Pasha departed for Cizre, where he would organize a similar induction ceremony for the regiments of the Mîran tribe headed by the notorious Mustafa Pasha.[77]

In June, after coordinating ceremonies and recruiting more tribes in the Diyarbekir, Mardin, and Siirt-Cizre areas, Zeki Pasha arrived in Van, where he was met by local Kurdish *agha*s and chiefs. The pasha must have been pleased to receive this greeting when he arrived, but frustrated at the numbers of the turnout. Indeed there were far fewer than had been anticipated due to deficiencies in cavalry mounts and also to the fact that many members of a single tribe had been enrolled in two, even three, regiments.[78] In spite of dwindling numbers, however, the pasha forged ahead with the ceremonies and presented the colors to the dozen or so regiments represented from the Van province in a spirited procession. He nonetheless appeared dismayed that each regiment had not more than twenty horsemen, who were a far cry from resembling a trained body of cavalry, "in spite of their having been put through a considerable amount of exercise for the occasion."[79]

The Erzurum ceremonies, held for the tribes in the Erzurum and Bitlis *vilayet*s about two weeks later, were much larger and included great fanfare. There, Zeki Pasha presented the twenty-four regimental colors to the tribes gathered from around the region. The entire force at the Erzurum garrison was paraded outside the Kars Gate and after the sultan's edict had been read, the chiefs, now designated as honorary colonels in the new force, each received their colors from Zeki Pasha.[80] Regular troops marched first in the parade, followed by the Hamidiye regiments, who numbered anywhere from 40 to 120 men per regiment, totaling perhaps 1,500 in all. Like their counterparts in Diyarbekir and Van, however, "with the exception of some of the Chiefs, the Kurdish horsemen had made little or no attempt at uniformity in any respect, and the great majority of their horses were of very inferior quality. . . . Most of them carried Martini and Berdan carbines, besides other very miscellaneous weapons, and . . . there were a large number of elderly men and very young boys in their ranks."[81]

The work that faced Zeki Pasha and others involved in the Hamidiye venture was not just to instill military discipline in the Kurds, but to help invent—through these ceremonies and other means—a new tradition in which tribal loyalties would be surpassed by and united with "supra" Ottoman loyalties. They were further designed to inculcate feelings of personal loyalty to the sultan himself. Deringil has described how Sultan Abdülhamid's regime would typically use decorations "as a form of investment in the goodwill it hoped they would foster in the recipient,"[82] a practice wrapped up in the larger emphasis on symbolic ceremony that became more widespread in the nineteenth century not only in the Ottoman Empire but in other parts of the world as coercive power declined. The imperial favors, decorations, and the pomp and ceremony surrounding their bestowal were elements of the Hamidian rituals designed, as Deringil has put it, to "win the hearts of sheikhs and notables" and to further bonds of loyalty and obedience.[83] In the case of specific groups of people, notably the Kurds and the Albanians, the sultan personalized these ties to the empire and his person by portraying himself as "the father" of these peoples—among Kurds *bavê Kurdan* (father of the Kurds), and among many Albanians *baba mbret*, or "father king."

These performances—part of what Scott calls the "public transcript" of power—worked on many levels. The authority of the Ottoman sultan was supposed to be supreme in every inch of the empire, but it clearly was not, as the Hamidiye venture was part of the larger attempt to incorporate the nonstate spaces and "tribal zones" that fell beyond the state's firm grasp. Instead of using sheer coercive power, the state engaged in these ritual acts of power as an "inexpensive substitute" for coercive force, "or as an attempt to tap an original source of power or legitimacy that [had] since been attenuated."[84] There were many audiences for these ceremonies: the Ottomans wished to impress European onlookers and to draft their Kurdish audiences into their performance of power by offering them a symbolic role in the power structure in a regulated form. But the sultan seems also to have been a consumer of his own performance.[85] And Hamidiye chiefs would manipulate the displays of investiture to their own ends by using this public transcript and performance of power to embolden their own grab for local authority and resources.

Hand-in-hand with the ceremonies and part and parcel of the modernization efforts was the issue of special uniforms to the Hamidiye regiments. While the ceremonies may have flattered tribal chiefs and heightened their status vis-à-vis their tribesmen, uniforms could be a visible symbol of the Ottoman state that all the Hamidiye tribesmen could (in theory) possess. The new uniforms were designed to replace the colorful traditional costumes worn by the Kurds, which themselves varied according to region and tribe. They were more subdued in color, and like their name implies, designed to lend a sense of uniformity and purpose to this group that was spread across a vast region and that had hitherto held no special loyalty for the state and had little sense of belonging to the larger Ottoman polity. Uniforms would strip individuals of "those traits that might interfere with routinized patterns of obedience" and they would also indicate "to the civilian population the distinctiveness of the military figure as the specialist purveyor of the means of violence."[86] It was intended that only those select men who wore the Hamidiye uniform and badge would legitimately exert power in the eastern borderlands, and here only at the behest and interest of the state. By empowering a small and controlled group among the larger population of Kurdish tribes, marking them with uniforms, the state hoped to dilute the number of alternative power holders in the region and to direct a more select group to represent its presence and interests. The uniforms were also intended to make the tribesmen appear less "tribal" and more like a modern Ottoman, with—it was hoped—the accompanying shift in loyalty and identity.

Various descriptions of the Hamidiye uniforms exist, which indicate that they were as similar to one another as possible, with some regional variations probably allowed by the Ottoman authorities to make the uniforms seem perhaps less alien and more palatable to populations used to varying headdresses and fabrics, which themselves were appropriate for use in different climates. For the tribes originating in the Bitlis and Caucasus areas, the newly issued uniforms consisted mostly of gray tunics or waistbelts of the ordinary officers' pattern, gray trousers with a narrow red stripe, topboots, and *kalpaks* (lambskin or fur caps/busbies) bearing the imperial arms. Ribbons of different colors tied around these fur caps were to distinguish the tribes from one another. Kurds from "Mesopotamia" wore a similar dress, but of darker cloth, and replacing the busby was a *kefiye* (a patterned scarf wrapped as a turban) worn fastened around the head by a broad band of camel's hair, to which was attached the imperial arms. Others wore a fur cap or band surrounding the traditional white cap in a kind of turbanlike fashion. Kurds from the Eleşgird region were distinguished by their "dark Circassian costume and badge on the kalpak."[87] Some of the wealthier Kurds wore taller kalpaks adorned with their badges, and specially decorated epaulettes.[88] Commenting on the freedom each regiment had been given in choosing its "distinctive garb," the traveler Lynch observed that "the result" was "an incongruous mixture of the braids and gold lace of Europe with the Georgian finery of a serried row of silvered cartridge cases, banded across the breast of a skirted coat."[89]

The flag ceremonies, uniforms, parades, and processions were all new instruments in the central government's arsenal of assimilation to bring the tribal nomadic Kurds into the fold of the modern state. In these endeavors they were not unique, but were employing the methods of their contemporaries in other parts of the world and were motivated by a similar worldview.[90] This was modern state building, with many features in common with states elsewhere in the world but with specificities that conjoined historically to flavor the Ottoman example. From the state's viewpoint, there were successes and failures in this mission, but as we will see below, whether success or failure (depending on the vantage point), these also constituted some of the contradictions of modern statecraft.

If their goal was to create a force to counter Armenian revolutionaries and their suspected supporters, in this state agents were partially successful;[91] however, if their aim was to assimilate and subjugate the Kurds themselves, in this they were largely unsuccessful.[92] While the state tried to manipulate the Kurdish tribes into becoming loyal "citizens" and behaving as such, it was the Kurdish chiefs who, in the end, were successful in taking what the state issued them and using it for their own purposes. In the final analysis, in many ways the tribal Kurds were able to perform an act of "symbolic jujitsu,"[93] subverting the state's wishes through the very tools and trimmings they had been given.

While it is certainly clear that the Hamidiye regiments were employed in military ventures against Armenians, and that they knew this was part of their mission,[94] it is equally evident that they did so only when they saw profit in it, not out of much patriotic zeal or a sense of loyalty to their patron. This became clear as early as December 1892, when the Hamidiye Badikan tribe was called out to suppress the insurgents in the mountains near Muş after they had defeated Ottoman troops who could not penetrate their snowy mountain strongholds.[95] But as the French consul reported, not only did the Badikan Hamidiyes *not* pursue the rebels, they actually served to hinder the efforts of the Turkish troops, and engaged in widespread pillaging across the plain. Here they struck peaceable peasants in Christian and Muslim villages alike and even attacked government troops who had come as reinforcements—all this with the rapid-fire rifles the government had issued to them.[96] Many Kurds who had been given arms for this purpose refused to use them on their immediate neighbors because they enjoyed good relations with them, and to kill them would be to destroy their own livelihood. It was easier, then, to deploy Hamidiye troops from further away as they would not have a personal or economic relationship with the target population.[97] Moreover, in some places, such as Siirt, for example, Kurds reportedly supplied the revolutionaries with provisions and some of the revolutionaries were able to use Kurdish homes to manufacture their weapons.[98] Elsewhere they were assisted by Kurdish chiefs in their arms-smuggling operations or through weapons they had purchased from them.[99]

The Hamidiye also used their uniforms to other ends. The uniform, at once a sign of prestige and power, was not actually as widely distributed as the Ottomans had planned, many Hamidiye tribesmen having only the "lambskin busby with brass badge" and no uniform at all. Those who did come into possession of a uniform donned it on all occasions until it was completely worn out.[100] The uniform and badge were prized by the tribesmen not because they were proud to wear them in a patriotic sense but because they brought privilege to their wearers. Locals were quick to discover that the Hamidiye tribesmen would always be backed by their powerful protector, Zeki Pasha, and could therefore take whatever they wanted from the population. As a result, the Hamidiye badge became such a hot commodity that local silversmiths were banned from producing it without authorization. The British Colonel Chermside observed: "Travellers in the interior have usually noticed in Kurdish villages and in the streets of towns a few men in the Hamidieh uniform or with the silver badge. This latter was, it is said, abused, being worn by Kurds with no title to it and not, therefore, invested with the privileges granted in return for their voluntary service. Local silversmiths in the Van district, and possibly all over the 4th Military Circumscription, have now been forbidden to manufacture it."[101] Government-issue rifles, which became widespread in the region, were not only not used for the purposes designed by those who distributed them to the Kurdish tribes; they were, in fact, sometimes used in direct opposition to these intentions. Hamidiye tribesmen employed them on occasion to attack the government's forces when they saw fit,[102] and others sold them to the very Armenians they were supposed to be fighting.[103]

While it is clear that the Ottoman administration formed the Hamidiye regiments partially with the "Armenian conspiracy" present in their minds, it is also evident that the members of the tribal militia could not be counted on to follow orders except when it suited them. While there were a range of individuals in Ottoman circles who were well aware of this fact and who argued that the sultan's Kurdish militia should be disarmed and dismantled, those who had the say in the matter decided not only to keep the units but to create more of them. It is certainly fair to ask at this point what the rationale was for keeping a force that was determined by many parties (state, local, and foreign) to be highly destructive and detrimental to the social and economic health of the region, which was very poorly trained, and which could not even be counted on as a viable military organization.

A review of the goals that the Ottoman government had in creating the regiments reminds us that in addition to serving as a force to counter Armenian activities, the tribal militia would serve as a means for the government to gain control over a region that had hitherto been relatively autonomous. Or, as Scott might suggest, it was part of the Ottoman state's larger project of expanding state spaces while incorporating or neutralizing nonstate spaces.[104] Once pulled into the fold, the Kurds would be settled, taxed, subject to conscription, and made more "legible."[105] Şakir Pasha, for one, believed that it was important to forge ahead with recruitment despite early problems because he felt that more widespread recruitment for the Hamidiye would also help settle tribes and assist the state in gaining census information. This was important so that they could find those tribes who were hiding members to prevent regular army recruitment—recruitment and censuses being intimately part of modern statecraft.[106] But when pushed for information, taxes, or conscription, the regimented Kurds simply refused. They were not pressed hard again.

Nor were the tribes that were attached to the Hamidiye ever trained rigorously to become bonafide troops. Two decades of reports from European (and Ottoman) observers repeated the same thing year after year: the Kurdish auxiliary regiments received little or no instruction or drills and were never regarded by any party as a serious military institution.[107] They were shock troops at best, and this only when it suited their purposes. Officers assigned to train them often did not know even the name of the tribal chiefs to whom they were assigned and made few attempts to train them.[108] In fact, "since the scheme was started," observers did not think there had been "a single attempt to drill or exercise Hamidiyés. The latter laugh at the regular officers, and these latter do not attempt to enforce any kind of obedience or discipline."[109] Şakir Pasha believed that in addition to these chain-of-command problems, some of the officers who were responsible for overseeing the tribal militia were unqualified, and others were in the pay of Kurdish chiefs.[110] On this level, the project seemed to be just one of many ideas the sultan and his advisors had that did not pan out. Viewed differently, however, military effectiveness may not have been the most prominent goal; rather, if the point was to fashion a loyal body of previously unruly tribes into a group that would remain attached to the central government, then military efficacy would not be so important.

A COMMON WORLDVIEW

The Hamidiye was certainly a "Hamidian" institution even though it was carried on by the Young Turks who came to power in July 1908. However, in many ways the two regimes, often posed in diametrical opposition to one another, proved to be rather similar. While there were attempts by the CUP-backed governments that succeeded the reign of Abdülhamid II to dismember this particularly Hamidian institution (it bore his name, after all), ultimately they decided to keep the organization, albeit under a different name. They also chose to use the regiments against Armenian revolutionaries, and to view them additionally in terms of their own modernizing and centralizing missions, which were not so different in the end from those of the sultan they had overthrown. After all, both regimes were concerned with the larger process of transitioning to modern (nation-) statecraft and were preoccupied with very similar concerns.

PRECEDENTS

The Hamidiye Light Cavalry did not represent the first time an imperial(ist) power had drafted one subject element for use against another, or even the first time the Ottomans had made military use of their Kurdish populations. And it was certainly not the first time that so-called warrior races were sought by imperial powers for their martial qualities. In fact, this practice goes back at least as far as Roman times, when Romans employed various Germanic tribes, whom they viewed as a barbaric but courageous military race, against one another.[111] Europeans first began to employ irregular troops on a large scale in the eighteenth century, sometimes drafting particular groups in their larger battles against other European armies. The Hapsburgs made use of some forty thousand Serbo-Croatian "Grenzer" troops during the War of Austrian Succession, and twice that number during the Seven Years' War.[112] Soon the French used irregular troops en masse, often giving this job to those deemed appropriate for such tasks as scouting, raiding, or sharpshooting—a judgment that often overlapped with ethnic stereotypes. In the Seven Years' War, for example, the French reserved the positions in the regular army for themselves and the irregular positions for Canadians, whom they regarded as having a "natural spirit" for such tasks.[113] The British are well known for their exploitation of colonized peoples in their military ventures, putting Scots and Irish to work close to home and Sikhs and Gurkhas abroad.[114]

The Hamidiye Light Cavalry was also not the first time the Ottomans had made military use of the Kurds. The Ottomans (and also, incidentally, the neighboring Safavids in Iran) had entered into military agreements with the Kurdish emirates within their domains from the beginning of their rule over Kurdish lands in the early sixteenth century. In the Ottoman-Safavid confrontation that took place in Kurdistan during the Ottomans' expansion eastward, Kurdish tribal troops led by their *mîrs* (leaders of Kurdish dynasties) assisted the Ottomans in inflicting the final defeats on the Safavid armies.[115] In the centuries to follow, both the Ottomans and the Safavids would often move their tribal populations, Kurds included, over vast distances either to recently conquered parts of the empire, or to regions under threat of attack. More recently, the Ottomans had employed considerable numbers of Kurds in the Russo-Ottoman War, although many of the Kurdish "troops" engaged during this conflict were hardly military assets to the Ottomans, having engaged in widespread looting and attacks on Armenians—a fact that was not forgotten by critics of the Hamidiye when it was proposed.[116] And most recently, the sultan had drafted "friendly tribes" in his campaign against Sheikh Ubeydullah following the war, and only a decade before the Hamidiye was created.[117]

The sultan had many precedents for the creation of his tribal militia, then, including ones from the Ottomans' own, and even quite recent, history.[118] But it was the Cossacks in Russia he declared to be the model for his new project.[119] The Russian Cossacks had been in existence as a developing community for centuries, but it was the military organization of the nineteenth century that Sultan Abdülhamid II had in mind as his model. The Cossacks were a "military caste" of excellent horsemen who acted mostly as frontier guards, and later, in the nineteenth century in particular, as personal troops of the tsar and as agents used in quelling internal threats. They performed their service in exchange for limited independence, concessions of land, and exemption from taxes and regular conscription.[120] It was in the nineteenth century that tsars began to nurture a special bond between themselves and the Cossacks as threats to their personal security increased. "Nicholas I emphasized this in 1837 when he bestowed the newly-contrived title of 'Most August Ataman of All Cossack Voiskos' on his heir [Nicholas II], beginning a succession of heir-atamans that extended to the son of the last tsar."[121] Henceforth, tsars would make ceremonial visits to the largest and most senior Cossack community—the Don. Later, as it became impractical for Nicholas I or future tsars to visit all the Cossacks due to the geographical expanse of their presence, "a symbolic handful of Cossacks could be brought to the precincts of the imperial family to serve as household guards . . . This not only put the tsar in direct contact with 'his' Cossacks, it provided an occasion to imply that he was one of them."[122]

Sultan Abdülhamid II clearly was alert to these aspects of Cossackdom in his creation of the Hamidiye regiments, and saw the key components of the Cossack organization and its relationship to the ruler as examples to emulate. Like the Cossacks, the tribal Kurds lived at the frontiers of the empire, were excellent horseman and had reputations for being great warriors.[123] Just as Cossacks received land grants for their services, the sultan believed that he could eventually settle the tribes and turn them into loyal agricultural producers, where they could replace, or better monitor, the "unreliable" Armenians who lived there.[124] But it seems likely that the features of Cossackdom that the sultan envisioned most for the Kurds was their service directly under the tsar as his "personal" servants—a close relationship of loyalty and patronage. Inspired by the Cossack example, the sultan even sent a group of Ottoman officers to St. Petersburg to learn Cossack-style drills, and these officers returned in 1896 having completed their training.[125] In the same year, plans were underway in the Ottoman Empire to create special Palace Guards from Hamidiye regiments, apparently in the image of the special Cossack household guards mentioned above.[126]

NOBLE SAVAGES AND SAVAGE NOTABLES

The Ottomans had employed Kurds for military purposes on numerous occasions over the preceding centuries, but what distinguished this latest mission from previous similar rounds of conscription was the worldview behind its promotion, and indeed its very modernity. An important aim of the Ottomans was to draw the Kurds under the umbrella of Ottomanism—to pull them "spiritually" into the Ottoman fold and to induce them to be loyal and obedient members of the Ottoman body. There were twin goals with regard to the Kurds, which were backed up by two views prevailing in Ottoman intellectual and ruling circles at the time (and, incidentally, these two views were mirrored by various European observers as well). First was the idea shared by most that the Kurds were a kind of "warrior" or "martial race."[127] Where the two visions of the Kurds split, however, was between those who believed the Kurds to be irreparable "savages" and those who adopted the "noble savage" view, both notions being common in American and European views on their native or colonized peoples.[128]

For those Ottomans (and European observers) who adopted the former view—that is, that the Kurds were inveterate barbarians[129]—the Hamidiye was indeed an institution to be feared, as it distributed weapons to those most likely to abuse them. They opposed bringing the Kurds into the Ottoman army as such and were disgusted by the institution on the whole. Indeed, from the very beginning, most high-ranking officials close to the sultan were against the idea.[130] The acting British consul at Diyarbekir wrote in February 1891 that the public in general and Christians in particular regarded the project with great misgiving. "They state, and with reason, that as these hordes have always been the terror and scourge of the peaceable inhabitants both Moslem and Christian, no one knows what they may do when incorporated into the army and provided with arms." He added that unless placed under the strictest discipline, the new militia might even cause "serious anxieties" to the government itself.[131] It was not only Christians and foreigners, however, who deemed the Kurdish tribes to be incorrigibly barbarian and a major threat. Another consul stated in his report on the subject that "this measure of organizing the Kurds is regarded by all Christians and foreigners, and by many Turks, with the greatest dread and anxiety."[132] The French consul at Erzurum averred that Muslim notables in that town regarded the Kurds as a "blood-thirsty, savage population, which is used to plundering and nomadic life" and which would "never submit to discipline straight off." He added that they had "no attachment to the Ottoman government" and that they did not even "identify with the Empire." These notables believed, therefore, that "the authorities [were] making a grave error in entrusting arms and giving military training to this population, which could then create a serious embarrassment to the government." They feared what would happen when they were armed and suggested that the honors bestowed on them would "only give them an exaggerated idea of their importance and [would] then render them even more difficult to follow."[133]

One Ottoman writer who penned similar thoughts in 1905 describes his deep feelings of mistrust for the Kurds, who (he alleges) nurtured the deepest hatred for the Ottomans and would sell them out to the Russians any day. He describes them as fickle, always ready to cross the border when things on one side are not going their way, only to return again when life on the other side fails to meet their expectations. His writing reflects his contempt for the Ottoman practice of bestowing ranks on the very same Kurds who were in the Russians' service.[134] Indeed one of the provincial governors also feared that the project would render the governing of Kurdistan, already a difficult task, even more challenging.[135] Of course the sultan would not tolerate criticism of his brainchild, and refused to believe that there was anything wrong with it. He routinely dismissed European reports on the militia as being written through Armenian-tinted lenses, and the complaints of Ottoman officers as stemming merely from jealousy of their colleague, Zeki Pasha.[136]

Critics were even more vocal as the years passed and the Hamidiye continued to participate in such unsavory activities as pillaging, land grabbing, and even murder. Due to the unsavory activities with which some Hamidiye commanders and the tribesmen they commanded became associated, the entire organization gained a bad name, and "the Kurds," it was judged, could not be civilized and would never display the order and obedience necessary to become viable troops and citizens.[137] Not only that, but they had begun to corrupt the regular officers and troops attached to their units, who "had taken up their bad habits."[138]

At the same time, however, there were many supporters in ruling circles as well as in the popular press of proposals to integrate their tribal peoples into the Ottoman army. Many of those in favor of incorporating Kurds in the Ottoman army, albeit as irregulars, were "social engineers," "liberals" who believed that the Kurds were backward, but noble, and had great skills to offer the military. They believed in their civilizing mission—that through service in the army, the tribal populations would learn discipline and would be able to channel their "warlike tendencies" in a direction sanctioned by, not opposed to, the state. They were also well aware of the fact that modern armies, while sometimes segregated and exclusive (shutting distrusted ethnic groups out of military power), can also often act as agents of assimilation and integration.[139] The sultan was himself a proponent of this view. In his political memoirs, he wrote on this topic:

In the event of a war with Russia, these Kurdish regiments, which were raised in an orderly fashion, can be of great service to us. Furthermore, the idea of "obedience," which they will learn in the military, will also be useful to them. As for the Kurdish *agha*s whom we have given the title of officer, they will be proud of their status and will strive for the discipline implied in the title. After a period of training, the Hamidiye regiments, which will be completed in this way, will in the end become a valuable army.[140]

It is nonetheless difficult to establish what the true opinions of observers were, for the Ottoman press in the Hamidian period is well-known for its strict censorship. Official journals had to support the sultan and his ideas; therefore, the Hamidiye tended to receive great praise, at least in the official press. Yet the worldview of the writers is what is striking. Shortly after the initial organization of the Hamidiye regiments, one journal praised the enterprise, arguing that the "nature" of the tribal peoples predisposed them to such a venture:

It cannot be doubted that, bold and intrepid as the Kurds, Chiefs and privates alike, are by nature and character, if they were regularly and continuously instructed and drilled by competent officers, and supplied with proper uniforms, arms, and the necessary horses, they would form a very effective division of the Imperial troops.

For the tribes of Kurds and Arabs within the limits of the Ottoman Empire, by reason of the conditions under which they live, of the localities where they dwell, abounding in pure air and water, and of their manner of life, are, for the most part, strong of body and constitution, and free from sickness and disease; and being strong of limb and in continual exercise, they are, from their earliest years, devoted to riding and the use of arms. In addition to this, owing to the existence of ranks among themselves, they are accustomed to discipline and obedience.

For all these reasons it will be recognized by all, great and small, that, if they be granted the protection and patronage of the Sultan, and be enrolled among the regular troops, they will justly gain much in esprit de corps, and become a brave and determined body of soldiers.[141]

The *Takvim-i Vekayi*, the official Ottoman gazette, also praised the effort, laying "stress on the good effects which this measure is calculated to secure. First of all," the journal submitted, "the nomad tribes will be thus brought within the pale of civilization, their hordes will be disciplined, and their proverbial bravery turned to good account for the benefit of the State."[142] The civilizing mission continued throughout the years of the Hamidiye. In 1896, the plan to bring select Hamidiye regiments to the capital was believed by the minister of war to be necessary in order to "tame" and "soften" the "peculiarities" of the Kurdish character through contact with the "civilizing influences of the capital."[143]

The opinion of Ottomans was mirrored by European authors who applauded the effort along similar lines. One writer praised the endeavor, arguing, "These irregular horsemen may fairly be compared with the Cossacks for capability to endure fatigue, and as to their methods of service and tactical formations; they are all born riders." He added that the tribes were "splendid fighting material, and will cost the State next to nothing: their value, however, will increase with their notions of discipline." The writer concluded: "We consider the raising of the Hamidié Cavalry to have been a most fortunate step, and think that the measures adopted will soon attain the desired end, more especially since they so fully recognise the tribal peculiarities of the people. When the necessary discipline has been infused, enormous masses of serviceable cavalry will have been added to the Osmanli ranks at a comparatively small cost."[144]

In their mission to turn "tribesmen into Ottomans,"[145] many elite Ottomans conceived of auxiliary civilizing and disciplining institutions to "educate" their respective tribal peoples, which would serve as an adjunct to the training they would receive as cavalrymen or soldiers. The well-known American-Indian boarding schools had a kind of counterpart, albeit a much smaller and less institutionalized one, in the Ottoman dominions. The Ottoman Imperial School for Tribes (Aşiret Mekteb-i

Hümâyûnu) was established shortly after the foundation of the Hamidiye regiments, again with the goal of assimilating the empire's tribal populations and especially fostering loyalty to the empire, and particularly to Sultan Abdülhamid II himself. The Kurds were not the only tribes targeted in this plan, but were to join Albanians, and especially Arabs, in learning discipline, loyalty, and basically, how to be good, civilized Ottomans. The idea was that the children of leading tribal chiefs would complete a course at the school, return home with ranks and honors, and thereby serve as a model for the youth of their tribes.[146] The school was part of the larger plan to ottomanize the tribal population, foster their allegiance to the center, achieve other benefits to the state, such as their eventual sedentarization and transformation into productive agriculturalists, and rescue them from the "darkness of ignorance."[147] It may also have fit into the sultan's larger policy of promoting orthodoxy, and indeed finding a means to turkify the non-Turkish populations.[148] The opening ceremonies of the school, in October 1892, were distinctly reflective of the worldview that was behind this school and its counterpart militia. In his speech in honor of the school's opening, the Ottoman minister of education emphasized the benefits of civilization that the students of the Tribal School would incur, and contrasted the "state of nature" the students were leaving behind in order to enter the modern civilization that faced them in the capital. The sultan's photographer joined in to capture the spirit of this speech in before-and-after shots of the students, meant to contrast their previous "barbarity" with their present "civilization."[149]

The connectedness of the two ventures—the Hamidiye and the Tribal School—was reflected not only in the registers, which showed a number of Hamidiye tribes whose children were enrolled in the Tribal School,[150] and not only in the worldview that was behind their creation, but also in very practical matters. Just as Kurdish tribes had been suspicious of enrollment in the Hamidiye when the organization was first proposed, so too were the tribes targeted for the Tribal School project, and there was similar pressure on local officials to recruit more students for the school.[151] And just like the Hamidiye never reached the desired numbers or military efficacy, so too was enrollment in the Tribal School a far cry from what the sultan had hoped.[152] Whatever the eventual realities, however, the visions were clearly connected. Ottoman sources indicate that it was planned from the very beginning to enroll the Hamidiye tribesmen in a military school so that they could be educated formally in military matters and return to head their tribes' regiments, but not at first in the Tribal School.[153] However, while recruitment may have been difficult among the Arab tribes in particular, Hamidiye tribesmen began to send petitions to the government asking to be enrolled in the Tribal School.[154] The minister of education opposed the idea and insisted that the school was intended for the Arab tribes and that the Kurdish tribes were supposed to enroll their children instead in a special cavalry class in the Imperial War School. But in the end the efforts of the petitioners were successful perhaps due to interventions by Zeki Pasha, who supported the Hamidiye requests, and an imperial decree was issued that allowed certain tribes to enroll students.[155]

The Tribal School was an essential part of the Ottoman government's larger efforts to reform and modernize, backed by the belief that with a little assistance, even the most backward elements of their society could be civilized. The Hamidiye and the Tribal School were both institutions created with these notions in mind, and while they were the major endeavors, there were smaller ones that also were to contribute to these larger goals. As Zeki Pasha toured the region in his efforts to recruit tribes for the new militia, he also met with other officials about their proposals to open schools in principal Kurdish villages.[156] Şakir Pasha, one of the original architects of the Hamidiye project, also believed in promoting educational reforms among the Kurdish population; in the mid-1890s he attempted to set up schools that would ottomanize, civilize, and develop them, all using Turkish as the medium of instruction.[157] And there were numerous plans to modernize roads, bridges, and other channels of communication, including a drive to build steam travel on Lake Van, although few of these actually ever materialized, to the great dissatisfaction of the inhabitants. All of these were part of the larger goal of assimilating and subjugating the Kurds, controlling the region (including monitoring and suppressing Armenian activities), and fostering bonds of allegiance between the sultan and the Kurds.

CONCLUSION: WHY THE KURDS?

As we have just seen, the Ottomans were joined by their counterparts across the globe in efforts to engineer, modernize, and protect their domains, and to invent new traditions of loyalty and identity. The Hamidiye was firmly a part of their attempts to do all of these. But we must ask: why the Kurds? And given that the Kurds were one of the groups the Ottomans wanted to better manage—indeed suppress—why empower them further?

As we have seen, the Hamidiye enterprise was part and parcel of the Ottomans' larger project to control and "civilize" the empire's tribal peoples and to establish bonds of loyalty to and identity with the Ottoman polity. This was a distinctive aspect of Sultan Abdülhamid II's reign, and was continued in many ways by this sultan's successors, the Ottoman Committee of Union and Progress (CUP). But the Kurds were not the only

Ottoman element to have a significant tribal or semi-nomadic population; Arabs, Albanians, Circassians, and Turcomans also had important tribal segments. We have seen above that the Ottomans' larger mission to sedentarize nomads and bring them into the Ottoman fold had all tribal groups in their sights, not just the Kurds.[158] The Tribal School included students from various backgrounds, and indeed Arabs constituted a more sizeable presence in that institution than did Kurds. But the Hamidiye, in the end, was almost uniquely Kurdish, with only a few of the sixty-four or sixty-five regiments composed of non-Kurdish (Arab and Karapapak) tribes.

There were, in fact, strategies at various times to incorporate Arabs and other tribal groups into the regiments. Indeed, the Hamidiye Regulations stated from the beginning that the regiments were to be comprised of "Arab, Kurdish, Karapapak, and Turcoman tribes."[159] But in actuality, these plans never materialized, and were clearly less important than the plans to enlist the Kurds. Early in the enrollment process Zeki Pasha did contact some very important Arab tribes in the Mardin region, not far from where the important Millî confederation enjoyed influence, perhaps when numbers were dwindling and he needed to boost enrollment. It is not known which party turned the other down in the end, but neither of the two powerful Shammar and 'Anayza tribes ended up enlisting men in the Hamidiye.[160] And Receb Pasha, the commander-in-chief of the Sixth Army Corps, which comprised the Arab lands bordering the Fourth Army Corps where the Hamidiye was based, was also commissioned to raise the Arab tribes in a similar formation.[161] A small effort was made to enlist a Druze regiment in Lebanon, but this similarly bore no fruit.[162] Several years later, there were reports that the government sought to enroll Albanian tribes, not in the Hamidiye, but in a parallel organization. In 1898 the British vice-consul of Üsküb (Skopje) reported a large contingent of Albanian chiefs visiting the area, supposedly with this goal in mind.[163] The British military attaché, however, explained that any such rumors of an Albanian formation along the lines of the Hamidiye was, for the moment, "entirely devoid of fact," adding his observation that many questions were raised, discussed, dropped, and raised again at the Yıldız Palace, quite independently of the War Office, and which never even reached the War Office until they assumed a "tangible form." In many cases, he noted, they were only entertained by the sultan, with no decision being reached, and hung up, only to reemerge for the same treatment when a relevant political question would bring the matter forth. The Albanian Hamidiye question was "an old one," as he cited, and many communications had passed from time to time between the Palace and assorted Albanian chiefs on the subject, but had never amounted to anything.[164] They never came to much because although enrolling the Albanian and

Arab tribes would certainly have been in keeping with the sultan's larger policy of controlling the empire's tribes and building bonds of loyalty to the empire and especially to his person, it was the Kurds in particular who were the primary target of the Hamidiye regiments.[165]

The reason for this is that the Kurds were the Muslim element that predominated in Armenian regions (the "Six Provinces") and along the threatened, fluid border with Russia and Iran. As this chapter has illustrated, a key priority in this manifold mission was the establishment of a means to counter Armenian revolutionary activities in the region, to protect that border from all threats—domestic and foreign—and to ensure the loyalty of the peoples who lived along the important frontier. All tribal peoples were targets of the government's efforts to control and/or sedentarize nomadic populations and to establish bonds of solidarity among the various Muslim groups in the empire,[166] which would be represented in the figure of the sultan/caliph himself, but the Kurds had the unique geographical distinction of proximity to large pockets of Armenians and to the fluid borders that could be crossed by Russians and Armenians from Russia, and to a lesser extent, Iran. This seems to be the most likely reason that symbolic institutions of decoration and privilege, while important practices, were not matched with a Hamidiye-like institution outside of Ottoman Kurdistan. Elsewhere there may have been fears that the population was drifting "spiritually" and needed unifying motifs to draw their hearts, if not their bodies, under the Ottoman (and indeed Turkish) umbrella.[167] But the eastern provinces were where a particular security threat was perceived at this time, where the borderlands were becoming "bordered lands,"[168] and the organization to counter the regional security breaches was, appropriately, a military one. In his political memoirs, Sultan Abdülhamid II himself acknowledged the importance of the Kurds in his scheme for internal settlement. Speaking of the need to limit the settlement of non-Muslims in the empire and the parallel need to bolster national strength, he wrote, "It is absolutely necessary to strengthen the Turkish element in Rumeli and especially Anatolia, and above all else to mold the Kurds in our midst and make them our own."[169]

It was the Kurds, then, who were practically the sole element comprising the Hamidiye regiments, but it should also be noted that not all Kurds were members of this privileged institution. Only Sunni Kurds were ever formally enrolled. Interestingly, however, there were at times plans to include Alevis, who formed a very significant minority especially in the Dersim region,[170] and Yezidis, who were a minority with a strong presence in the Sincar region of the Mosul province and in parts of the Van and Diyarbekir provinces. But the fact that the Ottoman government, or at least Zeki Pasha, solicited the Yezidis, and especially the Alevis, at all, invites comment.[171] It has hitherto been argued from many corners that a major feature of the Hamidiye was its overwhelmingly "Sunni-ness," and this has been taken by writers treating the subject as a sign of the sultan's anti-Alevi policies and his support for Sunni tribes in their attacks on Alevis as much as Armenians.[172] Given this new evidence, we must certainly rethink arguments for the former. Rather, I would argue, this is added testimony to the "Kurdishness" of the affair, and to the emphasis the sultan placed on building a network of Kurdish allies who would be loyal to him personally, and who would serve to counter any Armenian threat, even if this meant inviting non-Orthodox Kurds into the fold, although admittedly, it is more likely that the enthusiast behind the proposal was Zeki Pasha. It may also be an indication that the Hamidiye was backed by two different visions—one of the sultan, who was certainly committed to his policy of promoting orthodoxy, and the other of Zeki Pasha and Şakir Pasha, who envisioned loyalty as not resting so much in symbolic import but in material inducements.[173] The plans never materialized for the incorporation of either Yezidis or Alevis, but the fact that these plans existed in the first place is nonetheless worth mentioning.

The Hamidiye Light Cavalry was, then, a multifaceted mission, which was reflective of larger Ottoman preoccupations. As the empire had suffered many territorial and economic losses, especially in the century preceding the formation of these regiments, it looked for ways to protect the domains that remained and to prevent further losses. Sultan Abdülhamid II continued in the path paved by his reforming and modernizing predecessors to extend the state's reach domestically and to control not only the movements but the political and spiritual inclinations of its member elements. In its efforts to foster symbols and bonds of a supra-identity, the Ottoman government joined a world of others with similar goals and visions of their respective futures. The ideas behind the Hamidiye organization were distinctly reflective of the modern historical moment in which they were conceived and which, it was hoped, they would answer. Settling and controlling the tribes, creating bonds of loyalty, centralizing remaining Ottoman dominions, protecting them from the "Armenian threat," and ensuring that Ottoman proposals would match or beat any deals Kurdish tribes were offered by neighboring rivals, were all features of the Hamidiye project. And while the mission itself was manifold in aims, it was equally productive of outcomes that affected other broad spheres of local, regional, and empire-wide history, many of which occurred quite beyond what had been imagined by the militia's creators. It is to those other aspects of the Hamidiye and its moment that we now turn.

CHAPTER TWO

The Hamidiye Under Abdülhamid II, 1890–1908

★

Sometime around the occasion of his ten-year anniversary as Hamidiye commander, Mustafa Pasha, leader of the Mîran tribe in the Cizre region, claimed the unique distinction of being singled out for mention by Abdurrahman Bedir Khan in *Kurdistan*, the very first Kurdish journal. A dubious honor it was, however:

Before [Abdülhamid II] ascended the throne, the Kurds were knowledgeable and civilized people, having brotherly relations with Armenians and avoiding any kind of confrontation. Then what happened? Did [Kurdish] civilization and knowledge turn into barbarity, ignorance, and organized rebellion? Who else carries out the atrocities in Kurdistan but the members of the Hamidiye divisions, who are armed by the sultan and proud of being loyal to him? For example, there is Mustafa Pasha, the head of the Mîran tribe, within the borders of Diyarbekir [province]. He used to be a shepherd ten or fifteen years ago in his tribe, and was called "Misto the Bald." We do not know what he did to become a favorite of the sultan, but his talent in creating scandals appealed to the sultan, who thought that he would assist in shedding blood and hurting people. He made him a pasha and introduced him with the title of commander of a Hamidiye division. Now imagine what such a man is capable of doing—a traitor whose own son has even become an enemy to him, and a person who has outraged his daughter-in-law. Would he not butcher the Armenians and pillage the Muslims?[1]

This bizarre little passage, strangely enough, holds many clues about the power structure in southeastern Anatolia as it was changing in the late nineteenth century, particularly under Sultan Abdülhamid II. This chapter will trace the transformation of the local power structure of Kurdish society through the nineteenth century, with particular attention to how the Hamidiye organization impacted the changes underway. At the end of this chapter, the importance of this peculiar piece of text will be clear; the reader will be able to fully situate it in its historical context and understand the various roles the different actors within played in the story of the power struggle between the Bedir Khans and the Mîrans and between dynasty and tribe in the Kurdish-Ottoman tribal zone at the margins of the empire.

BACKGROUND: THE OLD EMIRATES

The Bedir Khans are perhaps the most legendary of Kurdish families. This has been due not only to the size and historical importance of this family, but also to the efforts made by the famous Mîr Bedir Khan's progeny to keep the family's name in circulation. The renowned Mîr Bedir Khan came to power in 1821 in Cizre, then in the Ottoman province of Mosul.[2] The emirate that Bedir Khan Beg ruled quickly distinguished itself in the history of Kurdish emirates for its size, its security, its "modernity," and its virtual autonomy. Since the time much of Kurdistan was incorporated into the Ottoman Empire in the early sixteenth century, Kurdish emirates had been of varying sizes and degrees of power relative to one another and also vis-à-vis the Ottoman and Iranian states that incorporated the emirates' territories into their respective empires. However, the structure of emirates like that headed by Bedir Khan Bey, their relative independence, and their general relationships to the Ottoman state were not simply distinctive features of Kurdish society, but were also intrinsic to the very nature of Ottoman rule over its periphery. Therefore, a brief look at the history of the emirate system in the Ottoman Empire is necessary in order to better understand and appreciate the significance of the Bedir Khan emirate in Kurdish and larger Ottoman history.

THE INCORPORATION OF KURDISTAN INTO THE OTTOMAN
EMPIRE IN THE SIXTEENTH CENTURY

Kurdish nationalist historiography tends to portray the relative autonomy that much of Ottoman Kurdistan enjoyed throughout a good part of its history as being solely a product of the Kurds' tenacity in maintaining their "independence" and ignores other factors that might explain why Ottoman rule over the region was minimal and largely indirect. Autonomy is considered to be a feature only of the imperatives of Kurdish society, and the Ottoman state is disregarded as an agent in this system.3 However, the flexible character of Ottoman rule over its periphery is also a major reason why the system was mostly successful. From the beginning of Ottoman rule over Kurdistan, this autonomy was not a unilateral imposition from either "side," but a mutually beneficial understanding between the Ottoman sultan and the local Kurdish chiefs, even if one side was more "equal" than the other. Both the Ottoman sovereign and the local Kurdish chiefs had vested interests in the agreement that set the tone for subsequent centuries of Ottoman rule over Kurdistan and the relationships between the Ottoman sultan on one side and various Kurdish chiefs and *mîr*s on the other. Therefore, while the sixteenth century is not part of the topic at hand, it is nonetheless necessary to explore the terms of this relationship as it was set during this period in order to better appreciate the issues addressed in this chapter.

The incorporation of much of historical Kurdistan into the Ottoman Empire in the early sixteenth century was based on a negotiation between the Ottoman Sultan Selim I and some twenty Kurdish *mîr*s in the context of the clash between the Ottomans and the new Safavid rulers in Iran, who were both expanding the territorial limits of their empires.4 The Battle of Chaldiran and its aftermath was a key event in the region's history, for it set the tone for subsequent Ottoman rule over the region. Already before the battle it had become evident to the Kurdish rulers that their fate would lie with one or the other of these two increasingly powerful dynasties, both of which sought ultimate rule over the region. The *mîr*s who had initially allied with and were subsequently arrested by Safavid Shah Ismail in the context of this imperial clash managed to escape and return to their lands. They were joined by others. Through the mediation of Idrîs-i Bitlîsî, a Kurdish notable in the service of Selim I, an agreement characterized by a later historian as "far-sighted" on the part of the Ottoman sultan was reached: the Kurdish chiefs would unite in assistance to the Ottomans and in return would be granted an autonomy that practically amounted to the level of rule they had previously enjoyed.5 As van Bruinessen has noted, "'Loyalty' may have been all that was required of them. In a frontier zone, after all, political (and military) allegiance is more important than the regular payment of taxes."6 Through this mutually beneficial alliance the Kurdish chiefs were able once again to secure possession of their former emirates, and the province of Diyarbekir, most of what is presently northern Iraq, and all the lands westward became Ottoman in name. The military accord continued to bear fruit for the Ottomans in subsequent campaigns against their neighbor to the east, during which further territories were annexed to the empire, with a more or less permanent border that was fixed with the Treaty of Zohab in 1639.7

The military alliance with the local Kurdish rulers was essential for Ottoman expansion in the region and for the maintenance of a permanent buffer against Iran. Furthermore, due to the remoteness of the region and the difficulties in governing a population that included a significant number of nomads who recognized no authority but that of their chiefs and *mîr*s, the sultan required a sort of administrative agreement as well. Nominal and indirect rule was better than no rule at all. However, in order to secure the continued allegiance of these chiefs, the Ottomans had to grant them significant privileges.[8] In 1515, Idrîs-i Bitlîsî, who had negotiated the deal between Sultan Selim I and the Kurdish *mîr*s, was given a sort of carte blanche in the form of blank documents bearing the imperial seal, to fill out with the titles of privilege, and to then report on the details regarding who was ruling which district and under what stipulations. The sultan's trusted intermediary was bestowed with additional "blank" documents to be used as "persuasion letters" for attracting additional Kurdish *mîr*s to add their names to the alliance.[9] Land-survey registers from the decade following the Battle of Chaldiran indicate that the areas ruled by the Kurdish *mîr*s were largely exempt from tax collection by the central authorities. Additional documents from the 1520s show that the administrative districts of Diyarbekir and the province of Kurdistan as well as some units called "Kurdish communities" (*cemâ'ât-i Kürdan*), which amounted to a region even larger than the districts included in the province of Diyarbekir, were administratively distinct; even those not referred to as "Kurdish communities" were called "provinces" rather than "counties," the usual Ottoman term for such administrative units.[10] Clearly the areas entrusted to the Kurdish *mîr*s were to have a different administrative relationship to the Ottoman state than their counterparts elsewhere in the empire.[11]

Although many details of this special status remain unclear, particularly with regard to how the relationship functioned in reality as opposed to in theory, a document from the aftermath of Süleyman the Magnificent's eastern campaigns outlines some of the concessions granted to the Kurdish *mîr*s. The districts and castles previously held by the *mîr*s, along with any additional assets given to them by the sultan, were effectively made their "property." They could be passed down to their generations of sons, and could not be interfered with by any administrator or tax collector, or even by the sultan's own sons, as long as the Kurdish chiefs remained loyal to the Ottoman state. The hereditary nature of these districts was emphasized, with a provision assuring that in the case that a particular *mîr* had no sons to claim his province upon his death, that province would be granted to another Kurdish chief and would not be offered to an "outsider." In return, the Kurdish *mîr*s were to remain loyal to this and subsequent sultans, to treat their subject populations in a just manner, and, in the event that contributions were required of them, they were to cooperate and act in concert with the governors of Diyarbekir and Baghdad and the other Kurdish notables.[12]

The numbers and status of individual principalities varied over the centuries to follow, and there are indications that the arrangement did not always operate in reality as it was outlined in the original grant.[13] The on-the-ground description of the administration of the Diyarbekir province provided in the travelogues (*Seyahatname*) of the well-known Ottoman voyager Evliya Çelebi indicates that most of the *sancak*s in the Kurdish regions actually functioned in a manner similar to those in other parts of the empire, with governors being appointed and dismissed by the state. Only some of them were autonomous hereditary governorships, or emirates, which were administered in the manner outlined by the original decree, mentioned above. But even these contained *timar*s and *ze'amet*s, the tax collection of which was recorded. There were, however, an additional five *sancak*s that were completely exempt from fiscal registration and tax collection, and the rulers over these districts maintained their inalienable right of possession. Evliya Çelebi further adds that in communications to the *mîr*s of these districts, the sultan even addressed them as "Excellency" (*cenab*).[14] Tezcan also points to discrepancies between the real and the ideal, noting that the changes in degrees of autonomy granted to a particular *mîr* over a particular district may have come about as a result of dynastic power struggles within the ruling families themselves.[15] There was also a fluctuating number of these principalities over the years,[16] which showed the continual process of negotiation and renegotiation of the relationship that was undertaken by the center and the local Kurdish rulers—a process that we see surfacing repeatedly over the centuries, particularly with the Hamidiye Light Cavalry institution at the turn of the twentieth century.

The Kurdish principalities were, then, less autonomous in reality than Kurdish nationalist historiography has suggested, but the regions in which they were located were nonetheless differently administered on the whole than were other parts of the empire, with significant sections of the region enjoying relative autonomy up to the nineteenth century, when centralizing reforms were pursued by sultans starting with and after Mahmud II. The flexibility with which the Ottomans ruled Kurdistan in a largely indirect and decentralized manner was successful from the points of view of the Ottoman state and of many local Kurdish emirates. The Kurdish notables negotiated a largely satisfactory arrangement for themselves, and the central Ottoman authorities displayed a pragmatic realism in their choice of ruling mode for the Kurdish regions. At a time otherwise characterized by a move toward centralization, the central Ottoman authorities realized that if they usurped too much authority from the local ruling families they might be faced with a serious rebellion or defection across the border.[17] Therefore, they kept just enough coercive power to maintain their more-or-less nominal rule, while at the same time thwarting the unification of local Kurdish magnates against the state, or preventing their defection across the border, by granting them significant privileges.

Nineteenth-century conditions, however, led the central Ottoman authorities to consider that they could no longer allow such a system of decentralized rule, and they embarked on a series of centralizing and modernizing reforms as part of their wider adoption of the practices and mindset involved in modern statecraft. However, in the midst of this novel drive for centralized power, at least in one part of the empire's margins one new emirate not only emerged but grew to be perhaps the most expansive and powerful of the Ottoman-Kurdish emirates.

THE BEDIR KHAN EMIRATE

Bedir Khan Beg, who came to rule over the Botan emirate around 1821, was later lauded by one of his many sons, Abdurrahman, as being not just a powerful ruler whose authority was vast and supreme in the region, but also a sovereign whose sense of justice was unmatched by previous and subsequent leading notables. Abdurrahman Bedir Khan painted the demise of his father's emirate as being not just the end of a family's rule but the end of justice, order, and security in the region: "Since my father left Kurdistan," he wrote in his journal, *Kurdistan*, in 1898, "the officials dispatched by the government to the villages and towns of Kurdistan are drinking the blood of the Kurdish people like snakes. The patrons do not know who their clients are, nor do the clients know who their patrons are. The Kurdish homeland is exhausted like a wounded body."[18] Although the sons and grandchildren of Mîr Bedir Khan had their own agendas for promoting a positive history of their father, some parts of this "eulogy" are, in fact, confirmed by other sources.

When Bedir Khan Beg took over the emirate,[19] he immediately set out to consolidate his rule over an entity that had previously been divided into "sister emirates" and that had been plagued by power struggles among its member tribal confederations.[20] It should be mentioned that one of these leading tribes, whose leader's death was ordered by Bedir Khan Beg during his campaign to consolidate his rule, was the Mîran. The significance of the passage from *Kurdistan* cited at the opening of this chapter will be clearer with this in mind. Brahîm Agha, the leader of the Mîran, had become powerful enough to take over some of the traditional functions of the *mîr*. Bedir Khan Beg ordered Brahîm Agha's death, and, aided by numerous loyal tribes, emerged victorious in the battle that ensued between his camp and the tribes allied with the Mîran. He was then the supreme ruler of the Botan emirate.[21]

This emirate distinguished itself locally for its expansive power that covered a significant part of historic Kurdistan by 1846 and also for its relative modernity. Inspired by his contemporary, Mehmed 'Ali in Egypt, Bedir Khan Beg worked to modernize his army and centralize command.[22] He created elite units recruited from all the tribes, who were now directly under his authority instead of under the traditional command of their respective chiefs, and even made military alliances with at least one government official.[23] With tribes under his authority, the influence previously enjoyed by the tribal *agha*s waned.[24] While Bedir Khan Beg's rule represented an affront to tribal supremacy, it was also clear to the Ottoman state that he was turning away from the traditional obligations of an *emir* to the sultan. The *mîr* declined to send his requisite tribal contingents when they were called up by the Ottoman army during the Ottoman-Russian war of 1828–29, and it is said that at one point he even had his own coins minted and had the Friday prayers recited in his name. All were acts that challenged the sultan's sovereignty.[25] By the mid-1840s, agents of the state were convinced that he could no longer remain at the head of his emirate. Significant privilege and autonomy had been part of the deal, but virtual independence had not.[26] The central Ottoman government, which had already been actively campaigning against the other Kurdish emirates, received additional pressure to bring down this large and powerful one after the massacres of Nestorians perpetrated by the *mîr*'s forces in 1843 and 1846.[27] Ottoman troops forced the final surrender of the *mîr*. The agreement pledged between Sultan Selim I and the Kurdish chiefs centuries earlier was not forgotten by later Kurdish *mîr*s such as Bedir Khan Beg, and he is reported to have brought this to the attention of the Ottoman authorities upon his capture.[28] It was clear, however, that a new policy had replaced the agreement, and the rebellious Kurdish *mîr* was brought with his entire family to Istanbul, where he received many honors and was then sent into exile.[29] The event marked the end of the Kurdish emirates and the beginning of a new era in the history of southeastern Anatolia.

CENTRALIZATION AND ITS DISCONTENTS

The destruction of the Kurdish emirates is part of the larger story of the Ottoman drive for centralization in the nineteenth century and would have important consequences for the future development of power struggles in Ottoman Kurdistan. Although targeted decentralization had worked well for the Ottomans for centuries, territorial losses in the eighteenth and early nineteenth centuries along with a diminished overall position in the global political and economic system convinced some in Ottoman ruling circles that reforms were necessary to turn the tides on this trajectory. The Hamidiye was created as part of the late nineteenth-century drive by Sultan Abdülhamid II for control of the empire's far-flung provinces and the transformation of the nonstate tribal zone into nontribal state spaces. However, in this wider centralization mission, the sultan had nearly a century of precedents to follow.

The Tanzimat-era reforms, which, for many constitute the focal point of mid-nineteenth-century Ottoman history, were a series of administrative measures taken by the central government aimed at modernizing, regulating, and centralizing the management of the empire. The major reform edicts of 1839 and 1856 are the most well known of the reform measures. The Hatt-ı Şerif of 1839 created new institutions to better deal with the exigencies of the day, while preserving, and reforming to a certain extent, the traditional state and religious institutions. The Hatt-ı Hümayûn of 1856 provided for the equality of all Ottoman subjects, regardless of religion, in "matters of military service, in the administration of justice, in taxation, in admission to civil and military schools, in public employment, and in social respect."[30] It additionally decreed that annual budgets would be strictly observed and that European capital and skills would be employed for economic improvements, and it codified penal and commercial law as well as provided for reform of the prison system. Keeping in the spirit of equality for all subjects, the 1856 decree also provided for the establishment of mixed courts for cases involving both Muslims and non-Muslims.[31]

The Tanzimat, although most closely associated with these two major reform edicts, was, however, much larger than this. The reform of the tax structure, which took place throughout the century and continued to unfold under Sultan Abdülhamid II, was also an important aspect of these measures toward change.[32] Additionally, sweeping bureaucratic reforms over the period resulted in the general transformation of the "branches" of government and their relationships to one another.[33] Accompanying the centralization of the bureaucracy were provincial reforms, which were enacted beginning in 1864 and were designed to integrate the administrative hierarchy, thereby increasing the possibility for central control while still delegating more judicial and administrative power to local councils and governors. The Provincial Law of 1864 further assured non-Muslims posts in the provincial government at all levels. In addition to securing greater control over the state's agents in the provinces, it was also hoped that these agents would, in turn, be able to strengthen their hand vis-à-vis the local population, particularly local notables and those from whom tax collection and conscription were difficult or impossible.[34]

But the centralization efforts were ineffective and/or differently applied in some parts of the empire; Kurdistan was one such place, where, instead of increasing order, general security, and the rule of law, they actually decreased in many parts. The central government had effectively destroyed the emirates—like that ruled over by Bedir Khan Beg—that had challenged its control; however, it had created no effective or strong institutions in their place. A power vacuum emerged, which was eventually filled, in part, by tribes that had been kept in check by the *mîr*s who had superseded the authority of tribal chiefs.[35]

THE RISE OF THE TRIBES

The emirates had been the most complex and significant political structures in Kurdish society in Ottoman times until they came to an end—a process that unfolded throughout the early nineteenth century, culminating in the destruction of the Botan emirate headed by Bedir Khan Beg. As an increasing number of emirates were dissolved, their component units—tribal confederations, and then simply tribes—progressively became the most important social and political units in the region. Yet instead of becoming more complex—that is, with tribes growing increasingly powerful and expanding their organization to replace the functions of the emirate—the opposite trend occurred. Martin van Bruinessen has identified this process, whereby "the tribal entities that we see articulating themselves in each consecutive phase of administrative centralization became correspondingly smaller, less complicated, and more genealogically homogeneous: emirates gave way to tribal confederacies, confederacies to large tribes, large tribes to smaller ones."[36] Mela Mahmud Bayazîdî, the Kurdish observer of nomadic Kurds in the wider Hakkari (Çulamerik) region, noted that many traditional leaders were left powerless.[37] The feuds of chieftains that used to convulse the country, as a British officer reported in 1885, were replaced by "a hundred petty quarrels among the descendents"; he believed this breakup of tribes into smaller units to be detrimental to the security of the region, particularly as clients—especially Christians—no longer enjoyed the same level of protection.[38]

The term tribe should not be meant to denote a primordial or unchanging social, economic, or political organization, and more specifically, nor should the term nomad be reified or treated ahistorically.[39] Kurdish tribes have experienced numerous modes of organization, ethnic composition, and relations with other tribes, settled populations, and state structures, in addition to a variety of "modes of production" in different times under various circumstances.[40] In fact, one of the most important observations about Kurdish society has been made by van Bruinessen, who has demonstrated that the features of given tribes, including their size, complexity, composition, and organization, as well as their relations with the outside world, have depended on and changed according to historical exigencies. The negotiations between a particular tribe and the state have strongly impacted tribes, and have even gone so far as to contribute to the dissolution of some tribes and the formation of new ones.[41] The availability of particular economic or natural resources has also been important.[42]

In the nineteenth century, Kurdish social organization underwent significant transformations and these shifts played a major part in the changes the local power structure endured. They also came about as a consequence of new concepts and practices of power by the central Ottoman government. As a result of the government's centralizing policies, which were backed by fresh visions of the state's authority vis-à-vis its various subjects, the Kurdish emirate system gave way to smaller units—tribal confederations and individual tribes. From the void left after the destruction of the emirates, tribal power emerged triumphant in most of the rural parts of the region.[43] Yet in many places the state did not step in to fill the void left by the deposed Kurdish "dynasts." Nor did the state accomplish its mission of centralized rule; indeed, in many regards and perhaps ironically, the Ottoman policy of centralization produced more decentralization than had previously existed.[44] The state continued to exercise indirect control, but this time increasingly through its new agents—individual tribal chiefs, in many ways carrying on a time-honored tradition.[45] At the same time, regional and global economic circumstances also impacted the new tribal formations as tribal units fought with one another for control over resources. Longrigg, who has also observed the "tendency towards [the] leveling, division, and disunity" of tribes, suggests that the process was assisted by the land-registry system and the purchase of entire estates by the sultan, as well as by such factors as the shifting of the Euphrates waters from the eastern to the western channel, which "had profound effects in displacing the tribes," and which "led to clashes, secessions, and invasions."[46] The periodic distribution of units of irrigable land by the government to tribal notables in exchange for a fixed rent gave rise to bitter feuds.[47]

The power structure in the Ottoman-Kurdish periphery experienced a significant transformation in the nineteenth century. At the beginning of the century, authority rested in the hands of the Ottoman state and its agents in some parts and the Kurdish *mîrs* in other districts. Although the officially recognized special status of the emirates in Kurdistan was different from the kinds of indirect rule practiced in other parts of the empire, it should be noted that Kurdistan was not necessarily unique in that many districts were virtually governed by local notables and even by renegade Ottoman governors who paid little heed to orders emanating from the center.[48] This had increasingly become the case throughout Anatolia and other parts of the empire.[49] With the centralizing reforms, however, the state attempted to take back its sovereignty by curbing the authority of local notables elsewhere in addition to those in Kurdistan.[50] In other parts of the empire, the state was more successful in imposing central control,[51] but in the Kurdish regions it was still too difficult to effectively govern from the center,[52] particularly given the fact that the destruction of the emirates had unleashed a new tribal dynamic. Gone were the former guarantors of security who also served as the link between the state and the local subjects.[53] First, the central government dissolved the province (*eyalet*) of Kurdistan in 1852, and attached it to the Anadolu Ordu Müşiriyeti. Provincial reorganization in the 1860s also was designed to increase the efficacy of local government. But administrative changes on paper still needed to be supplemented with effective means of governing the region in a manner that prompted more than paper changes. The state once again had to turn to local agents to collect taxes, fill local appointments, and act on its behalf. These agents were now the tribal chiefs.[54]

Now that the emirates no longer existed, local tribal chiefs sought sanction from the state in addition to a following from their own tribespeople, and they vied with one another for this power, with many chiefs of large tribes successfully achieving this goal.[55] Yet this struggle was accompanied by increased violence in the countryside as individual chiefs sought to expand their own power bases and their control over resources. The violence and insecurity that now mounted in the Kurdish and Armenian countryside was exacerbated by the new lack of a paramount authority to mediate conflicts. This role, which was formerly held by the *mîrs*, came to be filled in part by sheikhs, who could act as intermediaries. As such, they began to gather significant numbers of adherents, especially in areas where there were many (generally smaller) tribes or in areas where the nontribal Kurdish population was subject to a particular tribe.[56] Some chiefs were able to bolster their own prestige by alliance to a powerful sheikh, but in areas where large and powerful tribes held sway, the authority of the sheikhs was less significant and the power of the tribal chiefs became increasingly supreme.[57] The state had no choice but to recognize and co-opt the tribal power that had grown and proliferated in order to establish control and maintain security in Kurdistan.[58]

THE HAMIDIYE AND THE NEW TRIBAL "EMIRATES"

Until recent scholarship stepped in to question prevailing Western no-tions of "tribe" and "state" and their relationships to each other, the dominant discourse on tribes and states held them either as rungs in an evolutionary scale of social organization or as having inherently opposite aims and trajectories. Tribes were considered inferior to states in terms of political and social organization and states were assumed to have grown out of tribes, where applicable, but never the other way around.[59] In terms of their relationships to states, tribes have often been portrayed as inherently different from the state in terms of what their goals are; thus, the state always needed to suppress unruly tribespeople and force their detribalization. What recent scholarship has proposed instead is that there has existed a longstanding dialectical or symbiotic relationship between the two, whereby tribes and states have often contributed to the creation and maintenance of one another.[60] While this has long been the case for Kurdish tribes in the Ottoman Empire,[61] the political and social trajec-tories experienced by certain Kurdish tribes through their enrollment in the Hamidiye Light Cavalry illustrates this point most remarkably. The Ottoman government turned to certain tribes, particularly their leaders, at the end of the nineteenth century to further its own goals, and in the process dramatically impacted the face of the rural power structure in Kurdistan, a course that entailed the transformation of the tribal system and its relationship to the state. But the tribal chiefs who were clients of the state through the Hamidiye system were usually not unwilling parties to the deal; instead, they derived extensive rewards for themselves from this mutually beneficial association between tribe and state. Hence, not only were the interests of the enlisted tribes *not* in opposition to those of the government, but they became intimately connected, especially to one part of the Hamidian regime, namely the sultan himself and his supporters, chief among them Zeki Pasha. This process may be traced by following the path of the Mîran tribe and its leader, Mustafa Agha.

MISTO AGHA AND THE MÎRAN TRIBE

The name of Mustafa Agha's tribe, *mîran*, in Kurdish literally means "emirs." Name or no, the Mîran tribe did not, at least in recent history, produce any real *mîran*, at least not any recognized ones.[62] The tribe had, however, always been large and powerful, with near-*mîr* episodes. It had long been a significant tribe in the Botan emirate, whose chieftain was able to make important decisions in times when the emirate was led by a *mîr* who lacked charisma or power. In fact, Brahîm Agha, the chief of the Mîran in the early nineteenth century, had appropriated some of the traditional functions of the *mîr*, paying no tribute to the real *mîr* and acting as a mediator between other tribes in the emirate. Indeed, he refused to recognize the authority of the new *mîr*—Bedir Khan Beg—who rose to power in 1821, and this, as we saw above, resulted in his death.[63] Thus the enmity between these two Botan groups began. In spite of the brutal elimination of their leader, the Mîran continued to be one of the main Kurdish tribes in the region, and remained so throughout the nineteenth century. In 1886 the British Consul for Kurdistan wrote, "The Miran tribe is, though not the largest, by far the most influential of all the tribes of nomad Kurds who pass the summer in the highlands to the South of Lake Van and the winter in the plains about Mosul. The Miran Kurds are also the richest among these tribes and possess a considerable number of horses besides their flocks, whereas scarcely any of their fellows have horses though a few own mules."[64]

The rise to power of Misto Agha of the Mîran tribe exemplifies the relationship between the Kurdish tribes and the Ottoman state in the nineteenth century. The aforementioned account given by Abdurrahman Bedir Khan recalls the ascent of Misto Agha (or Misto Keçelo, Misto the Bald, as the writer called him) from being a mere shepherd in his tribe to tribal chief and decorated commander of the Hamidiye through the patronage of the sultan. Though Abdurrahman Bedir Khan's account is a bit exaggerated for rhetorical effect, it is not far from the facts.[65] Misto Agha was one of the first to join the Hamidiye, and thus managed to elevate not only his own standing in the tribe, but also the tribe's position vis-à-vis other tribes. Hamidiye members were allowed to pursue access to resources through any means at their disposal with either the complicity or the passive acceptance of the central Ottoman government. But Mustafa Agha was already the leader of his tribe when he joined the Hamidiye in 1891; he did not climb to the rank of chief through the Hamidiye as Abdurrahman Bedir Khan suggested. In fact, he had been the chief of the Mîran for several years. But he had risen to that station through the patronage of at least one Ottoman official around 1883–84. According to the British consul in the region, writing in 1886, "When, two years ago, the Diarbekir Vali was at Jezireh, Mousto (or Mustafa) in some way or other won his favour and was nominated chief of all these nomad tribes."[66] And thus the illustrious career of Misto Agha began.

Already the chief of a powerful tribe when recruitment for the militia commenced, Mustafa Agha agreed to join before its benefits became widely known and attracted further members. The British acting vice-consul reported that the Hamidiye proposal had been declined by the Kurdish chiefs, with one exception. It is stated by them that they suspect that the Government, under this pretext, would take them to Constantinople and keep them there as hostages. . . . The only one who accepted the proposition, and promised to form a regiment, is said to be Mustafa Agha, the powerful Head of the Miran nomad Kurds. The antecedents of this man do not inspire in the public mind much hope of an honourable career. He has been accused of incendiarism, murder, rapine, and all sorts of crimes; and it was only a few months since that he carried off several hundred head of sheep belonging to a merchant of Orfah, and, on being complained against, refused to obey the summons of the Mardin Governor, and the threats of the Governor-General were of no avail, and I am told that he is negotiating now with the Local Government for free pardon, as a reward for undertaking to form a regiment of dragoons.[67]

The Hamidiye was to be the biggest deal Mustafa Agha had been able to negotiate with the government (aside from his very chiefdom), but it was not the first. It seems that as soon as he received the backing of the Diyar-bekir *vali* and became leader of the Mîran tribe, Mustafa Agha began to aggressively build his power base and to bargain with the government.[68]

Mustafa Agha was not the only tribal chief, or *agha*, however, who was able to commit crimes with impunity. Since the breakdown of the emirate system, no strong power had stepped in to maintain order. In many parts of the region the government had to rely on the tribal chiefs to be their agents; although this often entailed little more than tax collection, it was an important enough activity to a government that needed the cash. Two years later, the governor of Mardin reported to the British consul that upon taking up his post, he found a list of some twelve hundred men, mostly *agha*s of villages and tribes, who had been accused of all sorts of offenses and were summoned to appear before tribunals, but had declined to obey and consequently were condemned by default. But, he wrote, the government was either "unwilling or powerless" to apprehend them, and since the taxes were collected through these chiefs, the governor thought it advisable to bring the case to the imperial government and "implore their pardon." He mentioned "Miranli Mustafa" as a case in point.[69]

"Mîranli Mustafa" is a working example for the present discussion as well. His career demonstrates how tribes came to be the most powerful social and political units in Kurdish society in the nineteenth century, often through the patronage of powerful government officials. It also illustrates how the creation of the Hamidiye accelerated the consolidation of local power and resources by certain tribes and leading individuals within those tribes who were able to exploit the threats that the state perceived and to milk the late nineteenth-century dilemmas of statecraft to their advantage. Although the Mîran tribe under the leadership of Misto Agha had "an atrocious reputation for all kinds of villainy" among locals, Ottoman of-ficials, and foreign observers alike, the reality is more complex.[70] As we shall see, the numerous acts of plunder and other crimes attributed to this and other Hamidiye tribes were based not on their inherent characteristics but on historical exigencies.

Kurdish tribes at the end of the nineteenth century numbered in the hundreds,[71] engaged in sundry occupations, possessed diverse skills, and had varied ways of life. Some were sedentary and excelled in agriculture and others were nomadic or seminomadic, the latter combining animal husbandry with some agriculture and the former living mostly off of the produce of flocks. The Mîran tribe likely oversaw in its "confederacy" several tribes that were at least partly engaged in agriculture, and were thus able to have access to the produce of these tribes through trade or through the tribute, often in kind, generally paid to the leading chief—in this case Mustafa Agha. The Mîran itself, however, seems to have been mostly, if not completely, nomadic. The tribe followed a seasonal migration between the Mosul plain, their winter quarters, and the region to the south of Lake Van, their summer pastures.[72] The British consul observed that the Mîran, like many other nomadic tribes that wintered in the warm and fertile Mosul plain, conducted their business as they were preparing to move on to their summer pastures. In the spring, the Mîran would convene in the town of Cizre, along with other tribes, to take care of their annual business. In this town they would pay their sheep tax; sell their wool, mohair, sheep, and other products; and purchase whatever they needed from the town before their long journey to the cool mountain pastures south of Lake Van.[73] Otherwise, business transactions were occasionally performed from their mountain camps in the vicinity of Van, where peasants and townspeople would visit them and purchase wool and other products.[74] The path of the annual migration brought the Mîran into contact with the government at Cizre, where there was a bridge they were forced to cross due to the swollen state of the Tigris in the spring. Here, the government, which otherwise had little access to migratory tribes such as the Mîran, was able to extract the sheep tax and levy heavy tolls for permission to cross the bridge.[75] Of course, after the Mîran men were enrolled in the Hamidiye, they became exempt from taxes, as did most other Hamidiye tribes.[76] The annual migrations were also generally fraught with conflicts between the nomadic tribes and the tribes and/or villagers whose lands they had to cross, and sometimes with the other migrating tribes they encountered along the way. Although territorial rights were specified according to custom,[77] conflicts nonetheless arose habitually, sometimes with great loss of life. Peasants protested that the tribes pillaged them in passing, or that the tribal herds ruined their crops. These complaints seem to have become increasingly frequent throughout the nineteenth century, as authorities were either unable or unwilling to address these grievances. Tribes such as the Mîran who were affiliated with the Hamidiye came to have added advantages during their annual migrations as well as during their times of encampment.

With the enrollment of the Mîran tribe in the Hamidiye, Mustafa Agha became commander of the two regiments provided by his tribe and was immediately made a pasha.[78] This undoubtedly increased his standing among his tribesmen even further. Enlistment in the Hamidiye also offered numerous other benefits to the new pasha and his tribe in the form of profit, protection, amnesty, and support against rivals. It was important to have a tribal leader who could come through for his people by keeping them fed, clothed, sheltered, protected from the outside world, safe from government excesses, and always at an advantage over neighbors. For Mustafa Pasha and others, the Hamidiye was the key to procuring these ends.

Economic advancement was a most important pursuit for the tribes, and enrollment in the Hamidiye was a ticket to profit and advantage over neighbors. The wealth of the Mîran, who were largely nomadic, resided primarily in their sheep. And with the rapid growth throughout the nineteenth century of the pastoral sector of the Ottoman economy, nomads and their sheep thus became increasingly vital to regional economies.[79] As an important tribe, the Mîran possessed a sizeable number of its own sheep. Like other regional tribes, the Mîran tended their sheep for the eventual sale of wool, skins, meat, and other important by-products (such as fats used for making soap and candles). It is also likely that they looked after the herds of local merchants and traders; desirous of the profits sheep could bring in, but lacking in the skills or wherewithal to care for them themselves, these merchants would contract with certain tribes for their custody.[80] In exchange, the tribes would receive a portion of the produce, whether in the form of newborn lambs, fleeces, or butter.[81] Those who did not entrust flocks to the nomads engaged in speculation: merchants would advance money to the tribes months before shearing in the expectation that the fleeces would be delivered to the party who advanced the money. This became an increasingly lucrative business in the later years of the nineteenth century, and was one that brought nomads and merchants into new and closer relationships with one another.

Since sheep were such an important and valuable sector of the regional economy, they were high on the list of items to be pillaged by those so inclined. Reports of sheep rustling became increasingly common during the later years of the nineteenth century. The Mîran tribe was certainly engaged in this pursuit as well as subject to falling victim to it, although the raiding party would have to be a tribe of equal or greater strength—and of these there were few in the region. Sometimes the raids were unprovoked, and sometimes they were retributive, punishing rivals who had made off with sheep and/or reclaiming stolen animals. Influential tribes like the Mîran, however, were not the usual targets of sheep rustling; their dependent villagers and less powerful neighbors were often the victims. While sheep raiding sometimes took on huge proportions, with thousands of sheep being pilfered in a single foray, most often it was on a much smaller scale; weaker neighbors often had fewer animals, but also fewer defenses.

Recovery of the stolen animals was immediately pursued by the owners. It was the responsibility of the chief to ensure that the stolen property was returned to its original owners who were members or clients of the tribe. Retributive raids often resulted in large loss of life. Sometimes, however, the victims of such theft would appeal to the government. Some officials dutifully pursued the thieves, successfully repossessed the stolen herds, and returned them. Others, however, would keep a portion for themselves upon recovery, or would sell them at the market, with the government pocketing the profits, ostensibly when "back taxes" were owed. Local governors who did their best to uphold the rule of law would, in addition to the recovery and return of the stolen property, also seek the punishment of the offender.[82]

Tribes that belonged to the Hamidiye were advantaged in many ways not only in the pursuit of property, whether lawful or not, but were also protected in practically every aspect of their lives. The Mîran and other Hamidiye tribes were safeguarded in their annual migrations—periods in which they raised and cared for their own animals as well as the sheep of merchants who had entrusted the tribe with their custody. Through their membership in the Hamidiye, not only were the tribespeople outfitted with advanced weaponry by the state, but they also enjoyed the benefit of armed escorts. These were often troops from the regular army, gendarmes, and police officers who were ordered to safely guide the tribe through dangerous territories traversed on the migratory route.[83] For example, during their annual migration, the Mîran tribe had to pass through the country associated with a longtime rival of Mustafa Pasha and his tribe, Aghayê Sor of the Şirnak region. The seasonal tours of the Mîran through the Şirnak district would generally be marked by fighting between these two rivals and their people. Aghayê Sor sometimes outright refused passage to the Mîran, who then had to make long detours. In this case, it was inevitable that the Mîran would retaliate for the inconvenience by attacking their rival's villages. Such affairs sometimes reached devastating proportions. Yet other times, the Mîran was able to make good use of government troops as escorts, and would not have to fear passing through unfriendly lands.[84] Aghayê Sor lacked Hamidiye connections and had no such advantage. When Mustafa Pasha stopped one time to raid some of

Aghayê Sor's villages on his way back to Cizre for the winter, the Şirnak *agha* was prevented by the government from retaliating. The British consul explained that Aghayê Sor "wished to take revenge, but was restrained by the Government; he has never consented to form Hamidieh regiments, and has usually been hostile to the Turks."[85] Meanwhile, "Mustapha Pasha, who commands a Hamidieh regiment [actually, two Hamidiye regiments], is given a number of *zaptieh*s [gendarmes] to accompany him to his summer quarters, and enable him to better ward off any attack from the Shernakh."[86]

There were other advantages accrued by Hamidiye tribes. In cases where a Hamidiye tribe was the victim of a crime, there was a better guarantee that the perpetrators would be pursued and punished by government forces, or that the tribe would have the backing of the government if it took matters into its own hands. Furthermore, Hamidiye tribes were largely assured freedom of action in any raid or other offense committed against a non-Hamidiye party.[87] Sometimes this impunity took the form of the government's simple "failure" to establish guilt or capture the malefactor—or so the government claimed. For example, trouble arose when Hamidiye troops were stationed in Derik, a town inhabited mostly by Muslims located between Diyarbekir and Mardin. The inhabitants, according to the British consul, "complain[ed] loudly of the conduct" of the Hamidiye troops who were encamped close to the village and were destroying the crops by "pasturing their horses in the young corn." Some of the villagers protested to the *vali* and received the "consoling reply" that they could inform His Excellency as soon as they suffered any "real injury." One of the villagers was killed by a Hamidiye tribesman.[88] At other times, there was outright collusion with certain government officials in a particular crime. Or, on occasion it was a bizarre mix of negligence and collusion. Take, for instance, the time when the powerful İbrahim Pasha, chief of the important Millî tribe and Hamidiye commander, plundered vast numbers of animals and other items from numerous villages attached to a rival. There was great pressure on the local government to recover the stolen assets, but instead of working to recapture the property lifted by the Millî chief and his tribespeople, local agents instead took the cattle and sheep belonging to innocent Kurdish villagers, rather than attempt to interfere with the protected pasha.[89]

There is ample evidence that the Hamidiye were the primary perpetrators of violence in the region, but they were not the only ones. As smaller tribes were squeezed by more powerful Hamidiye tribes who now enjoyed greater advantages that allowed them to survive and flourish, these weaker tribes also turned to raiding as a means of supporting themselves during increasingly tough times. Yet raids of this kind were not generally executed against strong tribes or against villages with powerful protectors, as retribution in this case would be sure and severe. Instead, they were carried out against even more vulnerable neighbors, most often unprotected settled villagers.[90] Having little to offer in the first place, they sometimes found themselves stripped of everything they owned after a single attack. One British consular officer sympathized with non-Hamidiye Kurds, and explained their raids as stemming from the exigencies of poverty: "The Kurds are a fine and intelligent race, but extremely poor. There not being sufficient arable land for cultivation, and having, rightly or wrongly, no confidence in the local authorities, they do not dare to leave their mountain homes in order to pursue a lawful calling and thus gain livelihood; but being compelled by the instinct of want, they commit all sorts of depredations, and thus become the terror of the districts surrounding the mountains."[91] One Kurdish tribesman expressed to a different consul his regret that he had to engage in plunder and theft to survive, saying that it was "from hunger, not from choice."[92] However, whatever reason there existed for plunder, tribes that were not enrolled in the Hamidiye were sometimes punished for their acts, while similar aggression on the part of a Hamidiye tribe effectively carried no penalty. At one point when non-Hamidiye tribes were engaged in large-scale plundering operations to the great detriment of the settled population, for example, the British consul observed that "as the Kurds in question have not been enrolled among the Hamidieh troops, the Government of this province has less compunction in using the forces at its disposal to punish the unruly tribesmen."[93] While the Kurdish regions in the nineteenth century suffered from violence and power struggles at all levels, then, the protection—and indeed the access to weapons—afforded to the Hamidiye tribes such as the Mîran aided in their pursuit of wealth and generally guaranteed their lives a higher level of security and safety than others enjoyed.[94] With such ease of action and pursuit of resources, tribes such as the Mîran were able to rapidly expand their power bases.

A minihistory of the Mîran tribe for its first decade in the Hamidiye illustrates this process. In 1891, Mustafa Agha received his commission as Hamidiye commander and traveled to Istanbul to participate in the induction ceremonies.[95] An account of Mustafa Pasha's reception in Istanbul is provided by a descendant of one Mustafa Pasha's contemporaries from Cizre. The account tells how the sultan wanted to meet and inspect the tribes who had just arrived in the capital, and of his particular encounter with Mustafa Pasha:

When he saw these powerfully built, majestic men from Cizre in different costumes, he said that he wanted to see them up close and inspect their manners, and he ordered that a dinner be prepared for them. He gave a banquet for these five hundred people coming from Cizre. Mustafa Pasha ordered his men not to eat with their hands and not to leave anything on their plates. . . . In a ceremony at the end of the dinner, Mustafa Pasha was given the Hamidiye regiments rank of pasha. He was also given many deeds of privilege, decorations, and banners. [The sultan] ordered him to form three regiments under his command.[96]

Mustafa Agha had solicited the Hamidiye commission himself when the government was actually recruiting the Kurdish tribes in the provinces of Erzurum and Van, the most important centers for the Hamidiye since they were borderlands and were home to the many of the region's Armenians. The Mîran leader returned from Istanbul a pasha,[97] and was presented with the Hamidiye standards in 1892.[98] After putting together his regiments, he constructed a barracks for them and began to choose his officers.[99] He then immediately set about using his new influence to consolidate his position in his tribe and to expand his wealth and power. In the spring of 1893, he ordered the murder of an important man in his tribe along with several other tribesmen. In spite of strong evidence against him, after a "thorough investigation," he was exonerated. Failing to find justice through the government, the victim's wife appealed to the chief of her family's tribe in Deh, who joined forces with their relative, Aghayê Sor, to take their revenge on Mustafa Pasha. Many lives were lost in the affray that ensued when, in the latter part of the spring, the Mîran passed through Şirnak on the way to their summer pastures.[100] Yet, as we have seen above, they were able to obtain government troops as escorts for their subsequent migrations, and would always, as a Hamidiye tribe, come out ahead of the non-Hamidiyes, Aghayê Sor and his people, and any other factions within his own tribe. This whole affair, incidentally, seems to have reflected a split in the Mîran tribe (or Çokh-Sor) itself. While the details remain obscure, what is clear is that Mustafa Pasha was able to use his Hamidiye connections to emerge victorious over any internal or external foes. He may even have used his new influence to eliminate others within the tribe, thus causing the split.[101] Whatever the case, he was favored by the government, and "not even questioned" in the case of the murders, while Aghayê Sor "received orders from higher quarters to make peace with the said Pasha."[102]

Mustafa Pasha also used his new authority to ensure that he could extract money and crops from villagers without fear of government retribution. One missionary at Cizre compiled a list of exactions from three Cizre villages as a sample he hoped would "serve as a good specimen of what is going on in all the villages about here during all the time [sic]." His list showed that Mustafa Pasha had not only extracted taxes far in excess of what was owed, but that he had also sent his sheep to eat up the villagers' late crops as reprisal for their lodging a complaint against him.[103] The same culprits were still at work two years later, according to numerous reports. In February 1895 the British agent at Mosul reported that the inhabitants of a Christian village in the Cizre district had complained to their patriarch that Mustafa Pasha and the other local *agha*s had plundered their village so many times that they were on the verge of having to vacate it, as their protests to the authorities had gone unanswered.[104] The consul at Diyarbekir added that Mustafa Pasha had ruined not only this village, "but also a great many other prosperous villages, both Christian and Moslem, in the neighborhood of Djézéré, and indeed, as he, together with his people, lives in the winter season in the district just mentioned, and migrates to the districts of Van in the summer, in passing backwards and forwards all the villages on his route sustain injury, and a great many become completely ruined." In spite of the many accusations brought against this Hamidiye commander, he was able to obtain acquittal "through the influence of a long purse."[105] The consular agent added that the Hamidiye chief had "also inflicted some injuries upon several innocent Moslems," who were on their way to Baghdad for pilgrimage. The latter had petitioned the government, but to no avail.[106] The consul summed up the situation in 1895, writing that Mustafa Pasha "was already a daring lawless man, and now that he belongs to the Hamidieh forces, he considers himself not amenable to public law or justice."[107]

Not content with acquiring wealth through these means alone, Mustafa Pasha also directed his tribesmen to hold up the rafts on the Tigris, sometimes allowing them to pass after paying a "toll," and other times pillaging them outright when the toll was not paid.[108] Sometimes both happened: the British consul at Diyarbekir reported that some raftsmen had recently come to file a complaint against Mustafa Pasha, who had not only exacted a toll from each raft, but had also dispatched his followers to await the arrival of the rafts as they floated downstream and to plunder them. His orders were carried out to "the consternation of the owners who had vainly imagined that by paying the toll demanded they could keep their goods."[109] The German traveler Paul Rohrbach described the far-reaching effects of Mustafa Pasha's control of the river traffic on the local economy:

When in 1901 I arrived in Musul, there was a severe cold spell. The streets were covered with a thick blanket of snow. The houses had been so aired out they were as cold and humid as iceboxes. Because no wood or coal could be found in the city, there was no choice but to put their faith in God. When I asked what the reason for this lack in fuel was, I found out that it was because Mustafa Pasha's men, who extracted a toll from the rafts carrying the wood and coal from the mountains, would forcefully take possession of the goods of those who did not pay the toll and would furthermore submit them to all sorts of transgressions. The same toll was extracted from goods brought from Europe via Samsun and Diyarbekir brought by camel or mule to the edge of the desert at Cizre. Especially during the time I was in Musul, the cost of many staples and goods coming from Russia and other countries, for example the price of oil, tripled and quadrupled.[110]

The year 1900 was a big one for Mustafa Pasha. Early that year, hostilities once again broke out between his followers and those under the authority of Aghayê Sor. The Hamidiye pasha and his Tay allies were clearly favored in the conflict, such that the *kaymakam* (governor of a *kaza*) of Cizre sent troops to defend Mustafa Pasha's Tay allies.[111] The Hamidiye tribesmen were not punished for the massacre of Aghayê Sor's people, but their non-Hamidiye rivals were prevented from retaliating.[112]

A few months later, hostilities once again erupted, and Hamidiye troops under Mustafa Pasha's orders attacked and razed some twenty villages in the Silopî section of the Cizre district, while killing over a hundred people. Finding no help from local governors, Aghayê Sor addressed a petition to the government, asking for protection against his tribe's attackers.[113] Apparently no response came, for just weeks later, Mustafa Pasha again assaulted Aghayê Sor's villages. According to the French consul, the latter *agha* complained to the Hamidiye commander in residence at Mardin, the brigadier-general Bahaeddin Pasha, who went to Cizre to conduct an on-site inquiry. But Mustafa Pasha, on the pretext of meeting with the Hamidiye high commander, instead had Bahaeddin Pasha captured and imprisoned. Zeki Pasha, the commander-in-chief of the Hamidiye regiments, demanded an explanation from Mustafa Pasha, who replied that Bahaeddin Pasha had come to take advantage of women and girls in his tribe. Bahaeddin Pasha was kept in Mustafa Pasha's makeshift jail for five days.[114] Later in the year, fighting broke out once again between the feuding groups, again with the destruction of some ten villages and many lives.[115] By the end of the year, Mustafa Pasha attacked the Yezidis again, killing five and carrying off numerous cattle and sheep. The British consul summed up the situation:

This Musto Pasha, taking advantage of his rank in the Hamidieh troops, continually ill-uses the inhabitants of the Jezireh, whom he treats as captives, and he and his followers seize whatever they choose from the merchants of Jezireh, either without payment or at half price and nobody dare say a word. Besides, he causes considerable loss to the trade between Mosul and Diarbekir by extorting money from the people in charge of rafts on the river, in consequence of which the number of rafts from Diarbekir and Djezireh has decreased. Owing to this the price of some articles has increased. The freight of rafts from Diarbekir to Mosul and Baghdad is now double what it was, owing to a rise in the price of wood for building and fire-wood, as Musto Pasha does not allow a raft or small float to pass down the river without extorting from each 15 or 20 mejidies. Complaints have been sent against him to Constantinople by the inhabitants, corroborated by the Valis of Mosul and Diyarbekir, but without result. The Sublime Porte refers them to Zeki

Pasha . . . who contradicts them, as His Excellency is interested in Musto Pasha and others, and occasionally his Excellency even strongly censures the said Valis for complaints against Musto Pasha and Hadji Agha.[116]

And thus it was that Mustafa Pasha ended the year 1900. It was also the year that he received the doubtful honor of being profiled in the Bedir Khan's journal, *Kurdistan*. One such article has been mentioned in the opening of this chapter, and while it is a colorful and interesting example of the prose devoted to protesting the Hamidiye and the regime behind it, it was not the only one.

The year 1900, then, might mark the beginning of a serious campaign against Mustafa Pasha and the entire Hamidiye system that encouraged and supported him and others like him. While Mustafa Pasha may have been the face of the "evils" of the Hamidiye for the Bedir Khans in particular, the members of this family who crusaded against him had many supporters from all ranks, all walks of life, all Ottoman religions and nationalities. They were complaining not just about an oppressive chief, but were against the entire system that helped produce and maintain him. It allowed these chiefs to expand their power and fill their pockets, and it also provided benefits to their tribes in the form of income and protection as well as advantage over rivals. And above all, they almost never had to report for duty. It is no wonder, then, that after all these benefits became widely known, tribal leaders flocked to join the Hamidiye, and others simply had the badge made illegally by silversmiths to look like they were in the militia. They, too, wanted the benefits. But not all people could be in the favored militia; privilege would be less dear if it were universal. Furthermore, most people wanted to live their lives without having to join or fear the Hamidiye Light Cavalry. Hence, there were numerous grievances against a system whereby favoritism and privilege determined justice. But before we examine the parties who had these complaints, it is important to take a closer look at the system in general in order to better understand these protests.

LITTLE *PAŞALIKS*, BIG PASHAS

As is clear from the preceding section, tribes that were enrolled in the Hamidiye Light Cavalry accrued enormous benefits from their association with this privileged militia. The license accorded to them by the Ottoman authorities allowed them advantages over other tribes in the pursuit of wealth and security. It also accelerated the nineteenth-century trend whereby larger, more politically complex units, like emirates, broke apart into smaller units, as tribal confederations, then simply tribes, became the key social and political units of the region. However, for a brief episode, mainly the period that the Hamidiye was alive and well, this trend became an extreme example of itself. A few individual tribes, increasingly becoming the key political units in the region, were growing so powerful through their Hamidiye connections and the advantages connected to them that they actually seem to have taken on the shape, authority, and functions that the emirates once had—with, of course, a few differences. It is evident that the Hamidiye tribes—large and small—gained countless returns for their participation in the tribal militia. These rewards mainly came in the shape of unfettered access to resources—license to illegally obtain wealth in its various forms with the complicity of the government and little fear of punishment by the law. Indirect aid came through the weapons supplied to the Hamidiye tribes, ostensibly intended for other purposes, and direct assistance through open acts of collusion. There is ample documentation that various Hamidiye members were supported in these ways. But there is one part of the story that remains to be analyzed. When we speak of "state support" what do we mean? Clearly there were numerous governors who tried their best to maintain the rule of law and the promotion of peace and security for all of their respective districts' inhabitants. How do such claims against "the state" stand when we know this to be the case? As the following section will demonstrate—entities such as "the government" and "the state" in the Ottoman context were indeed far more complex and less unitary than scholarship has portrayed them thus far.

First, we must distinguish between different actors, comprising different factions, within the Ottoman government. The frequently observed tension between the "Palace" and the "Porte" is one such distinction, but it is, of course, not so neatly drawn in reality, and is, in fact, much more multifaceted. Perhaps more telling is the distinction posed by opposition groups to the sultan, between those loyal to Sultan Abdülhamid II and those he determined to be disloyal to his personage, which was also a common Young Turk complaint.[117] The Hamidiye fits into this picture best when we consider the issue of loyalty. Not only does studying the Hamidiye provide insight into the transformation of local Kurdish power structures in the late nineteenth and early twentieth centuries, but it also helps us catch a few glimpses of larger Ottoman power issues. One section of the government—represented by one of the sultan's closest confidantes, the marshal Zeki Pasha—came to have vast powers over an entire section of the empire. What evolved was an interesting dialectic whereby there was neither a unilateral imposition of power from the central Ottoman government nor any single agent. Nor did the Kurdish social and political structure transform in a complete vacuum. Rather, the two impacted each other, and perhaps had broader ramifications for Ottoman society at large. The Hamidiye represented a fuzzy blend of state and nonstate power that was the result of an effort-bargain between some segments of the state and one of the groups that it wanted to control and incorporate at the expense of the groups that it viewed as larger "threats." This effort-bargain made it very complex to govern—and live in—the region.

It is expected that the sultan would have supreme reign over his own empire; yet the sheer power built up by his protégé, Zeki Pasha, requires a bit more explanation. Zeki Pasha was an Ottoman of Circassian origin, born in Istanbul in 1846. He entered into service in 1276 (1859/60), and although he began his career in the Palace already a captain before Sultan Abdülhamid II ascended the throne, he rapidly rose through the ranks after Abdülhamid became sultan of the empire, receiving decorations and promotions to major, then lieutenant-colonel, then colonel, and in quick succession, *liva* (brigadier) and *ferik* (divisional general), all by 1878. After serving in the Imperial Guard at Yıldız Palace and in the Balkans and Tripoli of Barbary,[118] in 1887, Zeki Pasha once again relocated, but this time to the region over which he would come to enjoy enormous control for the next two decades—the Fourth Army Corps (or in military terms, the "Russian frontier"). A special position seems to have been created expressly for Zeki Pasha, as *müşir muavinliği* (assistant field marshal). The British consul voiced the prevailing idea that this appointment was "but a step prior to his appointment as Mushir of the Fourth Army Corps,"[119] and in this he was correct. The following year, Hedayat Pasha, the current field marshal, had been dismissed from his post and was replaced by Nusret Pasha, who in his turn had to make way for Zeki Pasha after enjoying his post for only a few days.[120] From this point on, Zeki Pasha would be the commander-in-chief of the Fourth Army Corps, and, beginning in 1890, the top commander of the Hamidiye Light Cavalry as well. It is even possible that he had been selected for these posts when the original idea for the Hamidiye was submitted to the sultan as early as 1885. Whatever the case, Zeki Pasha rapidly became, in the estimation of one British observer, the officer highest in rank, and "by far the most powerful in influence throughout this part of the Turkish Empire."[121]

In spite of the common belief that Zeki Pasha attributed his rapid rise to Palace influences,[122] he did not invite quite the resentment any other nepotistic influence seeker might have incurred from his colleagues because he was, after all, a charismatic and capable leader. He was also ambitious, and through his combination of character traits and skills, he built himself into one of the most powerful men in the empire and maintained this position for two decades—a long time by contemporary Ottoman standards.[123]

It is difficult to know, without sources such as a memoir, what, exactly, Zeki Pasha had in mind for the Hamidiye. Therefore, one must imagine how he envisioned this body of Kurdish irregulars based on his record of command over them. He certainly put the militia together with his patron's goals in mind. But at the same time it is clear that he worked to build his own power base over an extensive expanse of the empire, and to promote the Hamidiye according to his own agendas and visions. Zeki Pasha cultivated this power base on two levels. On the one hand, he continued to convince the sultan of the necessity of the Hamidiye project, often exaggerating the "Armenian peril." As such he was able to maintain his high-ranking position. At the same time, he cultivated relations with local Kurdish chiefs by offering rewards or punishments, according to their behavior. Thus Zeki Pasha transformed himself into the single most important figure in the region for such a long period. This power meant that he pampered friends and had rivals and enemies punished or dismissed from their posts. In the process, he seems to have amassed a personal fortune.

On many levels, the Hamidiye was more the personal army of Zeki Pasha than it was of the sultan himself. The sultan had delegated almost full powers to Zeki Pasha in the formation and maintenance of this irregular body of tribal soldiers, and trusted him completely in the decisions he made regarding the Hamidiye, in spite of the criticism the Hamidiye received from many quarters. Indeed, as the sultan confided in his memoirs, "I believe that the Kurdish policy I have adopted is the correct one. Zeki Pasha, who has studied the regional conditions, has demonstrated the idea of organizing regiments of Kurdish Cossacks to be the most effective path [to achieving our ends]."[124] Accordingly, Zeki Pasha made good use of all the prerogatives assigned to him.

First, Zeki Pasha recruited by proffering rewards to those who joined; these incentives initially promised tax relief and often amnesty from past crimes. In nineteenth-century Kurdistan, where there was a breakdown in authority and, hence, an accompanying disintegration of public security, there were many "criminals" who could profit from this reprieve. While the centralizing mission described above was not complete, as was evident from this blatant power vacuum, it seems to have reached further into the lives of the region's people than hitherto supposed, as tax collection was, in fact, enforced in many parts of the Kurdish areas. Otherwise, tax exemptions would not have been such an enticing offer for tribespeople. Similarly, one must assume that if amnesty for crimes was a persuasive offer for some tribal chiefs, it can also be presumed that the state did have the power, when it wanted, to bring criminals to justice. Lastly, the offer of government rifles was also tempting. In fact, many of the tribes would sign up, take the weapons, and nothing would be heard from them again. Of course, this was not far from the Hamidiye standard, where most Hamidiye tribes were armed and were but rarely called upon to use their weapons for any government-directed military purpose. All of these rewards were among the initial attractions Zeki Pasha put forth to invite recruits.

Once tribes were enlisted, their leaders in particular were pampered and protected by Zeki Pasha. We have seen ample evidence of this in the case of Mustafa Pasha of the Mîran tribe. At the same time, those who objected were either censured, or worse; if they held official positions, they were dismissed from their posts. While appointments could only be made or taken away by the powers in the capital, Zeki Pasha often used his influence at the Palace to cause trouble for or dispose of his local enemies, in particular those who stood in opposition to his pet project. And of these there were many, right from the start. Ebubekir Hâzim Tepeyran, a former governor of the Mosul province, later confided in his memoirs that his own efforts to make the Hamidiye tribes (namely the Ertoşî) in his region abide by the law drew the great enmity of Zeki Pasha.[125] And in 1892, Zeki Pasha had the governor-general of the Erzurum province discharged and replaced. The deposed governor related to the British consul resident at the provincial seat that his fall was partly attributed to the hostility between himself and Zeki Pasha, who, with his strong Palace influence was able to get him dismissed. "This enmity arose," the consul reported, "chiefly from their divergence of opinion on the subject of the organization of the Hamidiyyé regiments, the Vali being, it is said, strongly opposed to the arming of the Kurdish tribes, as a measure which is likely to render the government of Kurdistan, if possible, a more difficult task than it has hitherto proved."[126] In the case of those who had stronger support at the capital or a formidable service record and were thus not as easy to dismiss, Zeki Pasha simply rendered their orders null and void when they conflicted with his own program. Other times, when he could not achieve the outright dismissal of a strong governor, he worked to discharge his allies. This is what happened in the case of the Erzurum governor, one of the higher-ranking officials in the region. His agenda was often in conflict with that of Zeki Pasha, and the latter simply tried to rob him of his supporters. The British consul reported that Zeki Pasha had the commander of the Erzurum division, who had a good service record and who got along well with the *vali*, removed and replaced with one of his own men. The consul believed that this was not only a military measure but "fresh proof" of the pasha's hostility toward the *vali*.[127] Zeki Pasha also employed a range of practices to undermine the efforts and authority of local officials who did not support the license he wished to accord to the

Hamidiye. The British military consul at Van reported how Zeki Pasha "tried to raise difficulties in the way of the Vali dealing with . . . Hamidié who commit crime." He achieved this through various means, one of which was to induce "the stoppage of supplies of money from outside to this vilayet for the payment of the troops."[128]

Almost everybody in the region feared crossing Zeki Pasha, or wanted to remain on good terms with him, at least in the beginning. Even the British consul at Erzurum, being aware of his power, decided to foster friendly relations with this commander while the Hamidiye was still in the early stages of its development: Consul Graves wrote in 1893 of his plans to travel to Erzincan, the seat of the Fourth Army Corps and the residence of Zeki Pasha. He believed it was highly desirable to take the opportunity to cultivate friendly relations as he acknowledged the pasha to be the highest-ranking officer and "by far the most powerful in influence throughout this part of the Turkish Empire," as the main civil authorities in Kurdistan were "notoriously dependant on his good will" for the maintenance of their offices.[129] The same consul, less than four years later, privately confided to his superior that he wished they could get Zeki Pasha moved from Erzincan. He believed his influence throughout the vast Fourth Army Corps had been "most pernicious," and that he was "the great obstacle in the way of well-intentioned Valis."[130] While powerful and popular governors were a small challenge for Zeki Pasha, he did feel a momentary slip to his authority in the period following the massacres of 1894–96, when Şakir Pasha was sent to make an official inquiry into the bloodshed and to oversee the reform project of 1895.

The carnage of 1894–96 claimed the lives of thousands of Armenian Ottomans. These events have often been mentioned by scholars over the past century, particularly in terms of being a prelude to the genocidal massacres and deportations of 1915–16.[131] The question of whether direct orders were given by the Ottoman government has been at the core of debates surrounding the Sasun and other massacres during this period. The purpose of the present discussion is not to review this discussion, but merely to touch upon Zeki Pasha's role in the slaughters and their aftermath, highlighting not only the extent of his influence but also his resilience, as he recovered after a period that apparently was characterized by multiple challenges to his authority.

There are conflicting reports about Zeki Pasha's hand in the massacres. Some reports claim that he attempted to stop them where he could, while others allege that he was the responsible party, giving orders to the Hamidiye and the regular troops he commanded to murder and plunder.[132] It is difficult to determine whether or not he issued direct orders to those under his command to perform the atrocities that were committed. However, given the sheer influence he enjoyed over the region, which was amply documented by various sources, it seems highly likely that he somehow shared in the responsibility of what had happened.[133] Not only European observers but also by members of the Ottoman government came to this conclusion. An official inquiry was ordered, and European diplomats meanwhile urged the implementation of the reform program, which had been on the drawing board for some time. Şakir Pasha was sent to conduct the official inquiry and to direct the reform program that was to follow.[134] But this appointment was perceived by Zeki Pasha as an enormous affront to his authority. The French consul provided a description of the tension between these two pashas:

For a long time, Zeki Pasha has been considered and came to consider himself as the primary figure of this part of the empire, when the sultan decided to send a commissioner furnished with extraordinary powers. The jealousy and rivalry between the two was nearly fatal. Zeki Pasha has a good service record; he has been running the Fourth Army Corps for over eight years and enjoys a good military name and a reputation for being a good organizer, which he earned for his participation in the creation of the Hamidié regiments. His alliance with the Sultan (one of his sisters being in the imperial harem, which allowed him to call himself the brother-in-law of the Sultan) has helped him a lot. Zeki Pasha has a touchy sense of pride: He was not able to see, without taking umbrage, the nomination of Marshal Shakir Pasha or valis like Mehmed Raouf Pasha, the vali of Erzeroum, who never was the creature of Zeki Pasha. Beforehand, most of the provincial officials were his devoted servants.[135]

Although Zeki Pasha was able to thwart the projects commissioned by officials who had agendas that differed from his own, Şakir Pasha represented the ultimate test to his authority. For some time following the massacres and the inquiries and reforms that ensued, many observed this apparent weakening in Zeki Pasha's power and concluded that his career in the region was soon to end. But this was not, in fact, the case, and Zeki Pasha managed to retain his influence and even build upon it in the decade to follow. The massacres and their aftermath would, however, prompt a review of the Hamidiye, particularly by Şakir Pasha, who submitted a report to the sultan that enumerated the various problems with the organization, and the subsequent issue of revised regulations in 1896 and 1897, which were designed to place the regiments under stricter control.[136] In fact, Zeki Pasha might even have been responsible for diminishing the authority of Şakir Pasha in the project, while maintaining his own good relations with the sultan.[137]

In the period following the reforms and the appointment of Şakir Pasha, the British consul reported that "Zeki's present attitude is rather a mysterious one. People are beginning to whisper that he is secretly disaffected against the present Government and the Sultan, and that he is meditating a 'pronunciamento' one of these fine days, if the scare of a war with Greece passes over."[138] Some even believed him to have special designs of becoming some sort of Muhammad 'Ali Pasha, or to have Russian support, ideas that gained currency in the years after the massacres.[139] Interestingly, this rumor was picked up by one of Zeki Pasha's protégés, the Hayderan chief Emin Pasha, who, after a run-in with his superior, telegraphed the Palace, "complaining that Zekki Pasha would not leave him in peace and was intriguing to make himself Prince of Kurdistan."[140] This was, of course, written because the disgruntled chief was irritated at Zeki Pasha's newfound—if temporary—strictness in dealing with him.[141]

While the gossip was obviously dismissed by the sultan and many observers, it is significant because it indicates how threatened Zeki Pasha's tenure over his post may have been, or at least how vulnerable it was perceived to have been. The British consul at Van observed that the fact that Emin Pasha, one of Zeki Pasha's most influential Hamidiye protégés, had turned on him, along with the order from the Palace that several prominent Hayderan chiefs (including Emin Pasha) be exiled (contrary to Zeki Pasha's wishes), indicated that Zeki Pasha's prestige and influence was suffering.[142] He also believed that Zeki Pasha was displaying a more conciliatory attitude toward local officials because he was feeling that his position was insecure.[143] Though Zeki Pasha's influence may, in fact, have waned somewhat after the massacres, he nonetheless continued to be supported by the Palace. It was reported that "the sinister designs attributed to [Zeki Pasha] have evidently so far found no credence at Yildiz [Palace], where he is apparently still in the highest favour and thoroughly trusted by the Sultan."[144] And given that he continued, until the Young Turk Revolution of 1908, to be able to promote the Hamidiye project and to protect the Hamidiye tribesmen from civilian courts, tax collectors, or other government officials, it is safe to say that Zeki Pasha managed to maintain his post with full authority.

But the sultan was still the supreme ruler. Zeki Pasha could not function this way unless the sultan believed it to be the best thing for the empire, his rule, or his person, or whatever the priorities of the moment were. In addition to his interests in promoting unity among the Muslim subjects of the empire,[145] Sultan Abdülhamid II's continued support of the Hamidiye seems to have been upheld through the constant reports of danger and exaggerations of the Armenian "threat" given by Zeki Pasha and many Hamidiye chiefs. Zeki Pasha persisted in arguing that the Hamidiye could and were countering this menace and could also help combat any Russian invasion should the need arise.[146] He also added another argument to this line of reasoning: that the Kurds were so powerful that they needed to be indulged, otherwise they could unite and rise against the government. According to the British consul,

Zekki Pasha, and a clique of military advisers of the Sultan, chief of whom have been Shakir Pasha and the late Dervish Pasha, have, for purposes of their own, built up a beautiful fiction on the subject of the Kurd tribes, which His Imperial Majesty is, no doubt, glad to believe, and which it will therefore be difficult to destroy. This is to the effect that the Kurds are a gallant and warlike race, personally devoted to the Sultan, though impatient of ordinary civil control; that their misdeeds in the way of rapine are grossly exaggerated by the civil authorities and in foreign Consular reports; and that to allow the said civil authorities to use repressive measures towards them would perhaps result in a civil war of great difficulty and doubtful issue. But if, on the other hand, the control of the Kurds be left to Zekki Pasha, they will not only remain faithful to the throne, but will furnish a splendid contingent of some 30,000 cavalry to serve as the first line of defence of the Empire in Asia and as a counterpoise to the "rebellious" Armenian population.[147]

Zeki Pasha also employed comparable arguments to achieve the dismissal of officials who meddled with the Hamidiye, by portraying them as traitors. According to a French consul, Zeki Pasha was able to obtain the discharge of a local governor who had acted against a Hamidiye chief. The incident report mentioned that when İbrahim Bey, the *mutassarıf* (governor of a *sancak*) of Bayazid, who was able to expel several Kurdish chiefs who had ruined Armenian villages in the region, turned his attention to Sheikh Halil, another Hamidiye *agha* (belonging to the Celalî tribe), he incurred the wrath of Zeki Pasha. He apparently obtained the dismissal of this official by telling the capital that he "was a friend of the Russians and Armenians, hostile to the Kurds, and a traitor to his country."[148] Zeki Pasha also accused British and Russian consuls, along with their "corrupt Christian [mercenaries]," of spreading nasty rumors about the Hamidiye.[149]

The Kurdish chiefs themselves contributed to the maintenance of this image of the local situation and the need for their role in it through false and exaggerated reports and other means. Mustafa Pasha, the Mîran chief, once telegraphed the sultan "the wildly improbable story that 10,000 Armenian revolutionaries had collected round Jéziré and were going to raise the standard of rebellion in company with the Shammars and a son of the late Bedr Khan Pasha, Ahmed of the Aga-es-Sor tribe." He did this so that he could carry out raids *not* against Armenian revolutionaries or even against Armenian civilians, in fact, but against non-Armenian Christian and Muslim villagers of his enemies.[150]

Sometimes, when it seemed that the Kurdish Hamidiye chiefs had simply gone too far in their exploits, or when they felt their favor at the Palace beginning to wane, they volunteered for special duties, such as offering to send troops to Yemen or Macedonia, or to the Hijaz to protect the railway, then under construction. Hüseyin Pasha, the infamous Hayderan chief, offered to conduct his Hamidiye regiment to Yemen in 1905 at the height of the Yemen crisis.[151] Of course many of these proposals were hardly sincere. They were often made just to curry the favor of the sultan at critical moments, or more cynically, to obtain further decorations and arms, only to find excuses to not go. Just two years earlier, Hüseyin Pasha was reported to have applied to the sultan directly for permission to bring his regiment to the capital, from where it would advance to Macedonia. Of course this proposal was put forth only after he had heard that İbrahim Pasha, head of the Millî tribe and also a Hamidiye commander, had been promoted to *liva* (brigadier).[152] And İbrahim Pasha volunteered his regiment to guard the Hijaz section of the Baghdad Railway.[153] His offer was made during a period of proposed expeditions against him at the height of his power. But Zeki Pasha tried to protect his Hamidiye chiefs from actually having to report for such duties. This, however, was not always motivated by concern for them, but rather out of a sense of embarrassment. When the minister of war, the "declared enemy" of Zeki Pasha, wanted to "demonstrate to the sultan that the enormous sacrifices that Zeki Pasha was making to support them from the Treasury, for over 14 years, was a true loss and that the enrolled Kurdish regiments had remained the same, the sultan suggested that he prepare some Hamidiye regiments for service in the capital as Imperial Guards." Zeki Pasha managed to dissuade him. According to the French consul, Zeki Pasha did not want to expose to his patron the holes in his Hamidiye "fiction."[154] After all, the conduct of the Hamidiye troops' stay in Istanbul in 1896 had certainly left a poor impression on some residents in the capital.[155] In the end, the sultan was convinced that regarding the Hamidiye, his trusted commander knew best; he seems to have left full prerogative to Zeki Pasha to run the Hamidiye operation however he saw fit.[156]

As for Zeki Pasha himself, it is again difficult to know exactly what he had in mind for the Hamidiye. Some local observers were convinced that he truly trusted in the validity of his project, and merely employed expedient means to realize it. The British military consul, Captain Maunsell, was convinced, first, that Zeki Pasha was trying to stamp out Armenian activities the only way he knew how, and second, that he believed there would be an encounter with Russian Cossacks in the near future. The Kurdish tribes were to be trained against these threats. He was single-minded in this goal, the captain supposed, and "sacrifice[d] everything towards this end . . . "[157] This may, indeed, have been the case, but it would only be a truly convincing argument if there was evidence that Zeki Pasha did his best to train the tribesmen as soldiers. Instead, there is striking testimony to the contrary: Ottoman and European sources alike repeatedly point to the worthlessness of the Hamidiye as a military organization and complain that training sessions were infrequent at best. Thus, it seems that even if the sultan himself saw the Hamidiye as a potential force against a future Russian invasion, Zeki Pasha first envisioned the militia for use against Armenian revolutionaries, who carried out their armed activities in small bands and were certainly not a standing army. Second, and perhaps most important, however, it was through the Hamidiye that he expected to obtain the loyalty of the Kurdish chiefs. The only way they could be used in the event of a war with Russia was to ensure that they would not, in fact, aid the Russians.[158] This effort-bargain was to be accomplished through appeasing and pampering them to ensure their continued loyalty. As a CUP officer later confided to the British military representative, "It is the fault of you foreigners. Why can't you leave us alone? The Russians are buying the Kurdish chiefs, and we have to bribe men like Hussein Pasha in this way to keep them away from the Russians."[159] Given the tribesmen's lack of formal training, it is unlikely that they could be expected to perform as soldiers.

What Zeki Pasha may have accomplished through the Hamidiye was a buildup of his own riches and power. During his tenure as commander of the Hamidiye, Zeki Pasha not only pulled together resources to establish himself as the single most influential figure in southeastern Anatolia, but he also used his position to amass great wealth. The *vali* of Bitlis confided to the British agent there that Zeki Pasha "was absolutely corrupt, and did nothing but extort money from rebellious Kurds, Kurdish Chiefs, and Hamidiehs as the price of his silence."[160] Elsewhere, this consul reported that Zeki Pasha was "fattening on the spoils" taken by his Hamidiye from the Armenians.[161] Two years before Zeki Pasha's career as Hamidiye commander came to an end, a different French consul remarked on Zeki Pasha's "colossal fortune," writing: "Upon his arrival to Erzindjian sixteen years ago, Zeki Pacha did not possess anything. Now he is worth a fortune of 12–15 million francs."[162] Even if the amount of Zeki Pasha's "fortune" was exaggerated, it does seem as if he left the venture a very wealthy man. More important, he was the most powerful man in the "Six Provinces" for nearly two decades.

"NEW TRIBAL EMIRATES"

Through their continued support from Zeki Pasha and the sultan, the Kurdish chiefs of leading Hamidiye tribes were able to develop little "emirates" of their own. Granted, these were not emirates in the traditional sense. They did not have the symbolic legitimacy that the classical emirates enjoyed, which superseded tribal and religious loyalties, nor did they have the "imperial" structure of the classical emirates.[163] They did not oversee an army, but rather had "members in arms."[164] And lastly, the tribes were a federation based on blood solidarity, or *'asabiyya*, while the emirates, perhaps weak because they lacked this *'asabiyya*, or strong because they superseded it, were families that ruled over many tribes. Having said this, it is nonetheless clear that certain of these powerful Hamidiye tribes, most notably the three that are highlighted in the present study, were able to expand their power bases materially and territorially, and to take on many of the functions and power that the classical emirates had, even if it was on different—and more modern—terms. And like the classical emirates, they did this through imperial patronage.

Through the cooperation of Zeki Pasha, who was himself fully backed by the sultan, Hamidiye chiefs were able to gain new standing in their tribes and to expand their power bases at the expense of non-Hamidiye neighbors and clients. When there existed tribes that were confederated, the Hamidiye tribe seems to have frequently taken over the dominant role, as in the case of the Mîran and its position in the Çokh-Sor confederation, described above; or else the tribe, due to its new prestige and power through its government connections and all the benefits that came with these connections, began to attract additional followers, who attached themselves to the tribe. This could include nontribal groups, who would join themselves to the tribe either directly or as clients who would pay a tribute, or it could consist of tribes, who would then ally with but become subservient to the powerful tribe. The most striking examples of this process are seen in the three tribes highlighted in this study—the Mîran, the Millî, and the Hayderan, whose commanders (tribal chiefs) also were among the few Hamidiye chiefs to bear the title of pasha.

The process described by van Bruinessen whereby larger, more complex social and political structures in Kurdistan gradually gave way to smaller, less complex structures, is exemplified by the Hamidiye. No longer subservient to the emirs, tribal chiefs took on new and increasingly powerful roles with the sanction of the state. However, the sheer power amassed by major Hamidiye tribes resulted in a situation in which emirates, albeit of a new sort, seemed to return to parts of Kurdistan, even if very temporarily. One British agent had a similar perception:

There is no doubt that the Hamidie movement, the appointing of tribal leaders as colonels of regiments, has had, and is having, great effect in consolidating various broken factions of Kurdish tribes, and mitigating, in a great measure, the want of unity and tribal authority which supervened when the great "derebeys" were exterminated by the Turkish Government fifty or sixty years ago. . . . The Turks have taken great trouble to get rid of any remnants of the old ruling families in Kurdistan, but now the various Hamidie cavalry leaders, themselves created and given rank by the Sultan, bid fair to occupy the places of the lost "derebeys", and this too with good arms and a certain organization supplied them by the Government.[165]

Thus it was that the nineteenth century began and ended with Kurdish emirates, albeit of different kinds. They were both sponsored and sanctioned by the state, this time concerned with clarifying and protecting its borders rather than its frontiers. In the case of the new "tribal emirates," however, there were various parties who suffered from this alliance, and many voiced their complaints. Locals enjoyed far more security of life and property under the old emirates than they did under the new.

We have seen numerous protests against the Hamidiye by British and French consuls on their own behalf. Of course, they were not the only ones to observe and criticize the Hamidiye and the entire system that supported these powerful units. There were copious grievances in Kurdish and other Ottoman circles as well, and these too were not only relayed by consular documents but also voiced through the medium of official reports and publications.[166] Of course villagers had plentiful objections, for they were the ones hit the hardest by this organization. Already squeezed by their own *agha*s and injured in feuds between rivals, their security and income decreased rapidly after the formation of the Hamidiye in many areas.[167]

While tribespeople from smaller or less powerful tribes were overcome by Hamidiye tribes with their new authority, even lesser Hamidiye tribes were also sometimes dissatisfied with the new order. The British consul at Van reported that non-Hamidiye Kurds complained that the sultan had "delivered them into the hands" of the Hamidiye; but even among the regiments, whom he believed had everything to gain and nothing to lose by the maintenance of the present regime, there existed "grumblers." The weaker tribes were oppressed by the mightier ones, and the *agha*s of the less powerful tribes were placed in military subordination to and "enslavement" by chiefs who were *miralay*s (colonels). He cites the example of Şekir Agha of the Ertoşî, who was likely the most influential Kurdish chief in the districts lying to the south and the east of Lake Van. This *agha* had approached the consul one day, complained about the sultan and the government, and asked him when he thought the Russians were going to take over as he and everyone else were "heartily sick" of the Ottoman government.[168]

Another anecdote illustrates the growing authority of the more powerful Hamidiye tribes over others in the manner complained about by the Ertoşî *agha*. In a feud that erupted between the Cibran and Hasanan tribes, the former having an alliance with the Bilikan tribe, a number of tribesmen directed by three chiefs in one regiment attacked their rivals, with an ensuing loss of lives and property. A victim of the plunder petitioned the *vali*, who referred the matter to Mahmud Pasha, the brigadier in general command of the Hamidiye, who reportedly told the complainant that he "could not be expected to sacrifice a regiment of Hamidieh for the sake of one village." In the end, however, some troops were eventually sent to arrest the offending tribesmen, but those given up for punishment were members of the weaker (Bilikan) tribe.[169] Poor Hamidiye tribesmen claimed that it was the Hamidiye with the "horse and gun" who took all the wealth.[170] A Bilikan tribesman, whose tribe was no longer in the Hamidiye by the time he expressed these words in about 1907, said,

Formerly . . . we lived with the Armenians like brothers. Religion was the only difference. Now we are always quarrelling, about I know not what. Are we in fault? Are the Armenians in fault? I know not—by God, I know not. All of us suffer, Kurd and Armenian alike. Soldiers come in every day, eat our chickens, beat our men, and demand taxes twenty-five years in arrear. How will it end? The Hamidieh rob us, the Vali robs us, the Mudir robs us. What are we to do? How are we to live?[171]

But the complaints extended beyond Kurdish and Armenian circles. The British consul at Mamuret'ül-'Aziz (Harput) explained how objections to the system were widespread and not confined to the *reaya* population. He cited the example of the *kaymakam* of Cizre, who had fled from his post because he was stripped of all power by the Hamidiye officers who were stationed there. Landowners, he continued, found that their losses had multiplied drastically since the creation of the Hamidiye. One Muslim official complained that the whole place might as well be called "Hamidiehland," as neither officials nor police had any power there.[172]

Local officials protested the system that prevented them from doing their jobs and that robbed them of their assigned prerogatives. The governor of Van confided to Sadettin Pasha, who had come to survey the province and promote reforms in 1896, that the Kurds would not listen to the government or respond to summons. They would say, "We are Hamidiye commanders and soldiers. We are not under the command of provincial governors, *sancak* governors, or *kaymakams*."[173] Provincial governors in particular resented having Zeki Pasha thwart their projects and challenge their authority. In the Ottoman Chamber of Deputies, Lütfi Fikri Bey, the deputy from Dersim, later noted the ongoing rivalry between Zeki Pasha and the governor of Harput, pointing out that "whenever the Kurds started warming up to the new governors, the marshal would become suspicious."[174] Ottoman regular soldiers also deeply resented the Hamidiye, as they were often wretchedly miserable, sometimes hungry and poorly clothed,[175] and suffered long bouts without pay while their tribal irregular counterparts were lavished with privilege and distinction. According to the British consul at Van, "Most military officers have no liking whatever for Hamidieh, as they are jealous of the titles and distinctions which the latter have won so easily, while they have to serve many years before attaining high rank."[176] In general, these officers were reported to have lost patience with the Hamidiye; they would "enjoy being told to take regular troops and 'hot' their quondam comrades in arms, who have treated them with great insolence in most cases."[177] One Takori chief bragged to Sadettin Pasha about his behavior. He said, "Four years ago if an officer came to our tribe we would tremble in fear. Now that the state has given us the ranks of lieutenant-colonel and major we don't listen to the government. In fact, if a battalion commander comes we say, 'I'm a lieutenant-colonel. You are beneath me in rank, shut up!'"[178] Another would wear his official uniform to town and tell the resident *kaymakam*, "Get up, *kaymakam*! I outrank you, and I'm a soldier," and would force the *kaymakam* from his chair and sit in it himself.[179] Some officers, such as in those in Malazgird, even tendered their resignation over the Hamidiye question, as they could not "stand seeing their brother officers shot at by Kurds with impunity."[180] Once again we might take the case of Mustafa Pasha, leader of the Mîran tribe, to illustrate these complaints.

OPPOSITION AND REINVENTION

The sons and grandsons of Bedir Khan Beg were especially vocal in the mounting opposition to the Hamidiye Light Cavalry and the faction of government that supported it. It is instructive to examine this opposition for the insights it offers into the Hamidiye organization and the theme of power in the Kurdish-Ottoman tribal zone.

A decade after the formation of the Hamidiye Light Cavalry, some of the sons of Bedir Khan Beg began an outspoken campaign of opposition against the Hamidiye and Mustafa Pasha of the Mîran tribe. They had already joined the growing movement against the sultan, who had created and supported them. We have seen how Mustafa Pasha and the Hamidiye were made subjects in *Kurdistan* by Abdurrahman Bedir Khan and his brother Mikdad Midhat, who conducted their campaign of opposition and published their journal from their residences in exile. While that piece was certainly colorful, it was not the only one. In fact, throughout the run of *Kurdistan* there were a number of diatribes against the Hamidiye organization, Zeki Pasha, and the sultan,[181] and indeed one very long article devoted to exposing the "harsh truths" about the Hamidiye organization appeared in the gazette. The piece suggests that in the hands of

Zeki Pasha, the Hamidiye troops committed many atrocities, detrimentally affected the Treasury, and initiated ethnic conflict among groups that had previously lived in peace with one another.[182] And in the same year, an article denouncing the Hamidiye was penned by Abdullah Cevdet, a member of the Kurdish intelligentsia as well as a member of the CUP.[183] The article, which appeared in *Droshak*, the official organ of the Armenian Dashnaktsutiun, located the creation of the Hamidiye in a longer line of Hamidian policies that intentionally spoiled otherwise friendly relations between Kurds and Armenians. The Hamidiye, he argued, was an organization in which

ranks of captain and major were given to shepherds and servants. Seeing this, the poor Kurds ran to enlist themselves and received free uniforms and weapons. With these privileges, a person like these shepherds and servants would kill not only an Armenian, but also their very own father. At the same time, Sultan Abdülhamid spread the rumors among the Kurds to the effect that the Armenians, in cahoots with the Russians, were going to massacre the Kurds, and after inciting the Kurds and making them fanatical, he telegraphed to Zeki Pasha the order to attack Dalvorik, and was able in this way to pave the way for an Armenian-Kurdish struggle.[184]

The crusade against the Hamidiye, thus, was well underway in Kurdish intellectual circles.[185]

While 1900 seems to be the year in which the movement of the Bedir Khans and their associates against the Hamidiye first came into print, it was not the beginning of this campaign. Indeed, in 1894, Abdurrezzak and Halil Bedir Khan reportedly visited their home (Cizre-Botan) clandestinely, presumably during a return trip from Russia, where they were in the Ottoman diplomatic service. While in Cizre, they accepted the protest of some "10,000 of their clansmen" against the formation of the Hamidiye.[186] This number seems ridiculously high, but the report is nonetheless suggestive. It appears that the Bedir Khans were active early on in the movement of opposition to the Hamidiye, and that they still enjoyed some influence in the region from which their family had been exiled decades earlier.[187] They were also apparently attempting to subvert the new hierarchy in state-tribe relations by building their contacts among non-Hamidiye tribes. The brothers may have been invited by their cousin, Mehmed Bey, and his sponsor, Aghayê Sor. The latter *agha* had, within the previous year or two, appointed Mehmed Bey Bedir Khan to lead his followers against Mustafa Pasha in the battles fought between these rival tribes.[188]

The opposition of the Bedir Khans to Mustafa Pasha picked up again around 1900, when the aforementioned article was published. The following year, Mustafa Pasha received a summons to go to Istanbul to appear before a criminal court, following a petition that was submitted to the *vali* of Diyarbekir and the sultan. This petition was signed by delegates of some twenty Muslim and five Christian villages in the area just west of Cizre, and outlined numerous wrongs to which Mustafa Pasha and Tahir Agha had submitted the inhabitants of these villages. But Mustafa Pasha managed to escape the trial—and punishment—by telegraphing the *vali* that one of the petitioners was in league with Abdurrahman Bedir Khan, "and by this convenient device . . . succeeded, for the present at least, in turning the tables on his accuser," as the British vice-consul stated.[189] Soon after that, Mustafa Pasha retaliated against Mehmed Bey Bedir Khan, who was resident in the Cizre region, by accusing him of being in league with the Shammar tribe (an Arab tribe) and the Armenians in planning a massive rebellion against the government.[190] Upon Mustafa Pasha's denunciation to the sultan and the *vali* of Mehmed Bey as a dangerous person who was inciting the Botan Kurds to revolt (apparently in concert with the Armenians and Shammars), Mehmed Bey was arrested and taken to Erzincan for questioning. From there he was sent back to Bitlis, where he remained in prison until orders came from the capital for his banishment. The British consul at Erzurum believed that Mehmed Bey may have been one of the intermediaries through which *Kurdistan* was distributed in the region.[191] Yet he also added in another report that Mehmed Bey "was a perfectly peaceful and harmless individual of no great influence or importance living quietly at Shakh,"[192] some five hours east of Cizre. Mustafa Pasha's accusation was possibly in retaliation for the diatribe against him in the journal, or perhaps because Mehmed Bey was friendly with Aghayê Sor, as the consul surmised. Whatever the case, Mustafa Pasha used his Hamidiye standing to discredit his rivals in the ongoing feuds. Naturally, the Bedir Khans opposed the Hamidiye and the sultan who created them and put power into the hands of their rival in this manner.

The hostility of the Bedir Khans to the Hamidiye and to Mustafa Pasha in particular seems obvious now that we know the history of both. Mustafa Pasha and his Mîran tribe were rivals, who now held power where the Bedir Khans had previously reigned over a largely independent emirate. The alliance of the Bedir Khans with Aghayê Sor, the enemy of Mustafa Pasha, also now makes sense.[193] But the opposition of the Bedir Khans to Mustafa Pasha, the Mîran, the Hamidiye, and the sultan who supported their adversary's new claim to power was not simply opposition for its own sake. Although most of the Bedir Khan family had been in exile since the time Bedir Khan Beg's emirate was destroyed by Ottoman forces in the middle of the century, the family still enjoyed a certain level of influence and respect from the people not only in their home base of Cizre-Botan, but over a broader stretch of the Kurdish regions as well. Over the years, the British and French consuls alluded to the support the family still enjoyed in the region, in spite of having been banished from it for nearly half a century. One consul noted the "superstitious reverence" with which Kurds to the south of Lake Van spoke of Bedir Khan Beg. The consul remarked, "There is no doubt that if one of these [sons of Bedir Khan Beg] found it possible to return, he could raise a considerable following, the moment being favourable."[194] Indeed, they found such opportunities on several occasions. Over the years, the sons of Bedir Khan Beg, whose family had been marginalized in the chain of command from the center to the periphery, did not cease their efforts to return to power, or at the very least to recapture for themselves a position in that center-periphery channel. In 1878, Osman and Hüseyin Bedir Khan made an attempt to reclaim their family's emirate. According to the British consul resident at Diyarbekir, the two *beys* escaped from their exile, and returned to Cizre. Taking advantage of the weakness of the government and the absence of troops following the Russo-Ottoman War, they managed to assemble several thousand followers, divided into two camps, and carried out their attack on the state from Cizre and Deh.[195] Although Ottoman forces were able to defeat the movement, it is nonetheless significant, for it shows that the family could still muster a following and that it displayed tenacity in their search for a means to return to power. Again in the early 1890s, Abdurrezzak Bey Bedir Khan seems to have explored the possibility of reviving his family's emirate.[196] There were various attempts, then, on the part of the Bedir Khans to breathe new life into their past emirate. The campaign against Mustafa Pasha and the Hamidiye must be viewed, in part, with this in mind.

On one level, members of the Bedir Khan family were pursuing their claims to power, continuing the feud with the Mîran in a traditional manner, yet on other and more significant levels they also represent political power as it would come to develop in Kurdish society in the twentieth century—through a fusion of ideas of identity, peoplehood, and borders with more "traditional" modes of seeking power. Starting from the last years of the nineteenth century, the claims of the Bedir Khan brothers to rule in Kurdistan were increasingly voiced through a nationalist idiom, beginning with their publication of *Kurdistan* in 1898.[197] Yet while the Bedir Khan name would come to be one of the most significant names in the Kurdish nationalist movement of the early twentieth century, for the years under review in this chapter it is equally important to note that the Bedir Khans were also Ottomans, concerned with the empire's larger issues and problems, albeit those that affected them more particularly. The Hamidiye was one such concern, but it was wrapped up in a larger movement of opposition to Sultan Abdülhamid II—a movement in which several Bedir Khans played a prominent role.

While the Bedir Khans were active in their opposition to the Hamidiye and to the regime that gave birth to this organization, they were far from alone in this.

The Hamidiye Light Cavalry was clearly viewed with contempt by many in the region, especially by those whose lives it touched the most—villagers and tribespeople, who, in some regions, referred to them with disdain as *tenekelis* (tin-plated men), as the traveler Lynch observed.[198] However, the cavalry for others came to represent Sultan Abdülhamid II's regime in general, whereby favors were lavished upon a small circle of individuals whom the sultan either already trusted or whose loyalty he was hoping to attract.[199] Military students and officers were among the first to join the ranks of this growing opposition movement; they, of course, came to be quite familiar with the Hamidiye organization and had ample opportunity to contrast their own often dismal lots with the favors and distinctions heaped on Kurdish chiefs by a sultan who was making an effort to win them over. We have seen the complaints of some of these soldiers. To this we should emphasize the connections of many officers with the Young Turk movement. Some of the officers serving in the eastern provinces concurrently with the Hamidiye were involved in the CUP, and saw their freedoms diminishing at the same time as the license accorded to Hamidiye chiefs was growing. For example, in 1897, over twenty Turkish officers of the Erzurum garrison were arrested for having been in possession of CUP publications and/or correspondence. They had already been removed from the capital when their "Young Turk" proclivities were suspected. Their comrades also found themselves facing stricter confines. The consul wrote,

Restrictive measures . . . and the arrests which have taken place cannot but increase the uneasy and discontented spirit already noticeable in military circles—a spirit to which free expression was given on the recent passage through Erzeroum of the detachment of Hamidiyé Cavalry returning from Constantinople, when officers of the regular army did not fail to contrast their own miserable situation with that of these fortunate recipients of Imperial bounty, who have come back with their pockets full of money, brave with decoration and presents, and loudly boastful of the favours which have been lavished on them.[200]

The Hamidiye came to be a very sore spot with many Ottoman officers. As a growing number of them became involved in the CUP, they shared their grievances against the Hamidiye and their commander with others in the movement. At one point there was even said to be a plan by some in the CUP to assassinate Zeki Pasha.[201] The British consul at Van reported in 1897 that he had been informed by an officer in the Ottoman army that the "Young Turk party" had considered the assassination of Zeki Pasha, but had been dissuaded in the end by Mizancı Murad Bey.[202]

The opposition of certain CUP members to the Hamidiye and its commander must be viewed in the context of Ottoman politics under Sultan Abdülhamid II. Abdurrahman Bedir Khan was an Ottoman intellectual as well as a member of a leading Kurdish family. He had ties to both communities and the Bedir Khani campaign against the sultan, Zeki Pasha, the Hamidiye, and Mustafa Pasha and the Mîran tribe must similarly be seen in this light as well.

The Bedir Khans' wish for Mustafa Pasha's downfall was realized in 1902, when this Hamidiye pasha was assassinated by the Bedir Khans' new allies, Muhammad Aghayê Sor and his men, who laid an ambush while the Hamidiye commander and his tribe were migrating.[203] The tribe thus lost the leader who had built such a personal relationship with Zeki Pasha, and in so doing had managed to advance his own and his tribe's position in the region. However, the tribe continued under the leadership of Abdulkerim, Mustafa Pasha's son, who was already commander of one of the tribe's Hamidiye regiments. Upon his father's death, it seems that Abdulkerim may have taken over command of the other regiment as well.[204] Observers noted that Abdulkerim also worked to enhance his tribe's position in the region through the same means as his father—plunder, intimidation, and murder. However, while he used as much violence, he initially met with less success now that he faced a greater alliance against him and his tribe. This coalition was partly the result of the Bedir Khans' efforts to bring about the downfall of Mustafa Pasha and his tribe. However, in spite of this mounting opposition, Abdulkerim and other Hamidiye chiefs managed to regain control over the mini-emirates that they had built through their Hamidiye connections until their imperial patron was overthrown and his confidante, Zeki Pasha, was dismissed from his post by the new regime.[205]

CONCLUSION

For the "Young Turks," who eventually succeeded in deposing the sultan and his trusted advisors, the Hamidiye was emblematic of the worst of the regime that they sought to dismantle. Although opponents of the Hamidiye under Abdülhamid II were not largely successful in achieving their ultimate goal of the full and final disbanding of this militia, their movement is nonetheless significant. The campaign of the Bedir Khans and their CUP comrades against the Hamidiye and its supporters century took place on many levels. It was an attempt by a former ruling family to return to their previous influence using traditional channels, but it was also a reflection of the modernity of their political programs and activities.

The movement was conducted using new means—publications, political organizations, and finally a constitutional revolution. Indeed, with the spread of modern communications, the "public transcript" of power became ever more public, and various parties engaged with it to assert their own programs. Under Abdülhamid II, Hamidiye chiefs employed their knowledge of the empire's perceived threats and the sultan's concerns to their advantage. Together with Zeki Pasha they put on a smoke-and-mirrors performance to magnify these threats and to justify their unique empowerment, which was otherwise so detrimental not just to the practices of the state, as Joel Migdal would say, but also to the idea of the state, and indeed the state's very image at home and abroad. But the opposition also engaged with the public transcript of power as they deployed new technologies of communication—particularly in print media—to press for their own claims. What is interesting, and what we will find in the next chapter, is that the discourse of the public transcript changed somewhat after 1908 when a representative government was in place; the raw terms of power, however, did not. For all of its interest in dismantling the Hamidiye program, in the end the CUP promoted a very similar agenda to the regime that it had staunchly opposed. Although many in the Second Constitutional Government perceived the irony in the state's empowering of a group that it ultimately wanted to assimilate and better control, events on the ground caused them to feel that they had no choice but to abandon their efforts at reform and to return to the Hamidiye program that had dangerously emboldened new agents in the Kurdish-Ottoman periphery. After all, both regimes faced similar contradictions in modern statecraft.

CHAPTER THREE

The Tribal Light Cavalry Under the Young Turks, 1908–1914

★

The year 1908 was a crossroads in the history of the Hamidiye, just as it was a turning point in various other facets of Ottoman life. For many, it was a year of hope. The "Young Turks" had succeeded in reinstating the Ottoman constitution of 1876 and promised sweeping reforms. In the provinces where Hamidiye Light Cavalry units were based, many people eagerly greeted the news of the constitution and rejoiced as heartily as did their compatriots in the capital. It was reported, for example, that "doubt and disbelief in the news" had initially put a check on open displays of feeling at Harput; but when at last word of the recent events at the capital arrived there by the mail a semi-official celebration was held and crowds of Muslims and Christians "paraded the town, which was illuminated and decorated, amidst the greatest enthusiasm." In Erzurum, a "general rejoicing" took place among both the soldiers and the civilian population. The prevailing feeling was described as "universal satisfaction and relief." And lastly, in Diyarbekir, the local consul reported that people were universally in favor of the constitution, with the exception of fanatics and "corrupt officials."[1]

These, however, were mostly the reactions of urban residents in the region, and indeed the consuls failed to report that some among them were ambivalent if not outright hostile to the new developments. For the rural population, the response was more mixed. Although it was met by some with as much joy as it was by their urban counterparts, for others, news of the constitution was received with a measure of indifference. Many people had little faith that their situation would actually change for the better, and some, like the Hamidiye chiefs, were worried it could indeed change for the worse.[2]

On one level, the fears of these chiefs would prove to be correct, at least in the short term. The Hamidiye would, after all, be transformed in the initial period of the CUP's rule, when the new regime took resolved steps to curb the power of the tribal chiefs, which had grown so great under the previous regime. However, these policies spurred Hamidiye chiefs, whose power, property, and privilege were now threatened, to join the political scene described at the end of the last chapter. They responded to the aggressive campaign of the new government with their own moves by establishing and joining political clubs and engaging in many other means—ranging from professed loyalty to protest to open rebellion—to protect the precious power they had built under the ancien régime. At this most critical moment in their rule, the CUP leaders felt that they could not alienate this powerful element, and decided that they continued to need their support and alliance. Hence, on other levels although the patronage and indeed the name of the Hamidiye changed under the new regime, the organization and the power structure with which it came to be identified remained the same in significant ways; the many promised reforms and reorganizations fell to the wayside in face of the staunch opposition offered by the Hamidiye and other Kurdish chiefs and notables. Thus, by the time of the Balkan Wars, it seemed that the two regimes, often posed in contradistinction to one another, were not so dissimilar after all. The ultimate goals of both regimes, after all, were to create a centralized and controllable nation out of the remaining Ottoman dominions and to temper the influence of foreign powers and threats. This chapter will trace the unfolding story of power in the Ottoman tribal zone for the years 1908 to 1914 by outlining the aims of the central regime, again using the Hamidiye as a lens through which to view the issues at hand. The chapter will also treat the question of power as it unfolded on the ground quite beyond the reach of the government. Modern means of communication and organization begun during the Hamidian period flourished after 1908, and political parties, clubs, and platforms turned into new venues to bargain for authority among diverse groups and individuals in the Kurdish regions, including the Hamidiye chiefs.

THE FIRST TO GO

Many in the new regime recognized the problems involved in empowering a group that ultimately made it more difficult for the state to govern effectively, and indeed that defied not only state practices but also the very "idea of state."3 They did not believe that this effort-bargain was really a bargain in the big picture. Hence, shortly after the constitution was announced in 1908, the French consul at Erzurum reported that the Hamidiye would be one of the first things on the agenda when the Ottoman deputies convened.4 The question of the Hamidiye was certainly linked to the larger issue of reforms that faced the new government. For those who had benefited from the system that had flourished under the previous regime, modifications were, naturally, unwelcome. Indeed, the Hamidiye chiefs were one such group who would be the first to be affected by changes initially promoted by the new regime.

First on the agenda was the dismissal of Zeki Pasha, which took place in August 1908.5 Zeki Pasha's removal from office was likely no surprise to most, as he had been one of the closest confidantes of the sultan, whose regime was abhorred by the CUP and their sympathizers. Zeki Pasha had even tried hedging his bets in the years immediately preceding the constitutional revolution; seeing that the Young Turks were gaining in power, he attempted to cultivate friendly relations with some of them as early as 1906. The French consul reported then that Zeki Pasha, "fearing the upcoming overthrow of the current regime, is taking his precautions in showing himself favorable to the ideas of the Young Turks."6 Indeed, at the time, the CUP central committee sent a congratulatory letter to Zeki Pasha, whom it believed was assisting its cause; in reality the marshal was doing his best to suppress the revolutionary movement and to demonstrate his utter loyalty to his imperial patron.7 When the moment came, then, as a figure so closely identified with the outgoing regime, he could not be allowed by the new government to remain at his post.8 According to the British consul resident at Erzurum, the "retirement" of Zeki Pasha gave immediate hope to Muslims and Christians alike "that the long reign of licensed brigandage, for it can be called nothing else, with which the name of Kurdish Hamidié Cavalry has come to be identified in these parts at length to [*sic*] be brought to an end."9 And indeed, it seemed that with the dismissal of such an influential figure, things were going to change.10

"THE GREATEST NATIVE PERSONAGE IN KURDISTAN"

Described by the British ambassador as "only second perhaps to the dismissal of the famous Zekki Pasha" was the news of the government's decision to conduct a campaign against İbrahim Pasha,11 leader of the Millî tribe and Hamidiye commander, who had grown into one of the most powerful figures in Kurdistan and who oversaw what some called a "little empire."12 Like Mustafa Pasha, İbrahim Pasha used his Hamidiye connections to expand his power base; he combined his mounting authority with government resources to advance his own agenda, particularly in the case of feuds with neighboring tribes. İbrahim Pasha was able, just as Mustafa Pasha had been, to increase his wealth, especially through the number of clients he was able to attract through his growing strength and prestige. This, however, is what appears to have set him apart from Mustafa Pasha. Whereas the latter apparently exploited his own clients extensively, instead of only raiding the clients of rival tribes, İbrahim Pasha seems to have enjoyed a better reputation for his treatment of the peasants and smaller tribes absorbed by the Millî. He was also a noted "protector" of Christians during moments when their lives were in particular danger.[13]

We may compare the two Hamidiye pashas further. The authority of Mustafa Pasha and the Mîran tribe began to wane around 1900, not because they enjoyed any less protection from their patrons, Zeki Pasha and the sultan, but because they had attracted such a coalition against themselves for the brutal methods that Mustafa Pasha had used to enrich himself over the previous decade and a half. By contrast, just when the Mîran were beginning to decline around the year that marked the century's turn, İbrahim Pasha and the Millî were growing stronger than ever. Around 1900 the tribe began to show a heightened level of activity in the quest to expand their resources and attract clients. But part of this process necessarily involved feuds with neighboring tribes upon whose territory or clients the expanding tribe was encroaching, or from whom the Millî were beginning to take more "business." The two, after all, often went hand-in-hand. Most of these feuds were naturally with neighboring tribes. In the case of the Millî, the main rivals were primarily the Kîkî, the Karakeçi, and the Shammar (an Arab tribe). To complicate things, the first two tribes mentioned were also Hamidiye tribes and therefore enjoyed the advantages associated with membership in the militia. The latter, while it was not a Hamidiye tribe, often entered into alliances with the two former tribes, and was thus able to enjoy some of the benefits by proxy.[14]

Advantages through association were not generally enough, however, to support İbrahim Pasha's rivals. It is evident that although the Millî was certainly a less populous tribe than any of its aforementioned adversaries,[15] it was the most important Hamidiye tribe, or confederation, in its region. It is also clear that İbrahim Pasha had built a significant following, even by this point. Like other powerful Hamidiye commanders, he used his standing with Zeki Pasha and the sultan to his advantage in these feuds. This was the case during raids that were carried out back and forth between the people of İbrahim Pasha and one Osman Agha throughout 1900.[16] Apparently in hopes that he would be able to heighten his footing vis-à-vis his rival, Osman Agha went to the capital with the intention of persuading the central government to allow him to form a Hamidiye regiment from his people. But owing to "the adverse influence" exercised by Zeki Pasha, his efforts remained unsuccessful.[17] İbrahim Pasha's other main foe, the Shammar,[18] also a non-Hamidiye tribe, similarly failed to enlist help when it faced the Millî. The Millî carried out a major raid against one section of the Shammar—a raid which resulted in some loss of life as well as in the theft of a thousand camels and fifteen thousand sheep. In response, the Shammar leader, Sheikh Faris, telegraphed the capital that the Hamidiye leaders İbrahim Pasha and Mustafa Pasha (Mîran) must be controlled; otherwise, he said he would retaliate. However, once again the powerful Hamidiye chief was able to win out against his non-Hamidiye rival. Apparently in dread of a coalition of the Shammar and its allies against his tribe, İbrahim Pasha addressed telegrams to Zeki Pasha and the Palace to the effect that he faced great danger of a combined attack, and that the Shammar tribe was being incited by the British. He was thus able to enlist the support of the government: First the government sent Bahaeddin Pasha to effect a peace between the two, and when this failed, troops were sent to protect Viranşehir, İbrahim Pasha's "capital."[19] Hence, İbrahim Pasha was able to expand his influence and make use of additional government resources through his Hamidiye connections, becoming perhaps the most powerful figure in the region, second only to Zeki Pasha himself.[20]

By 1901, one British consul remarked that İbrahim Pasha "administers a little empire of his own, which reaches to within an hour or two of Urfa."[21] The feuds of the Millî against their rivals, which were generally over raids and encroachment on pasture lands, continued over subsequent years. As one tribe lost access to certain lands due to a feud with a different tribe, it began to encroach on the lands of another, bringing old tensions to the fore.[22] But gradually İbrahim Pasha was able to manage his feuds and to expand his authoritative and coercive power such that few dared to attack his territories. İbrahim Pasha also continued to develop his "empire" by attracting new clients, some of whom were groups who volunteered to attach themselves to the more powerful protector, and others who were intimidated by his tactics of persuasion. He would reportedly send his agents to villages all the way to the outskirts of the city of Diyarbekir, for example, offering them the chance either to pay tribute or to be plundered. Interestingly, many of these villages belonged to notables resident in Diyarbekir and some were even the "property" of government officials. Yet in either case, all agreed to pay the tribute.[23] This is further indication of the authority that İbrahim Pasha enjoyed in the region.[24] To ensure his continued support from the Palace and to keep in the sultan's favor, İbrahim Pasha also offered special services to his patron. In 1904, for example, the tricky task of reconciling two feuding Hamidiye chiefs arose. Urgent orders were telegraphed from the capital to effect a peace between İbrâhim Pasha of the Millî and Halil Bey of the Karakeçi, both men in positions of high command in the Hamidiye.[25] Perhaps to get an edge over his rival or perhaps to guarantee that he remained the most influential of the Hamidiye chiefs in his region, İbrahim Pasha volunteered his men for service in Yemen, where they would join the Ottoman military expedition to bring a different far-flung region into the fold.[26]

While İbrahim Pasha had, by 1901, already been able to build a little empire of his own, by 1905 his position was stronger than ever before, as stated by one observer.[27] He did this through a carefully maintained policy of keeping up good relations with "persons of influence at Constantinople and with his military chief at Erzinjian," while ignoring local authority. At the same time, he was "invariably courteous to Europeans" and careful to "retain the confidence of the native Christians," of whom increasing numbers were settling and enjoying protection in his capital, Viranşehir.[28] İbrahim Pasha became so influential that, in addition to gathering large numbers of villages under his protection, he was also able to absorb numerous other tribes under his wing, including even tribes that had formerly been his rivals, like the Karakeçi. The "reconciliation" that had taken place was, of course, to the advantage of the Millî, with the result that Halil Bey, the Karakeçi leader, came under İbrahim Pasha's protection with nearly his whole tribe behind him.[29] Soon after that he was able to absorb a section of the Shammar, his former foe, expanding his influence to a virtual tribal emirate. He controlled the trade of Viranşehir, and profited enormously from it.[30] According to Sykes, who had extensive contact with İbrahim Pasha, his influence even spread far beyond his immediate environs, with Kurds from various religious backgrounds as far as Malatya and Erzincan regarding him as their chief and taking their disputes to him rather than to the courts.[31]

Already the head of this powerful conglomeration of tribes and villages, İbrahim Pasha was able to raise yet two more regiments from his people, perhaps in reward for his offer of service in Yemen. In August 1905, the British consul reported that a *miralay* from the Palace had arrived from the capital bearing an imperial decree that sanctioned the formation of two new Hamidiye regiments under the Millî chief.[32] Now, besides his previously held regiments (numbers Forty-one, Forty-two, and Forty-three), İbrahim Pasha also commanded the newly created Sixty-third and Sixty-fourth Regiments.[33] And in addition to his own—now five—regiments, he was also the real authority, though not on paper, behind several other Hamidiye tribes in his region, notably the Kays, an Arab tribe, which provided two Hamidiye regiments (Fifty-first and Fifty-second).[34]

Soon, a coalition formed against this powerful chief. However, this league was not nearly as powerful or as diverse as the one that had formed against Mustafa Pasha just a few years earlier. This one consisted mainly of a group of Diyarbekir notables, whose interests were threatened by the powerful Hamidiye chief, who now could attack their villages all the way to the gates of Diyarbekir.[35] The notables addressed a telegram to the Palace requesting the exile of İbrahim Pasha and further tried to enlist the support of local Christians, who seemed rather unwilling to join the movement against him. Interestingly, whereas the European representatives had come out entirely in favor of dismantling Mustafa Pasha's authority, and indeed that of the Hamidiye in general, in the case of İbrahim Pasha, their support rested not with the opposition, but with the Hamidiye pasha himself as they blamed the Diyarbekir notables for the sad state of affairs in the region and believed that the pasha protected Christian interests.[36] His efforts to cultivate friendly relations with Europeans seem to have achieved their goal. The quarrel was "settled" not by the exile of the Hamidiye commander, as the notables had hoped, but through an imperial commission sent to mediate the dispute.[37]

But tension mounted between the Diyarbekir notables and İbrahim Pasha once again in 1907. The British ambassador reported in November of that year that his conversations with the grand vizier and other sources pointed to a serious crisis in Diyarbekir. It became known that İbrahim Pasha's men had overrun the entire countryside surrounding the city, and were even reported to be at the city's gates with some sixteen thousand armed tribespeople. The Muslim notables of the town revolted, seized the telegraph office, and sent a message to the Palace demanding the suppression of İbrahim Pasha as well as measures for the reform of the local government.[38] An imperial decree was issued to the effect that İbrahim Pasha should be sent to Aleppo until a commission of inquiry could determine a just course of action.[39] Once again, however, İbrahim Pasha was able to count on the support of two more British agents, who, like their colleague, blamed the Diyarbekir notables for the situation, remarking that the notables were "much worse in reality" than İbrahim Pasha,[40] that the charges against him were largely fabrications of the notables, and that his removal would lead to greater disorder, as competition for power among his rivals would ensue.[41] In the spring of 1908, however, the local administration summoned the Diyarbekir notables and communicated to them the contents of a new imperial decree. Administrative reforms were announced and pardon was granted to the notables who had taken part in the demonstration the previous November, albeit with orders that they were "not to do it again." Troops were then sent to İbrahim Pasha's places, presumably to arrest him and enforce his departure for Aleppo, which had been ordered several months before.[42] However, the next month İbrahim

Pasha once more made a good effort to gain the graces of the sultan by demonstrating his loyalty by offering to send some of his Hamidiye regiments to the Hijaz, to protect the Baghdad Railway, which was then under construction.[43] His services were reportedly "accepted with profuse thanks from sultan."[44] And once again, İbrahim Pasha was able to hold on to his position and escape banishment or any other form of punishment.

On the eve of the Young Turk Revolution, İbrahim Pasha was one of the most powerful figures in all of Kurdistan. One of the British agents in the region, who had the opportunity to visit him, wrote a lengthy report that offers a glimpse into several issues at play in this study, power relations in particular. In it, he described the extent of İbrahim Pasha's authority, which he had gained after becoming the Hamidiye chief of five regiments, thus reversing the trend whereby the tribes under the Millî, which had lost influence several decades earlier, had fallen "into the hands of the Eshreffs [notables] of Diarbekir, Mardin, and Aleppo." Now, many of these tribes had come back under İbrahim Pasha's wing. He noted the "flourishing condition of the lands under his protection," and was particularly impressed with how well the Christian populations of his district lived, compared to people in other regions. Indeed the consul was so awed by İbrahim Pasha's authority that he even suggested that the British government could consider him—rather than the local government—a resource in the region for protecting the security of the region, particularly Christians. And İbrahim Pasha, for his part, discreetly sought support from the British government, as he seemed to sense the instability that reigned on the eve of the Young Turk Revolution. European agents in the region were rarely sympathetic to Kurdish chiefs—particularly Hamidiye chiefs—but İbrahim Pasha seems to have been an exception.[45]

With his main rivals crushed and others kept at bay, by mid-1908, İbrahim Pasha's "empire" stretched all the way to Nusaybin, where the Shammar tribe had formerly prevailed. The British consul remarked that "his triumph over his enemies has been complete and crushing and he is now by far the greatest native personage in Kurdistan."[46] This was stated just weeks before the revolution; the new leaders, when they came to power, could not allow such a powerful figure to challenge their authority.

THE PASHA'S LAST STAND

Soon after coming to power and immediately following the dismissal of Zeki Pasha, the new government issued orders for the arrest of İbrahim

Pasha.[47] Without delay, the Hamidiye pasha set out eastward from Aleppo, where he had been waiting to proceed to the Hijaz with one of his regiments, but soldiers were dispatched to prevent him from joining up with the rest of his tribes. He nonetheless managed to reach Viranşehir, his "capital," where his force then swelled to some four thousand to five thousand armed men.[48] He arrived just days after his eldest son, Abdülhamid, had celebrated the sultan's Day of Accession and the reinstatement of the constitution by offering a feast to the *kaymakam* and military officers and illuminating the town. When İbrahim Pasha reached his destination, he and his forces faced a large number of government troops. The two sides agreed to not enter the town armed, but the tentative peace was soon to be broken. A brawl broke out in the bazaar between a soldier and some civilian assailants. Both sides ran for their arms and severe fighting broke out, which lasted for three days. İbrahim Pasha then cut off the water supply, hoping that he could force the soldiers to evacuate.[49]

During this time, İbrahim Pasha drafted a desperate letter to the British vice-consul resident at Diyarbekir in which he sought support from the only party he believed might be his ally. İbrahim Pasha's "only friend," Consul Heard, did communicate the letter to his superior in Istanbul. But the British ambassador had a different regard for the pasha in trouble. The ambassador condescendingly acknowledged the pasha's "fair share of the barbaric virtues," but concluded: "Whatever may have been the personal merits of Ibrahim, it seems beyond question that this resolute suppression of a Chief who by dint of lawlessness had raised himself to a semi-independent position would have a far-reaching effect in awing and tranquillizing the Kurds throughout Anatolia."[50] The new power in Istanbul was supported, then, in its campaign against İbrahim Pasha by the British representatives in the capital.

Stripped of his rank and facing orders for his capture dead or alive, İbrahim Pasha agreed to surrender to Şahin Bey, the commander of the Aleppo Esterlis (Muleteers). According to several sources interviewed by Consul Heard, İbrahim Pasha directed his men to leave their arms in their tents while he went over the details of the surrender with Şahin Bey in his tent. However, while the two were discussing the surrender, İbrahim Pasha's Hamidiye troops were fired upon by some officers of the regular army. İbrahim Pasha's men then ran for their weapons, but were attacked by shock troops. Seeing that the situation was now beyond repair, İbrahim Pasha then made a dash for Heleli. After their flight, the regular soldiers, rival tribes, and shock troops plundered Viranşehir, then Heleli, and finally some surrounding villages, attacking some of their inhabitants as well. İbrahim Pasha only made it as far as Sufaya, a twelve-hour march from Heleli (the "capital" of his Yezidi ally, Hasanê Kenco), where he surrendered not to the Ottoman troops, but to dysentery, on September 27. His son, Abdülhamid, managed to reach the vicinity of Nusaybin, where he was finally surrounded by hostile tribes and forced to capitulate. He sent a message of surrender with İbrahim Pasha's first wife, Xatûna Xanse, and was soon after arrested.[51] From prison, Abdülhamid Bey addressed a petition to the government in which he described his father's great services to the empire, how he had rendered his region safe and prosperous, and how his father had delivered the region from the grip of the notables, who were now conniving against them. Engaging in the "public transcript of power," he called on the government to hold true to its constitutional principles and to act in the name of justice.[52] Perhaps due to his professions of loyalty to the new regime, and also perhaps because of representations made by his British supporters, the grand vizier sent orders to release Abdülhamid Bey and his brothers from prison.[53] However, the government continued to send expeditions to forcibly seize all of the Millî's sheep and other animals, on the pretext that the late pasha owed a huge debt to the government.[54] The government also rearrested the sons of İbrahim Pasha, and continued to detain the late pasha's wife at Mardin; Xatûna Xanse apparently could have served as a protector of her tribe.[55] Divested of government protection, the tribe was now also open to combined attacks carried out by neighboring tribes. These assaults were indeed perpetrated in the months to follow, with extensive destruction and looting.[56] The tribe was now in the position of a non-Hamidiye tribe. Deprived of its leaders, its wealth, and particularly its government support, the power the Millî held just months before was now gone.

CRACKDOWNS AND EMISSARIES

The new regime not only brought down the most influential Hamidiye chieftain soon after coming to power, but it did so thoroughly and brutally. At the same time, it had carried on an expedition against the Kurds of Dersim, who were not enrolled in the Hamidiye.[57] Arrests of additional leading Kurdish notables, including other powerful Hamidiye chieftains, such as those from the powerful Mîran tribe, also followed,[58] and were publicized in the *Takvim-i Vekayi*, where the central government hoped it would demonstrate its seriousness in instilling law and order by disseminating its public transcript of power.[59] What is more, many Kurdish chieftains were evicted from the Armenian villages they had taken over in the course of the preceding years.[60] The Hamidiye was to change as well. It was not entirely abolished, but was to be reformed. In November of 1908, the government announced that the militia would now rank as reserve militia, answerable to civil courts for civil offenses, and would face military tribunals only for military crimes. The tribes were not to be fully disarmed, but were to return their government-issue rifles.[61] The following year the crackdown persisted, particularly after the overthrow of Sultan Abdülhamid II from his throne. For the tribes that had benefited so vastly under this sultan, his removal from power was devastating.

The new regime was firm in its attempts to establish itself in the tribal zone; in this regard it was no different from the regime that it had replaced. But military expeditions and arrests were not the only methods it employed. The central government also sent emissaries to convince the leaders of the Kurdish tribes that support of the new regime would be in their interests. It employed every tool in its arsenal to establish its control and authority. Kurdish intellectuals had played a prominent part in the Young Turk movement from the start; indeed two of the four "founders" of the CUP, Abdullah Cevdet and İshak Sükûti, were Kurds. Now, as discontent among such a powerful group mounted, the new regime called upon its Kurdish supporters to reach out to their compatriots and draw them into the fold of the new regime.[62]

Although the CUP's popularity had been mounting in the Six Provinces in the years preceding the revolution, it was never widespread by any stretch of the imagination. Shortly after the reinstatement of the constitution in 1908, the British ambassador remarked that the active propaganda of the CUP had still not been extended to the "distant Asiatic provinces." To remedy this, the central government dispatched telegrams and delegates "to explain to the populations the true significance of the constitutional movement."[63] But cooperation was still not forthcoming, and the leaders of the new regime made a decision to call upon their Kurdish allies.

The central committee chose Seyyid Abdulqadir, an influential Kurdish chief from Şemdinan, one of the sons of Sheikh Ubeydullah, the leader of the famous uprising of 1880. Although he had not been resident in the region for some time, Seyyid Abdulqadir was reported to be still held "in great repute" by all the Kurdish chiefs and to wield great influence among them.[64] Seyyid Abdulqadir arrived in Van in mid-October 1909, where he and the *vali* planned a series of discussions on the constitution and "counsels of obedience" to the new government that he would give to Kurdish chiefs of the region.[65] Nearly all of the Kurdish *agha*s in the Van province reported to the summons and arrived in Van shortly afterward. The string of meetings, which lasted a couple of weeks, was attended not only by Kurdish chiefs but also by Armenian community leaders. The lectures given by Seyyid Abdulqadir were designed to convey to his Kurdish "constituents" the advantages of supporting the present regime, the need to settle the question of the appropriation of Armenian lands by Kurdish chiefs, and to bring about a sort of friendship and understanding between Kurds and Armenians. At what was described by the British consul as "an important meeting" held on November 1, 1909, the Kurds and Armenians swore friendship and mutual aid. And at the final meeting, which the *vali* also attended in person, a formal document embodying the resolutions adopted by the Kurdish chiefs was drawn up, and all who were present signed it. The British consul at Van reported the document as bearing the following resolutions:

1. A promise on the part of the Kurds to live in friendship with their Armenian brothers, to work for the union of all elements, and to help the Government to punish wrong-doers.

2. An engagement to settle the question of the ownership of land claimed by Armenians. By this engagement the Kurds bind themselves to hand over next spring the lands now in their possession, of which Armenians possess and produce the "Tapu" (title-deeds), and in the case of lands claimed by Armenians who cannot produce the "Tapu" to leave the matter to the Government to settle.

3. To establish and further industries in the vilayet, and to spread education by opening schools in the various villages.[66]

Similar "lectures" were given elsewhere in Kurdistan, such as Dersim, where troops sent on a punitive expedition dispatched messages requesting the convention of some thirty-five tribal leaders, who reported to government officials at the military camp and were given the "necessary advice" about obeying the new regime.[67] The well-known Kurdish intellectual, Said-i Kurdî (aka Said-i Nursî), also traveled throughout the region to explain the benefits of the constitution to numerous individual tribes.[68] The government thus used the various means at its disposal to reach out to its Kurdish population in the borderlands. At times it used force, and at other times it commissioned influential Kurds to act on its behalf. Both means, however, were part of a determined effort to bring the region into the fold, just as the preceding government had done,[69] but this time with purportedly different goals in mind.

THE HAMIDIYE REORGANIZED

While the initial plans for the Hamidiye were multifaceted, and certainly included as part of their mission the stronger incorporation of Kurdish tribal society into the Ottoman fold, this aspect of the venture was taken even further when the CUP was in power. The new regulations for the

Hamidiye as they developed in the Second Constitutional Period reveal much about the notions of those now in control of the government. They, too, idealized the Hamidiye as a *mission civilisatrice* for the Kurds—an organization through which they would be introduced to order, modernity, Ottoman citizenship, and now, more than before, Turkishness. The larger vision took the process of "making up people" to another level. Now it was not simply Armenians whose identity was crystallizing as such, but also those of Muslim groups, namely Kurds and Turks. The new regime's relationship with this Kurdish tribal militia played an important part in this story.

The Hamidiye was one of the first things on the agenda when the constitutional regime stepped into power in 1908; however, aside from ordering a reform of the Hamidiye later the same year and collecting government-issue rifles, there were few other changes made to the tribal militia until late in 1909. The units simply were considered "suppressed," although it seems that in reality this meant little to those who were part of the group. The first change after the overthrow of Sultan Abdülhamid II in 1909 was symbolic and significant: the Hamidiye were no longer to be called the "Hamidiye," after their former patron, but were now to be known as the Tribal Light Cavalry Regiments (Aşiret Hafif Süvari Alayları)—a more neutral name for a "neutralized" organization. This change was to communicate firmly and clearly to those tribes who formed the regiments that their former patron was no longer there to oversee and protect them. It was unmistakable that a new regime with different rules was now in control. By December 1909 orders had been issued from the field marshal's office that all officers of the regular army who had been attached to former Hamidiye regiments should return to the headquarters of their respective regiments and proceed with the reorganization of the newly named body. Lieutenant-Colonel Mahmud Bey, accompanied by a military veterinarian, departed on a tour of inspection and recruitment. The British consul at Van reported that Kurds from the surrounding districts flocked to Van, showing "great eagerness" in enrolling themselves. Plans were then made for the distribution of the ten-shot Mauser rifle, which the regular troops at Van had recently discarded in favor of the five-shot, followed by a period of drill.[70]

When Mahmud Bey returned from his tour of inspection in February 1910, he reported to his superior that the Hamidiye regiments had only existed on paper. Mahmud Bey discovered that each regiment, which had been inscribed in the official registers as having at least five hundred armed and mounted men, was in reality composed of a handful of tribesmen, these being mostly the personal retainers of the tribe's chief. He also found that they lacked military training and that few tribesmen had arms (since these had been collected by the government already) or horses. Just as it had been under the old regime, it was in the interest of the chief to record himself having some five hundred, or even one thousand armed and mounted tribesmen, when in reality he could only provide fifty or sixty. The chief could never achieve high rank, decorations, and privileges if he commanded so few men. He would also be ineligible for government weapons, which he could use for his own agenda. The British consul reported that the first inspection conducted under the new regime had "revealed the truth."[71] This was a detail that had long been known to Ottoman and European observers, but one that Zeki Pasha had always succeeded in masking from the sultan. In this case, the facts were reported to the authorities, who then shot the messenger, so to speak; the commanding field marshal was displeased with the report and dismissed Mahmud Bey from his post as inspector.[72]

The British military attaché's report offered a similar view of the Hamidiye as that given in the report drafted by the former inspector, Mahmud Bey. Captain Tyrrell indicated that the abolition of some units along with the retention of others was, in fact, strange, given that some, which never existed or which were never revived, were to be abolished or retained. The regiments' organization was always very loose and in many cases "imaginary." Hence, the "abolition, like the inception, was chiefly an affair of paper." Some, he acknowledged, were in fact more than a mere sham, but even many of these had disintegrated when the Young Turk government had undertaken its punitive expedition against İbrahim Pasha in 1908, or when the leaders of other Hamidiye tribes fled across the border to escape imprisonment during the new crackdown on Kurdish chiefs.[73]

Whether or not the new commander-in-chief of the Hamidiye acknowledged the facts as stated by his own officer or the British observer, he did proceed with the reorganization of the Tribal Regiments.[74] In April 1910, Mustafa Effendi, the *redif* major at Bitlis, reported to the British agent in charge that in addition to instructions received from headquarters to reorganize the militia, a special military commission had been appointed and would soon be assigned the task of investigating the situation and carrying out plans for reorganization.[75] The new regulations planned to replace all former Hamidiye officers who were illiterate with officers in the regular army. Kurdish tribesmen who had horses of the required height would be taken into the Tribal Regiments, while those who had no horses would be drafted into the regular army. Each province would be divided into "ethnographical" zones, or districts based on a particular tribe's territory. The Tribal Regiments would be armed and drilled four months each year. Another officer reported to the same British agent that the "health and economic conditions of the Kurds" would also be taken into consideration in determining who would form part of the Tribal Regiments and who would be drafted into the regular army.[76] In July, several staff officers and census officials set out on the tour of inspection. Emin Pasha, the commander of the Erzurum Division, stated that the Tribal Regiments were necessary due to the inadequacy of the Ottoman army's regular cavalry force, and that the expediency of utilizing the Hamidiye militia had been "admitted in principle."[77] A new school for subofficers at Erzincan was being designed, and plans included the education of those young Kurdish *beys* who had already received an elementary education. The graduates of this school would serve for a time in the regular army and would then be commissioned as officers in the Hamidiye Regiments as vacancies occurred.[78] Soon after this, orders came from the Ministry of War for the abolition of Hamidiye tribes that were sedentary, as these would now be regarded in the same light as settled populations for recruitment purposes. Only migratory tribes would form the Kurdish militia, and the name was accordingly officially changed to "Tribal Light Cavalry Regiments."[79] With the change thus effected, the official numbers of enrolled regiments would be reduced by a predicted half.[80] This indeed took place in the Diyarbekir province, where the numbers of the former Hamidiye regiments were drastically reduced after the president of the Commission of Inspection recommended the disbanding of some of the Millî regiments as well as the regiments provided by the Karakeçi and Ertoşi tribes (the latter actually belonging to the province of Mosul).[81]

These tentative proposals and recommendations were reworked and codified along with many others in a new set of regulations on the Tribal Light Cavalry Regiments in 1910.[82] The new regulations were significant on many counts: They revealed the new government's emphasis on implementing a stricter and more modern order among the Kurdish tribes and also highlighted its new focus on classifying and ordering the peoples in its borders—a project that belonged to modern statecraft. First, they provided for the formation of Tribal Light Cavalry Regiments from the nomadic and seminomadic tribes in various parts of the Ottoman Empire. These tribes were not specifically noted as Kurdish tribes in the regulations, but it seems that once again, the body was targeted almost uniquely to the empire's Kurdish population.[83] Second, they provided for a new Tribal Regular Cavalry Regiment. The tribal soldiers in the regular army would train with other *redif* regiments during times of peace, but would detach into separate "Tribal *Redif* Cavalry Squadrons" (Aşiret Redif Süvari Bölükleri) in times of war. This seemed to be an intermediary step between the former irregular system for the tribes and the regular army for settled populations who had always been subject to conscription. The document also provided for the inspection of the existing "sixty-four-and-one-half" tribal cavalry regiments, and ordered that this number would be "reduced to a reasonable limit." In fact, the number was projected to be reduced from sixty-four or sixty-five regiments to twenty-four, a more reasonable figure for the actual regiments. Later, the name was once again changed, this time simply to Tribal Cavalry Regiments (Aşiret Süvari Alayları).[84]

The provisions for the recruitment of the new tribal units showed a firm commitment to monitoring the tribes, keeping records, and ensuring that conscription would be regular and thorough. Some allowances for tax exemptions were made, but tribal soldiers were no longer exempt from the sheep tax and the tithe. Regular officers could count on the government to supply them with their horses, equipment, and weapons, but tribal officers needed to provide for their own knives, swords, uniforms, and other equipment in addition to their horses. Perhaps aware of the abuse of the Hamidiye badge in the days of Sultan Abdülhamid II, the new regulations forbade tribal officers from appearing in uniform when not on active duty.[85] Penalties were also severe for those who failed to show up for drill or battle. The new document clearly attempted to introduce its own order in the Kurdish regions.

The section on officers plainly revealed the modernizing visions the CUP had in mind for the Kurds in particular and for the empire and its armed forces in general. On the one hand, the new scheme threw a few bones to the existing order. It allowed tribal officers already in possession of rank to maintain that rank as they took over their new regiments (although if they were not in possession of a certificate, they would only receive one-quarter pay). It further permitted those tribes not populous enough to form more than a few squadrons to keep their present rank, although it would now be considered "honorary." Lastly, it acknowledged the social hierarchy in Kurdish society by maintaining hereditary posts and tribal custom. It did so by stipulating that commanders of the Tribal Regiments, in the event that they were tribesmen and not soldiers appointed from the regular army, could only be sons of chiefs or influential men. At the same time, many of these concessions had clauses that rendered them largely unattractive to those who had enjoyed vast benefits under the previous system. Furthermore, the regulations illustrate how the CUP envisioned slowly incorporating the Kurds into mainstream Ottoman civilization through education and "social engineering." The sons of these chiefs had to fill certain requirements in order to be appointed to fill vacancies as they arose: they were to have been prepared in the military school and to have received a diploma, to have obtained certificates upon completion of their probation in the regular cavalry, or to have been trained in tribal noncommissioned-officer schools. Plans for these schools were also outlined in the regulations. Added to certificate requirements was one last, but revealing, clause: tribal officers would have to read and write Turkish.[86] The assimilating drive of the new government and its move toward a more uniform nation-state identity was clear.[87]

Before the regulations were even formally drafted, the British military attaché had reported in January 1910 that the reorganization of the former Hamidiye regiments was "chiefly political, as these regiments are of little military value,"[88] a largely valid statement—and indeed prediction. However, it does seem that the goals of those charged with the task of reorganizing the Tribal Regiments was, in fact, to turn this group of "warlike tribesmen" into a disciplined force amenable to the new laws of the land, and they initially set about this task with great zeal, even if the momentum would soon fade away. Before the ink of the new regulations was dry, military organizers in Erzurum began to create a model regiment of cavalry to train the new Tribal Light Cavalry, and men from Erciş, Karakilise, and Diyarbekir were summoned to Erzurum for this purpose in early January 1912.[89] Shortly after that, tribes were recruited for the new tribal militia. Many tribal leaders initially believed that it was a chance for them to form a bond with the new regime, to once again use the support of the government to advance one's own tribe. Some were thus eager to enroll. The Mîran tribe led by Mustafa Pasha's son, Abdulkerim, along with several tribes attached to them, enrolled in 1912 and were sent to fight in the Balkan Wars.[90] In the meantime, perhaps hoping for a commission in the newly organized cavalry, İbrahim Pasha's son Halil Bey, who now headed the Millî tribe, offered to purchase an airplane for the Ottoman military and to present it in the name of his tribe.[91] Halil Bey and Dirî Bey, the head of the Karakeçi tribe who was now considered a wanted outlaw, also offered their services in the Balkan Wars and were dispatched to eastern Thrace.[92] There is little information about the Tribal Regiments under the CUP during this period, and I have not come across any full lists mentioning all the tribes that were enrolled. From the scattered information found in archival reports and published sources, however, it seems that most of the tribes continued to be those that had been enrolled under the previous regime.[93] Drills were planned for the fall of 1912,[94] and some more tribes received orders to fight in the Balkan Wars.[95] Regulations continued to be amended in 1913 and 1914.[96] By late 1913, it was reported that some twenty-five regiments were in the course of being organized.[97] In 1914, the government continued to take an interest in the Hamidiye regiments, now more than ever, as their military potential seemed increasingly important. Two reports submitted to the Ministry of War in 1914, however, reveal the continued mixed feelings about the organization. One was very positive, stating that it was an important project worth developing on many fronts, and even expanding to include Dersim tribes.[98] The other, while more critical of the regiments, nonetheless suggested that in spite of their ignorance and inability to fight defensive wars, the militia's tribesmen were good horsemen and sharpshooters, always ready for battle. After being submitted to the necessary reforms, the writer concluded, they could be of service, especially in when they were on the offense.[99] So it was, then, that in 1914 recruitment among the border tribes continued, as the authorities hoped to turn them into forces capable of supporting the frontier companies of the regular army.[100] Those now in charge also hoped for a new bond between the government and the Kurds, but continued to envision the reorganized cavalry as part of a larger attempt to bring the Kurds into the fold and to modernize the region. There were also efforts to introduce education in the region and to use the Tribal Regiments to advance its spread.[101]

Within six months of the new scheme, however, the remodeled organization proved to be very unpopular among many tribesmen, as it had brought few of the benefits they had hoped for, instead seeming to be a significant burden on the resources of their tribes. The regulations also provided scanty concessions to the chiefs, who were so used to extended privileges. A letter from a missionary in the Mardin region pointed out that the recent raids on Christians were carried out by newly enrolled tribes who were trying to recuperate for themselves the losses they had incurred not only through their failure to cultivate their crops on time but also through their expenditures on saddles and other equipment.[102] Others, like the Hayderan, were displeased with the fact that they were consolidated into a single regiment, and the various *agha*s who had commanded the regiments before were now without their former commissions.[103]

Although recruitment would continue for the new Kurdish Tribal Regiments, and although efforts to promote the original goals of the constitution were still sporadically made, some in power seemed now to be acquiescing to the local power structure as it was, rather than attempting to change it. They realized that many of their moves were unpopular, and were causing many influential Kurdish chiefs to flee the already underpopulated region by crossing the border to Iran, where a less centralizing government was in power.[104] Most, however, did come to appreciate the significance of the Kurds if they ever united, which previously seemed like a remote possibility, but which now increasingly appeared to be a stronger likelihood. The new regime responded to the reaction in the provinces, and, likewise, those in the provinces continued to rethink their position vis-à-vis the new regime; both were transformed in the process.

RESPONSE AND REINVENTION II

Just as there were both supporters and opponents of Sultan Abdülhamid II among various elements of Kurdish society, it would similarly be a mistake to present the situation in the Kurdish periphery after 1908 as one of "the government versus the Kurds." The reality was far more complex than this. The new regime also had its fair share of supporters and opponents in diverse Kurdish circles.[105] Initially the distinction between advocate and adversary fell upon rather clear lines: those who had benefited under Sultan Abdülhamid II viewed the new regime with suspicion, if not outright antagonism; those who welcomed the CUP in power were often the people who had suffered the most under the previous sultan. These individuals tended to be the elements of society with the least protection against the tribal chiefs who were armed and supported by Zeki Pasha and the sultan, but the cut was not always strictly along class lines. Intellectuals, statesmen, and army officers who had been alienated by Sultan Abdülhamid II also welcomed the new government, at least initially, until the Turkish nationalist and authoritarian tendencies of the new regime became clear.

After news of the constitution was announced, there was a flurry of activity in the capital and the provinces by Ottomans of all stripes, who immediately began to organize political clubs, parties, programs, and various kinds of publications, all of which had been severely restricted under Abdülhamid II. In addition to being part of more general Ottoman political parties, Kurdish intellectuals in the capital also formed a Kurdish club, the Kurdish Society for Mutual Aid and Progress (Kürd Teavün ve Terakki Cemiyeti; KTTC), and published a gazette, the *Kürd Teavün ve Terakki Gazetesi* (Kurdish Journal of Mutual Aid and Progress; hereafter *KTTG*), which printed articles in Ottoman and Kurdish (just as *Kurdistan* had done) and functioned as the society's official organ. Similarly, Kurdish clubs in the major towns in Kurdistan also were established following the proclamation of the constitution. However, although the clubs in Diyarbekir, Bitlis, Van, Muş, Mosul, and other towns in the region were affiliated with the club in the capital, there seem to have been significant differences in the agendas promoted by their respective members.

The remainder of this chapter will analyze the multifaceted response to the new regime among Kurds, again using the Hamidiye as the lens through which to view this issue, as each informs the other. By examining Kurdish publications in the Second Constitutional Period and by analyzing archival reports at the same time, one can arrive at a better picture of the new power dynamics in Kurdish society. A few points will emerge in the subsequent discussion. First, we find that the CUP's new policies regarding the Hamidiye are indicative of its more general "Kurdish policy." No longer did the government seek to support certain tribes at the expense of others (overtly, at least). Instead, the new regime's general aim was to extend its reach into its various peripheries, and to use education, military service, and other institutions to create a more uniform, loyal, and controllable citizenry; the new Tribal Cavalry was to serve this larger mission. The policy had both backers and adversaries among various Kurdish elements. However, we also find that during the first few years of the CUP's rule, alliances would switch, and lines between supporters and opponents would blur. Some who had promoted the CUP when it first came to power would withdraw their support and others, who had previously opposed it, would be drawn in to back the government. By the end of the period under review in this study, however, we find that although the faces of power in the tribal zone did not change much during these years, the vocabulary of power did: now politics—particularly the politics of peoplehood—would be the means to accessing power in the margins of empire. It would also result in the alienation of many others in the same region. But all parties would engage with the new public transcript of power that now emphasized loyalty to the new regime and the empire-nation over loyalty to the sultan.

POLITICS AS UNUSUAL

Shortly after the reinstatement of the constitution in 1908, the overlap between opponents of the Hamidiye and proponents of the new regime was clear and distinct from the supporters of the Hamidiye, who tended to oppose the new government. Outright opposition was not immediately forthcoming, however, as many waited to test the new regime, its policies, and indeed its strength. But when Hamidiye chiefs saw the most powerful among them—İbrahim Pasha—toppled, and the subsequent (although tentative) proposals to abolish the Hamidiye entirely, they also began to see that the new regime might not back them in their former path to influence and wealth. They, too, began to gather and organize, but now politically. At the same time, after the proclamation of the constitution, in Istanbul Kurdish intellectuals inaugurated their new club, the KTTC. They supported the new regime and took advantage of the opportunity to publish diverse articles in Kurdish and Ottoman for themselves and for distribution among their countrymen in Kurdistan. This club has been hailed by Kurdish nationalists as being a progressive club, which was also organized largely to promote a nationalist agenda. This picture is not completely accurate, especially when one considers the club's provincial branches. By reading the articles alongside consular reports and official Ottoman publications, the reader finds that members of the club in the capital seem to have had largely different visions than those in the provinces, although there was certainly cross-affiliation. While they all emphasized the well-being of the Kurds, they had different visions of the future and of the kind of government they hoped to support, and diverse opinions on what "well-being" for the Kurds meant.[106]

The Hamidiye is the lens through which I have chosen to examine various issues in Ottoman and Kurdish history not simply for the sake of convenience, but because it happened to be an important lens through which Kurds, Armenians, and other Ottomans of different backgrounds themselves viewed power, their relationship to the state, their interaction with their neighbors (along with their changing notions of *who* these neighbors were), and their visions of the future. Although in the very inception of the idea of the Hamidiye one goal in the manifold mission was the modernization and stronger incorporation of Kurdish society into the Ottoman fold, under Zeki Pasha's leadership, however, this "civilizing" mission was largely abandoned in favor of other aims. His primary concern was to build up a loyal and powerful group of influential Kurdish leaders who could contain Armenian revolutionary activities and, in case of need, join a coalition against a Russian invasion. It was a program of inducing and ensuring loyalty to the Hamidian regime. In the eyes of the CUP's central committee, however, the Hamidiye was envisioned more strongly, if it was to be retained at all, as a means—just like education—to discipline, incorporate, and assimilate the empire's Kurdish tribal population. Kurdish intellectuals supported most of these objectives although they certainly opposed the assimilating tendencies. After the proclamation of the constitution and the subsequent dismissal of Zeki Pasha and the destruction of İbrahim Pasha, they did view the "new" Hamidiye as a means through which tribes could be modernized and educated.

One contributor to the *KTTG* penned a series of articles on the Hamidiye in which he also discussed the militia in these terms. The emphasis in his articles was on the reformed tribal cavalry, not the Hamidiye as it had been under Zeki Pasha. Acknowledging that "one hears complaints about these regiments from time to time," he placed the blame for the problems caused by the organization not on "the inherent characteristics of the Kurds themselves," but on its former "commanders." After uprooting this leadership, the author continued, the organization under the constitutional regime would be a blessing for the Kurds and the Ottomans, for it would be through the Hamidiye that Kurds would become educated and acquire brotherly bonds with other soldiers. Similar to the premises held by the author's CUP comrades, this author also drew attention to the Kurds' "natural" abilities in the field of horsemanship. He stressed how important a good cavalry was for warfare, and hence, how important the services of the Kurds would be to the Ottoman army. All they needed, he concluded, was "education, along with theoretical and practical instruction." The reformed Hamidiye, under the leadership of the new government, would be the means to this end.[107] Said-i Kurdî wrote about the Tribal Regiments in analogous terms. Said-i Kurdî argued that the two most important things for Kurdistan were national unity and religious knowledge, but these would only occur through the spread of the technologies of civilization. And he considered the Tribal Regiments to be "the foundation and the school" for this goal, and especially the means through which Kurdish tribes would build brotherly bonds. He argued that grudges and clashes had arisen as the result of a nomadic lifestyle, the failure of the state to assert itself in the region, and also, by contrast, the state's oppression when it did make its presence felt. For these reasons, he argued, the situation deteriorated, and the region was torn by internal strife. He deplored how Kurds balked at modern education and technology, but emphasized their importance in curing the ills plaguing Kurdish society. The role of the Tribal Regiments in all of this was to be the vanguard of modernity, opening the roads to education and modern civilization. "To sum up," he wrote,

if the union which is the bond and element of life for every nation, especially the Kurds, were a palace, its deep foundation would be the Tribal Regiments and the military service which defeats all titles would be its firm roof. The Tribal Regiments will be a very sparkling and striking school for technical knowledge and a giant industrial factory for education, which can be likened to a petrol depot that would illuminate that palace of union and accord and serves as the circulatory system of nations. The government, which will be the master, if it provides an order matching the abilities of the regiments, how wonderful it will be—just what we've been after.[108]

Praise and support for a new and reorganized Tribal Regiments poured forth from the pages of the newly revived Kurdish press. Writers wished to emphasize the importance of the Kurds in the larger Ottoman context, and perhaps wished thus to ensure that Kurdistan would not be forgotten when money for education and modern facilities was allotted by the new government. They wanted the new government to know that the Kurds had something to give, and they sought to convince the Kurds that the new order had something to offer them as well.

However, not all writers supported the broad changes underway in Kurdistan, particularly the new regime's crackdowns on Kurdish notables. Seyyid Abdulqadir asserted that the previous regime had fomented discord among the various tribes and their non-Muslim neighbors, and that therefore the new regime needed to pay special attention to Kurdistan in its efforts to promote "national unity." He alleged that at the time of his writing, however, non-Muslims, perhaps still in the mode they were forced into under the previous regime, were now inventing complaints against their Kurdish neighbors. Seyyid Abdulqadir criticized the crackdown carried out by the CUP on various Kurdish chiefs in response to these grievances, and he saw the proposed changes to the tribal militia in the larger context of this "persecution" of Kurdish chiefs. Writing at a time when their complete abolishment was one option that was on the table, Seyyid Abdulqadir wrote that it would be a mistake to completely disband the units, and instead proposed that the government commission experts reform the troops. He added that the entire eradication of the militia was "an undeniably political move."[109]

Although Seyyid Abdulqadir was a friend of the constitutional regime and would later act as an intermediary between the new government and the Kurdish notables, this did not stop him from voicing the frustrations of many Kurdish chiefs who were rapidly being alienated by the new regime as it tried to promote order throughout the empire in the months after it came to power. But some Hamidiye chiefs did not rely on the agency of others to enunciate protests on their behalf, preferring to submit them directly to the journal. Several letters to the editor of *KTTG* are from Hamidiye chiefs who were dismayed with the recent change in their status. In a letter to the journal, the head of the Karakeçi tribe, Halil, expressed outrage at having sacrificed the lives of many of his tribesmen in obeying official orders to suppress İbrahim Pasha, and then being repaid for his services with imprisonment on "old charges." He was particularly irked that he was held "in a gendarmerie ward when . . . wearing official military uniform."[110]

The famous Hamidiye pasha from Patnos, Hayderanî Hüseyin, had his own record to set straight. He wanted to deny certain charges to his Kurdish readers, particularly those who were close to the new government, and wrote that he did not commit the various murders attributed to him by the *Manzume-i Efkâr* journal, notifying readers of his intention to bring charges of slander against the paper.[111]

Other tribal leaders wrote to the journal with praise for the new regime and expressed their intentions to cooperate with the new government. A letter sent by the chiefs of the Harûnan and Reşkotan tribes likened the constitution to the Tree of Paradise, with justice, equality, and fraternity for fruit. The writers told their audience how, when the constitutional regime was explained to them by the *mutassarıf* in Kurdish and Turkish, they "shed tears of joy" and vowed to sacrifice themselves for the "well-being and happiness of [their] beloved country."[112] And the Hevêrkî chief from the Midyat area drafted a letter with his associates from Nusaybin in which they praised the constitution and vowed to cooperate with the collection of weapons then underway.[113]

The Kurdish journals were not, however, the only forum for the tribes' declaration of loyalty to the new regime. Many tribal heads chose a more direct route to communicate their messages, submitting them not only to a gazette of their "own" people but to the government directly. The telegrams they sent to the Ministry of the Interior, which were reproduced in the *Takvim-i Vekayi*, the official Ottoman journal, showed the same demonstration of commitment to the new regime. One such telegram written by leaders of the Babus and Şirvan tribes of Bitlis declared that although certain members of their tribes had engaged in brigandage under the old regime, this was only because of the bad behavior of the officials and also because of the ignorance of the Kurds. However, a number of such individuals had surrendered themselves to the subgovernor, declaring that they had regretted their past deeds and affirming their loyalty to the constitutional government. They were especially moved, they claimed, by the speech given by the subgovernor, Süleyman Faik Bey, in Turkish and Kurdish.[114] In Siirt, the tribal heads of the Pencinar, Bişarê Çeto, and Batwan tribes similarly surrendered their weapons to the *mutassarıf*, and resolved their feuds "with strong advice . . . [entering] into the true path to obedience and civilization," kissing one another in the presence of the subgovernor.[115]

The various articles and letters printed in the Kurdish journal and *Takvim-i Vekayi* in 1908 and 1909, a sample of which have been cited above, are noteworthy on a few accounts for the purposes of the present discussion. First, they indicate the extent to which the Hamidiye and the regime that had supported it had played a role in the lives of many Kurds in the region, whether positive or negative. The Hamidiye was a symbol of either corruption or the strength of "the Kurds," depending on the person voicing the opinion, and it was also a means through which these things would be achieved. Second, these letters give the reader a sense of the impression made by the new regime upon certain Kurdish chiefs, particularly those in the tribal militia. These chiefs saw that the order under which they had previously benefited seemed to have completely crumbled, and their words deplore this fact while at the same time phrasing their thoughts in such a manner as to seem as if they are welcoming the new regime. As Scott points out, "Subordinates offer a performance of deference and consent while attempting to discern, to read, the real intentions and mood of the potentially threatening powerholder."[116] At the same time, the new regime—the new power holder—was, in Scott's words, producing a "performance of mastery and command while attempting to peer behind the mask of subordinates to read their real intentions."[117] While this kind of power performance may not have been entirely new, what was novel was the manner in which it was conducted—through modern political parties, platforms, organizations, and publications, at least on the surface; behind the scenes, however, various parties were struggling for power in the margins of empire.

The *KTTG* was founded by Kurdish intellectuals in the capital who were largely supporters of the new regime and who were now able to take advantage of the relative freedom after the revival of the constitution was declared in 1908. They did so by using print as a medium for political activity, as did many of their non-Kurdish compatriots. Yet the voices in the journal were not only those of the Kurdish intellectuals resident in the capital, who backed the new regime and its principles, but also those of tribal chiefs and others in Kurdistan, who read and contributed to the journal. But just as the opinions in the journal were diverse, so too were the agendas of the Kurds who established and joined the numerous "Kurdish clubs" that were also established after the constitution. These clubs, like the main Istanbul headquarters of the club, have also been hailed by many scholars as progressive and/or nationalist clubs. Yet again, just as we have found the opinions in the *KTTG* to cover a range of views, we also find a similar variety of agendas by those who sponsored and participated in the Kurdish clubs in the capital and in towns in Kurdistan.

The "Kurdish club" in Istanbul (KTTC) was set up shortly after the return to constitutional rule was announced in 1908. In spite of the fact that there had been numerous Kurds in the Young Turk movement, it seems that some in the new regime regarded what it saw as "the Kurds" with as much suspicion as the Kurds who had benefited under the previous regime likewise viewed the new government. Therefore, a number of Kurdish community leaders felt it was important to show their support for the new regime right away, to dispel myths that "the Kurds" were a homogeneous body uniformly against the new regime. The founding of the new club must certainly be regarded with this in mind. Observers writing about the opening ceremonies and meetings point to this in their accounts of the events. An article from *Stamboul* reported that the resolutions adopted during an initial meeting of the Kurdish club at the Hagia Sophia Mosque in Istanbul included getting rid of the "calumnious allegations of the journal *Feyz-i Hurriyet* against the loyal Kurdish population," and publishing in the press that it was "only the *agha*s who are responsible for the misfortune of the Kurdish country and the vexations from which their Christian compatriots suffer."[118] Those present also affirmed that those Kurdish notables known for violence were not to be elected to the Chamber of Deputies, and they resolved to initiate a letter-writing campaign to this effect. Other resolutions emphasized the importance of education and establishing schools in Kurdistan, among other things.[119] Statements in the press, cited above, make more sense with this information. Many Kurds were afraid that the Hamidiye had irreparably tarnished the reputation of Kurds as a group and were fighting to emphasize their loyalty and potential as citizens in the new order. As they engaged with the public transcript of power they needed to draw attention to their fidelity to the new regime and to separate themselves from the previous leadership with which Kurdish chiefs had been so closely identified. These proclamations had been heard at the first meeting of the new Kurdish club in the capital, held at a reading café (*café de lecture*) in Istanbul's Vezneciler neighborhood. One "Colonel Süleyman" reported that in the speeches, the Kurds vowed to "fight to their last drop of blood to uphold the tenets of the Constitution which guarantee the security and peace of their dear homeland, goodwill and the progress of all Ottomans." They further confirmed that "they had no idea, no intention of going against either the Constitution, nor of hindering the patriotic interests of the CUP." They also pledged to renew the traditional bonds of friendship between Kurds and Armenians, which they claimed had been ruptured by bad government under the previous regime.[120] Such were the voices of Kurds in the capital. Their articles make a bit more sense with this in mind.

In Kurdistan itself, however, sentiments seem more complicated. Shortly after the foundation of the KTTC in Istanbul, branches of the organization were established in numerous towns in Kurdistan, including Diyarbekir, Bitlis, Muş, Van, Erzurum, and Mosul. The Diyarbekir branch, for example, was inaugurated in December 1908 "with great pomp and ceremony" and included the procession of dervishes bearing religious banners through the city, speeches made by prominent individuals including the *vali*, and the music of a military band. Thousands of people attended the ceremony.[121] While these branch clubs seemed officially to espouse the platforms adopted by their parent club in Istanbul, the actual agendas of the club's provincial members were rather different.[122] These were urban notables and tribal chiefs who were witnessing their own destruction—the recall of their patron, Zeki Pasha, and the expeditions against İbrahim Pasha and other Hamidiye chiefs, as well as numerous arrests of their numbers. Mostly, they saw their power bases and the wealth that they had accumulated in land and resources threatened before their very eyes. Some Kurdish chiefs joined the clubs ostensibly as supporters of the new regime so that they would appear in favor of it, and not, then, suffer the consequences meted out to their counterparts from other tribes. But there is evidence that for them, the so-called "Kurdish clubs" carried a different meaning and that their members had different concerns from their compatriots in the capital.[123] The British contact at Diyarbekir reported that by the time the Kurdish club had opened in that town, support for the CUP was dwindling and also that townspeople expected the new club to be far stronger than the local CUP branch itself. He added that while the Kurdish club was in contact with its parent club in Istanbul and supposedly took orders from the club in the capital, its patrons seem to have had their own agenda. For example, members of the local club stated to the British contact that they had received orders from their central body at the capital to keep on friendly terms with the Christians. But he felt that "the general tendency of the movement" did not "seem to comply with such an attitude."[124] Some members of the club in places like Diyarbekir were hostile to the new regime, which they believed was no longer interested in upholding the tenets of Islam, and they made such demonstrations on numerous occasions.[125] But members of the Kurdish clubs in provincial centers were not the only ones who were suspicious of the new regime. Members of the CUP clubs themselves were assessed by the European observers present in these towns to actually be barely lukewarm to the new government. In fact, the British agent at Diyarbekir believed that members of the Kurdish club nurtured fewer hostilities against their Christian neighbors than did the local CUP.[126] The CUP was weak in the Kurdish regions and was challenged, to the extent that it was at all different, by the branches of the Kurdish clubs. Other opposition clubs also sprang up, such as the Muhammadiyye club, which, while short-lived in Diyarbekir, nonetheless spread to other places such as Harput.[127]

Given this reaction in the provinces, the CUP in the capital deemed it necessary to both proceed with the crackdowns on those individuals in Kurdistan who challenged their authority and at the same time to appeal to them through emissaries such as Seyyid Abdulqadir. And politics continued in Kurdistan. Although the Kurdish clubs were officially disbanded sometime after the countercoup of 1909, they did continue to function clandestinely. As many people in the provinces grew increasingly resentful of the new regime and its policies, they looked for ways to overthrow the "infidel" government.[128] Former Hamidiye heads were among the chief organizers of movements against the government. In Diyarbekir, for example, an American missionary reported that two Hamidiye colonels formerly connected to İbrahim Pasha were wearing their uniforms as if on active duty and were telling Kurds to rebel, since the government was powerless to stop them anyway.[129] Resistance took other shapes as well. The British consul at Erzurum reported an interesting incident involving a "mysterious personage, known among the Kurds as 'Ibrahim Pasha,'" who had been spotted in various parts of the Erzurum province and who was received with great deference by the various Kurdish chiefs of the region, who vied with one another in "showing him hospitality"; one Hamidiye colonel "had not only given him a valuable horse but had also insisted on taking off his boots for him." None of the authorities could ascertain who this mysterious figure was until a lapidary at Erzurum offered a clue. He said that the secretive stranger had ordered a seal bearing the inscription *İbrahim, Hamidiye Light Cavalry.* The *vali* ordered the engraver to complete the order, and when the stranger went to claim his seal, the *vali* had him arrested. The individual finally confessed that his name was actually Ali ibn-Sayid, and that he had been entrusted by the Kurdish club of Diyarbekir "with the mission of conveying letters and messages to all the Kurdish tribes with the object of bringing about a general rising against the new regime."[130]

Organized opposition to the new regime continued to exist, although it was hardly united or strong enough to cause the government immediate concern. But there were other means of protest and resistance as well. The remnants of the Millî tribe, along with some of its Yezidi associates, contemplated converting to Christianity, an act that was likely to attract the sympathy of European powers.[131] Occasionally, others tried to acquire European citizenship using different means. One Eyüb Efendi, a Kurdish notable at Muş, addressed a petition to the British embassy in Istanbul on behalf of some forty to fifty families, stating their desire to become British citizens in order to escape the tyranny of the Young Turk government. But the Ottoman officers of the town reported that this individual had been the mayor of Muş under Abdülhamid II, whose men had expropriated many lands from Armenian peasants under the old regime. They believed the petition was merely a ploy on the part of Eyüb Efendi to avoid the impending collection of large sums of taxes and arrears he owed to the government.[132]

While these were largely isolated incidents and were only loosely organized at best, they do signal the strong dissatisfaction with the new regime current among various sectors of the Kurdish elite in the provinces. But many Kurdish intellectuals of the capital were also becoming disgruntled with the new regime. Although there existed different visions for the future, again what seemed to unite various Kurdish opinions more than anything was a dislike of present conditions. This discontent turned into a political movement, which was gradually spreading throughout the provinces.[133] The hidden transcript would no longer be entirely hidden, and it would begin to be "spoken directly and publicly in the teeth of power."[134]

It became clear to many in the provinces that the expectations many had held for the new regime were not to materialize. Armenian, Kurdish, and Turkish peasants, who had seen their lands usurped by Kurdish chiefs in the countryside and by Turkish and Kurdish notables in the towns, initially held great hopes for the new government when it promised to enforce the restoration of their lands and the punishment of their oppressors. But by 1912, suspicions that had been increasing until then were confirmed. Prior to the elections of 1912, the government released a number of Kurdish chiefs and notables who had been convicted of numerous crimes, a move the British agent interpreted to be political as those in power were trying to curry favor and support for their party before the upcoming election. He also reported that the CUP officials of places like Diyarbekir had told those who had usurped lands from Christians not to worry, that they would not have to return them after all.[135] Apparently included in the new amnesty of former criminals was Abdulkerim Bey of the Mîran tribe, who again was made a commander in the new Tribal Light Cavalry in a showy ceremony.[136] As discontent increased in the region, the government tried to curry favor again among the former Hamidiye chiefs and paid special attention to the Tribal Regiments in the months to follow.[137]

The moves of the government to court powerful Kurdish notables in the region were deemed necessary by those in power because they were faced with an opposition of a new kind. Once again, a significant part of the opposition to the government was led by Bedir Khan family members. As active members of the CUP, they had rejoiced when the CUP came to power and when the sultan was deposed. However, after a couple of years of CUP rule, they, too, began to gather in opposition to the new regime, albeit through different channels than those followed by their Kurdish compatriots, described above. The new Bedir Khani opposition to the regime continued to be characterized by journalistic activity, as it had been under the previous regime when Abdurrahman Bedir Khan and his brother used their journal, *Kurdistan*, as a voice of opposition to the sultan. Of course the Bedir Khans were certainly not alone in this. However, those Bedir Khans who became active in the opposition to the new regime did not rely solely on print to organize followers, but decided to promote their own candidates in elections, now that this was an option available to them. Second, and perhaps more important, other Bedir Khan family members toured the region gathering support for what was becoming—for some—a movement for independence.

At first, the Bedir Khans, like many other Kurdish compatriots resident in Istanbul, were concerned with the promotion of education among the Kurds. In 1911, Bedri and Midhat Beys made a tour of the Cizre-Botan region, preaching "modern ideas" among their fellow countrymen and encouraging the masses to enroll their children in primary schools.[138] Meanwhile, Abdurrezzak Bedir Khan was making plans to return to Cizre and stand as a candidate during the upcoming elections.[139] Hüseyin Pasha and Hasan Bey also toured the region gathering support for what was then an unknown cause. At this point, all of the Bedir Khans enjoyed the support, albeit lukewarm, of the government.[140] By July 1911, however, the British agent at Diyarbekir reported that the Bedir Khans (Hasan Bey and either Hüseyin or Mustafa Bey) who had just arrived in Botan were combining their efforts with those of Bedri and Midhat Beys, who were already in the region and seemed to "have started on a political activity on a line quite different from that, which at first they appear to have professed to be their object: i.e., the education of the Kurds of the Bohtan region, their original birthplace."[141] The French Dominican mission head at Siirt reported that the Bedir Khans had been "propagating anti-Turkish ideas among their ignorant compatriots, trying to prepare them to follow in future the example set by the Albanians in demanding some sort of administrative autonomy for Kurdistan." He further stated that they were distributing pamphlets printed in Kurdish, claiming Botan and Cizre as the property of their glorious grandfather Bedir Khan Bey, which had "been usurped by the Turks in an infamous manner." The Dominican priest observed that the Bedir Khans exercised great influence over the Kurdish masses in the region. However, the British agent commented that the Bedir Khans' nationalist propaganda, even if it were allowed to carry on unhindered, would "take a long time to bear any fruit in rousing the Kurds from their present torpor to a fair measure of national consciousness."[142] Of course the Bedir Khans seem to have been aware of this fact, as were other likeminded Kurds in the capital. The efforts of the organizations they and their associates established in the capital around this time, along with the publications of these Kurdish committees, were designed, in part, to spread ideas of Kurdish autonomy and to promote an increasingly ethnic and nationalist identity among Kurds.

At the same time as they were active in Botan agitating for Kurdish autonomy, which seemed to also be a revival of their family emirate, Hasan Bedir Khan moved on to Siirt, where he stood as the candidate for the Hürriyet ve İtilâf Fırkası (Party of Freedom and Understanding), the opposition party. According to numerous observers, Hasan Bedir Khan was very popular among his Christian and Muslim constituents in Siirt, and was even hosted at Siirt by a leading Christian notable, Şemmas Abboş. The government, however, attempted to intimidate the population into voting for the official candidate. The French Dominican priest at Siirt reported that the *kaymakam* there was "distinguished by his efforts in this regard" by moving about the town with a revolver threatening people that they would "suffer harm if they did not vote for the official candidate." In the end, Hasan Bey still won the majority of the votes, but the government then declared the elections to be null and void, and repeated instructions to the town to elect the CUP candidate. Hasan Bey fled the region after this "big-stick election."[143]

The Bedir Khans were largely defeated in their efforts to come to power in the region either through elections or through an autonomy movement. By 1914 the British consul reported that the confederation that had been attempted by Kurdish tribes the previous year under the Bedir Khan family appeared "to have been a complete failure."[144] This letdown did not stop members of the Bedir Khan family from continuing their efforts to either revive the family emirate or promote an independent Kurdistan. Abdurrezzak Bedir Khan was particularly active in the following years in trying to gather Russian support for an independent Kurdish entity until he was executed in 1918.[145] Other Bedir Khans would become involved in the period following the First World War, when they played key roles in the movement for Kurdish independence. However, for the period under review, what is significant is that they were only one of many groups of Kurds who were caught up in organizing against a government that seemed increasingly unsympathetic to an entity that was becoming known as "the Kurds." This body was diverse and had a range of complaints, but what unified its members was their opposition to the government—a resistance that originally began as a protest of the Hamidiye and the regime that backed it, but that now included members of the very same former Hamidiye regiments.

CONCLUSION

In 1914, the British consul submitted a long report on the situation in the Kurdish provinces. Parts of the report described the various points around which Kurds were united in opposing the government:

Up till now the Kurds have received no benefit from the Young Turk Government; nothing has been done to improve the material condition of this part of Turkey, and on the other hand taxes are more rigorously collected than under the old regime, whilst the tribal cavalry has been deprived of the privileges it used to possess. Added to this the Vilayet has suffered from a constant succession of new Valis since the constitution, so that there has been no continuity of policy; the last Vali, Ahmet Izzet Pasha, himself a Kurd, was on good terms with the Chiefs, and kept down brigandage to a great extent by his personal influence, whilst the present Vali has hunted down and shot several brigands and shown that he means to keep order with a firm hand. Owing to this the Kurdish Chiefs are uncertain as to how they stand, and there is no doubt that many of them look upon the present regime with mistrust and suspicion. The failure of the Turkish army in the last war and the continued occupation of the neighbouring Persian province by Russian troops has lessened the respect of the Kurds for the Government at Constantinople and increased the prestige of Russia. . . . The loyalty, partly religious and partly the result of benefits received, which the Kurds felt for Abdul Hamid, is no longer given to the present Government; in its place is a feeling of uncertainty as regards the future, and a belief that the Young Turk government cannot for long hold the empire together. Unless the Turkish government gives more attention to the development of this part of Turkey, and brings the Kurdish Vilayets into closer connection with the western provinces of Asia Minor, and unless it establishes a common bond by bringing the tribes into closer relationship with the regular army and thus makes use of the Kurdish military spirit, it seems inevitable that this feeling of dissatisfaction should go on increasing. Though there is no reason to anticipate any united action on the part of the various Kurdish tribes against the Government, yet, if present conditions continue and develop, in the event of the Eastern frontier of Asia Minor becoming the scene of hostilities against a foreign power, it is probable that the Turkish Government would no longer be able to count on the loyalty and active assistance of many of the Kurdish tribes.[146]

Later that year, the consul was proved correct on some counts and wrong on others. He was accurate in his assessment of the causes for the growing discontent among various Kurdish groups; however, he underestimated their ability or will to unite in rebellion. In 1914 parts of the opposition did, indeed, coalesce into an antigovernment movement centered in Bitlis. Although the movement was crushed, with many of the leaders receiving death sentences, what is important is that it revealed the extent to which various groups of Kurds in the provinces were displeased with the new government. Many former Hamidiye chiefs suffered setbacks to their privileges,[147] but many other Kurds felt that the new regime had also let them down by neglecting to come through on its original promises to modernize the country, found schools, and improve facilities. They had been hoping that the new regime would promote the general well-being of all inhabitants through the enforcement of justice and the rule of law and the maintenance of security for their lives and property. The British consul was correct in stating that the government sent mixed messages to the Kurds. On the one hand, many tribal chiefs did find their privileges curtailed by a government that tried to grasp its far-flung provinces with a firm hand. On the other hand, others saw that the central authorities needed to keep working with the Kurdish power structure as it was, as they required the support and alliance of tribal chiefs to conduct government in the region.[148]

Although power began to be accessed through new channels (political parties, print media, etc.), the substance of power and power relations seems not to have changed drastically, except in name. It is true that the organization known as the Hamidiye Light Cavalry no longer figured into the power equation as it had under the sultan. After all, it had now lost its most vigorous protectors, Zeki Pasha and the sultan himself, and the goals in forming the new Tribal Regiments were not completely dissimilar from those of the previous regime. The very intimate connection of the Hamidiye to Zeki Pasha and the sultan was replaced by a more impersonal relationship between the new regime and the Kurdish chiefs. Nonetheless, the tribes and the state continued to need one another for support; indeed, the conundrum faced by the new regime—how to establish control over this borderland without reinstating the authority of the group it ultimately needed to disempower—continues to be faced by the government in present-day Turkey as it deals with the Village Guards problem.[149] Power relations moved beyond ethnicity and often created strange bedfellows, but at the same time the processes through which the state attempted to gain administrative power helped to create and crystallize these very emergent ethnic identities. Nonetheless, these identities did become real, although their formation was also helped along by changing relations over land and property relations. This was literally the very ground on which the power struggle unfolded, took shape, and on which its material basis rested.

CHAPTER FOUR

The Hamidiye and the "Agrarian Question"

★

In 1908, with the reinstatement of the constitution and the change in government, Hüseyin Pasha of Patnos, chief of the powerful Hayderan tribe and commander of several Hamidiye regiments, began to feel some heat. While Kurdish Hamidiye chiefs like Hüseyin were waiting in the first days of the new order to see what, if any, changes would affect their lives, it soon became clear that indeed a new era in the relationship between the Hamidiye chiefs and the government was about to begin. Early in 1909, Hüseyin Pasha drafted a letter for publication in the newly established *Kürd Teavün ve Terakki Gazetesi* (Kurdish Journal of Mutual Aid and Progress; *KTTG*). He was worried that he was about to join the list of Kurdish chiefs who were being arrested for crimes committed under the previous regime, or at least that his name was being associated with certain crimes. He wrote,

To the Kurdish Club of Union and Cooperation,

In an article in *Manzume-i Efkâr*, which was quoted in number 5240 of the newspaper "İkdam," it says that six years ago I killed the *kaymakam* of Adilcevaz by setting him on fire with gas in his house, and that I also killed the acting lieutenant-colonel at Erciş, Rağib Bey, with a dagger in the middle of the night fifteen days ago. I was in Istanbul when the Hamidiye lieutenant-colonel, Said Bey, was killed at Adilcevaz. The murderer of the aforementioned is someone by the name of Kel Mehmed of Ştak [Şatak], who is still confined at Van after confessing in court. The murderer of Rağib Bey, who was killed at Erciş, was a soldier by the name of Niğdeli Mehmed, and after making this clear to the appropriate authorities, the murderer is in prison. I am currently in the process of opening a case against the editors of the *Manzume-i Efkâr* newspaper for attributing these killings to me, and for wagging their tongues in other ways. I request that they publish nothing outside the simple truth. Your obedient servant.

[Signed] Chief of the entire Hayderan tribe, Hamidiye Brigadier General, Hüseyin.[1]

The following year, Hüseyin Pasha fled across the border to Iran, taking with him many of his tribespeople and many more valuable animals.

It soon became clear that in addition to escaping punishment for various crimes, other factors were also at work. In fact, Hüseyin Pasha, or Kör Hüseyin [Blind Hüseyin] as he was otherwise known, was playing a game with the government. He was making a bold demonstration against the new regime and also attempting to strike a deal. It was important to the government that he return because when he crossed the border he took valuable human resources away from an already underpopulated region, and more important, he took with him numerous animals—"Ottoman property," as the state saw it. It also was evident that the flight of Hüseyin Pasha and his associates, as leaders of the largest and most powerful tribe in the region, was stripping the frontier of its "protectors." It was soon apparent that the government wanted Hüseyin Pasha to come back, not so much to prosecute him as to ensure that the valuable resources he had carried off during his flight would be restored to the Ottoman dominions, that he would remain a loyal and powerful entity in the threatened borderlands, and that he would not permanently cross over to the other side, physically or politically. The modern state needed to assert its jurisdiction and to instill the concept of a nonporous border into its citizens. If fighting prosecution was all Hüseyin Pasha had in mind in his escape, it should have been easy for him to return; but instead he wanted to make sure that the numerous lands he had usurped from the peasantry in his domains over the preceding decades, which were in the process of being returned to their original owners, would be handed back to him instead.

The previous two chapters have followed the transformation of power in the eastern Ottoman margins of empire by tracing the careers of two leading Hamidiye commanders and Kurdish tribal chiefs, Mustafa Pasha of the Mîran and İbrahim Pasha of the Millî. By following their stories, it has been possible to explore a number of key historical processes involving the relationships of the Ottoman administration and the various segments of Kurdish society as well as the social and political transformations in Kurdish society in which the Hamidiye played a role beyond the original visions of its creators. Part of what was at play in the changing power structure was a process, for convenience dubbed "tribal re-emiratization," which was intimately connected to the Hamidiye Light Cavalry. Mustafa Pasha Mîran and İbrahim Pasha Millî were two of the most important figures in this development. The process may have begun before the Hamidiye was first organized, but this Kurdish tribal militia and its fuzzy connections to state power advanced this dynamic in major ways. The "reformist" regime that came into power in 1908 weighed the "threats" confronting the Ottoman state. But its decision makers determined—albeit reluctantly—that in order to manage the risks that it perceived to be more serious (i.e., Armenian nationalism and Russian encroachment), the state needed to maintain or reinstate the power of this new brand of Kurdish *mîr*.

The present chapter will chart the path of Hüseyin Pasha, the third key Hamidiye pasha whom we can identify with this process, in order to highlight what was at the crux of the power struggle explored above. Hüseyin Pasha Hayderanî's career is representative of what rested at the heart of this often violent struggle—the changing nature of the conflict over resources and the grab for land. His name surfaced more than any other in the myriad documents that relate to what became known as the "agrarian question." It is therefore worthwhile to explore this connection in order to arrive at a better understanding of the complicated story that has unfolded thus far. By probing this question through the career of Hüseyin Pasha and other Hamidiye chiefs, this chapter also advances the important suggestion that the violence which overwhelmed much of the region during the period under review was the result, not of primordial ethnic or religious conflict or simply of government orders, but of struggles over concrete resources.

Additionally, this chapter will illustrate how the transformation in land tenure practices—a process that was already underway in the region—was impacted by the Hamidiye organization, and concomitantly, so was the structure of Kurdish society. Although the land-grabbing that came to be associated with this violence did not emerge with the organization of the first regiments and did not end when the militia was eventually disbanded, the Hamidiye moment represented a significant chapter in the history of modern property relations in the region. Hamidiye chiefs played a crucial role in the land grab that was part of the larger process because they were allowed special status and they used the strong backing of the government to advance their agendas. Although the government did not initiate the process whereby large tracts of land were confiscated by Kurdish chiefs who were most often affiliated with the Hamidiye cavalry, it did support it in order to advance its own projects. There were assorted means of acquiring property and many of these methods necessitated at least the indirect complicity of the government, which wanted for its own reasons to promote the appropriation of peasant holdings by Kurdish tribes. Unable to effectively control and tax a remote and largely mobile population, the government looked to remedy this problem through the settlement of pastoral Kurdish tribes. Forced settlement seemed to yield few results, and was, moreover, a step the government feared would incur more ire from a population whose loyalty was sought. Attracting tribespeople to settle and become landowners would bring a solution to this matter without disaffecting the tribes, and could further act as a means to break the power of the chiefs by making the state the official granter of lands and the state's agents the intermediaries through whom relevant transactions would be conducted. The process was certainly no plot on the government's part, but it was furthered to the government's ends; in turn, the state's policies also affected the extent and depth of the problem.

THE "AGRARIAN QUESTION"

Shortly after the Ottoman constitution was reinstated in 1908, a new "question" added itself to the list of the many "questions" debated by Ottomans as they pressed for changes under the new order. The "agrarian question," as it came to be known by Armenian leaders and European diplomats who took a keen interest in the matter, was actually, however, not truly an agrarian question. It was not about land reform in the usual sense, nor was it about how to promote agricultural productivity or good land-use practices. Rather, it was a euphemism for the matter of the Armenian lands usurped during the previous decades mostly by Kurdish tribal chiefs. The Hamidiye was intimately connected to the "agrarian question" from the time of its creation, and so too would the resolution of the land question be linked to the larger matter of what to do with this Kurdish tribal militia.

The matter became a "question" in 1908, and had turned into a full-blown problem by 1910. Most of the correspondence about the so-called agrarian question is from these first years of the Second Constitutional Period. However, for the individuals and collectivities whose lands had been overtaken by Kurdish *agha*s, the matter did not begin in 1908. Rather, 1908 merely represented an opportune time for them to press for justice in the new era of freedom. The issue they came to protest loudly had been ongoing for decades before, even if it was not considered a "question" by anyone in any position of authority. For those who suffered dispossession, however, it was not a mere political issue, but a matter of survival, and had been so for decades.

MATTERS OF CHANGE

For historians of late Ottoman history, the Young Turk Revolution of 1908, which heralded the reinstatement of the Ottoman constitution and proclaimed along with it a new period of hope for many Ottoman citizens, was a momentous occasion for most Ottomans and was particularly meaningful to Ottoman Armenians, whose political committees had worked closely with the Young Turks to bring about the events of 1908. Armenian participation in the Young Turk movement is generally recognized for the goals Armenians hoped to achieve for their community, namely, their desire to be treated on equal footing with Muslim Ottomans in educational, military, political, and social matters. Armenian-Kurdish relations are also considered as figuring prominently in the Armenian discourse of the period, as Ottoman Armenians pressed their government (and indeed sought representation from European diplomatic circles) to commit to protecting them from violence at the hands of neighboring Kurds.[2] However, one of the most important of Armenian claims in the new constitutional era—the restoration of Armenian lands that had been usurped by Kurdish *agha*s over the preceding years—is rarely mentioned as a significant and emotional issue of the day.

This gap in the literature has left students of the period with the impression that the violence that plagued southeastern Anatolia was either a matter of the state versus "the Armenians," and/or "natural" ethnic conflict between two different religious and cultural communities, each of which had different visions, divergent goals, and uncommon paths. What the research conducted for this study indicates, however, is that the matter of usurped Armenian lands was actually one of the most important issues that spurred Armenians to action. Furthermore, this research also suggests that the violence protested by Armenians and their European supporters was often closely linked to the land question, even if this connection has not been widely acknowledged yet. Last, this chapter proposes that while the battle to return Armenian lands was the most publicized of the land restoration movements as the Armenians found vocal and active support in their European diplomatic advocates, theirs was not the only campaign in the region. A number of Kurdish peasants similarly lost their lands to Kurdish *agha*s, many of whom were affiliated with the Hamidiye, and also fought for their restoration.

The Importance of Land

For nomadic and seminomadic Kurdish tribes, land use was traditionally viewed as an association between a tribe and a particular territory with specified grazing rights that grew out of a combination of traditional tribal law, Islamic jurisprudence, and Ottoman land practices.[3] While the term *traditional* cannot do justice to the wide range of complexities in land-use practices as these were also varied and evolving, a major transformation did take place in the nineteenth century concerning the social organization of tribes and settled communities and their relationships to land. This transformation was spurred by the centralizing policies of the Ottoman state on the one hand, and the appearance of the world capitalist market on the other.[4] These forces eventually produced a shift in the nature of the regional economy and the positions of the various agents within that economy. For tribes whose means of existence centered primarily around pastoralism, this meant the transfer to a predominantly agricultural economy, which further necessitated (and was, at the same time, partially caused by) the need to end their nomadic lifestyles and to settle. For those communities who were already sedentary and engaged in agricultural pursuits, the transformation brought in the long term a shift from largely autonomous household or clan units to cultivation by dependent individuals and families who now worked as tenants and sharecroppers,[5] a transition that became widespread during and after the period under review. Most important for the topic of the present chapter is the general transformation in the value of land and accompanying land ownership practices and relations that evolved as part of these larger changes.

The area of geographical Kurdistan most studied with regard to issues revolving around land-use practices and relations is southern Kurdistan, specifically the Ottoman province of Mosul. Various authors working on this region (Batatu, Haj, A. Jwaideh, and Longrigg) have helped us create a picture of this general transformation. There are few comparable studies for regions further north; it appears, though, that there were at least some general similarities. After all, Mosul was an important commercial center not only for those in close proximity but also for those further away. Furthermore, the Hamidiye's role in the transformation of property relations and the grab for land also serves as evidence that what these authors working on Mosul have found for that region may also stand as true for the Anatolian provinces to its north.

Mosul and other parts of the larger hinterlands to which it belonged were affected by the advent of the world capitalist market. By the nineteenth century, changes in global trading patterns were certainly felt in these regions, and as the demand for agricultural goods increased, so did the value of land. But while world market forces doubtless affected economic exchange and property relations in Kurdistan, perhaps more immediately felt were the changes instigated by the Ottoman state in the nineteenth century. As Samira Haj has noted for Iraq, by "the second half of the nineteenth century, a bankrupt Ottoman state was setting in motion new policies to secure its domination and to ensure higher returns for its treasury."[6] The central Ottoman government attempted to take over regional markets in parts of its Kurdish periphery and their trade-related infrastructures, including trading centers and routes. The state also tried to capture the power base of nonstate merchants in the system, which included tribes.[7] According to Haj, tighter control meant that fixed-sum rents replaced the *iltizam* (proportional rent) system, and heralded the development of the *tapu* system, a new kind of tenure based on lease holding. As such, individuals now received legal and heritable rights, with ultimate ownership remaining in the hands of the state.[8] The Ottoman Land Code of 1858 was the document that introduced the new form of tenure on an empire-wide scale. However, it was not formally promoted in Kurdistan until around 1870 (and several years later in some parts, or indeed not at all),[9] when Midhat Pasha, the governor of Baghdad (who was also the co-architect of the Vilayet Law of 1864), pushed through sweeping reforms in the province he governed.[10] These provincial reforms, which were also administrative in nature, were intended to give the state the control it sought over land and the fruits of the land.

Finally, the central Ottoman government worked to expand agriculture throughout the region and gain a tighter control over its dominions and resources through the sedentarization of the nomads who comprised a significant segment of the region's population.[11] Attempts to settle nomads were not new to Ottoman history. Indeed this mission has featured prominently in the state's actions in the region during different moments throughout its rule over Kurdistan (and it was not just Kurdish tribes or tribes in Kurdistan, but tribes all over the empire whose settlement was sought).[12] And, as with previous campaigns to settle tribes, the state's agents employed different means, ranging from outright forced settlement and relocation to gentler methods including offering tribes incentives to settle. Separate policies were introduced to different (kinds of) tribes, and the responses of these tribes also varied—some cooperated while others resisted. Those nomadic tribes whose existence continued to be dependent on animal husbandry and long-distance trade balked the most, as forced sedentarization challenged their very livelihood. In these cases, the government used the policy of cooptation as a means of achieving its goals. Haj cites examples whereby Ottoman governors made deals with the heads of leading tribes: in exchange for their settlement and their adoption of agricultural pursuits, they secured special privileges and appointments. In one case, the Ottoman governor offered the leader of the 'Anayza tribe special lease-holding (*tapu*) rights as well as the governorship of a local district. When the Ottoman governor attempted a similar deal with the head of the Shammar tribe and when the latter refused to cooperate, the governor had the tribal chief replaced as head of the tribe by his more malleable brother, who in addition to becoming head of his tribe, was also made a pasha.[13]

THE HAMIDIYE AND THE GRAB FOR LAND

The Hamidiye Light Cavalry was certainly part of this larger carrot-and-stick means employed by the government in its dealings with the empire's Kurdish tribes. Since it was not only the settlement of the Arab tribes (mentioned by Haj) that the state sought, but also the sedentarization of tribes in general—Kurdish tribes included—this certainly figured into the equation when the Hamidiye was created. Here's how it worked for Hamidiye tribal chiefs: Land in general was becoming more valuable due to the onset of agrarian capitalism. The Ottoman government sought better control over its dominions and also wanted more ways to add to its bankrupt treasury. Better control over its agrarian population meant higher returns for the treasury and the ability to collect these returns. This involved censuses to know who, how many, and where they were and what they could pay; more efficient and secure means of tax collection; and greater "governmentality," or "administrative power" in general. Fewer hard-to-control nomads would allow the government to better monitor larger segments of its population and get taxes from them and would also boost agricultural productivity. In Kurdistan there were many such nomads as well as a growing number of immigrants from the Caucasus. The Hamidiye would be a means to solving some of these goals. The state could offer something to chiefs as incentive for them to settle: land, which was now becoming a valuable resource, one over which fresh disputes were created with the new *tapu* system.[14] As Haj has noted elsewhere for tribes of lower Mesopotamia, "the leading tribal houses adopted a land-grabbing strategy as they came to recognize that the new regime of power was to be founded on the direct control of the land and agricultural pro-duction."[15] The privileges associated with membership in the Hamidiye played a particularly important role in this wider process.

While there were certainly instances in which Ottoman authorities made outright land-for-settlement deals with important tribal figures, in other cases, such as those involving Hamidiye chiefs, the process worked in a subtler manner. Rather than continue the discussion in abstract terms, it would be instructive to follow this process by focusing on specific epi-sodes of land-grabbing in which the Hamidiye were generally involved. By highlighting the activities of Hüseyin Pasha Hayderanî, the reader can see how the special privileges associated with membership in the Hamidiye allowed certain tribal chiefs to take over the land of their neighbors and clients. In the course of this land-grabbing they increased their own power, wealth, and standing. The reader will also see how and why the state's policies and practices helped this process along in both direct and indirect manners.

HÜSEYIN PASHA, THE HAMIDIYE, AND THE "AGRARIAN QUESTION"

Hüseyin Pasha's name figured prominently in consular correspondence on the "agrarian question" when it officially became a "question" in 1908 after the Young Turk Revolution. Documents from 1908 forward show that over the years Kör Hüseyin (or Blind Hüseyin, as he was known locally) had appropriated numerous lands from the villages in and around his immediate domain. Establishing the exact means by which he carried out this feat is a bit trickier, however, since it seems that official observers remarked on this process as such only after it was identified as a "question" in 1908. Nonetheless, through a careful reading of this body of consular and official state correspondence, it is possible to find clues as to how this process unfolded and how Hüseyin Pasha and other Kurdish chiefs were able to come into the possession of numerous valuable agricultural lands by dispossessing the peasants who lived on them.

Overall, Kör Hüseyin's career is similar to that of the other Hamidiye chiefs who were the focus of previous chapters. Hüseyin Agha (as he was known before he became a pasha) was a lesser chief of the large Hayderan tribe, which lived in the Ottoman-Iranian border region with sections on both sides of the border.[16] He had a rather villainous reputation, and in the late 1880s was sought by the authorities in connection with various charges of raiding and plundering. Hüseyin Agha would also rise from being a subchief in his large tribe to the paramount head of the tribe and one of the most powerful figures in the region through his Hamidiye connections, and he too was able to begin his rise before the institution was even created. According to one source, Hüseyin Agha became *kol müdiri* (director of security) of the town of Patnos and its neighboring villages after assassinating a relative who had held the post.[17] Hüseyin Agha was one of the first to enroll in the Hamidiye, and enlisted under similar circumstances as others, such as Mustafa Pasha. It seems that the governors of Erzurum and Van provinces had demanded his arrest after receiving numerous complaints against him from people in the Eleşgird district, but, according to the British consul at Erzurum, "he spared no expense to obtain the good-will of the authorities here, and it is known that he gave to, and received from, the President of the Criminal Court of Appeal various valuable presents."[18] Originally summoned to Erzurum to answer for his crimes, he was, however, "shortly afterwards sent back to his district to collect information as to the number of horsemen it could furnish to the new Hamidiyé cavalry,"[19] and soon thereafter claimed he could enlist some two thousand men. Although the number was exaggerated, the British consul estimated that Hüseyin Agha nonetheless "certainly could produce a considerable body of men well mounted and armed with Martini rifles."[20] This offer was too valuable for the government to pass up, and he was enrolled in the first stage of recruitment in January 1891. He traveled to the capital in 1891 to attend the special induction ceremonies,[21] received the rank of general of brigade (*liva pasha*),[22] and subsequently began a rapid rise in rank and power. Through the protection afforded him by Zeki Pasha, his patron, and the general privilege brought to Hamidiye commanders, Hüseyin Agha, now a pasha, rose from being a mere subchief in his tribe in 1891,[23] to "the most powerful *agha* among the Haydaranli tribes," as he was described by the French consul in 1896.[24] Indeed, as the head of one of the leading Hamidiye "tribal emirates," he was now one of the most influential figures in the region. By 1903, the *kadı* (a judge, who was then acting *kaymakam*) of Adilcevaz confessed to the British consul that "the Government was Hussein Pasha; that they were all in his hands, and that litigants knew it was no use troubling him (the Cadi), but were in the habit of taking their cases direct to Hussein Pasha for decision. He said that Hussein Pasha was always supported by the Vali, who depends on him . . . for money to help carry on the Government."[25]

In his first years as Hamidiye commander, Hüseyin Pasha seems to have been responsible for a good deal of bloodshed in the region. Some of the violence during these years came as the result of raids on neighboring villages, but much of it was an effect of some large-scale intertribal feuds waged between the Hayderan and other Kurdish tribes in the Van and Erzurum provinces, chief among them the Sibkan tribe. Indeed Hüseyin Pasha, who was deemed to be the aggressor in most of the affairs,[26] was summoned by the Van governor to his province in 1892, then to Erzurum in 1894, so that the authorities could persuade him and his rivals to put an end to the intertribal warfare that was costing so many lives.[27] During these years, Hüseyin Pasha was attempting to expand and consolidate his power, and to this end he made good use of his Hamidiye privileges. The French consul noted in 1896 that he had been arrested and incarcerated several times at Bayazid for his numerous misdeeds, which were reported to include robbery, pillage, and assassination. Yet each time he managed to leave prison promptly, "thanks to the golden key that opens all doors."[28]

When Hüseyin Pasha was summoned to answer for his crimes in 1890–91, he left with a position in the newly created Kurdish cavalry, the rank of pasha, and the accompanying prestige rather than the shackles that were originally intended for him. Similarly, in 1894 when he was called to account for his attacks on neighboring tribes, he was not punished but was instead entrusted with official military orders to proceed to Muş, where his regiments would work to put down "the Armenian rebellion" brewing in the mountainous region of Sasun.[29] He may even have volunteered his services for this mission to avoid punishment, as he would also do several times in the future. Over the course of the next year, Hüseyin Pasha would become one of the parties most connected with the massacres of Armenians that bloodied much of Kurdistan during the years 1894–96. Although little is known about any official orders he may have been given in putting down the Sasun rebellion, it can be surmised from the available sources that the Hayderanî Hamidiye forces he commanded were also responsible for a significant amount of "extracurricular" violence against Armenians in his own districts, and indeed, he became notorious for his involvement in these sanguinary activities.[30]

Hüseyin Pasha was called to account for his role in the massacres, as were many other Kurdish chiefs, but due to his Hamidiye connections, his protection by Zeki Pasha, and his abundant use of intimidation tactics, he managed to escape punishment for the part he played in the violence (as did many other Hamidiye *agha*s). Already at the end of 1895, it was reported that "the authorities do not seem willing to court martial him, under the pretext that no Armenian or Kurdish witness would be willing to testify against him. In reality, they fear upsetting a powerful Kurdish tribe."[31] Some provincial governors, notably Şemseddin Pasha of Van and Rauf Pasha of Erzurum, repeatedly tried, however, to obtain the exile of Hüseyin Pasha and two other influential Hayderanî chiefs, Emin Pasha and Haci Timur Agha, the latter of whom was actually not a Hamidiye officer.[32] Under pressure from European diplomats, who were urging reforms and conducting inquiries into the massacres, local Ottoman officials took steps to comply with demands to bring those responsible for the massacres to justice. By the end of 1896, Zeki Pasha summoned the "Haydaranli trio" to Erzincan, the seat of the Fourth Army, for an inquiry.[33] The governors of Erzurum and Van were joined by the European consuls in their wish for the permanent banishment of these men, but doubted that such a punishment would ever be dealt: "I hope this measure . . . will this time be followed with a sufficient disciplinary sanction," wrote the French consul. "But," he continued, "Marshal Zeki Pasha has shown to the present such an indulgence for the Hamidièh officers that he will have to be coaxed to produce the necessary severity, in my opinion."[34] In the spring of 1897, the Russian consul at Van reported that Hüseyin Pasha was then claiming that not only did he *not* perpetrate any violence against Armenians, but that he had actually been "instrumental in saving large numbers of Armenian villagers" in the *kaza* of Adilcevaz during the "disturbances" of the previous year.[35] However, approximately one month later, the British consul averred that Hüseyin Pasha did not deserve the eulogies passed on him. The *vali* had held his brother, Sultan Bey, personally responsible for the protection of certain villages, and the Armenians were forced to sign a petition he had drawn up. The ex-*vali* of Van, Şemseddin Bey, said he had paid no heed to it as he knew the Armenians had signed it under pressure.[36] But Zeki Pasha was more easily persuaded, or rather, likely used the document, along with the pretext of needing more Hamidiye troops on the Iranian border, to have Hüseyin Pasha released in August 1897.[37] He was not allowed to return to his home until the following year, but when he did, it was apparently worth the wait; as the British consul asserted, in addition to the remission of his exile, Hüseyin Pasha had "obtained fresh proofs of Imperial favor in the shape of further decoration," and promotion to the rank of full colonel in the Hamidiye cavalry.[38] Although Hüseyin Pasha had a brief falling-out with his patron shortly after he returned home in 1898, he was able to emerge unscathed from the affair. He was now in a position to continue with the expansion of his power base and acquisition of resources largely unhindered until numerous claims were brought against him a decade later under the new regime by peasants whose lands he and his associates had appropriated.

Hüseyin Pasha and other Hamidiye chiefs used sundry means to acquire the land, animals, and possessions of their weaker neighbors and clients. The most blatant manner in which they took over land, animals, and other property was through direct violence or threats. But there were numerous other strategies. Raids were a common means of acquiring moveable property such as animals and household goods, and were generally, but not uniquely, carried out by tribal Kurds. A raid would be executed against the individuals or community whose property was sought, and if the latter were unable to defend themselves—as was usually the case—the raiding party would take possession of the goods they demanded. Consular reports describe countless cases of this kind of assault. However, only in Bayazîdî's narrative on the customs of nomadic Kurdish tribes do descriptions of raids and other types of theft appear, and it is a valuable source for this reason. According to Bayazîdî, theft was a common occurrence, taking place not just in settled villages but also in the encampments of nomadic Kurds, where night watchpeople were posted with their weapons to keep an eye out for thieves and raiders.[39] Travelers were especially vulnerable to raiding parties, who would send guards to a hilltop to be on the lookout for travelers, and if they were deemed worthy of robbing, the guard would send a signal, sometimes using a handkerchief, to his cohorts, who would descend upon the travelers. The victims were generally not killed, but simply blindfolded, tied up, and made to stay in a ravine until nightfall when the thieves could escape.[40] Consular reports also confirm that while property loss was often enormous, in most types of assaults victims were generally only killed when they resisted.[41]

Christians and Muslims alike suffered from these attacks. Targets were chosen for their weakness and inability to protect themselves, not because of their ethnic or religious background. The Hayderan tribe was notorious for its raids even before Hüseyin Pasha came to lead it.[42] However, when Hüseyin Pasha took over the tribe, these forays increased, as he knew that with his Hamidiye connections he was assured freedom of action. He and his associates carried out numerous raiding and plundering missions, some of which involved Armenian victims, such as the attack on Iğdır in 1891, in which the Hayderan raiding party killed an Armenian priest and made off with as much property as the raiders could carry.[43] Other raids involved Kurdish victims. One report tells of a petition of three Kurds from Eleşgird against Hüseyin Pasha. The report adds, "For five or six years Hussein Agha has been the terror of the inhabitants of Alashgird, both Christian and Mussulman."[44] When one of these Muslims, Sheikh Nuri of Patnos, complained, Hüseyin Pasha had him murdered.[45]

Not only were the homes and villages of both Christian and Muslim peasants targets for raiders, but it seemed to them that nothing was sacred; there were also a good number of churches that were pillaged during the years in question,[46] with thieves stealing anything of value in them. Hüseyin Pasha allegedly played his own part in this activity right from the beginning of his tenure as Hamidiye pasha. A report from October 1890 alleges that his retainers plundered the Mezop monastery near Erciş in the Van province.[47] However, Christian churches and monasteries were not the only holy sites that whose sacred status failed to deter thieves. Some thieves stole from mosques,[48] and Hüseyin Pasha's men even went so far as to rob some Muslim students at their school.[49] Although evidence for incursions of this kind can be found in sources stemming from long before the period in question, they seem to have increased significantly in the nineteenth century with the destruction of the Kurdish emirates and the general insecurity that arose as a result of the power vacuum left in its place. Moreover, these types of assaults also appear to have been even further on the rise after the creation of the Hamidiye.

Raids and other kinds of theft, however, generally only yielded moveable property. There were a number of other things that could be stolen or pilfered by parties attempting to enrich themselves, key among which were tithes and taxes. While urban notables and officials were traditionally those placed in the best position to win the bids for tithes, as tribal chiefs grew more powerful they also entered their bids to farm the taxes of the villages in and around their domains. Hamidiye chieftains were especially advantaged in this regard, managing to strong-arm the bids through their government connections and intimidation tactics. Hüseyin Pasha often used such maneuvers to browbeat officials into handing the bids to him. The British consul at Van reported that Hüseyin Pasha was able to buy up all of the taxes of the Armenian villages in the Adilcevaz and Erciş *kaza*s, with "no one having the hardihood to bid against him."[50] He also used the collection of tithes and taxes as a pretext to rob villages of numerous other possessions.[51] Hüseyin Pasha's Hayderanî associate Emin employed similar tactics, reportedly purchasing the tithes of twenty-four villages at approximately one third of their real value, having "frightened off all competitors."[52] Sometimes the government granted Hamidiye officers the right of tithe-farming in lieu of pay, as was the case in the Muş region, for one.[53] It was also the case for Riza Agha, a Hasanan Hamidiye captain from the Malazgird district, who was allotted tithes as "pay" for his services in the Hamidiye. One informant confided to the British consul at Bitlis that no one dared to bid against Riza or other Hamidiye chiefs at the tithe sales.[54]

Even when the government made attempts to rectify this situation by forbidding the sale of tithes to Hamidiye officers, the latter nonetheless managed to circumvent the order using other means. In 1897, after reforms were ordered for the entire region, the British consul reported from Bitlis:

The Porte's directions for the non-sale of village tithes to the Hamidiehs are evaded without difficulty. The latter purchase the tithes in the names of other Kurdish villagers or compel the Armenian peasants to negotiate the transactions on their behalf. The result is that Fatullah Bey, the Hamidieh Commander, who is notorious as a brigand, an oppressor, and an ill-doer, is this year the farmer of many villages, a measure which is diametrically opposed to the orders of the Sublime Porte and the principles embodied in the scheme of Anatolian reforms.[55]

The French consul later offered a similar view of things, writing in 1905 that when the Porte prohibited the sale of tithes to these Kurdish chiefs, the latter just had "straw men make their purchases" with the result of a massive loss of revenue from the Kurdish regions of these provinces. He chalked this up to the "complacence of Yildiz towards these turbulent chiefs and the open protection accorded to them by the Marshal

[Zeki Pasha]," who would intimidate local officials.[56] On other occasions Hamidiye officers would simply extort more taxes even after they had already been collected by proper government agents.[57] These abuses continued either with the collusion of officials, or elsewhere in spite of their attempts to rectify a situation that was damaging not only to the villages in question, but also to the government's treasury.[58]

Not only did tax-farming improprieties deprive the treasury of potential income, but they worked to transform the peasantry into tenants. The British agent at Bitlis reported: "A further grievance lies in the farming of tithes, which displays all the abuses usually attached to the system. In this district the farmer of the tithes often acts in concert with the tax-gatherer, and the latter compels the villager to borrow back at high interest the tithes which he has just paid to the former." He continued, describing how Armenians in particular were being reduced to farming contracts with "the more favored Kurds" by which they undertook to serve for bare shelter and sustenance.[59] However, another observer suggested that the expression "absolute impunity of Mussulmans who wrong Christians" had to be qualified; in his experience the "incidents connected with taxation" applied to all elements of the population.[60] This situation was harmful to Christian and Muslim, Kurdish and Armenian, peasant alike.[61]

There were further means of tampering with the local economy to one's advantage. Grain hoarding and speculation were other such activities. There is certainly evidence that these tricks were in practice before the Hamidiye was created, as in the case of grain hoarding by members of the Diyarbekir administrative council, which indeed provoked a riot by townspeople in 1880.[62] But they seem to have spread from the urban notables, who were the usual suspects in such activities, to tribal chieftains, especially Hamidiye chieftains, after the creation of the tribal militia. The British agent reported that Hüseyin Pasha joined the mayor of Van in hoarding wheat to force the prices higher in 1899.[63] He seems to have worked out an additional deal whereby the government would go to him for their wheat purchases. However, the British consul believed that Hüseyin Pasha may not have been building up stocks of grain entirely for his own benefit, but at the behest of Zeki Pasha, who wanted to ensure a supply of wheat for his soldiers in case of a campaign in the spring.[64] But it should also be mentioned that Armenians, when they were in the position to do so, attempted to stockpile grain as well, as some did in the province of Van the following year.[65] Reports of grain hoarding continued throughout the period in question, although it is unclear which notables— urban or rural—were actually heading the various "grain rings." In 1907, for example, the British consul at Van stated that various tithe buyers and corn speculators had managed to collect large stores of corn, which they were holding for higher prices, an act that caused the price of grain to ascend nearly to famine rate.[66] British agents reported such "corn rings" in other regions as well.[67]

Raids, grain hoarding, and other means of theft may have been lucrative, but they yielded little when compared with the profit that land could bring. As the head of the Kîkî tribe confided to the British traveler Sykes, İbrahim Pasha liked raids "because they amuse him, but they do not lead to riches as does fellaheen business and farming."[68] Therefore, the form of property theft that would prove to be the most significant, and which turned into an actual "question" beginning in 1908, was the usurpation of land by notables and officials of all kinds, but especially by Kurdish Hamidiye chieftains. This grabbing of land, like the many other forms of theft practiced in the region during the Hamidian period, did not begin with the creation of the Hamidiye,[69] although these forms of theft certainly were helped along in significant ways by it.[70]

Even though there is ample evidence that such land-grabbing activities occurred quite outside the massacres and with victims not limited to Armenians, the importance of the Armenian massacres of 1894–96 in this process cannot be overstated. Sources signal that these bloody events were significant in the history of southeastern Anatolia in the late Ottoman period not only for political reasons, but for social and economic ones as well, as they effected the large-scale transfer of agricultural properties from Armenian peasants to Kurdish tribal chiefs, notably (although not uniquely) Hamidiye chieftains. This was the case throughout the region, as numerous reports from all parts of southeastern Anatolia indicate. In Malatya, it was stated that the land and crops belonging to Armenians there were being appropriated by Muslims in various villages, who declared openly that they would no longer pay their debts to "infidels."[71] In the aftermath of the massacres the British consul in Van stated that Kurds had taken over most of the villages in Erciş after most of the village inhabitants had fled to other regions.[72] It was later observed that after the massacres, "lands of emigrating and fugitive Armenians, being considered as 'mahlul' (unowned) [escheated] by the Department of Cadastre here, have been granted or sold to Moslems."[73] Occupation after the massacres was the case in numerous parts of the region, including sections of the Harput (Ma'muret'ül-'Aziz) province, where the British agent pointed as an example to the village of Ilic, whose lands had been seized by Muslims since the eruption of violence.[74] Sources detail the process whereby Armenian villages and even ecclesiastic establishments had been wholly taken over by Kurdish magnates especially after the creation of the Hamidiye, and particularly during the massacres.[75]

Hüseyin Pasha also seems to have begun his career as a land-grabber during these years. In 1895 his tribe was reportedly responsible for the total plunder of the Armenians of Adilcevaz and some in Erciş as well.[76] In 1896, Hayderanî Hamidiye tribesmen engaged in a massive plundering campaign in several villages in the Ahlat district.[77] And after the massacres, Hüseyin Pasha and other Hamidiye chiefs even managed to steal the cattle sent by relief groups to Armenians whose belongings had been destroyed or stolen in the violence.[78] Even nearly a decade later, the Armenian *murakhas* (representative) of Adilcevaz reported in a letter, "In this Caza, Hussein Pasha, Chief of the Haideranli Ashiret and a Mir Alai of Hamidieh . . . ever since the year of the famous massacres, has seized, and taken possession of, the goods and revenues, the property and fields of the Armenians."[79] Hüseyin Pasha used the massacres as the initial foray into land-grabbing, and he continued it for years after.

While the massacres provided the context and opportunity for this widespread appropriation of Armenian property, the usurpers banked additionally on the fear of the victims that such an event would happen again. In the aftermath of the massacres, where lands were not forcibly taken over, villagers were coerced into signing them over to Hüseyin Pasha and other Kurdish chieftains in exchange for protection. In 1898 the British consul at Bitlis recalled several instances in 1895 of villages having ceded lands to powerful Kurds in this manner.[80] Another report from 1897 suggested that the appropriation of land by Kurds was continuing on a broad scale in the villages of Ahlat and Bulanık districts, where Christians were forced to give up their fields in return for Kurdish protection and to hand over documents stating that they had parted with their lands for value. Although the villagers, the consul noted, were glad to do this as it afforded them at least temporary protection for what remained of their property, the practice was leading to the ultimate expropriation of all the Christian families.[81] In some cases, villagers signed over their lands after the massacres in exchange for the moveable property they had lost during the looting. Although it is unclear precisely what these peasants (of the Başnik village in the Silvan district of Diyarbekir province) were thinking, it seems that they did not believe that such a transfer would be permanent. However, by 1899 the transfer of lands became legal, "not withstanding the opposition of the owners," as the consul pointed out. A decade later not only were the peasants still unable to obtain their return, but they also found the gardens adjacent to Başnik, to which their usurpers had "no shadow of a legal claim," nonetheless occupied.[82]

Hüseyin Pasha gained lands through various similar means after the period of the massacres, and even clashed with officials who tried to prevent him from doing so. In 1901, the British agent at Van reported that the acting *kaymakam* of Patnos was a strong man and that his methods, along with the presence of small detachments in the villages around the region, were "displeasing" to Hüseyin Pasha. This Hamidiye chief wanted some villages to be given over to his entire jurisdiction, and to this end he induced the villagers of Kiazuk to make their village over to him and to convey a telegram to the *vali* that they were "quite satisfied with the arrangement."[83] In this instance the *vali* apparently managed to restore the property in question. In most cases, however, Hamidiye chiefs such as Hüseyin Pasha were able to acquire property through these and other means. Hüseyin Pasha appears to have been especially successful in this endeavor, and was described by the British consul already in 1900 as dominating much of the *kaza*s of Erciş and Adilcevaz.[84]

Although the massacres and their aftermath formed a significant chapter in the history of land-grabbing in southeastern Anatolia, usurpers capitalized on the fear and poverty of peasants in general to find sundry means for acquiring their property, and relied on the relative inability of the peasants to protect themselves. In the case of Hamidiye chieftains, who were generally allowed extensive freedom of action by the authorities, the grab for land proceeded quite rapidly during the period under review. Moreover, if we look at the history of land-grabbing beyond the era of the massacres, we find that Christians were not the only victims. Indeed, there were numerous Muslim peasants who were dispossessed of their land and property by Hüseyin Pasha and others like him, who used various methods to acquire their lands. Many Alevis of Dersim, for example, were transformed into tenants in a manner similar to their Armenian neighbors, but these villagers—unlike many Armenians—had no European protectors to advocate on their behalf.[85] Other Kurds found themselves stripped of their lands by Hamidiye chiefs as well. Hüseyin Pasha, for one, seized the pastures of *reaya* Kurds in the Van province,[86] and later was so bold as to take over the lands not only of Kurdish peasants, but also the villages of less powerful *agha*s.[87] Indeed, in a retrospective glance at the "agrarian question," the British consul remarked in 1911 that the Armenian land question was actually "not so prominent as the more difficult question of the settlement of claims of the Raya Kurds who demand the restoration of the lands taken away from them by their chiefs and Aghas. It appears that at the time of the formation of the Hamidie cavalry the power and influence of the Kurd chiefs and Aghas became greatly increased through the favour shown them by Abdul Hamid. These chiefs then began gradually to appropriate the land and property of the Raya Kurds and to reduce them to a state of serfdom."[88]

A number of peasants were forced to cede their lands to Hamidiye chiefs such as Hüseyin Pasha because of sheer poverty or indebtedness.

In the Bitlis province, for example, it was reported that "the peasants are selling their fields for a mere song to the Kurds, as they have no means of cultivating them, and are reduced to living on 'gilgil,' a species of coarse millet, which causes constipation and frequent illness, and many have died from that cause."[89] In other cases, the property of peasants was acquired through tax-farming abuses, as we have seen above. As peasants became increasingly impoverished and indebted to their *agha*s, they were forced to sign over their lands to them in lieu of the taxes they could not pay. In addition, numerous properties were taken over by Kurdish notables and tribal chiefs when debts, often petty, went unpaid by the villagers. This was accomplished through forceful takeover, and sometimes with the complicity of the courts.[90]

On other occasions, peasants were stripped of their land through simple fraud. In Sasun, for example, it was said that the Badikan Kurds were claiming a good deal of land now occupied by Christians in Sêmal and Geliyêguzan. They were supporting their bid by certain papers they claimed were some seventy years old. The *mutassarıf* and the local government seem to have accepted their word but the Christians themselves were protesting the decision and were about to appeal to Bitlis and the Istanbul. These old papers were apparently invalid.[91] A later report detailing the numerous means used to deprive peasants of their lands further mentioned that false creditors were able to acquire lands after submitting bogus evidence to the courts.[92]

Usurpers also employed other means. In the village of Hormuz in Bitlis, it was reported in 1907 that "several Kurdish families took up their abode last summer . . . and endeavored to squeeze out the Armenian families, but, owing to the representations of the Acting British Vice-Consul, were ejected."[93] They returned, however, and managed to set up a permanent home.[94] Elsewhere in Bitlis it was stated that ten Armenian villages of Tadig were entirely in the hands of the sheikh of Hizan, who had reduced them to "complete servitude," and whose numbers had fallen by half "to make room for the Kurds."[95]

Government agents were often openly complicit with the land-grabbers. Some Armenian lands were taken over directly by the government and sold to Muslims at the lowest possible price in return for taxes. This appears to have taken place quite often between 1904 and 1908 in the *sancak*s of Bitlis and Muş. Armenian properties were also put on the market by the Agricultural Bank at lower prices in return for debts the peasants owed to the bank. According to a later report, "the whole plain of Mush, including the districts of Bulanik and [M]elazgerd, has cruelly been a victim to the machinations of the Agricultural Bank, the directors of which have invariably been local men of great power and tied by relationship to notorious chiefs. Armenian ignorant peasants have contracted loans under the old régime, and, as they have not been able to fulfil the conditions, the bank has taken advantage in getting the land out of Armenians and selling them to Kurds."[96]

By the turn of the twentieth century, observers clearly identified a general trend of dispossession. A report by a British officer at Van is interesting for the details provided surrounding some of the means through which lands were taken, and is thus worth describing at length. In 1902, Captain Tyrrell surveyed the four *kaza*s comprising the *sancak* of Hakkari and remarked that, in Elbak, the Hamidiye could do "pretty well what they like." Şerif Bey of the Şikak tribe, who, like other Hamidiye chiefs had not been the chief of his tribe, gained vast power after receiving government rank and support through his Hamidiye connections. As such, he was now looked upon as the chief of the Şikaks on the Ottoman side of the border. Both Christians and non-Hamidiye Muslims complained of his tyranny, and these grievances were not limited to the peasantry. Indeed one Sheikh Hamid, a landowner near Başkale, confessed that even his villages were not safe, that Şerif Bey could seize them in the same way as he had taken many Christian villages. He described how average tribesmen and low-ranking Hamidiye officers had followed these examples. A common manner they employed to seize property was to build a house near the desired village, claim that they were the masters of that village, draft a petition to this effect, and force the village representatives to sign it. The government then handed the rights over to that person, and the peasants became his sharecroppers. This happened, as he noted, in many cases with Hamidiye Kurds.[97]

The transfer of land from Armenians to Kurds, most of whom were members of Hamidiye tribes, often happened not as the result of direct appropriation but through semilegal sales. Taxes were rigorously collected and villagers were forced to mortgage lands and future crops to pay them. Although this was not a new situation, it was becoming more prevalent. Tyrrell described the transfer of land from Armenians to Kurds who were not pressed for taxes to the same extent, who also largely evaded the sheep and cattle taxes, and who were thus able to buy out the Armenians. He believed this applied chiefly to the Hamidiye nomads, who were protected against even the local government. Cases were repeatedly brought to notice of Kurds settling in Christian villages, having first acquired their lands in this way. In making their complaints the people always informed the consul that there was an order to the effect that Hamidiye Kurds were not to be allowed to settle in Christian villages. But as far as he could determine, there was no such order. The *vali* attempted to temper this process, and in several cases the efforts of Hamidiye Kurds to acquire Christian villages were frustrated. But the fact remained that Kurds acquired land legally using these methods, and it was very difficult, therefore, to turn them out.[98]

Other transfers of land were the result of simple harassment. A report from Cizre mentioned that two Hamidiye regiments under arms were "doing as they like." One Kervan Agha had forced the Takyan villagers to promise to sell to their village. If this was allowed, the consul feared, all the Christians in Silopî would be compelled to leave.[99] Hence, the villagers were harassed to the point where they had to desert their land, as was the case of the village of Duman in the Erzurum province, which "was abandoned by its Armenian inhabitants who could not support any longer the vexations to which a Hamidiye officer, a Kurd named Khallo, submitted them. He had come a few years ago," it was stated, "and settled himself by force."[100] Out of fear of such harassment, peasants would contract with powerful protectors, but in the process would often lose their properties to the people who were supposed to be protecting them from the usurpers as the price for such "protection."

By 1908, Hamidiye chieftains had developed a full-blown system for acquiring resources and setting the limits of their influence. Their "new tribal emirates" seem to have been acknowledged by one another in terms of recognized "zones of influence." As the British agent reported, "The districts of Akhlat and Bulanik are divided into zones of influence among the notorious Hamidié officers for the object of near or future plundering and depredations. Major Riza Bey, for instance, must not raid any more the Armenian villages on the shore of Lake Van, which is described as to be in the zone of Major Sabit Bey, and vice versa."[101] It should also be mentioned that Armenian peasants were squeezed not only by Kurdish *agha*s, but also by members of their own community. The French agent believed that a number of Armenian peasants in the Muş district were being compelled by Armenian revolutionaries to sell their animals and fields in order to purchase weapons.[102]

The fact that Armenian revolutionaries were indeed active only served to work against the wider Armenian community in the long run because the peasants were pressed in the manner just described, and also because their activity gave rise to pretexts to rob Armenians of their goods by those seeking to capitalize on the "Armenian question." Muslim and Christian peasants both suffered at the hands of powerful tribal chiefs, each seeking to expand his influence and wealth, as members of both communities spiraled into deeper and deeper pits of poverty and as Kurdish chiefs acquired whatever goods or land they had left through force or extortion. At the same time it should be noted that Armenians were particularly vulnerable simply because of the existence of the "Armenian question."

Victims of raids, extortion, tax abuse, and land usurpation included both Christian and Muslim peasants (and sometimes members of weaker tribes) who were unable to protect themselves. But the Armenians had the added disadvantage of being subject to denunciation as traitors (not to mention the fact that they were not allowed to bear arms). Those who sought to take possession of their neighbors' property could use blackmail to gain custody of the goods (by threatening to denounce the latter to the government) or could simply take the desired property and claim after the fact that the victim was a revolutionary.[103] Kurds were also denounced by their neighbors, as in the case of Mustafa Pasha and others, who would condemn their adversaries as traitors. But the Armenian question was so potent and evocative at the time that accusing someone of being a revolutionary or sympathizer was a sure means to his downfall, and a powerful weapon through which usurpers could expand their holdings.[104]

The trend whereby numerous Kurdish and Christian peasants became dispossessed of their lands and other properties and were reduced to tenancy or forced to emigrate was part of a historical process, and was not a conspiracy. However, there are indications that some in the government wanted to perpetuate the process for ends they believed would strengthen the state's hold over the region. By allowing nomadic and seminomadic tribes largely unfettered access to resources, including the land of settled peasants, the central Ottoman government was able to accomplish many of its goals. First was the permanent settlement of the nomads, a mission that was sporadically sought from the first days of Ottoman rule over the area. Second, appeasing powerful Hamidiye chiefs in this manner would permit the government to gain the support and alliance of the Kurdish chiefs, who threatened to move their people and flocks over the border to "greener" pastures or who could be enticed by a better deal from Russia. For these reasons, it was a historical process that ended up working out well for the state in certain terms (despite its destructiveness on the economy), but there is no evidence to claim that it was intentional from the start.

Having said that, in the case of Armenian lands in particular a number of European observers believed that there were some in the government who decided to pursue actively the policy of uprooting Armenians from their lands and settling Kurdish tribes or Muslim emigrants from the Caucasus on these lands, while at the same time forcing the emigration of what was perceived by some to be a dangerous population.[105] In 1906, growing numbers of Muslim emigrants streamed into the empire from the Caucasus, many of whom were directed toward Muş,[106] where authorities were particularly anxious to uproot Armenians from what was then an important center of Armenian revolutionary activity. The following year the British consul reported that there were problems settling these immigrants, and that in some cases the commission set up to deal with them forced Armenians of Muş and Bitlis from their homes. Those who were not directly pushed out felt they had no choice but to emigrate to Russia, and sought permission to do so.[107] In 1898, the French consul reported:

I am informed that the Vali just received from Constantinople the order to propose to the Muslim population lands in the Armenian provinces of the Empire. The very confidential circular, which contains these instructions, had been, according to what is confirmed to me, addressed to all the Governors General.

The secret with which one guards this affair up to now makes information difficult to gather; I only know that a commission has been instituted to this effect to compile a list of destitute Muslims of the country and to formulate the demands of concessions for those of them who decide to profit from the government largesse.[108]

The British consul had the same impression, some five years later. His report is interesting as, in addition to showing the often gray lines where dispossession was actually legal in some cases, it also indicates that he, too, believed that the government was playing some sort of active role in the process. He cited the case of a Taqurî Hamidiye chief, Nîmet Agha, who had acquired his village through the Agricultural Bank using questionable means, and who had taken over the land of a Christian village. Although the consul confessed that some cases were certainly exaggerated, an inquiry could not be conducted because he was a Hamidiye officer. The consul then suggested that

a Hamidie Kurd occupies a curious position in relation to the law. Even when his behaviour is such as to earn the censure of the authorities, there is something which screens him from punishment, or even from interference. I have been told here most emphatically that it is a fact that orders have been issued secretly from Constantinople (not recently) that a Hamidie Kurd is to be settled in every Armenian village. Such a proceeding would, if carried out, mean the gradual decimation of the Christians, who cannot long remain in their own village on these terms.[109]

The consul concluded that the aim of the government was to "curry favor" with the Kurds and to foment unfriendly relations between themselves and the Christians.[110] The Sasun district, which was where the massacres of 1894–96 began, seems to have been a region particularly targeted for this policy. The French consul reported that "the civil and military authorities of Mouch have requested the cooperation of the Kurds in evicting the Armenians of Sassoun and [have] distributed arms amongst them.[111] The following year, his colleague stated that "the Turkish authorities seem now to have a well-established plan: install Kurds in the villages or in what is left of the villages of Sassoun and Talori and 'uproot' the Armenians of the mountain and distribute them throughout the plain where they will doubtless be easier to completely destroy if the occasion presents itself."[112] The French agent at Van voiced similar beliefs in his summary of the land question in 1906:

In order to keep an eye on the revolutionaries, the Government has installed Hamidiés in a large number of localities, who have taken over the best lands; they have occupied the houses that were temporarily abandoned by their owners during the massacres. When the latter returned, they were not able to evict the new occupants. They complained to the authorities, who took no action. Such acts took place in the villages of Haspestan, BoasKessan, Azara, SalaKuna, and so forth. It is obvious that the goal of the Government is to annihilate the Armenian population, and to supplant them with Muslims, whether Turks or Kurds. In the same spirit, and also to settle and subjugate the Kurdish nomads, it has had the Hamidiés purchase lands located in Christian villages and sold by the Agricultural Bank. These newcomers act as if they had conquered the land. Their *agha*s forced the former owners to work their lands and to build their houses.[113]

This mission continued in the Muş region into 1908, when the British consul reported that Armenian families were being evicted from four villages and were being quartered on other Armenian families. Plans were underway for the same action to be taken in other nearby villages. This was apparently being done to make room for Hamidiye regiments.[114]

The overall process whereby land and other resources changed hands from peasants to powerful Kurdish *agha*s began before the onset of "the Armenian question" and before the creation of the Hamidiye. But by the late nineteenth century the Hamidiye had largely come to be identified with the process, which began perhaps a decade later to become a "question" that was itself linked to the larger Armenian question, not only for the European agents in the region who saw the protection of Christians as a pressing concern, but even in the minds of some in the central Ottoman government. Although Kurdish and other Muslim peasants (and indeed other non-Armenian Christians) were victims of this process, when the Young Turk Revolution ushered in a new era of freedom, it was the "Armenian agrarian question" as it came to be known that demanded attention. Armenian activists and their European advocates actively pressed for the return of lands usurped from Armenians over the preceding decades. However, although the "agrarian question" became a euphemism for the question of specifically *Armenian* lands, it should not be forgotten that there were others, non-Armenians, who had lost their lands in a similar manner, and who also agitated for their return after the proclamation of the constitution in 1908.[115] Although their voices were not heard as much as those of the Armenians, whose political leadership was now allied with the recently empowered Young Turks and who found support in European diplomatic circles, it is nonetheless important to recognize them.

THE "AGRARIAN QUESTION," 1908–1914

Immediately after the reinstatement of the second Ottoman constitution in 1908, Armenian political and community leaders pushed for the return of the Armenian lands that had been usurped by Kurdish tribal chiefs over the previous two to three decades. They now had a name for their cause—"the agrarian question." While Armenian leaders had many reforms they wished to urge on the new regime, the "agrarian question" was perhaps the most important. Indeed, several observers believed that it had been a key issue drawing Armenians to become revolutionaries in the first place. Even before "the agrarian question" as such surfaced, it was reported: "Armenians are gradually being ousted from their villages, and their lands are falling into the hands of Kurds"—a point stressed by the revolutionaries.[116] By 1908, then, when the "agrarian question" became a clear-cut grievance, the Dashnakists, for example, had numerous complaints and demands they wished to be addressed, but most of their pleas were for the immediate arrest and punishment of those *agha*s who had taken Armenian lands.[117] In the months following the proclamation of the constitution, Armenian peasants, also emboldened by the initial positive measures taken by the new regime, pushed harder for the return of usurped lands and the resolution of the "agrarian question." In the new climate of peace in August and September, hundreds of protests were made by Armenians in hopes of getting back their lands that had been seized.[118] The government immediately began to make inquiries, and followed up by issuing orders for the return of these lands and, in some cases, the arrest of the usurpers. Hüseyin Pasha became an instant target for the policy, but he was only one of many ordered to give back their illicitly obtained territories.

The new regime began at once energetically to address this matter that was so important to its Armenian constituents as well as to European onlookers. Almost immediately, orders began to emanate from the capital for the eviction of Kurdish chiefs from the Armenian villages in which they had illegally settled. However, the matter would become quite complicated for all of the parties involved. Just as the process of land-grabbing had been closely associated with the Hamidiye and the license accorded to its members by its patrons, so would the "agrarian question" remain intimately linked with the question of the Hamidiye and its role under the new regime. Moreover, by extension the "agrarian question" necessarily became connected to the larger matter of the state's relationship with the Kurdish *agha*s who had grown so powerful during the Hamidian period.

Hayderanî Hüseyin Pasha, as we have seen, built what I have referred to as a "new tribal emirate" through his Hamidiye connections, which allowed him to expand his zone of influence and ownership. As one of the chief usurpers of Armenian lands, his name naturally figured prominently in the various exchanges on the "agrarian question" beginning in 1908. Indeed, he was one of the first land-grabbers to be sought by the new regime in connection with such activities.

Soon after the new regime came to power in 1908, orders were issued from the capital for the eviction of Hüseyin Pasha's people from thirteen Armenian villages in the *kaza* of Adilcevaz, where he had settled them after taking over the lands from what were probably Armenian owners. The British consul described the people to be turned out as Hüseyin Pasha's people, whom he had settled in villages during and since the massacres and who had no title-deeds or other rights to be there.[119] The Hamidiye chieftain and his associates were summoned by the *vali* to appear before him in Van. Believing the new regime to be serious about its measures taken in this regard, the Hayderanî chiefs responded and proceeded to Van without incident.[120] However, in his "interviews" with government officials in Van, Hüseyin Pasha quickly picked up on something that would prove to be extremely significant in the years to follow: just as officials under the former regime had different agendas, so did members of the new government. Some were dedicated to the ideals of the Young Turk Revolution, yet others remained secretly loyal to the ancien régime. Hüseyin Pasha sized up the situation and determined that not much had really changed since the constitution was proclaimed, and sent his people back to the villages from which they had been evicted. It turned into a battle of wills at that point, for the *kaymakam* again expelled the Kurds from the villages and again they returned. Counting on his protection from the military commander at Erzincan, Hüseyin Pasha sent him a telegram, whereupon the latter in turn sent a telegram to the *vali*, which the British consul characterized as "tactless." It told the *vali* to "salute the Kurds and leave them in peace."[121] Elsewhere he noted that they "were not be punished and that they were to retain their plunder."[122] The *ferik* reportedly "ignored the telegram, explaining it as the act of an adherent of the ancien régime, ignorant of the country and of the Turkish character."[123]

The one-step-forward-two-steps-back manner in which the resolution of the "agrarian question" proceeded from 1908 to 1913 reflected the tumultuous nature of politics practiced by the various groups that were either trying to establish or to hold on to power. For the Kurdish and Armenian peasants who had lost their lands and other properties to usurpers the issue was of pressing concern. For the government, it seemed to be a question of working out its priorities, placing some agendas higher on the list of concerns than others. But for the *agha*s who had appropriated vast stretches of land over the preceding decades, the matter became equally complex. In the end, a status quo would be reached, or rather returned to, by the government and *agha*s. But perhaps more interesting than this final result is tracing the process whereby this came about.

From 1908 to 1910, the central Ottoman government and many of its local governors appeared intent on bringing about a just resolution to the "agrarian question" and took a number of energetic, and even aggressive, measures in this regard. First, the government ordered the return of usurped lands and the arrest of leading land-grabbers like Hüseyin Pasha.[124] However, state agents who soon realized the sheer complexity of the matter were forced to pause for a moment to conduct inquiries into a situation that now looked as if it would not be solved by such simple steps. One of the most difficult problems was determining what lands had actually been occupied illegally—an exceedingly tedious task given that land-grabbing had proceeded over the course of several decades in manners that were not always as simple as straightforward cases of usurpation. Many of the territories in question were acquired through what appeared to be legal means, wherein peasants actually signed over papers to the new owners either under duress or in exchange for protection. The government attempted to refer the matter to the courts, but since in many cases the usurpers were able to produce deeds to the disputed lands, Armenian leaders and their European supporters recommended that the matter be resolved administratively through decrees, rather than through the legal system. After all, it seemed to produce few results in favor of the dispossessed tenants.

The inquiries conducted were intended to sort out the matter and to deal with specific lands claimed by known individuals, rather than simply issuing a general directive that seemed to have little force behind it. Numerous petitions were filed by claimants almost immediately after the constitution was proclaimed.[125] These grievances, which came from all over the region, were submitted not only by Armenians but also by Kurds who had been similarly stripped of their lands. In Hüseyin Pasha's domains, for example, a year after the Hamidiye chieftain was ordered to return the lands in Adilcevaz to the Armenians from whom he had taken them, Kurdish peasants in the Bayazid *sancak* brought complaints to the *vali* against the Hayderan chieftain who had forcibly seized and retained their lands. Their claim prompted the *vali* to make a tour of the region to investigate the allegations. The *vali* was probably additionally eager to repossess the government taxes that Hüseyin Pasha had been collecting and keeping for himself.[126] In 1910, the central government ordered the provincial governors to make further inquiries into the question of Armenian lands and directed them to produce a clearer picture of specific disputed lands. According to the French consul, realizing that the government did not even have "a single official figure to even approximate the lands taken from the Armenians by the Kurds," the Armenian patriarch was obliged to produce the information.[127] The Ministry of the Interior was also reported to have made plans to send agents to the region to try to settle the land question.[128]

As a result of the petitions filed by various claimants and the efforts of the authorities, some disputed lands were actually returned. In the Bitlis province, for example, it was reported in September 1909 that peace and tranquility were prevailing in the Muş plain; that thanks to energetic measures taken by local governors and the courts, relations between Kurds and Armenians were friendly; and that in the new atmosphere of peace, occupied Armenian lands were being reinstated and were already being cultivated, and numerous Armenian villages were being restored to their original owners.[129] Similar reports from other provinces showed that land was being returned to dispossessed Muslim peasants as well (although, as we will see below, the positive developments in this regard would, in the end, not be far-reaching).[130]

The steps toward land restitution were further accompanied by other efforts on the part of the government to promote general peace in the region and to encourage Kurdish chieftains to cooperate with the new regime and its efforts to restore the lands that some of them had usurped. As mentioned in Chapter 3, Hüseyin Pasha and other influential Kurdish figures were summoned to Van in November 1909 to attend the series of lectures given by Sheikh Abdulqadir, whom the government had asked to encourage such chieftains to support the new government, to promote friendly relations between Kurds and Armenians, and especially to cooperate in efforts underway to resolve the "agrarian question." The latter resolution, which was adopted by the group at its final meeting, allowed for "an engagement to settle the question of the ownership of land claimed by Armenians. By this engagement the Kurds bind themselves to hand over next spring [in May] the lands now in their possession, of which Armenians possess and produce the 'Tapu' (title-deeds), and in the case of lands claimed by Armenians who cannot produce the 'Tapu' to leave the matter to the Government to settle."[131] Many officials under the new regime were committed and sincere, helping to bring about positive changes in the relations among communities and a more general peace in the region; however, it should also be noted that discontent was brewing among those parties, namely the Kurdish *aghas*, who had the most to lose as a result of these endeavors. Almost immediately, resistance to efforts to restore disputed lands to their original owners was offered up by numerous Kurdish chieftains.

The case of Hüseyin Pasha is again instructive, for it reveals the extent to which the resolution of the "agrarian question" was actually a process of negotiation between the state and the diverse elements it sought at various times to either control or appease. It is also instructive as to the means used, in turn, by these various elements to influence the state's policies and actions. Although there were general directives issued for the return of Armenian lands, the sources tell us that Hüseyin Pasha actually became one of the first usurpers to be called on by name to return the lands he had appropriated. Over the next few years, Hüseyin Pasha and others would employ a range of strategies intended to secure their retention of the disputed lands.

In the early days of the constitutional regime when the central government and its provincial agents were still enthusiastic about promoting change and pursuing the return of the disputed lands, Hüseyin Pasha and his associates responded to their summons to Van and informed authorities that they would cooperate fully. As the British consul later reported, "Finding that the Government was in earnest they came, and have agreed to surrender all lands to which they have no official title-deeds, while in doubtful cases, if the former owners are forthcoming, the Courts are to decide the question."[132] However, in spite of his professed willingness to cooperate, Hüseyin Pasha nonetheless ordered his people to return to the lands from which they had been evicted, as was mentioned above. While at Van, he came under the impression that the government was not as earnest as he had initially perceived it to be, and he felt confident that he would be able to proceed with the resettlement of his people in the disputed villages. However, the government forged ahead with its efforts to arrest and exile Hüseyin Pasha and his associates.

To obtain his release, Hüseyin Pasha pursued four strategies. First, he solicited the support of the high military commander at Erzincan, who telegraphed the *vali* on Hüseyin Pasha's behalf. The governor ignored the telegram so that Hüseyin Pasha was forced to devise a different plan. This time, he decided to draw upon a scheme that had worked well for himself and other Hamidiye chieftains in the past: when they had felt that their favor with the government was waning, they would offer their regiments for service in whatever campaign required men at the time. Hüseyin Pasha had put forward his services in this capacity twice before,[133] and in 1908, he once again offered his help in hopes of obtaining favor with the new regime. He thought he might find a bargaining chip that he could use in negotiations with government agents on the question of the disputed lands.

The British consul reported in November 1908 that Hüseyin Pasha had sent a telegraph to the capital in which he offered to raise an astounding sixteen regiments for service in Bulgaria. However, as the consul reported, the proposal was "politely declined" by the minister of war.[134]

At the same time as Hüseyin Pasha was trying to obtain the good graces of the government to advance his goals, he also engaged in discussions with other parties he believed could help achieve his pardon. Strange bedfellows, Hüseyin Pasha and the other Hayderan chiefs entered into a preliminary bargain with Armenian leaders, who were trying to ensure the election of their respective candidates in the upcoming vote. Leaders of the Dashnaktsutiun party used various means, including intimidation and threats, to try to secure the election of their candidate, Varhad Papazian, called "the Doctor." To further this goal, they even began soliciting the votes of the very same Kurdish chiefs they had ordered arrested and whose return of Armenian lands they had demanded.[135] The British consul at Van reported that "several Kurdish Aghas, who have been summoned to Van by the Acting Vali to answer for their misdeeds, have actually asked Aram [a Dashnak leader] on what terms he will secure their pardon." The consul continued: "The Tashnak have been intriguing with these Haideranli Chiefs, promising to procure their pardon, on condition of their voting for the election of 'the Doctor' as Deputy, and their punishment otherwise."[136] Although the agreement was only short-lived, the fact that Hüseyin Pasha was willing to consider it shows how desperate he was to consider any option that might secure his release from prison and his eventual ability to retain the disputed lands (not to mention the irony found in the Armenian leaders' willingness to collude with their pronounced "enemy" to secure votes for their candidate). In the end, Hüseyin Pasha and the other influential people in his tribe decided "to vote for no Armenian," as the Hamidiye chieftain confided to the British consul, "and to probably put up a Kurdish candidate for their own district."[137] This seems to have been Hüseyin Pasha's fourth strategy: he apparently did supply a candidate, who, along with those nominated by other tribes, were granted spots in the electoral college where they could elect a deputy who would work toward creating laws favorable to their interests.[138]

The "agrarian question" was intimately connected to larger issues facing the new regime and the various groups in the empire. However, while the resolution of the "agrarian question" was certainly related to political commitments made by members of the new regime, at the same time the manner in which the "agrarian question" was investigated and pushed toward resolution also prompted parties to act politically in their turn. Hüseyin Pasha and other Hamidiye chieftains now faced what they perceived as persecution by a new regime that sought to curb the vast privileges they had enjoyed while their patron, Zeki Pasha, was still in charge. The "agrarian question" may have only represented one part of the privileges they were now being asked to surrender, but it was nonetheless an extremely important one since it touched the livelihood that tribes in the process of settling were newly enjoying.

Hüseyin Pasha and others, while still attempting to conduct business in the ways they had previously practiced (through intimidation, threats, and bribery), now began to add political maneuvering to their list of strategies they could employ to protect their interests. Hüseyin Pasha was just one of several powerful tribal chiefs who put candidates up for election, and in so doing, acquiesced in a sense to participate in the new regime they opposed. At the same time, Hüseyin Pasha was also one of many influential Hamidiye chieftains who began to agitate politically by establishing and joining political associations whose members could form a coalition to protect their interests. The Kurdish clubs of the provinces were established by those individuals who had built up enormous stores of wealth and power thanks to the license accorded them under the previous regime, and who sought to protect this wealth and influence through almost any means at their disposal. The reasons for establishing and joining the provincial branches of the "Kurdish club" were many, but chief among them was the agrarian question, which spurred those affected to action. According to the British consul at Van, for example, the Kurdish club of that town had as its principal member Kurdish *agha*s of "bad character"—Hüseyin Pasha, Emin Pasha, Mustafa Bey, and Kop Mehmed Bey of the Hayderan tribe. He added that they and others feared "for their illicit gains under the new regime."[139] After interviewing a couple of Hamidiye chieftains in the Van vicinity, the consul reported that the Kurdish *agha*s who had joined the Van club had "no love for the new regime," which threatened their "despotic power as chiefs," and curtailed "their right of pillage." He submitted that the average tribesman, on the other hand, who had not profited much by the raids (as the "lion's share" always went to the *agha*, as he said) welcomed the constitution for the chance of freedom it would offer. However, he added, reports of the Armenians' wish to confiscate their land, to "interfere with their religion and harems," and to punish all the *agha*s had been "adroitly used by reactionary agents" to upset the tribesmen.[140]

In spite of Hüseyin Pasha's varied attempts to protest and circumvent the return of his lands to their rightful owners and to avoid prosecution, governors under the new regime forged ahead with their efforts to restore lands in his domains and elsewhere to their former owners. In December 1909, the *vali* of Erzurum traveled to Bayazid to look into the complaints filed against Hüseyin Pasha by Kurdish and Christian peasants.[141] The petitions against chieftains like Hüseyin Pasha continued to stream into governors' offices all over the region, and they remained busy conducting inquiries and attempting to restore lands for quite some time. In April 1910, for example, it was reported that "the minute" the new *vali* came to town he was encircled by some 150 dispossessed peasants of Çukur and was required to look into the immediate settlement of the land problem. The same report added that unanimous complaints were also being made by Armenian and Kurdish peasants in Muş against oppressive notables, Hamidiye officers, and other expropriators in Malazgird and Bulanık.[142]

In cases where government agents persisted in their efforts to investigate and resolve the agrarian question, a number of *agha*s whose lands had come under dispute and scrutiny tried other means to protect their interests. Hüseyin Pasha, who had just witnessed the arrest of numerous outlaws in Van province, was one who decided to flee into Iran with his people and herds in December 1909. In February 1910 the British ambassador reported that a number of Kurdish chiefs had anticipated government action against them and had escaped across the border. Hüseyin Pasha was thus joined in this act by many other Kurdish chieftains named in the report. However, once in Iran, Hüseyin Pasha sent a telegram to the sultan claiming that his flight was due to the persecutions he had received at the hands of the *vali* even though he had been guilty of no violence since the reinstatement of the constitution.[143] The consul continued, surmising that the true motive for his departure was the possibility of having to give up the lands he had stolen and of having to pay the government the arrears of taxes, which he had for some time been illegally collecting.[144] An additional reason for Hüseyin Pasha's border crossing may also have been that he intended to use it as a bargaining tool. He could not have been unaware that while the defection of chiefs would, as the British ambassador believed, facilitate the settlement of the Armenian lands question, he was also sensitive to the fact that it might embarrass the Ottoman government in other respects. The Armenians (ironically) were alarmed, fearing that it would leave them open to constant raids, and the Ottomans themselves were under the impression that many more Kurdish chiefs would follow Hüseyin Pasha's example. "By denuding the Turkish frontier of its protectors" they would eventually compel the government to seek a compromise by offering a general amnesty and a remission of all debts.[145] The politics of the borderlands—unique to the modern nation-state—were complicated indeed.

The government did seek such a compromise in the end. In just a few months the governor of Van began to ask the chiefs who had fled across the border to return. He told them that they would not be harassed if they came back, and added that they would have an additional period of grace before their lands were seized. With such an offer on the table,

Hüseyin Pasha, apparently finding that he had more to gain from returning than from staying in Iran, came back to Van and was accorded a big
welcome by the *vali* himself to the great dismay of many. According to the
French consul, "When the news that Hussein Pasha was returning came,
the Kurdish population, the *rayas* (peasantry) of Patnoz, Ziyaret, Mollah
Ibrahim, Kaynici and other villages sent protests against his return to
Tutak demanding the protection of the authorities. But one doubts that
such protection will really be effective, as the miserable situation of the
peasantry has only been improved in principle since the constitution [was
reenacted]."[146] Hüseyin Pasha was forced to take up residence in Van
upon his arrival in May. "The truth is," wrote the consul, "Hussein Pasha
fears that if he goes home, he'll be poorly received by the Armenians and
the Kurdish *rayas*, whom he has equally mistreated and exploited."[147]
Indeed, Kurdish peasants in some places were apparently in open revolt
against their landlords, refusing to work until their lands were restored.
Over six hundred petitions against Hüseyin Pasha and his associates
poured into the offices of the governor. When they heard he was about to
come back, the Kurdish peasants joined with their Armenian neighbors
who were arming themselves in preparation to protect themselves and
defend their properties.[148]

However, by June 1910 the British consul stated that

the alleged decision of the Government to compel Hussein Pasha of Patnotz and
his compeers to pay their arrears of taxes and to return their ill-gained possessions
to the rightful owners has not been carried out, nor is there now any question of
depriving these brigands of their rank and privileges, although these have long
ago been forfeited by failure to comply with the Government's exhortations to
return from Persia within a specified lapse of time. And no better indication of
the frame of mind of these chiefs (and of the Government) could be adduced than
the fact that, on their refusal to pay the sanitary dues leviable on their crossing
the Ottoman frontier, the authorities received a hint from head-quarters not to
press their claims.[149]

In 1910, then, all of the complexities surrounding the agrarian question
came to a head. In fact, a significant portion of consular correspondence
in 1910 was devoted solely to following the increasingly heated agrarian
question. It became clear to the government that they could not afford to
fully alienate the Kurdish chiefs, whom they considered powerful protectors of the borderlands, and who yielded great influence in their domains.
However different from the Hamidian regime the new rulers claimed to
be, their wider concerns were much the same and they engaged in a similar effort-bargain with these military and cultural brokers in their borderlands. Hüseyin Pasha may have been the first clear case where the
government had to at least partially abandon its efforts to return the

usurped lands, but it was not the last. In the general manner described in Chapter 3, the government continued for the next few years to grant concessions to prevent the alienation of such an influential group, which it feared would join forces and organize a revolt or would be seduced by the Russians. An interview of the British military representative in the Ottoman capital with a high-ranking CUP military officer added another layer to what the British consuls had suspected for some time, that is, that the Russians were intriguing among Kurdish chiefs. "The mere possibility of this," he wrote, "certainly makes it most difficult for the Turkish Government to alienate these Kurdish chiefs by redressing the Armenian grievances about their lands."[150]

But such fears were not the only reasons the agrarian question could not be resolved; there were other issues facing governors as well, namely the reality that they could not simply dispossess countless Kurds from lands on which they had settled, sometimes for decades, and which they had productively farmed. At the same time, they could not leave the Armenians (and other Kurdish peasants) completely without compensation. Then there was the matter of trying to determine who the rightful owners had been. After all, not all lands had been usurped outright; many had been taken over through legal means, or at least through fraudulent maneuvers that looked legal. Additionally, there seemed to be little uniformity in the manner and regions in which the Land Code was applied. It was a terribly knotty problem. In order for the reader to understand the depth of the complexities, it will be instructive to examine the correspondence of 1910 in more detail and to highlight the diverse facets of the agrarian question that emerged in the various reports.

May 1910 had been the month agreed upon by Kurdish and Armenian leaders in the province of Van for the return of the lands taken by Kurdish *agha*s from Armenian peasants. Hüseyin Pasha, as we have seen, crossed over into Iran shortly after the "Kurdo-Armenian Congress," which he had attended and whose decisions he had sworn to uphold. His flight to Iran signaled, however, his intentions to try any means possible to circumvent the agreement. More important, however, the conditions that led the government to not press so hard for the adjustment of the issue seemed to be the real problem for those who sought the restoration of their lands. After all, it was natural that Hüseyin Pasha and others did not want to return the properties that represented continued wealth.

Until 1910, it seemed that the process of land restoration had been yielding a good deal of satisfaction among many Armenians in several regions. However, although these successes continued, it became clear that instances of land restoration were increasingly few and far between, and that whatever gains materialized were being rapidly offset by numerous setbacks to the proceedings. First there was the matter of the "grandfather clause," which seems to have been enacted, or at least enforced, in the spring of 1910. According to the French consul, the unilateral orders for the administrative settlement (as opposed to the settlement in courts) of the agrarian question underwent a "change in mood" when the Council of State "abruptly" decreed that this only applied to lands seized before 1325 (1908–9), and that therefore current claims were not valid.[151] Soon after, it became evident that the administrative orders to return lands were increasingly abandoned in favor of sending petitioners to courts, which rarely seemed to offer rulings in their favor. In some cases, it was simply too difficult to prove ownership, due to the host of problems surrounding the title-deeds. But in other cases, even when petitioners had clear title-deeds indicating their rightful ownership of the disputed properties, the courts frequently continued to deny restitution to the deed holders, "in spite of protests of Armenian and Kurdish agricultural peasantry." Observers believed that "unwarrantable misdeeds [were] being committed by the local tribunals in [sic] behalf of the oppressive Kurdish chiefs."[152] Even in cases where peasants were allowed, as a result of either an administrative or a court order, to repossess their lands, they were unable to pay the compensation to the *agha*s and were therefore unable to reclaim their lands. The compensation had been something that even the Armenians had agreed was fair in principle (even though they felt that this reparation should come from the treasury, not from their own pockets),[153] but in many cases the peasants were simply unable to produce the necessary funds.

In some cases, peasants simply gave up. The British agent at Bitlis reported: "The Christians have ceased lately of addressing themselves to the local courts for agrarian disputes; they are almost sure to lose their case in the arbitrary proceedings of the courts."[154] The French consul concurred with his British colleague, adding that the peasants who had lost their lands were poorly received, and that they were afraid to testify against their *agha*s.[155] In other instances, they were intimidated into dropping their claims. This was the situation in Bitlis, where, as the British agent reported, "Some eight days ago a telegram from Hazzo (sanjak of Mush), addressed to the acting vali here, stated that one Armenian was killed there by Kurds for land disputes. . . . Five days ago one Kurd was killed in Shatak (kaza of Bitlis) by Kurds, again for the land disputes."[156] He continued in a later report, mentioning that "in consequences of the land disputes between Christians and Kurds in the sanjak of Sairt, anarchy is reported as prevailing in Khargan and Bervari (kazas of Sairt), where Moslem chiefs are killing Christians with a view to intimidate the latter and cease their protests."[157]

A few examples will illustrate these numerous problems surrounding the restoration of usurped lands. First is the case of villages in the Ergeni district of the Diyarbekir province, where the British agent there reported that two civil inspectors arrived to investigate the land question. Locals complained to him that "their activity was confined to interviewing local officials" and that they had no confidence that the mission would extend beyond these conversations. He then cited several specific instances in which owners with title-deeds to villages had been unable to obtain their possession. One specific case stood out as typical:

After the events of 1895, twelve Armenians of the village of Bashnik, in the caza of Silivan, pledged their lands to the late Seveddin Pasha and his cousin, Bedri Bey, in return for the restitution of looted property. In 1899 the legal formalities for the transfer of these lands to the names of Seveddin Pasha and Bedri Bey were carried out, notwithstanding the opposition of the owners. These lands are now occupied by Bedri Bey, and the sons of the late Seveddin Pasha. In addition, the gardens adjoining Bashnik village, to which Bedri Bey and the sons of Seveddin Pasha have no shadow of a legal claim, are at present occupied by their followers.

He concluded that "although some land cases have . . . been settled directly by the vali as an administrative measure ('iradeten'), the general policy of the Government has been to refer the complainants to the courts, which are as a rule incompetent and unwilling to deal with such cases."[158] Disputes in Çarsancak in the province of Harput (Ma'muret'ül-'Aziz) uncovered further complexities involving the restoration of usurped properties. According to the British agent there, the constitution had renewed the hopes of the peasantry that their lands, which had been seized by various *aghas* over the preceding decades, would be restored. So the peasantry continued to agitate for the return of their lands. In the fall of 1909, the peasants at Peri, the seat of Çarsancak, applied to the authorities for deeds to their lands, submitting a petition signed by thirteen hundred Christian and Muslim peasants. Although the *kaymakam* of Peri favored the petition and worked to bring the case to his superiors for settlement, the commission at Hozat had some difficulties determining which lands were registered and in whose name. The *vali*, to whom the findings were forwarded, told the villagers that their interests would be safeguarded, but at the same time he instructed the *kaymakam* to return only those lands whose original owners had title-deeds, and referred all other cases to the courts. The villagers protested but the question was nonetheless shelved. A few months later, when the heads of local Armenian communities, the principal *beys*, and ten villagers were invited to Mezre to discuss the matter, the commission was greeted by some five hundred villagers crying, "[ya] derdimize derman, [ya] katlimize ferman"—a remedy for our ills or an order for our death. The *vali* promised that the matter would be settled in a fair manner, but after the villagers departed, the administrative council told the *beys* and *aghas*, "'The land is yours, retain or evict the villagers.'" Indeed, after that, numerous peasants were expelled. These peasants then organized protests and strikes, in which they were joined by their neighbors. The orders nonetheless were upheld, although the *vali* predicted that he would eventually be able to return some lands to the peasants if he was able to exploit a complication in the deeds. After all, many of the disputed lands that were now claimed by the local *beys* and *aghas* had not been properly surveyed, and hence there were certain territories that would be up for distribution.[159]

In 1910, then, it became clear that the numerous complexities surrounding the agrarian question were proving to be overwhelming and were causing a good deal of inertia in the process. The agreement made by the Kurdish and Armenian leaders in 1909, "from which so much was hoped at the time," was suspected of being "a grand farce" already by the spring of 1910.[160] By the end of the year it was clear that even where government officials were doing their best to bring about a just resolution to the ongoing matter, there was more talk than action. This was made most clear in the report on the *vali* of Bitlis, who, upon taking up his post there in 1910, addressed the Armenians and Kurds assembled in connection with the agrarian question in the *nahiye* of Çukur, telling "them in a violent language that 'he would sacrifice himself as a "fedai" in defence of the rights of the peasantry, and that he would blow up with dynamite usurpers and oppressors like Hajhi Nedjmeddine Effendi of Bitlis.'"[161] Due to the overwhelming problems surrounding this complicated issue, one of which seemed to be the *vali*'s inability to find support from the central government to deal with the matter as he saw fit, it was soon clear that he was not going to do anything of significance to settle the matter.[162]

The unproductive manner in which the agrarian question's resolution proceeded stemmed partially from the complications surrounding proof of actual ownership and the means to compensate those whose lands were being repossessed, but also from the government's inability or unwillingness to commit to a full resolution of the problem for other reasons. These factors were intimately tied to the new "Kurdish policy" the constitutional regime was in the process of elaborating.

Although it may not have been evident from the first days of the constitutional regime, the agrarian question rapidly became intertwined with the government's attempts to work out a "Kurdish policy." The main goals of the central administration with regard to its Kurdish population, particularly the nomadic tribes, was to ottomanize (or indeed turkify) and control them using a variety of means. A general military conscription that extended beyond the Hamidiye tribes was one tactic; education was another. Expeditions against those Kurds who refused to submit to the orders of the new regime were also widely carried out. Here, the central government was trying to make it absolutely clear that it alone possessed the monopoly on violence, and it would seek to discipline and punish those who refused to recognize the new order. These were general measures, but there were also other ways in which the question of landholding figured into the new balance the central government was trying to work out between the state and the Kurds in the tribal zone.

An important goal of the new regime was to break the power of leading tribal chiefs, many of whom had built extensive networks of influence through their Hamidiye connections. But much of the wealth and authoritative power that these Hamidiye (and other) chieftains enjoyed was now based on their landholdings, many of which had been usurped from Kurdish and Armenian peasants outright, or which had been acquired through other legal or fraudulent means. To repossess the lands from these chiefs would be to take away much of the power that was associated with ownership. Such measures would additionally demonstrate to the population that it was the government that held ultimate power, not the tribal chiefs. However, the policy extended further than this. In fact, not only did the government want to break the power of the tribal chiefs by taking away their land, but it also hoped to settle the tribespeople of these powerful tribes and to make each tribesman a farmer with a small holding of his own, a plan not unlike the one envisioned by the previous regime. This would serve as a way to fracture the authority of the chiefs by robbing them of their means to control the wealth in their regions. This was the plan of the *vali* of Van, as reported in 1910 by the British consul, who apparently admired the *vali*'s initiatives:

> The vali has an idea . . . that the Kurd tribesmen, removed from the feudal authority of their chiefs, will prove peaceable and useful subjects. He says that under the old régime, the chief of a tribe held all the land of the tribe and the tribesmen might be considered his slaves. He was their sole court of appeal and they knew no other authority. He now wishes, if possible, to make each Kurd tribesman a proprietor and to encourage him to rely more and more on the Government authorities for protection and justice. By this means the power of the chiefs which was always evil, will be broken, as they will find themselves without followers.[163]

The policy was also connected with the settlement of tribes, which was strongly desired by the new regime. The government even allocated sufficient "empty" land in these districts for the tribes to colonize.[164] It was further associated with the government's wish to plant Muslim Circassian immigrants in the region.[165]

In order to give lands to Kurdish tribesmen and Circassian immigrants, the desired result of which would be their permanent settlement and their "national" self-identification as Ottomans rather than as members of a tribe, the government could not, then, afford to follow through fully with its measures to restore lands to Kurdish and Armenian peasants who claimed them; in fact, as we shall see below, in some cases the government took it upon itself to seize the lands for distribution to the nomads and immigrants.

At the same time, even in the midst of efforts to make some restitution to peasants, these measures caused an enormous strain on relationships among communities in the region. Reports from all over the six *vilayet*s pointed to rising tensions between Armenians and Kurds over the land question. The British ambassador called the relations between the two communities "cold," stating that the land question continued to be "the one absorbing problem."[166] Commenting on his recent tour of the region in the fall of 1911, the British agent also reported on his tour through "Vostan, Mush, Kighi, Peri, Erzingan, Chemishgezek, Khozat, and Kharput. In almost all the districts where Armenians were to be found the still unsettled land question was a source of much complaint and bad relations between the Armenians and Kurds."[167] Of course, even though the conflicts between Armenians and Kurds received the most press, there were also numerous disputes between Kurdish peasants and Kurdish *agha*s over land.[168] Emergent ethnic identities began to take shape during the process of conflict.

Kurdish-Armenian (or Muslim-Christian) relations would spiral downhill—in good measure because of these land conflicts. But relations between Armenians and Kurds, and peasants in general and the *agha*s from whom they claimed land, were not the only ones that were tense. A mounting hostility also was forming between the government and those Kurdish chiefs whose lands were the target of repossession. The chiefs' discontent increased until the government feared it would face a serious rebellion. Powerful Hamidiye chieftains like Hüseyin Pasha corresponded with other influential Kurdish chiefs like Haci Musa Bey of Muş about joining forces to rebel against the government that was threatening their privileged status, attempting to take away the material basis for their power.[169] These *agha*s were intimidated by the numerous actions the new government had taken to conscript them, make them pay taxes, put a check on the benefits they had enjoyed as Hamidiye chieftains, and remove other privileges they had amassed and enjoyed under the previous regime. But key among the complaints was their fear that the material basis for their influence—the vast holdings of land they had acquired over the course of two or three decades—was in jeopardy. Additionally, it was not only the power they derived from holding such lands that was at stake, but many of them had made significant investments in these territories. As the British consul later pointed out, Hüseyin Pasha's case was complicated, for even though he had seized numerous properties—dozens of villages, in fact—from Kurdish and Armenian peasants, he had invested a good deal in them. Indeed, the British consul wrote that Hüseyin Pasha, "in spite of his past misdeeds," was a rather progressive landowner for the region, having carried out certain improvements in his villages. Patnos, he said, "though a squalid enough place," compared well with any outlying Kurdish or Armenian village he had seen. He described it as having a mosque, a school, a number of shops, and two or three decent houses "amongst the warren of squalid hovels which make up a village in this district."[170] And lastly, due to the fact that a growing amount of land was being snatched up as private, the amount of grazing land to which nomads had access seems also to have been diminishing.

Hence, although the government's fears of a full-blown "Kurdish movement" were a bit premature, as the level of organization required for such a rebellion had not been achieved, the fact that the danger was at least somewhat real prompted the central government to drop the demands it had placed on the Kurdish chieftains. At this precarious moment in their history, when they felt external threats endangering their territorial sovereignty, government officials and Ottoman intellectuals urged all parties to handle "the Kurds" with care, so that Kurdistan would not become another "Albania," as many feared.

The agrarian question figured prominently in this equation. Writers in the popular Ottoman press urged Armenians to be careful as they advanced their claims and warned them of the dangers of pressing too hard. They urged Armenians not to act rashly and to employ more careful language when speaking of their "usurpers." In the *Tanin*, for example, one writer submitted that "even when speaking of usurpers, too great freedom must not be used. Because otherwise the principal people in the country will say to themselves 'this new Government will sooner or later take its vengeance and destroy us,' and, becoming scared, will naturally be the cause of disastrous events."[171] They counseled the Armenians to be patient, saying that the agrarian question would eventually be settled, but that for now it was best not to alienate the Kurdish *aghas*.[172]

Members of the government also thought it unwise to estrange this powerful element, and began taking measures to alleviate their concerns and appease them in a manner not unlike that of their predecessors under Sultan Abdülhamid II. Since many of the grievances the Kurdish *aghas* held stemmed from the government's attempts to resolve the agrarian question by depriving the *aghas* of the lands they had acquired, many of the steps taken to appease these *aghas* also involved land. Such a policy was already evident in the welcome that Hüseyin Pasha received upon returning from Iran. The

British agent found it was not difficult to believe that the stance of the government vis-à-vis the Kurds was weakening. He averred that evidence for this claim was "afforded by the virtual capitulation of the authorities to the fugitive Kurdish chiefs," who had returned to Ottoman territory as "honoured guests."[173] But Hüseyin Pasha was not the only influential Kurdish chieftain whom the government thought it best not to disaffect by pressing too hard for the return of their lands. Numerous reports of this trend as a general policy streamed in from all over the region. By 1911, the British consul felt that the government's policy regarding the agrarian question tended toward an intimate understanding between the Kurdish chieftains and the government, "at the expense of the Armenians."[174] By 1912, it was reported that the CUP agents had promised Kurds that the lands and villages that they had usurped from Christians would not, in the end, be returned.[175] Of course, it was not coincidental that such promises were being made in the midst of heated elections. Such guarantees made to powerful Kurdish chiefs, who could gather numerous votes, were not inconsequential.[176]

The agrarian question was thus intimately tied to the government's attempts to control the Kurdish chiefs and at the same time to guarantee their support at a precarious moment when the empire's territorial integrity was being threatened. The Kurds were viewed as a group that could potentially ally themselves with the Russians, could cross over to Iran, or could simply cause problems through an internal rebellion. A process unfolded whereby Kurds became "marked" citizens, not just plain Ottomans. They were constructed as a group that needed to prove their loyalty (although they certainly were involved in that construction). Yet some officials decided to bypass that step and merely made it in their interest to remain loyal. This occurred at the greater expense not only of the lives and livelihoods of its Armenian citizens as well as subordinate Kurdish groups but also at the expense of the state's own sovereignty and international image. The agrarian question also played a role in the struggles between political groups, as each sought to advance itself by gathering support for its party in exchange for promises related to land. This often created unlikely bedfellows, as when Hüseyin Pasha and other Hamidiye chieftains entered into an alliance, albeit one that was short-lived, with Dashnaktsutiun leaders in the elections of 1908, and it again played a part of the politics in the election of 1912.

CONCLUSION

One goal of this chapter has been to explain some of the violence that plagued the eastern Ottoman borderlands during the years under review.

As far as the Armenian massacres are concerned, few accounts to date have attempted to clarify what the violence was about, instead relying on the assumption that violence by Muslims against Christians was normal and expected, if not intrinsic. In reality, there were other factors at play. Concrete material gains were at stake; violent offenders often had economic motives for their deeds, and were not merely acting out perennial ethnic hatred. Having said that, we note that the very violence that did take place worked to "transform people's sense of self, community, and history."[177] In other words, the violence that occurred and the new identities that began to crystallize as a result of these events "transformed the existing situation and created a new mode of historical action that was not intrinsically part of that situation."[178] What started out as a conflict over resources was ethnicized during the unfolding of the conflict itself as memories of what "they" did to "us" or fears of what "they" will do to "us" took shape.[179] We should not take the ethnicity in ethnic conflict as sui generis; as Mann puts it, "If ethnic groups do become more homogenous as conflict escalates, this is precisely what we must explain."[180]

Violence did not start with the creation of the Hamidiye, nor did it end when the militia was finally disbanded. At the same time, the land-grabbing that was associated with some of this violence did not commence with the Hamidiye and nor did it cease after the Hamidiye was finally dispersed. However, the Hamidiye remains an important part of a longer development of new and modern property relations in the Ottoman Empire. Members of this tribal militia played a significant role in the land-grab that was part of this process because they were allowed a special advantage in the race to acquire resources by the unlimited support they received from the state, which, for its own reasons decided to engage in this effort-bargain with select Kurdish chiefs. The land-grabbing phenomenon and its associated violence was a significant aspect of the social and political dynamics of Kurdish society at the turn of the twentieth century, and it clearly impacted the changing nature of power in the Kurdish- and Armenian-inhabited Ottoman tribal zone. The wider background of land-grabbing, violence, and emergent ethnic conflict came to play an important role in the Armenian genocide that occurred during the First World War, and indeed has much to do with shaping Turkish-Kurdish relations to the present day.

CHAPTER FIVE

The Hamidiye and Its Legacy

★

THE FIRST WORLD WAR AND THE PEACE SETTLEMENT

If the Hamidiye Light Cavalry had not already made enough of a name for itself in the preceding two and a half decades, the organization certainly gained a good deal of repute, albeit ill, for its activities in the First World War. This is because of the close link many observers and later scholars have drawn between the Kurdish militia and the Armenian genocide. The Tribal Light Cavalry was reconstituted as Reserve Cavalry Regiments and put under the command of the regular army.[1] Little is known about the participation of these regiments in the First World War, although it can be stated that some regiments were employed in different theaters of battle during the war, albeit mostly in eastern Anatolia on the Russian front.[2] The Mîran tribe, for example, served there and was deployed as far away as Bulgaria.[3] Most, however, seem to have been based in Hınıs, Eleşgirt, Erciş, Viranşehir, or the Van region.[4] One eyewitness noted that the Hamidiye units—with their broken rifles—were dispatched against the far superior Russian forces, against whom, not surprisingly, many lost their lives.[5]

The Kurdish militia also played a role during the war in the Ottoman operations against the Armenians.[6] Armenians in Russian service were wreaking vengeance upon the Kurdish population that had caused them so much grief over the years, and Russian forces had initiated "ethnic cleansing" operations around Bayazid and Eleşgirt, which certainly prompted Kurdish militia members and others to participate in the massacres of

Armenians that were part of the Armenian genocide. McDowall has also suggested that "the Kurds were constantly reminded of their own potential weakness and vulnerability by the connections their Christian neighbours enjoyed with the hostile European powers. It is no accident that the atrocities were worse the further east one went, where the Russian danger was the greatest, and those areas where tribes gave protection to Armenians were well away from the battlegrounds. In short, most Kurds involved in the massacres probably felt it was a question of 'them or us.'"[7] Nuri Dersimi wrote that Armenians were telling Kurds, "Hey Kurds, wherever you may go you will never be safe from us."[8] Many Kurds nurtured a longstanding fear—probably going back to 1895–96, when there were rumors that the Europeans would assist the Armenians in establishing their own *"beylik"* in Kurdistan[9]—that their region was about to become an independent Armenia. Some Kurds might have acquiesced to commit such acts of violence against their Armenian neighbors because they feared what would happen to their lands if the Armenians once again took possession of them. The Armenian nationalist discourse that spoke of Armenian independence and a "Greater Armenia" compelled many Kurds to believe what was voiced by the Kurdish poet Hacî Qadirê Koyî: "I swear by the Koran, all sense of honour is gone. Should there be an Armenistan, no Kurds would be left."[10] The agrarian question was still burning at the outbreak of the war, contributing to a general decline in friendly relations between Kurds and Armenians. Additionally, with Armenians no longer on their lands because they had been either deported or killed, Kurdish tribal chiefs would not only be able to keep the disputed lands but would actually gain more of them. This was especially clear after the chiefs were formally permitted, in 1915, to occupy "abandoned" Armenian property.[11] Although the Armenian genocide is not a focus of this book, the Hamidiye Light Cavalry and particularly its land-grabbing activities are certainly important parts of that story, and my study hopefully contributes to our attempts to better understand the nuances of genocide—particularly the motivations of perpetrators beyond state orders or ethnic or sectarian factors. We have seen that Hamidiye members simply ignored state orders when to collaborate with Armenians served their interests better, but did not hesitate to use their state backing, or indeed use the pretext of Armenian revolutionary activity, when they could profit from them instead.

A number of Kurdish tribes fought in service of the Ottomans, then, but there were others who were now fully disillusioned with the state and attempted to enter into a sort of alliance with Russia (or who responded to Russian overtures). In doing so they hoped to win freedom from the Ottomans, perhaps in the form of an independent Kurdistan, although this group was admittedly rather small. The nationalist movement that developed during the war was a strange mix of Kurdish figures: the Bedir Khans, who had long promoted nationalism, and their former foes, a group that included former Hamidiye chieftains like Hüseyin Pasha, who opted to hedge their bets elsewhere.[12] During the postwar period, however, a Kurdish nationalist movement truly blossomed, as different segments of Kurdish society looked for ways to chart out their future. Nationalism was not the course sought by all or even most at the time, but it did become an increasingly significant movement for a growing segment of Kurdish society, beginning in 1918 with the end of the war.

A direct link has often been posed in the literature between the Kurdish clubs of the Second Constitutional Period and the Kurdish nationalist organizations that formed after the war, but the connection is not as clear as has often been suggested. As we saw in Chapter 3, there was a distinct difference between the main Istanbul club and the provincial "Kurdish clubs" during the first part of CUP rule. Members joined the provincial branches, not so much because they espoused Kurdish nationalism as an ideology, but because they were attempting to protect the privileges they had enjoyed under the previous regime and joined organizations they believed might help them do so. This was in contradistinction to the Istanbul club, whose members, largely comprised of Kurdish intellectuals and educated notables, were familiar with the ideology that was becoming increasingly meaningful to Ottomans of various backgrounds: nationalism. It should be clarified, then, that the postwar Kurdish organizations and the programs and journals they founded are perhaps more directly related to their precursor in Istanbul and not to any provincial branches, and it should also be pointed out that many who espoused nationalism in the late-Ottoman period saw no irony in declaring themselves to be simultaneously Ottoman and Kurdish—they did not, in other words, have separatist inclinations.[13] Having said this, significant changes were underway during the postwar period, when Kurdish nationalist organizations were not simply continuing in the footsteps of the clubs that had existed before the war but were increasingly based on the realization, prompted largely by the declaration of Woodrow Wilson's Fourteen Points, that nationalism was becoming the language of legitimacy, the idiom through which various social and political battles would be fought. Membership in the nascent Kurdish nationalist movement was itself varied, however, and included diverse members of the Kurdish elite.

The Greek invasion of Anatolia in 1919, however, put a temporary damper on the Kurdish nationalist movement. The Ottoman Empire was being invaded, and many Kurds, like other Ottoman nationals, felt more patriotic. In many cases, this loyalty was elicited by the figure now increasingly viewed as a national leader, Mustafa Kemal Pasha, who sought alliances with Kurdish figures and brokered deals with them that were designed to alleviate any fears the latter had about the emerging republic. Numerous Kurdish leaders provided assistance to Mustafa Kemal's forces during the war, including some Tribal Light Cavalry regiments.[14] For some, the incentive may have been patriotic,[15] but for others, as Olson has pointed out, the change of attitude was because they predicted that they would need the support of Mustafa Kemal and his government to be able to claim the disputed lands and the newly usurped Armenian lands.[16] Others believed that it was the key to securing certain demands, like assurances that Kurds would be able to have a say over the nature of the new state's rule over the Kurdish-populated regions. At the same time, however, other Kurds engaged in anti-Kemalist propaganda and began to promote a Kurdish nationalism that was now separatist, a new direction in the larger picture of Kurdish identity politics. The former Hamidiye chieftain, Halit Bey of the Cibran tribe, who had also fought for the Kemalists until 1918, was an important figure in this development.[17]

While a variety of responses to the war and the subsequent Turkish War of Independence manifested themselves among various segments of Kurdish society, equally mixed were the feelings of the emerging leadership of the Turkish independence movement regarding the new "Kurdish question." Kâzım Karabekir's series of reports on the "Kurdish question," penned in 1920, reveal this ambivalence. They also help us to better understand the politics involved in the decision over whether or not to make use of the Kurds in the Turkish military, and under what conditions. There were debates in the newly created Turkish Grand National Assembly (Türk Büyük Millet Meclisi; TBMM) over what to do with the tribal military organizations, with some in favor of retaining them and others in favor of abolishing them. Karabekir was one who was staunchly against incorporating the Kurds into the military under any circumstances, at least until government institutions and control, as well as modern infrastructure, could take root in Kurdistan. Karabekir believed that arming the Kurds was dangerous, and was convinced that the actions of some (i.e., taking up arms against the government or offering assistance to enemy forces) spoke for the intentions of *all* Kurds. Therefore, he concluded, incorporating the Kurds into the military in *any* manner would be a hazard to both domestic and foreign policy as well as for the "moral and material" well-being of the country.[18] His discourse echoed that of the debates that surfaced in the early years of the Hamidiye's formation. Indeed, the parameters of these debates persisted well into republican years and arguably still exist in some form today.

The ambivalence of the Turkish military and political leadership toward the Kurds would continue to be a feature of the government's emerging Kurdish policy. Like the Ottoman leaders from whose tradition they came, they viewed the Kurds as a backward and potentially treacherous element that needed to be modernized, and, now with the issue of nationalism taking prominence, to be severed from their Kurdish identities and turkified. In truth, these policies would be codified as law after the creation of the republic, but as far as the tribal militia was concerned, the ambivalence with which Karabekir's reports regarded the "Kurdish question" would persist as a prominent feature of the government's Kurdish policy. Although Karabekir and others spoke out against incorporating the tribal Kurds into the military, what was left of the Tribal Cavalry would indeed be employed in various theaters of battle for at least a decade to follow. Like their Ottoman counterparts, the Turkish state weighed its "threats" and attempted to neutralize one segment of these hostile elements by handing them weapons and authority so that they could be transformed into an arm of state power in this vast, remote, and largely inaccessible borderlands region. This calculation produced disturbing consequences as it played out from the 1980s to the present with the creation of the Village Guards, who were supposed to combat PKK (the Kurdish acronym for Partîya Karkerên Kurdistan, or the Workers' Party of Kurdistan) operations in southeastern Turkey but who have in many ways undermined the very state authority they were intended to represent. The Hamidiye Light Cavalry was an important part of the larger story of the effort-bargain made between the Ottoman, then Turkish, state and its Kurdish population. It serves as a major link between the dismantled empire and its main successor state and represents dynamics that continue to play out today.

After independence was achieved, the new leadership of the Turkish republic soon began overtly to promote a series of policies that resulted in the alienation of a large segment of the Kurdish population. Until the Turkish republic was declared, Mustafa Kemal had emphasized Turkish-Kurdish and Muslim unity in his various communications with the Kurds, even if privately high-ranking figures such as Karabekir spoke otherwise. However, this public discourse soon changed. The elections for the new Grand National Assembly in 1923 revealed that the government would not allow Kurds to field the candidates of their choice. Most appointments in the Kurdish regions were filled by Turks. There could no longer be any official reference to "Kurdistan," and Kurdish place names were replaced with Turkish ones. In 1924, the Kurdish language was officially banned, and finally, the last bond holding the Kurds and Turks together—the caliphate—was abolished.[19]

In response to these measures, Kurdish opposition to the new regime became increasingly widespread as a popular movement. These developments helped change the social composition of Kurdish nationalist organization that had been founded in 1921, Azadî, whose members had until then included mostly educated notables. Now it had little trouble attracting adherents from broader segments of Kurdish society, especially through the networks of religious orders throughout Kurdistan. In 1924, the leadership of Azadî, which included some prominent former Hamidiye chiefs, began to plan the uprising known now as the Sheikh Said rebellion. Although the government caught wind of the plans and were able to arrest several ringleaders before the uprising took place, the rebellion nonetheless occurred the following spring.[20] The revolt failed for numerous reasons, and the aftermath was brutal for Kurds of the regions involved. And soon, the state's repressive policies extended to Kurds who had not even participated in the rebellion and may even have assisted the government in suppressing it.[21] Huge numbers of Kurds were deported from the region and several massacres were reported. But perhaps due to a desire to clean up its reputation abroad, in 1928 the Turkish state began to allow some Kurds to return home and promised to restore land to their former *agha*s. These measures were, at the same time, accompanied by new turkification initiatives.

In response, a new Kurdish political organization called Xoybûn emerged from among exiled Kurdish dissidents,[22] a group that included some former Hamidiye commanders as well as some *aghas*. The latter had, until the deportations of the *agha* class, been loyal to the Kemalist regime. Hüseyin Pasha Hayderanî fit both bills: the former Hamidiye commander had assisted with the suppression of the Sheikh Said revolt, but was nonetheless not spared from deportation.[23] Indeed the head of the Ağrı Dağ (Ararat) revolt, İhsan Nuri Pasha, had supported the Kemalists until 1924, when their policies regarding the Kurds alienated him along with many others.[24] The leadership of Xoybûn soon gathered forces to bring about the famous revolt of Ağrı Dağ, a rebellion that aimed to establish an independent Kurdistan. Like the previous revolts, however, this rebellion was crushed. It would be the last major revolt until the events of Dersim in the mid-1930s.

Robert Olson has drawn the connection between the Hamidiye and the Kurdish nationalist movement of this period. He has argued that the Hamidiye regiments must be seen as "an important stage in the emergence of Kurdish nationalism from 1891 to 1914, serving as a fulcrum of Kurdish power for over two decades."[25] According to Olson, Kurdish tribesmen became acquainted with ideas of nationalism through their service in the tribal militia, which made them travel outside their immediate domains, and through their contact with fellow Turkish and Arab officers, who were familiar with ideas of nationalism. He also suggests that the education of Hamidiye chiefs' children in Tribal Schools exposed them to new ideas, which included nationalism. "The Hamidiye," he argues, "gave an opportunity for Kurds to experience and fathom the wider world."[26] Olson's point is certainly well-taken, but I would suggest a different take on the link of the former Hamidiye chieftains to the emergent nationalist movement. They were not actually widely traveled, as Olson suggests, and could not have embraced nationalism—if and when they did—because of their exposure to the wider world, as few actually enjoyed this experience. Instead, a number of Hamidiye chieftains had seen the vast privileges they had enjoyed under Sultan Abdülhamid II gradually eroded, or at least threatened, under the regime that followed. Disgruntled, they began to engage in opposition movements, some of which were ostensibly national-ist. Yet the Hamidiye chiefs and other influential Kurdish figures were not only upset by the threats they faced with regard to the property they had acquired, as well as by the challenges to their traditional and newfound freedoms, but they also simply felt the state ignored them when it came to funding the latest improvements in communications and education from which they, too, hoped to benefit.

Hüseyin Pasha expressed this mix of complaints to the British agent at Van already in 1914. Commenting on his lengthy meeting with the militia chieftain, Consul Smith recounted how Hüseyin Pasha regretted the pass-ing of the old regime, not because the Armenians found new freedom, but rather because he was made to surrender several villages without adequate recompense and because he had made a considerable number of improve-ments, funded out of his own pocket, which were not remunerated. He fur-ther complained of the reorganization of the Hamidiye cavalry, whereby the numbers were reduced, several regiments were merged into one, and their former privileges were much curtailed. Although these reforms were indeed a dead letter, the chiefs were unwilling to relinquish control over their own regiments, which were combined and in many cases overseen by Turkish officers. The Kurds, he further explained, were also much an-gered by the government's recent military operation against the Sheikh of Şemdînan. In fact, the recent outbreak of typhus among the Turkish troops nearby was believed by many Kurds to be some sort of divine retribution for this expedition against their sheikh, and they were just waiting for the *vali* himself to be struck with paralysis. However, while these may have been the usual complaints, Hüseyin Pasha further added that he (and the Kurds in general) blamed the government for the backward state of the province. Comparing the state of Ottoman Kurdistan with the "flourish-ing" condition of the provinces in the Russian Caucasus, he described his homeland as "bare and empty" and complained that the government did nothing for the welfare of the Kurds. He said that the Armenians had European advocates but the Kurds had no sponsors and felt that the only path open to them was to come together under a Kurdish leader. Interestingly, Hüseyin Pasha seemed to welcome European inspectors to the region but feared that they would end up taking more lands away from the Kurds and giving them to the Armenians and that the Kurds would be turned out of their homes with no compensation. Lastly, the bonds of loyalty and privilege Kurds enjoyed under Sultan Abdülhamid II had faded away under the new regime, and on the brink of war, they were convinced that since the Young Turk regime could not hold the empire together, they should take their fate into their own hands.[27]

Thus, some members of the Hamidiye indeed did join forces with new Kurdish nationalists, but not so much, as Olson suggests, because they had been exposed to new ideas while in service to the Ottoman state. After all, until the second decade of the twentieth century few Hamidiye tribesmen were even employed as troops, their voyages to Istanbul undertaken in the recruiting process were short-lived, and very few seem to have been enrolled in military schools. Rather, they joined because their wealth and power was threatened and because in all likelihood they thought that they would flourish better in an autonomous or independent setting. At this point, with the exception of a few ideologues, the motivation was largely political and economic rather than ideological. Of course after the leadership of the new republic had severed the last remaining link—a shared religious identity—and instituted more aggressive turkification and deportation programs, the movement did become increasingly ideological for many Kurds. But the fact remains that Kurdish nationalism during this period truly began as part of a power struggle and as a movement of resistance to centralizing reforms and challenges to the strengthened tribal system that the Hamidiye Light Cavalry institution had encouraged under Sultan Abdülhamid II. All of these factors combined, then, prompted some former Hamidiye chieftains and other Kurds to join the Sheikh Said rebellion and—for those who were not captured and executed by the new government following the rebellion or subject to the deportation policy—to maintain resistance, as in the case of the Ağrı Dağ revolt, against the state.

The Tribal Light Cavalry formally disappeared as an institution some time after the First World War and the Turkish War of Independence, although an exact date for the end to this institution is difficult to ascertain. After the outbreak of the First World War, the different Light Cavalry tribes went their separate ways. There is evidence that some Tribal Light Cavalry regiments remained allied to the state and were used, in part, to suppress the aforementioned rebellions well into the republican period.[28] One source claims that families of former Hamidiye chieftains who did not participate in any rebellion of the early republican period continued to draw their pensions until the 1950s, when the last immediate relatives died.[29]

THE VILLAGE GUARDS

While the Kurdish tribal militia seems to have formally ceased to exist in the republican period—even though some units were called to suppress the revolt at Ağrı Dağ—a similar institution was created in the form of what is now known as the Village Guards. The Village Statute, written in 1924–25, provided for village guards to protect and defend villages.[30] The system seems to have been created in response to the Azadî movement and the events leading up to the Sheikh Said rebellion, and there is evidence that efforts were made to add to the numbers of the group after subsequent rebellions, notably the revolt at Ağrı Dağ.[31] There is little information on this early republican institution, but it appears to have been an important reflection of the Turkish government's ongoing efforts to address the dual aim of finding a means to suppress local rebellions and inducing local elements to remain loyal to the state by providing them with official positions, arms, and a salary. Its significance also becomes clear in retrospect when we consider it in the context of the legacy of the Hamidiye and also as a precedent for the more recent Village Guards organization.

In 1984 a new rebellion brewing in the Kurdish regions of Turkey erupted into an armed uprising, which would be waged for over two decades. The PKK, which had formed several years earlier, now gained enough membership and strength to carry on armed operations against government and military targets in Turkey.[32] This new domestic security challenge was perhaps the first in six decades that threatened Turkey's territorial integrity. In response, already in October 1984, Prime Minister Turgut Özal announced that "in addition to the security forces, citizens, too, want to intervene against those who disrupt peace and tranquility in the villages, adding that under an existing law, the *mukhtar*s, the councils of elders, and village guards can be given police powers."[33] Within six months, the Turkish Grand National Assembly approved a bill allowing for the creation of a new system of temporary village guards (*geçici köy korucuları*).[34] The Village Statute of 1924–25 was amended to provide for this organization. A precedent for such an organization had existed in the early republic (described above), and indeed a very contemporary parallel appeared just across the border in Iraq, in the form of the *fursan* units—Kurdish tribes in the employ of the state to serve in the war with Iran and also to operate against antistate Kurdish tribes.[35] However, it soon became clear that it was the Hamidiye Light Cavalry that served as the model and precedent most accessible in the minds not only of the creators but also of the observers. Indeed, journalists made a ready connection, and a new interest in the original militia sparked a few scholarly articles devoted to the Hamidiye, for now it became not only an institution of the past but a contemporary reality.[36]

There are certainly differences between the two organizations, and most of the popular and academic articles treating the subject have drawn points of comparison largely on superficial terms.[37] But the similarities between the organizations are indeed plentiful, and moreover are suggestive of important aspects of historical continuity, particularly with regard to the relationships between the state and Kurdish tribal and nontribal populations, and also concerning the power dynamics within Kurdish society. Although the Hamidiye Light Cavalry resided in a more distant past, it shared in many of the dynamics of the present-day militia conflicts. Some of the key points in common include the nature of violence, challenges to state authority and security, damage to the state's international reputation, and the overall sense that the state had created a monster it could no longer control. In both cases the state harnessed on-the-ground conflicts to its own ends, exacerbated the violent nature of these conflicts, and, counter to its intentions, formed even greater threats to its own authority, security, and reputation. And in both conflicts the state was left with the dilemma of how to disband the militia forces without generating an even greater problem. In the case of today's Village Guards, the Turkish state cannot dismantle the militia until it creates an alternative source of income for the tens of thousands of guards who have no other means of making a living in the war-torn region of Kurdistan.[38] Both cases reside within the history of the larger Middle East, and the Kurdish region in particular. But an understanding of these dynamics can help to unpack other historical and ongoing conflicts elsewhere in the globe—such as the one in Darfur, which shares similar dynamics—and perhaps also to contribute to their resolution.

CONCLUSION

Although they might not have realized it at the time, the journey to the capital made by the Kurdish chiefs in 1891 would end up having a significant impact on the history of the Ottoman Empire in its final years, and indeed, to a certain extent, on the histories of at least two of its successor states, mainly Turkey but also Iraq. At once anxious and excited at the honor of meeting with their sultan and caliph, the chieftains may have known that their own lives would change somehow after this momentous event; but they could not have fathomed at the time the larger part the Hamidiye organization would play in the transformation of the power structure to which they belonged and of the wider society in which they lived, and in the state-society relations that continued to unfold in the empire's successor states.

It appears that most states are confronted with various threats to their territorial integrity and to their monopoly on violence, authority, and power. And while it may seem ironic that one remedy for these threats is to empower a group that ultimately undermines the state's bid for authority, many states have continued to make these effort-bargains with often criminal groups to the detriment of their own sovereignty, international image, and especially the security of their citizens. These kinds of effort-bargains have appeared across centuries past, but the arrangement worked out with the Hamidiye in the Kurdish-Ottoman tribal zone was born from and played out under distinctly modern conditions. Their story sheds light on numerous contradictions in modern statecraft.

The setting was the "tribal zone," the "edge of empire," the threatened borderlands that were a sort of "nonstate space" that the state needed to neutralize and incorporate. The condition of locals frequently residing beyond the grasp of the state's administrative and authoritative power—as Giddens might say—was exacerbated under these uniquely modern circumstances. Threats from the outside mounted, and states were in the process of delimiting their borders and demanding not just tribute but *loyalty* to the nation-state-in-the-making. As such, internal threats appeared to be just as menacing as those that loomed from across the border. In its attempts to manage one of these threats—that of Armenian nationalism and revolutionary activity, which had sometimes clear and sometimes assumed support from outside—the Ottoman state opted to draft another suspect group into its orbit and harnessed an on-the-ground conflict over local power and resources to its own ends.

Select Kurdish tribal chiefs played a key role as military and cultural brokers in this process. But they were also agents in the affair and used their state backing to prosecute their own bids for local hegemony; as such, the state's "blueprints" for the project often had unintended results. These *aghas* deftly engaged with the "public transcript" of power and used various platforms and media to manipulate the state's biggest fears to their own advantage. They read and used the catchwords of this transcript to perform acts of deference and speak words of loyalty that magnified the Armenian threat and, hence, their own importance to the state. Along with the support of Zeki Pasha, these militia chiefs worked to turn the state's discourse on their activities into one of sanction and approval. This study has attempted to read beyond and analyze these performances, for, as Scott suggests, "the public transcript, where it is not positively misleading, is unlikely to tell the whole story about power relations. It is frequently in the interest of both parties to tacitly conspire in misrepresentation."[39]

The terms of this collusion between segments of the state and certain Kurdish elements could not have played out the way it did, however, had modern identity politics not been at work. The Ottoman Empire was an empire, but it was also thinking in many ways like a nation-state, and nation-state identities are historically constructed through a process. Through this process, markers are given to those who belong, those who do not, and those who might belong, but "never quite," as they do not inhabit the nationalist core.[40] As Ottomans began to ask that nation-state question, "Whose country is this anyway?"[41] Christians, particularly Armenians, were judged as "marked citizens" by those who questioned their loyalty. Muslims became the "we" that needed no articulation.[42] This process was not self-evident on the ground, however, and it was the very process of conflict over things that were largely nonethnic in nature that helped local actors—Kurds and Armenians—crystallize their emergent identities and see their conflict in ethnic terms. However, in this process through which minority and majority were historically constituted[43]—as indeed they were—the "we" that began to need no articulation began to be Turks. And Kurds—as a target of "internal colonization, often glossed, as it is in imperial rhetoric, as a 'civilizing mission'"[44]—were granted characteristics of the "marked" citizen who needed to demonstrate their loyalty and, in Pandey's words, the "sincerity of their choice" to remain Ottoman—then Turkish—citizens.[45] Kurds continue today to be the major group of "marked" citizens in Turkey, and the story told in this book certainly played a role in the history behind this situation. The effort-bargain made by the Ottoman state and certain Kurdish tribes helped to reify the Kurds as a group and to popularize and codify in many ways the state-elite image of them—once reserved for "tribes" but now made into ethnic stereotypes—as backward, barbaric, and of questionable loyalty.

Although the story told in this book ends with the genocide of Armenians and the making of Kurds into a minority—viewed later as a stateless—group, we must emphasize the contingency of these events. As such, we must question accounts that simply read backward from the later results (which themselves continue to unfold). For those Kurds who were perpetrators in the atrocities, as Michael Mann proposes, "murderous cleansing is rarely the initial intent of perpetrators,"[46] and this is especially true of those Kurds who participated in the deportation and murder of their Armenian neighbors (and we should remember that many more not only refused to participate but also protected their neighbors). But each case of genocide has its own specificities, and as Akçam rightly points out, we must also focus on understanding the perpetrator group, not just on the victims.[47] For the main group of perpetrators—those Unionists who organized mass violence—it is certainly true, as Akçam has convincingly demonstrated, that ideology, particularly of Turkish nationalism, played a key role.[48] But there were a variety of reasons for *Kurds* (some of the on-the-ground perpetrators) to take part in the atrocities. As we have seen, it was certainly not the culmination of ancient hatreds, although a history of past enmity was undoubtedly created during and after the violence began to unfold, which helped in part to create further context for more violence or for its justification. And although ethnic identities began to crystallize during the wider processes described in this book, we must be careful in assessing blame and victimhood on attributes of grouphood alone. As Mann notes, accounts that emphasize the collectivity of actors are deeply flawed. The views therein are *"nationalist,* since it is nationalists who claim that the nation is a singular actor . . . whole nations or ethnic groups *never* act collectively."[49] The collusion across ethnic lines between Kurds and Armenians and between the state and other groups of Kurds also emphasizes the point that these "strange bedfellows" may not have been so strange after all, and that we must look beyond ethnic explanations when we attempt to decipher power struggles underway on state, local, and state-society levels.

Scholarship on states and state-society relations has become increasingly sophisticated in recent years, but the more ambiguous dynamics therein have not yet been finely delineated, and to the extent that they have, these works have generally been confined to the wider field of political science; historical studies have yet to venture far into that realm. This book has attempted to bridge this gap—to provide what I have found to be a complicated and interesting story in the past that has a continued legacy in the present, and to tell this story using a wide range of sources and with the help of certain interdisciplinary theoretical tools.

The dynamics that I have described in this book are specific to late-Ottoman Kurdistan but they also describe some of the dealings with other parts of the Ottoman "tribal zone" where Ottoman officials worked out similar policies and practices as part of their larger state-building efforts.[50] These dynamics at the same time are mirrored not only in Ottoman successor states, but elsewhere in the world where states have handed over the reins of state power to threatening groups in an attempt to manage those threats that are perceived as being even more menacing, particularly in the peripheries of state power. In most cases, disturbing—indeed disastrous, often genocidal—results have ensued, the majority of which have involved great loss of life, security, and prosperity. The Village Guards system in Turkey certainly comes to mind, but better known may be the example of Darfur in Sudan.[51] It is true that many of these dynamics play out in border regions that are often remote or less accessible to traditional state power, but as this study has shown, it is essential to historicize the political geography in question so as not to make deterministic or causal assumptions about the dynamics of particular locales without understanding why certain processes unfold at particular times with unique consequences. Finally, I hope this study contributes to identifying the ingredients of violent conflict and identity construction. In this study I have found that conflicts hitherto explained as having an ethnic or communal basis started out, in fact, as struggles over concrete material resources but became ethnicized in the process. My findings will hopefully help us decenter identity and nationalism from its place of primacy in scholarship on conflict, while also showing where and how they have played a role. Recent scholarship that has gone far in rethinking the inherent nature of conflict between groups has been important, but in its efforts to draw attention to the fact that diversity did not necessarily mean discord it has often ended up airbrushing actual conflict out of the picture. Here I hope to have dealt with these episodes of conflict in a manner that may not only help the readers of this book to understand them as they unfolded in the past, but to contribute to their resolution in the present and future. After all, the Mustafa Pashas, İbrahim Pashas, and Hüseyin Pashas of a century ago—and the state actors behind them—have names and faces today, as do the victims of the past and present. To close with words from Michael Mann: "Perpetrators of ethnic cleansing do not descend among us as a separate species of evildoers. They are created by conflicts central to modernity that involve unexpected escalations and frustrations during which individuals are forced into a series of more particular moral choices. Some eventually choose paths that they know will produce terrible results. We can denounce them, but it is just as important to understand why they did it. And the rest of us (including myself) can breathe a sigh of relief that we ourselves have not been forced into such choices, for many of us would also fail them. . . . Murderous cleansing comes from our civilization and from people, most of whom have been not unlike ourselves."[52]

Appendix: Map of Hamidiye Regiments,

ca. 1900

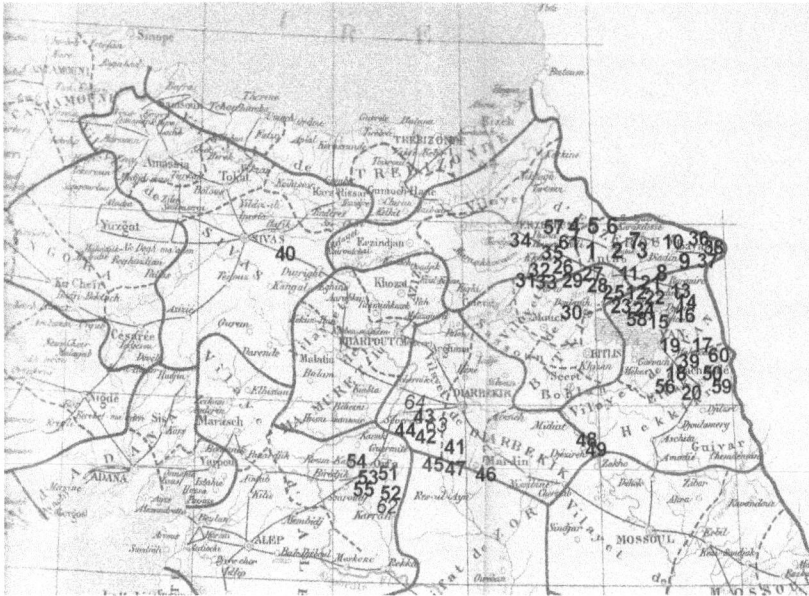

This is truly a rough-and-ready map. The background is taken from Vital Cuinet, *La Turquie de l'Asie*, vol. 1, on which I have superimposed the numbers corresponding to the regiments (see Klein, "Power in the Periphery," appendix A). However, it should be kept in mind that this is only a rough estimate of where the tribes were located, as the various sources sometimes provide conflicting information (in cases where there was a serious conflict I have italicized the number of the regiment), and furthermore, are imprecise about the exact locations of the tribes themselves. Moreover, many of the tribes were migratory, and covered regions larger than those indicated by their regimental headquarters. Therefore, this map should only be considered a general idea as to the locations of the Hamidiye tribes.

Notes

ABBREVIATIONS

AA   Affaires Arméniennes.
AIR   Records of the Air Ministry and Ministry of Defence, at the
            Public Record Office (London).
BOA   Başbakanlık Osmanlı Arşivi (Başbakanlık Ottoman Archives,
            Prime Ministry Archives; Istanbul).
CAB   Records of the Cabinet, at the Public Record Office (London).
CC   Correspondence Commerciale, Archives du Ministère des
            Affaires Étrangères (Paris).
CPC   Correspondence Politique et Commerciale, Archives du
            Ministère des Affaires Étrangères (Paris).
FO   Records of the Foreign Office, at the Public Record Office
            (London).
MAE Nantes Archives du Ministère des Affaires Étrangères (Nantes).
MAE Paris   Archives du Ministère des Affaires Étrangères (Paris).
MD   Archives du Ministère de la Défense (Château de Vincennes).
OAYC   *Osmanlı Arşivi Yıldız Tasnifi: Ermeni Meselesi* (Ottoman
            Archives Yıldız Collection: The Armenian Question). 3 vols.
            Istanbul: Historical Research Foundation, 1989.
PRO   Public Record Office (London).

INTRODUCTION

1. Russo, "La formation des régiments de cavalerie kurde Hamidié," esp.
34–37 (my thanks to Vincent Lima for bringing this article to my attention);
Hampson to White, Political no. 108, Erzurum, Nov. 14, 1891 (FO 195/1729);
Chermside to White, Confidential draft no. 16, May 5, 1891 (FO 195/1718).

2. Chermside to White, Confidential draft no. 16. May 5, 1891 (FO 195/1718). The Italian consul at Erzurum also had such suspicions (Russo, "La formation des régiments de cavalrie kurde Hamidié," 35).

3. Maunsell to de Bunsen, no. 40 (*sic*: should be 41), extracts, undated (Sept. 16, 1900) (FO 424/200; FO 195/2082). Maunsell seems to have been mistaken about Kurdish nationalist sentiments among the Hamidiye tribesmen at this time, but was not off-base to express concern over their utility to the state.

4. Some of the ideas in this chapter were explored briefly in Klein, "Çevreyi İdare Etmek."

5. This is the title Reşat Kasaba created for a panel he organized (and in which I participated) at the annual MESA conference, Nov. 2008. I borrow it, as it aptly describes the dynamic.

6. Wigram and Wigram, *Cradle of Mankind*.

7. See, for example, Zohrab to Elliot, no. 63, Confidential, Erzurum, Sept. 18, 1876 (FO 195/1100).

8. The Turkification mission, although somewhat present in the mind of the sultan and his associates at the time of the Hamidiye's creation, became more evident particularly after the Ottoman Committee of Union and Progress (CUP) came to power in 1908.

9. For example, Kévorkian, introduction to Russo, "La formation des régiments de cavalerie kurde," 31–32. It should also be noted that although Kévorkian employs the same argument in his *Les arméniens dans l'Empire ottoman à la veille du génocide* (cowritten with Paul B. Paboudjian), 48–49, he does recognize the other factors, many of which I will treat below, as elements of the Hamidiye project.

10. This is the impression readers may get from a number of texts, including Gürün, *Armenian File*; Anadol, *Tarihin Işığında Ermeni Dosyası*; Gazigiray, *Osmanlılardan Günümüze kadar Vesikalarla Ermeni*; and McCarthy, *Death and Exile*. Armenian sources generally work to establish the culpability of the state in these events, and in so doing, often fail to mention the extensive death and destruction suffered by Muslims during the war, which occurred sometimes at the hands of Armenians. The "Turkish nationalist" authors take the matter to the other extreme, usually describing only instances of Armenians killing Muslims and not acknowledging the fate that befell the Armenians themselves. While these authors do not wrongly draw attention to the suffering of Muslims during the war, which has so often been ignored by Western writers, their narratives nonetheless are designed to deflect all attention away from any official role in the massacres. To the extent that the massacres of Armenians are discussed, which is rarely, the Kurds seem to be a convenient target for blame. This line of reasoning has also, however, at times posed a challenge for this official line, which, until recently, maintained that there was no such thing as a Kurd, that they were really Turks. In his short piece on the Hamidiye, Gültepe, for example, claims that the Hamidiye regiments were comprised of "Turkmen" tribes. See his "Hamidiye Alayları," 47.

11. Tepeyran, *Hatıralar*, 227, 388.

12. For example, Aytar, *Hamidiye Alaylarından Köy Koruculuğuna*.

13. This approach may be represented by Kodaman in his *Sultan II: Abdül-hamid Devri Doğu Anadolu Politikası*, particularly his chapter on the Hamidi-ye, which appeared separately as an earlier publication titled "Hamidiye Hafif Süvari Alayları"; and Talay, *Eserleri ve Hizmetleriyle Sultan Abdülhamid*; and Duguid, "Politics of Unity." Other authors include Sırma, *II. Abdülhamid'in İslâm Birliği Siyaseti*; and Tepedelenlioğlu, *Hürriyet'in İlanı ve II. Abdülhamit*.

14. Çay, "Türk Milli Bütünlüğü İçerisinde Doğu Anadolu," 23 (cited in Ergül, *II. Abdülhamid'in Doğu Politikası ve Hamidiye Alayları*, 5).

15. Giddens, *Nation-State and Violence*.

16. Migdal, *State in Society*, 20; parentheses in original.

17. Ibid., 49.

18. Ibid., 12.

19. Brown and Fernandez, "Tribe and State in a Frontier Mosaic," 177. The authors' observations on the colonial relationship in Peru apply here.

20. Bragge, Claas, and Roscoe, "On the Edge of Empire."

21. Balta, "Military Success, State Capacity," 21.

22. Ateş, "Empires at the Margin."

23. Adelman and Aron, "From Borderlands to Borders," 814–41.

24. See, for example, Karpat and Zens, eds., *Ottoman Borderlands*.

25. Giddens, *Nation-State and Violence*, 4, 50, 90, 119–21.

26. Giddens makes an important distinction between ruling and governing (ibid., 57).

27. Scott, *Seeing Like a State*, 186–87.

28. Ferguson and Whitehead, eds., *War in the Tribal Zone*. See also Özbek, "Policing the Countryside," 47–67. In this interesting article the author looks at gendarmeries in the Ottoman Empire in the context of managing the border-lands and its larger state-building project. Aksakal, in his *Ottoman Road to War in 1914*, also notes the connection between the state's sense of "geopolitical danger and domestic vulnerability" and how many in ruling circles saw milita-rization as the path to modernity (2–3).

29. Scott, *Seeing Like a State*.

30. Ibid., 82, 184.

31. The title of Douglas's fifth chapter (*How Institutions Think*, 55).

32. Ibid., 100.

33. Ibid., citing Ian Hacking.

34. A process described elsewhere by Ferguson and Whitehead, "Violent Edge of Empire," in Ferguson and Whitehead, eds., *War in the Tribal Zone*, 14.

35. See Klein, "Kurdish Nationalists and Non-Nationalist Kurdists."

36. Douglas, *How Institutions Think*, 102.

37. See Adelman and Aron, "From Borderlands to Borders," on this point.

38. See, for example, the work of de Waal, "Tragedy in Darfur"; Berdal and Malone, eds., *Greed and Grievance*; and Ballentine and Sherman, eds., *The Po-litical Economy of Armed Conflict*. Some Ottomanists whose works stand out in this regard are Makdisi, *Culture of Sectarianism*; Philliou, "Communities on the Verge"; Gingeras, *Sorrowful Shores*; and Yosmaoğlu, "Counting Bodies, Shaping Souls."

39. Ferguson and Whitehead, eds., *War in the Tribal Zone*, xvii.

40. Pandey, *Routine Violence*, 14.

41. Douglas, *How Institutions Think*, 63.

42. Mann, *Dark Side of Democracy*.

43. Ibid., 112.

44. Foucault, "Governmentality," in *Foucault Effect*, 87–104.

45. Abou-El-Haj, *Formation of the Modern State*.

46. Borrowing Partha Chatterjee's phrase ("Nationalist Resolution of the Women's Question," 236).

47. My thanks to Ken Lockridge for helping me to develop this point.

48. See Kühn, "Imperial Borderland as Colony."

49. Powell, *Different Shade of Colonialism*.

50. Scott, *Seeing Like a State*, 82.

51. See also Bragge, Claas, and Roscoe ("On the Edge of Empire," 111) on this point.

52. Deringil, *Well-Protected Domains*.

53. In the words of Scott, *Domination and the Arts of Resistance*, 98.

54. Giddens, *Nation-State and Violence*, 7–8.

55. Scott, *Domination and the Arts of Resistance*, 21.

56. Guha, "Prose of Counter-Insurgency."

57. In Scott's words (*Domination and the Arts of Resistance*, 3).

58. In the words of Bragge, Claas, and Roscoe ("On the Edge of Empire," 110).

CHAPTER ONE

1. Ottoman Government, *Tensikat-ı Askeriyye Cümlesinden Olarak Hamidiye Süvari Alaylarına Da'ir Kanunnamedir*, 2.

2. See my introduction to this book. Van Bruinessen's treatment of the Hamidiye, while brief, is one of the most insightful, and indeed helped inspire me to do this study (in *Agha, Shaikh and State*, esp. 185–89).

3. Sultan Abdülhamit, "Türk-Rus Harbinden Sonra [1898]," in *Siyasî Hatıratım*, 91–92.

4. W. Jwaideh, "Kurdish Nationalist Movement," 212.

5. Olson, *Emergence of Kurdish Nationalism*, 1–7; Jwaideh, esp. 212–67. Kodaman also notes that the sultan organized "friendly" tribes against Sheikh Ubeydullah's forces ("Hamidiye Hafif Süvari Alayları [II. Abdülhamid ve Doğu-Anadolu Aşiretleri]," 437). It should not be forgotten that just prior to the Sheikh Ubeydullah rebellion, the government had worked to suppress a revolt led by Hüseyin and Osman Bedir Khan, of the famous Bedir Khan family. A very interesting, more recent, analysis by Sabri Ateş problematizes some of the positions held by these and other authors and argues that we should see this rebellion in the context of the important task of demarcating the frontier with more fixed and less fuzzy borders, that is, from a borderland to a bordered land (Ateş, "Empires at the Margin," chap. 5).

6. Dasnabedian, *Histoire de la Fédération révolutionnaire arménienne*," 21–25.

7. Ter Minassian, "Role of the Armenian Community," 109–56; Ter Minassian, *Nationalism and Socialism*; Nalbandian, *Armenian Revolutionary Movement*, esp. 90–220; and Suny, *Looking Toward Ararat*, 19.

8. In the political memoirs attributed to him, Sultan Abdülhamid II complained bitterly about the attention the Armenians were drawing to the empire with their distorted grievances, and believed that they had no grounds for complaint (Sultan Abdülhami[d], *Siyasî Hatıratım*, 72–73).

9. These documents are reproduced in Ergül, *II. Abdülhamid'in Doğu Politikası ve Hamidiye Alayları*, 50–52.

10. *Löbells jahresberichte*, 327, mentions that the idea arose in 1885 (my thanks to Baki Tezcan for translating this piece for me). The bug may even have been put in the sultan's ear by Ottoman officials who were most familiar with the region (see Hamid, Governor of Van, to HIM Report, Nov. 24, 1884, in *OAYC*, 3: 322–33; and Hamid, Governor of Van, to HIM Report, Dec. 16, 1886, in *OAYC*, 3: 334–51. In 1887, a post was carved out for Zeki Pasha, who would become the commander of the tribal regiments, and in 1888 there is direct mention of plans to raise regiments composed of Kurdish tribes based on the Cossack model. Şakir Pasha, who had served as ambassador to Russia from 1878–89, is most likely the figure who proposed the idea of forming Kurdish tribal regiments after the Cossack model to the sultan (see Karaca, *Anadolu Islahâtı*, 173–74). British Colonel Chermside submitted a report on the plan in 1888, which indicates his awareness of a Cossack-like cavalry planned for the empire's Kurdish tribes (Chermside to White, Report A, Erzurum, Dec. 22, 1888 [FO 195/1617, FO 195/1652]). Doğan Avcıoğlu suggests that it was Zeki Pasha, who, after returning from a trip to the eastern provinces, proposed to the sultan that they form regiments of the Kurdish tribes after the Cossack model (*Milli Kurtuluş Tarihi*, 1085–86, cited in Ergül, *II. Abdülhamid'in Doğu Politikası ve Hamidiye Alayları*, 44).

11. Foucault, "Governmentality," 87–104.

12. These were all goals envisioned by Şakir Pasha (Karaca, *Anadolu Islahâtı*, 174–75).

13. Most sources list sixty-four regiments, but Avyarov lists a sixty-fifth (Avyarov [Avriyanof], *Osmanlı-Rus ve İran Savaşlarında Kürtler, 1801–1900*, appendix, 55). The number given by the reform regulations of 1910 is sixty-four and one-half, the half regiment being the sixty-fifth regiment mentioned by Avyarov (Ottoman Government, *Aşiret Hafif Süvari Alayları Nizamnamesi*, and the English translation: "Tribal Light Cavalry Regulation," enclosed with Tyrrell to Lowther, Istanbul, Dec. 30, 1911 (FO 195/2386). Ergül also puts the number at sixty-five, basing his information in the military yearbook for 1908 (although he seems unsure whether it was actually sixty-four or sixty-five) (77). For a full list of these tribes see Klein, "Power in the Periphery," app. A.

14. Kodaman, "Hamidiye Hafif Süvari Alayları (II. Abdülhamid ve Doğu-Anadolu Aşiretleri)," 439. See also Kévorkian, introduction to Russo, cited above.

15. And the extent of this role has been partially challenged by Verheij in his article "'Les frères de terre et d'eau.'"

16. Cuinet, *Turquie de l'Asie*, vols. 1 and 2.

17. A fascinating catalog of Armenian life, replete with statistics, maps, and photographs, can be found in Kévorkian and Paboudjian, *Arméniens dans l'Empire ottoman*.

18. See Stone, *Academies for Anatolia*; and Kocabaşoğlu, *Anadolu'daki Amerika*.

19. Dasnabedian provides a map of the routes used by Armenian revolutionaries to transport men and munitions. The following lines are detailed in the map: (1) Salmas (in Iran) to Van (via the monastery at Derik), with an extension in the direction of Sasun (via Lernabar, south of Lake Van; (2) Nakhchevan to Van directly (via the monastery of Thadé or Stépanos Nakhaveka); (3) Erivan to Van directly (via the Ararat region); (4) Kars to Ahlat (via Eleşgirt); (5) Kars to Sasun (via Pasin, with an occasional branch toward Garin); and (6) Batum to Sasun via Kars (p. 66). Additionally, the memoirs of Minas Ter Minassian (aka Rouben) also mention Ahlat, Sasun, and Pasin as points that revolutionaries traversed or rejoined after crossing the border (Rouben, *Mémoires d'un partisan arménien*, 47).

20. The main focus of Armenians living in Russia at this time was the liberation of Ottoman Armenia. They were much more preoccupied with the conditions of Armenians in the Ottoman Empire than they were with their own situation in Russia (see Nalbandian, *Armenian Revolutionary Movement*, esp. chap. 6).

21. A very interesting first-person account of Armenian revolutionary activities and goals can be found in Rouben (*Mémoires d'un partisan arménien*). The English version, which appears to be largely, but not entirely, similar to the French version is also a great source (Rouben, *Armenian Freedom Fighters*). The French version has translated a few more pages from the original multivolume work. See also Nalbandian, *Armenian Revolutionary Movement*; esp. 90–220; and Dasnabedian, *Histoire de la Fédération révolutionnaire arménienne*.

22. In the year that the Hamidiye was established (1890), for example, the first chamberlain wrote to the grand vizier's office about the sultan's perception of the situation:

It is needless to declare that, with the exception of the Hejaz, in all localities of the Glorious Ottoman Lands Armenian [*sic*] can be found. Of a certain locality, whose inhabitants are predominantly Kurdish, and whose name came to be known as Kurdistan since ancient times, some malignant mouths have been talking as Armenia. Though these ill intentions are cast with the purpose of creating an Armenia, just the way used in the earlier formation of the vilayet of Danube, i.e., a certain principle was established to determine the boundaries; the locality known as Kurdistan is there today, and the Muslim folk inhabiting it is incomparably more numerous than the Armenians. Consequently it is not at all right to change the name of the locality into Armenia, and furthermore it is not at all possible to draw boundaries that would include Armenian localities, under the heading "vilayets inhabited by Armenians." (First Chamberlain, signed as Süreyya to the Prime Ministry, Aug. 11, 1890, in *OAYC*, 3: 192–93)

23. It should be noted that while the Russians were not actively invading the region, they certainly were trying their best to gain a foothold in it through various activities, especially in their support of Armenian revolutionary activities. Armenian revolutionaries coming from Russia were noted to be in Hınıs (Graves to Sir A. Nicolson, no. 19, Erzurum, June 27, 1893 [FO 195/1804] and other places). There are even reports of Russians contacting Kurdish chiefs, some as far in the interior as Dersim, during the 1880s (Chermside to White, Report A, Erzurum, Dec. 22, 1888 [FO 195/1617, FO 195/1652]). Ahmad also provides a full chapter on the various interests of the Great Powers in the Kurds and the lands they inhabited, and provides a rather detailed account of the Russian interest in the region (*Kurdistan During the First World War*, 25–36).

24. Of course, there was not always a direct overlap between Armenian population centers and locales where revolutionaries either hid or operated. The following are some of the main (but not only) places where Armenian revolutionary activities are noted in consular reports to have taken place: Eleşgirt, Başkale, Arabkir, Sasun, Palu, Bergiri, Hakkari, Saray, Bitlis, Erzurum, Hoşab, Karakilise, Harput, Egin, Diyarbekir, Ahlat, Van, Toprakkale, Patnos, Delibaba, and other points along the frontiers.

25. BOA YMM 48/39 2 (9 Şubat 1306/12 Şaban 1308 [Feb. 21, 1890]), reproduced in Ergül, *II. Abdülhamid'in Doğu Politikası ve Hamidiye Alayları*, 53.

26. One British agent believed that the line of Hamidiye regiments across the southern boundaries of Kurdistan was an arrangement that served "the double purpose of affording a further check on the Kurds and of weakening the Arabs by preventing the possibility of a combination on any large scale on their part." He continued later in the report, noting,

> It is generally supposed that the Hamidieh regiments have been raised to act as irregular cavalry in time of war but as regards the Hamidieh of this district it is possible that this use for them might be only a secondary one. During the last war with Russia, the Turkish Government was anxious about the actions which the Kurds and Arabs might take, and special precautions were taken by the Vali of Diarbekir, Abdurrahman Pasha, to keep them quiet and to avoid giving them any excuse to make trouble; for example, troops sent from Diarbekir to Bitlis, instead of taking the direct route by Zor, made a wide detour to the north through Lije and Mush. In the event of another war with Russia it is considered not improbable that the centre of strategical importance may be shifted from Erzeroum to Bitlis, in which case the routes leading from the Mediterranean to the Bitlis region, passing through Urfa and Diarbekir, will be of the greatest importance. A glance at the map will show that these lines of communication are exposed to two dangers, i.e., to attack by the Arabs from the South, and the Kurds from the north; moreover[,] from Birejik to Bitlis and from Mardin to Bitlis, the country traversed is mountainous and inhabited solely by Kurds. It is therefore of great military importance that in time of war the inhabitants of these tracts

of country should not act against the Government. The Government seems to have seriously occupied itself with this question. The best solution might appear to have been to subject the Kurds and Arabs by ordinary administrative methods, or by force if necessary, but either method in dealing with these people would have been attended with serious difficulties, and there is much to recommend the system chosen, i.e., that of utilizing the well-known intertribal feuds of the Kurds and Arabs, which renders it comparatively easy to create a system which makes a combination against the Government very difficult. (W. J. Anderson, Report, Diarbekir Vilayet, March quarter 1902, Apr. 2, 1902, PRO FO 195/2125)

27. There were two main groups of Hamidiye—one along the frontiers with Russia and Iran, and the other in northern Mesopotamia. Kodaman ("Hamidiye Hafif Süvari Alayları [II. Abdülhamid ve Doğu-Anadolu Aşiretleri]," 450) has argued that the second (Mesopotamian) group was intended to counter British influence, but I have not found much evidence that this was a true concern at the time, or, if it was, it was certainly subservient to other goals.

28. What this means is that the number of regiments did not grow beyond sixty-five, and likely shrank in reality, even if not on paper. The number of regiments also may have fluctuated over the years, with some smaller tribes dropping out or being reabsorbed by larger tribes.

29. Interestingly, the Wigram travelers, in interviewing an Assyrian in the region of Hoşab, were told by their informant that "there were Armenian villages here once . . . but . . . the Kurds turned them out" (Wigram and Wigram, *Cradle of Mankind*, 234).

30. Dasnabedian, *Histoire de la Fédération révolutionnaire arménienne,"* 66.

31. Van Bruinessen, *Agha, Shaikh and State*, 186. A similar relationship was also forged with other groups, notably the Albanians, who called him *baba mbret*, or father king (Skendi, *Albanian National Awakening*, 341).

32. See the brief biography of Zeki Pasha written by Colonel Chermside, the British military attaché to the Ottoman Empire (FO 195/1794).

33. On conscription in the Ottoman Empire see Zürcher, "Ottoman Conscription System."

34. Devey to White. Confidential, Van, Nov. 24, 1890 (FO 424/169); and Siouffi to Goblet, Mosul, Mar. 8, 1889, Annex to dispatch no. 36 (MAE Paris, CPC Turquie/Mosul/3); Lamb to White, no. 8, Van, Dec. 24, 1885 (FO 195/1521); Safrastian to Shipley, Bitlis, Dec. 15, 1906 (FO 195/2222).

35. Wigoureaux to Ribot, Erzurum, Nov. 15, 1890 (MAE Paris, CPC Turquie, Erzeroum, vol. 7).

36. See Ergül on this point (*II. Abdülhamid'in Doğu Politikası ve Hamidiye Alayları*, 55).

37. Wigoureaux to the Minister of Foreign Affairs, Erzurum, Nov. 8, 1890 (MAE Paris, CPC Turquie, Erzeroum, vol. 7).

38. Acting Vice-Consul Boyadjian to Acting Consul Hampson, Confidential, Diyarbekir, Feb. 24, 1891 (FO 424/169). Ahmad also suggests that some viewed the initiative as "demeaning," while others, drawing on their past experiences with the Ottoman government, believed the venture to be bait, as the authori-

ties "frequently resorted to trickery" in their dealings with the tribes (*Kurdistan During the First World War*, 55 and n. 17). As we shall see below, this fear would prove to be well founded. Incidentally, the Ottoman state was not the first to employ the practice of taking tribal chiefs hostage for the good behavior of their tribes. Kurdish *mîrs* who, before the destruction of the emirates, often ruled over many tribes, would take important members of the tribe, often a brother or son of the chief, to remain "in the service of the *mîr*" (*xizmetê mîr*), where they were, in fact, well-treated hostages, according to van Bruinessen, *Agha, Shaikh and State*, 164–65.

39. Devey to Hampson, Confidential no. 23, Van, July 20, 1891 (FO 424/169; FO 195/1729).

40. Ahmad, *Kurdistan During the First World War*, 54. Ahmad continues, describing how several senior officials were dispatched to the Kurdish regions to enter into discussions with influential persons, "dispensing magnanimous promises in the name of 'the Muslim Caliph' to them, telling them that he had decided to confer many gifts, honours and grants on chiefs whose men joined the new formations. A special appeal in the name of the Sultan was distributed throughout the Kurdish areas in which he addressed himself to the 'faithful Kurds, defenders of Islam', urging them to hasten to respond to the 'sincere' calls to 'sacred duty'. The 'noble title' of the new formation was highlighted everywhere as, it was claimed, conclusive evidence of the sovereign's great concern and 'magnanimity.'"

41. Karaca, *Anadolu Islahâtı*, 175–76.

42. Hayderani (the nephew of Hamidiye commander Hüseyin Pasha]) "Aşiret Mektebi ve Aşiret Alayları," 147.

43. Wigoureaux to the Minister of Foreign Affairs, Erzurum, Nov. 29, 1890 (MAE Paris, CPC Turquie, Erzurum, vol. 7). See also Hampson to White, Erzurum, Jan. 30, 1891 (FO 424/169); and Memorandum on the formation of the Hamidiye regiments, translation, enclosed with White to the Marquis of Salisbury, Confidential no. 68, Istanbul, Feb. 24, 1891 (FO 424/169); and BOA YMM 48/83-4 [1891] (reproduced in Ergül, *II. Abdülhamid'in Doğu Politikası ve Hamidiye Alayları*, 56–57). Hayderani adds that the officers also received pay for their services in addition to arms ("Aşiret Mektebi ve Aşiret Alayları," 147).

44. BOA YMM 48/83-2 (reproduced in Ergül, *II. Abdülhamid'in Doğu Politikası ve Hamidiye Alayları*, 55–56). Zeki Pasha seems to have wanted to offer the voyage as a "carrot" to as many tribes as expressed interest in going, but Şakir Pasha put a limit on the number who could go, and allowed only two additional tribesmen from each regiment to accompany their chiefs to the capital (Karaca, *Anadolu Islahâtı*, 175).

45. ASDMAEI, AP, Armenia, b.325, fasc. 1891, no. 204/22, from Trebisonda 28.3.1891 in Russo, "La formation des régiments de cavalerie kurde Hamidié," 36 (italics added). The two officials from Istanbul mentioned in this passage are noted by the British consul at Trabzon as being Colonel Vehbi Bey, of the Imperial Palace, and Lieutenant-Colonel İsmail Bey, of the War Office (Longworth to White, Trabzon, Mar. 28, 1891 (FO 424/169; FO 78/4344).

46. Extract from "Tarik" of [Istanbul] Mar. 30, 1891, translation by British official (FO 424/169).

47. Chermside to White, Confidential draft no. 16, May 5, 1891 (FO 195/1718).

48. The *selâmlık* was the public procession of the sultan to the mosque for Friday noon prayers.

49. Undated memorandum signed "Selim," from the Başbakanlık Osmanlı Arşivi, Yıldız Evrak Odası (my thanks to M. Şükrü Hanioğlu for providing me with this document, which sadly lacks dossier numbers).

50. Longworth to White, Trabzon, May 23, 1891 (FO 424/169).

51. Memorandum by Colonel Chermside, June 6, 1891 (FO 424/169). Chermside further notes that "in addition to these, numerous decorations, 4th and 5th classes, of the Osmaniye and Mecidiye, were bestowed, and money gifts of 5 liras . . . to the more important aghas, and of 3 liras . . . to retainers." The gifts from the sultan were proudly displayed to guests. The traveler Lynch described his visit with Ali Bey, the son of Haci Yusuf, and now the head of the Sibkan tribe, who, in addition to wearing his imperial decorations on his chest, showed his guests "a cigarette case, of gold encrusted with jewels, the gift of the Sultan, accompanied by an autograph letter" (*Armenia*, 2: 268).

52. Altay, *10 Yıl Savaş ve Sonrası (1912–1922)*, 55. It is not clear whether these items were presented at the Istanbul ceremony.

53. Chermside to White, Confidential draft no. 34, Istanbul, Aug. 21, 1891 (FO 195/1718). Ergül also notes that the top command posts were often given to officers from the regular army (*II. Abdülhamid'in Doğu Politikası ve Hamidiye Alayları*, 58).

54. Memorandum by Colonel Chermside, June 6, 1891 (FO 424/169).

55. Longworth to White, Trabzon, May 23, 1891 (FO 424/169), and Memorandum by Colonel Chermside, June 6, 1891 (FO 424/169). See below for further descriptions of the new uniforms.

56. ASDMAEI, AP *Armenia*, b.325, fasc. 1891, r. no. 310/114, il Ro. console d'Italia Francisci al ministro degli Affari esteri, Trebisonda 22.5.1891, quoted in Russo, "La formation des régiments de cavalerie kurde Hamidié," 36. This consul added that he didn't believe the change in clothes would accompany a change in discipline.

57. Memorandum by Colonel Chermside, June 6, 1891 (FO 424/169).

58. Memorandum by Colonel Chermside, June 6, 1891 (FO 424/169). Chermside states that this second lot (numbering 52 or 53) reached Trabzon on May 21, departed for the capital aboard the Austrian Lloyd steamer Medea on May 23 and reached Istanbul on May 27 accompanied by the same officers who escorted the first group. Just like their countrymen whose paths they crossed, they also were quartered with their retainers in barracks, attended the *selâmlık*, and in general were treated much like the men of the first lot. Among other smaller tribes from the Pasin, Başkale, and Hakkari districts, the second group also included the Hayderan, which was the largest Kurdish tribe and one which enjoyed influence in Ottoman and Iranian Kurdistan, and the Mîran and Millî

tribes (Chermside to White, Confidential draft no. 34, Istanbul, Aug. 21 1891 [FO 195/1718]).

59. Ambassador White writes: "There is a great deal that might be *a priori* objected to the probable success of such a scheme, but it is no use talking to his Ministers about it as they have nothing to do with it, and would never venture to speak to the Sultan unfavourably of a scheme upon which he looks upon [*sic*] his personal work" (Sir White to Marquis of Salisbury, Confidential draft no. 68, Istanbul, Feb. 24, 1891 (FO 424/169).

60. Chermside to White, Confidential draft no. 34, Istanbul, Aug. 21, 1891 (FO 195/1718).

61. See also Deringil, "Ottoman Twilight Zone," 17, esp. n. 20. The Ottoman Cabinet also convened to discuss taxation of Hamidiye members and determined that only those members who had completed their military service would be exempt (BOA, YMV 72/81, 6 Kanun-i Evvel, 1890).

62. One such threat was reported by Mrs. Bishop to the archbishop of Canterbury in a letter recounting the perceptions of one Mr. Richardson, an American missionary in Erzurum, who, while at Erzincan, witnessed the newly commissioned recruits riding "through the Christian quarter making gestures as of cutting throats, saying to the Armenian merchants, 'Your time has come now; hitherto we have not had the co-operation of the Government, but we have it now.'" (Mrs. Bishop to Archbishop of Canterbury, Bournemouth, Apr. 17, 1891 [FO 424/169]).

63. Hampson to White, Erzurum, Nov. 7, 1891 (FO 195/1729; FO 424/169).

64. Wigoureaux to Cambon, no. 1, Erzurum, Jan. 9, 1892 (MAE Nantes, Série D, Erzeroum, 1883–93).

65. Acting Vice-Consul Boyadjian to Acting Consul Hampson, Confidential, Diyarbekir, Feb. 24, 1891 (FO 242/169). In his work on Şakir Pasha, Karaca points out the tension between Zeki Pasha and Şakir Pasha over the matter of pardons being conferred on lawless chiefs (*Anadolu Islahâtı*, 175).

66. Giddens, *Nation-State and Violence*, 7.

67. Van Bruinessen, "Kurds, States, and Tribes," 169–70.

68. Hampson to Fane, Political no. 16, Erzurum, Feb. 27, 1892 (FO 195/1766; FO 424/172). See also Kodaman, "Hamidiye Hafif Süvari Alayları (II. Abdülhamid ve Doğu-Anadolu Aşiretleri)," 447; and Ahmad, *Kurdistan During the First World War*, 56.

69. Bergeron to Ambassador Cambon, no. 3, Erzurum, July 2, 1892 (MAE Paris, CPC Turquie, Erzurum, vol. 7; MAE Nantes, Erzeroum, no. 873 [1883–93]). Petitions to join the Hamidiye would continue to build over the years to follow. The Ottoman Archives houses, for example, some of these petitions. One tribe from the *sancak* of Mardin proclaimed themselves to be loyal and faithful, and ready to sacrifice themselves for the sultan and the state. Another tribe (Sinanî) from the Bitlis province claimed that they had seven thousand men in their tribe who were ready to take up arms (in the Hamidiye), and desired the permission to do so (BOA Yıldız Esas Evrak, Kısım A-Zarf 21, carton 131, Evrak no. 21/4 (cited in Ergül, *II. Abdülhamid'in Doğu Politikası ve Hamidiye Alayları*, 73). Kodaman reproduces these letters in full in his work ("Hamidiye

Hafif Süvari Alayları [II. Abdülhamid ve Doğu-Anadolu Aşiretleri]," 459–62). What the letters illustrate is how hard many tribes tried to sell themselves, their abilities, their numbers, and their loyalty to the sultan and Zeki Pasha in order to join.

70. Chermside to Ford, no. 9, Istanbul, Mar. 19, 1892 (FO 195/1759; FO 424/172).

71. Graves to Ford, no. 38, Erzurum, June 22, 1892 (FO 195/1766; FO 424/172). Sadettin Pasha, who was sent to survey the Van region in 1896 also met one very elderly Hamidiye *kaymakam* of the Şavli tribe; this man could barely hold his head up (Önal, ed., *Sadettin Paşa'nın Anıları*, 27–28).

72. Nearly a decade after conscription began, the minister of war (Reza) noted the problems associated with hugely inflated Hamidiye numbers (BOA, Y.PRK.ASK 134/3, July 11, 1899).

73. Even Emin Agha, who had been charged with raising two regiments from his huge Hayderan tribe, which boasted some twenty thousand families, could not even put together the numbers to form a single battalion (Ahmad, *Kurdistan During the First World War*, 56).

74. Wigoureaux to Ambassador Cambon, no. 21, Dec. 5, 1891 (MAE Nantes, Série D, Erzeroum, 1883–93. See also MAE Paris, CPC Turquie, Erzeroum, vol. 7.

75. As noted by the Italian consul in Trabzon (see Russo, "La formation des régiments de cavalerie kurde Hamidié," 39).

76. Wigoureaux to Ribot, no. 7, Aug. 1, 1891 (MAE Paris, CPC Turquie, Erzeroum, vol. 7). See also MAE Nantes, Série D, Erzeroum, 1883–93.

77. Boyajian to Hampson, no. 16, Diyarbekir, May 10, 1892 (FO 195/1766; FO 424/172). I have not been able to find any further description of the ceremonies held at Cizre.

78. Fitzmaurice to Hampson, no. 18 (should be no. 13), Van, June 6, 1892 (FO 195/1766; FO 424/172). An example of this seems to have been Reşid Bey's Kizkanlu (Kasikan) regiment of the Pasin district, which, by 1894 seems to have received orders to disband. According to Consul Graves, his "enemies" reported him to the capital, claiming that he had a "sham regiment" and that "as his own men were too few in number, & he had picked up odd lots in about thirty different villages, many of whom were enrolled elsewhere already, to make up the necessary strength" ("Extracts from letters [to Chermside] on the Hamidiye Cavalry," Chermside to Currie [Ambassador], Istanbul, June 4, 1894, draft no. 32 [FO 195/1837]).

79. Fitzmaurice to Hampson, no. 15, Van, June 11, 1892 (FO 195/1766; FO 424/172).

80. The titles given to the Hamidiye chiefs is often confusing. Most were given the rank of colonel, or lieutenant-colonel, but a few, such as Mustafa Pasha Mîran, İbrahim Pasha Millî, and Hüseyin Pasha Hayderan, were given the title of pasha. However, it should be remembered that here the title pasha did not imply that they were recognized as military pashas, or generals, but rather, implied a high civilian rank.

81. Graves to Ford, no. 38, Erzurum, June 22, 1892 (FO 195/1766; FO 424/172). See also the very colorful description provided by Bergeron, Consul to Ambassador Cambon, no. 3, Erzurum, July 2, 1892 (MAE Paris, CPC Turquie, Erzeroum, vol. 7; MAE Nantes, Série D, Erzeroum, 1883–93.

82. Deringil, *Well-Protected Domains*, 35.

83. Ibid., 37. See also Kodaman on the point about stroking the egos of the chiefs as part of the larger mission to induce them to recognize the strength and patronage of the government ("Hamidiye Hafif Süvari Alayları [II. Abdülhamid ve Doğu-Anadolu Aşiretleri]," 437–38).

84. Scott, *Domination and the Arts of Resistance*, 48.

85. See ibid., 49.

86. Giddens, *Nation-State and Violence*, 230.

87. Longworth to White, Trabzon, May 23, 1891 (FO 424/169); Memorandum by Colonel Chermside, June 6, 1891 (FO 424/169); and Chermside to White, Confidential draft no. 34, Istanbul, Aug. 21, 1891 (FO 195/1718?).

88. Mayevski, *Van ve Bitlis Vilayetleri Askerî İstatistiği*, 196.

89. Lynch, *Armenia*, 2: 5.

90. Klein, "Tribal Militias from the Wild West."

91. Dasnabedian mentions several skirmishes that took place between Armenian revolutionaries and Hamidiye troops and also notes that they posed certain setbacks to the revolutionaries' plans (*Histoire de la Fédération révolutionnaire arménienne*, 65). This is corroborated by the account provided in Rouben's memoirs (*Armenian Freedom Fighters*, 47).

92. However, it should be mentioned that the tribal elements supported by Sultan Abdülhamid II were, in the end, loyal to him, and strongly opposed the Young Turks who overthrew him. This could also be counted as a success for the regime of this sultan. Furthermore, Verheij has also pointed to the sultan's success in creating a great popularity for himself among this element ("'Les frères de terre et d'eau,'" 238).

93. In Scott's words (*Domination and the Arts of Resistance*, 98).

94. Immediately after their return from the capital during the initial organization, the British agent at Erzurum reported that many of the new Hamidiye tribesmen openly stated that they had been appointed to suppress Armenian activities. Whether or not they were given these instructions explicitly is difficult to determine, as there seem to be few records that state this, but it is clear that the tribesmen believed this to be their mission (Hampson to White, Erzurum, Feb. 28, 1891 [FO 424/169]).

95. The Badikan tribe of Muş is mentioned in several sources as belonging to the Hamidiye, but it does not appear on any of the official rosters. This is an appropriate point to note that while some tribes (such as the Mîran, Millî, and Hayderan) were constant members of the Hamidiye, others seem to have enrolled and dropped out, with still others filling their places. Unfortunately, the names of some of these tribes at present cannot be determined.

96. Gilbert to Ribot, Confidential, Aleppo, Dec. 21, 1892 (MAE Paris, CPC Turquie, Alep, vol. 9).

97. Shipley to O'Conor, no. 51, Erzurum, Nov. 16, 1903 (FO 424/205). This situation continued in Sasun for years; indeed, a report from 1903 also mentions the difficulties the government had in persuading Kurds of Sasun to assist them in suppressing Armenian revolutionary activities there.

98. See, for example, Shipley to O'Conor, no. 51, Erzurum, Nov. 16, 1903 (FO 424/205).

99. Wratislaw to Hardinge, Confidential draft no. 27, Tabriz, Dec. 28, 1903 (FO 424/206); and O'Conor to the Marquess of Lansdowne, Confidential draft no. 285, Istanbul, Apr. 18, 1904 (FO 424/206).

100. Chermside to Ford, no. 30, Istanbul, Dec. 15, 1892 (FO 195/1759; FO 424/172).

101. Memorandum by Colonel Chermside (October 21, 1893) (FO 424/175). Years later the abuse of uniforms was still a problem. The British consul at Van reported in 1901 that orders had been given only allowing officers to wear the Hamidiye badges all the time. Noncommissioned officers and troopers were to be banned from wearing the badge except for during training exercises. This measure was taken after the acknowledgment that the wearing of the Hamidiye badge had become widespread even among Kurds who had nothing to do with the organization (Satow to O'Conor, no. 27, Van, Dec. 2, 1901 [FO 195/2104]).

102. See, for example, telegram from Bapst, Therapia, July 11, 1898 (MAE Nantes, Série E/116).

103. Elliot to Currie, Private, Khoi, Iran, Apr. 8, 1898, (FO 195/2021); Elliot to Currie, no. 18, Tabriz, May 5, 1898 (FO 195/2021; FO 424/196); Cambon to Hanotaux, Pera, July 19, 1897 (MAE Paris, CPC, Politique Intérieure Turquie, vol. 73). See also Dasnabedian (*Histoire de la Fédération révolutionnaire arménienne*, 65), the memoirs of Rouben (*Armenian Freedom Fighters*, 114–15, 121–22, 125–27, 175), and Report by Mark Sykes, enclosed with Maunsell to O'Conor, no. 36, Istanbul, June 12, 1905 (FO 424/208).

104. Scott, *Seeing Like a State*, 186.

105. Ibid.

106. Giddens, *Nation-State and Violence*, 227–30.

107. See, for example, Chermside to Currie, Istanbul, Dec. 6, 1894 (FO 424/178; FO 195/1837) and Chermside to Currie, Istanbul, Apr. 8, 1895 (FO 424/182). And in his memoirs, retired general Fahrettin Altay, who had firsthand experience with the Hamidiye, writes that in spite of the grand plans for them, they existed "only on paper, [and] for years these regiments were neither educated nor disbanded. To the contrary, they were spoiled and were, as a result, out of control, and in some towns those [young men] who came of age were registered in these regiments and were thus able to escape military service" (*10 Yıl Savaş ve Sonrası (1912–1922)*, 55).

108. Tyrrell to O'Conor, no. 43, Van, Dec. 24, 1903 (FO 424/206); Mayevski, *Van ve Bitlis Vilayetleri Askerî İstatistiği*, 196.

109. Chermside to Currie, Istanbul, Apr. 8, 1895 (FO 424/182), citing a report from Consul Graves dated Jan. 30, 1895.

110. In Karaca, *Anadolu Islahâtı*, 178. Indeed, some even questioned that the Hamidiye truly existed as a force at all. Lynch wrote of his interview with Riza Beg, the Hamidiye Hasananli chief, who gave "very evasive answers" to the questions Lynch posed about annual training of the militia. Lynch concluded, "one hears so very much, and one sees so very little of this formidable Hamidiyeh! Melazkert is a kind of headquarters for the force; and I feel sure that, if

even one regiment were in actual existence, it would have been paraded for our benefit" (*Armenia*, 2: 276).

111. A point made by Holm, "Militarization of Native America," 463. See also Young, *Minorities and the Military*, esp. 5–7.

112. Nicolai, "Different Kind of Courage," 54.

113. Ibid., 60.

114. Holm, "Militarization of Native America," 463.

115. Van Bruinessen, *Agha, Shaikh and State*, 144.

116. Acting Consul Hampson to White, Erzurum, Jan. 30, 1891 (FO 195/1728; FO 424/169).

117. See Kodaman on this point ("Hamidiye Hafif Süvari Alayları [II. Abdül-hamid ve Doğu-Anadolu Aşiretleri]," 437).

118. Moreau, in her "Bosnian Resistance to Conscription in the Nineteenth Century," 129–37, submits that the Bosnian reserve cavalry regiments, which were originally created in 1836, but which were not actually a true force until the 1860s, may have served as a precedent for the Hamidiye Light Cavalry. I have found no other evidence to confirm Moreau's suggestion; however, her point about the regiments being created to obtain the loyalty of local notables is certainly well-taken, and her article shows that there were indeed certain similarities between the Bosnian and Kurdish regiments. There was also a short-lived effort to recruit locals into an infantry formation in Yemen from 1880 to 1882, and indeed this organization was called "Hamidiye soldiers" (Asâkir-i Hamidiye). Although there were some similarities with the Hamidiye organization under discussion in this book, particularly in regard to the state's efforts to recruit locals in the periphery to manage local threats, the organization was apparently not organized tribally and, as far as I have been able to discern, did not serve as a precedent for the Hamidiye Light Cavalry in the minds of those who created the Kurdish militia (see Cengiz Çakaloğlu, "Yemen Halkından Yerel Askerî Teşkilat Kurma Denemeleri").

119. Many in touch with Ottoman ruling circles were aware of the sultan's vision of the Hamidiye as some sort of Kurdish Cossack brigade. See, for example, Acting Consul Hampson to White, Erzurum, Jan. 30, 1891 (FO 195/1728; FO 424/169); White to Marquis of Salisbury, Confidential draft no. 68, Istanbul, Feb. 24, 1891 (FO 424/169); and Acting Vice-Consul Boyadjian to Acting Consul Hampson, Confidential, Diyarbekir, Feb. 24, 1891 (FO 424/169).

120. See Ure, *The Cossacks*; Longworth, *The Cossacks;* and McNeal, *Tsar and Cossack.*

121. McNeal, *Tsar and Cossack*, 1.

122. Ibid., 2. See also Ure, *The Cossacks*, 205. This distinctive relationship cultivated in nineteenth-century Russia between the tsar and the Cossacks was consecrated in a statue erected in Novocherkassk in 1904, which represented the "official myth of tsar and Cossack, of mutual loyalty and generosity, the warrior-cast providing self-sacrificing valour and the monarch rewarding them with land and privilege" (McNeal, *Tsar and Cossack*, 1).

123. One British traveler was also under the impression that the Russians had reduced a number of Kurdish tribes in its territory to subjection and had

"even made excellent irregular cavalry out of the wild riders of which they are composed" (Creagh, *Armenians, Koords, and Turks,* 201).

124. Indeed this notion was attributed to the sultan when he first encountered the tribal leaders during their initial visit to Istanbul, where he told them that they would abandon their nomadic lifestyle as part of the venture (undated memorandum signed "Selim" from the BOA, Yıldız Evrak Odası).

125. BOA, Y.MTV 138/92 (16 Mart 1313 [Mar. 28, 1897]): Minister of War Reza reports on the returnees from training in Russia to be used in training the Hamidiye in the Fourth and Fifth Army Corps, and recommends that the returnees be promoted to the rank of captain. Using documents from the Ottoman Archives, Deringil has also been able to illustrate how seriously the Ottomans took their Cossack model ("Ottoman Twilight Zone," 16, esp. n. 15).

126. Several documents in the Ministry of Foreign Affairs Archives mention these plans and record the journey of some Hamidiye regiments to the capital in the summer of 1896 (MAE Nantes, Série E, Affaires Arméniennes/113). These plans, never truly implemented, were again revived in 1905 (Srabian to Boppe, no. 89, Erzurum, Sept. 1, 1905 [MAE Nantes, Série E/118]).

127. Enloe has described the paradigm she refers to as the "Gurkha syndrome," in which the "perfect 'martial race'" was an ethnic group that produced men who were both martial *and* loyal." But,

the combination is not a natural one when, typically, the group only recently has waged protracted battles against the recruiting institution. They key ingredient necessary to make martial traits and allegiance compatible is *dependency.* By making an ethnic group dependent, the state élite can move it from the outer rim of the security map to a circle closer to the core. Those groups which have been defeated have little access to central authority and are frequently outnumbered within the newly consolidated state system. It is such vulnerability that permits recruiters to absorb them into the military with little fear of subversion or mutiny. . . . Furthermore, they are often objects of suspicion or contempt in the eyes both of other ethnic groups and the state élites. They are urged to see military service as a vehicle for gaining respect, legitimacy and protection in the larger social order of which they are now, albeit reluctantly, a part (*Ethnic Soldiers,* 27).

128. Klein, "Tribal Militias from the Wild West" and "Noble Savages or Savage Notables?"

129. Indeed for some "Persians and Turkis," as one traveler observed, the Kurd was "a sort of 'bogey-man,' used for frightening children and even grown-up people" (Harris, *From Batum to Baghdad via Tiflis,* 227).

130. See Kodaman on this point ("Hamidiye Hafif Süvari Alayları [II. Abdül-hamid ve Doğu-Anadolu Aşiretleri]," 443).

131. Acting Vice-Consul Boyadjian to Acting Consul Hampson, Confidential, Diyarbekir, Feb. 24, 1891 (FO 424/169).

132. Hampson to White, Erzurum, Apr. 4, 1891 (FO 424/169).

133. Wigoreaux to Ribot, no. 111, Erzeroum, Apr. 11, 1891 (MAE Paris, CPC Turquie, Erzeroum, vol. 7).

134. M[ehmed] 'Arif, *Başımıza Gelenler,* 264–65. The writer concluded,

"Our administrative officials and military should have acted in a proper manner to eradicate the barbarity and ignorance of these people. If the number of those whose ideas are educated and whose characters are refined are multiplied, then they would render huge services to the Islamic community." The British consul had a different opinion, however. Writing in 1890, Consul Devey, in a long report that was designed to clear up the many false reports circulating in England that the object of the Ottoman government was to exterminate the Armenians, added: "In respect of the Beys and Aghas mistaken notions are prevalent, such as that the Turks fear them, or that they occupy formidable strongholds, and are strong enough to resist a military force, and hate their nominal masters; these ideas are clearly erroneous; the Kurds are not less loyal and trustworthy than other Ottoman subjects, though in rare parts of the mountain fastnesses they inhabit, the influence of the Government is scarcely perceptible. As to their 'hating their nominal masters,' perhaps, under present conditions, indifference, mingled sometimes with a touch of contempt, more accurately represents the state of mind of some Kurds" (Consul Devey, "Memorandum on the Misleading Views respecting Armenian Affairs disseminated by paragraphs periodically recurring in certain Newspapers, in particular the 'Daily News,' and upon the Condition of the Kurds and Armenians generally," enclosed with Devey to White, Van, Jan. 12, 1891, PRO, FO 424/169).

135. Graves to Ford, Confidential draft no. 48, Erzurum, Aug. 12, 1892 (FO 195/1766; FO 424/172). Indeed, in his memoirs, the former governor of Mosul, described the Hamidiye as being one of his most recurring "nightmares" (Tepeyran, *Hatıralar,* 317).

136. Sultan Abdülhami[d], "Kanun-u Esasi [1894]," in *Siyasî Hatıratım,* 74–75.

137. Deringil notes that the "imperial chief of staff continued to report that various *Hamidiye* tribal commanders 'did not show the necessary characteristics of command and responsibility'" ("Ottoman Twilight Zone," 18).

138. Ibid.

139. Derisziger and Preston, "Polyethnicity and Armed Forces," 3.

140. Sultan Abdülhami[d], "Kanun-u Esasi [1894]," 75.

141. Extract from the "Envar Sharkié [*Envâr-ı Şarkiyye*]" of Erzurum, Feb. 20, 1891, translation (FO 195/1728; FO 424/169).

142. Extract from the *Levant Herald* of Apr. 3, 1891, "The Kurdish Cavalry" (FO 78/4344; FO 424/169). The *Salnâme-i Vilayet-i Bitlis* (1310/1892) similarly hailed the Hamidiye as "one of the most distinguished and good works of the government" (162).

143. The Ottoman minister of war confided this to the British military attaché (in Currie to the Marquess of Salisbury, no. 25, Istanbul, Jan. 11, 1897 (FO 424/191).

144. "The Development of the Military Strength of Turkey," by Captain O.B.S.F. Shore, 18th Bengal Lancers, translated from the *International Revue* for Nov. 1893 and *Die Reichswehr* for February 1894 (FO 78/4561).

145. In the words of Rogan, *Frontiers of the State,* 14.

146. Rogan, "Aşiret Mektebi," 85.

147. Quoted in Akpınar, *Osmanlı Devletinde Aşiret Mektebi*, 20. Mardin has also pointed out the "Ottoman civilized man's stereotype that civilization was a contest between urbanization and nomadism, and that all things nomadic were only deserving of contempt" ("Center-Periphery Relations," 170–71).

148. Deringil, in his *Well-Protected Domains*, and Kodaman have emphasized the Hamidiye, the Tribal School, and similar endeavors in the context of the sultan's pan-Islamic (read orthodox) policies, and Kushner has pointed to the sentiments of Turkish nationalism, or Turkism, in the Hamidian period (*Rise of Turkish Nationalism*).

149. Again, see Rogan, "Aşiret Mektebi," esp. 91–92. These were similar to the before-and-after photos that were proudly displayed by architects of the Indian boarding schools in the United States. It seems that there were not too many children from Kurdish tribes who actually attended the school, at least not the numbers projected in the initial plans, but we do know that there were provisions made early on (1890) for at least four boys from the Cibran tribe to attend not the Tribal School, which had not yet been created, but the Imperial Military Academy (BOA YMM 48/83-4, reproduced in Ergül, *II. Abdülhamid'in Doğu Politikası ve Hamidiye Alayları*, 56–57). Although Rogan's information leads us to believe that the Kurdish population of the school was relatively smaller than that of other groups, Hasan Sıddık Hayderani, who was himself a student at the Tribal School, writes that more than half of the two hundred students enrolled were Kurdish. His is also an interesting source for understanding the daily life of the students, as he mentions their daily routine, and the subject of their quarrels with other students (147–48). Hayderani was the nephew of Hayderan Hamidiye commander Hüseyin Pasha and the son of Mehmed Sıddık Bey, who was also a Hamidiye commander of the tribe.

150. The lists provided in Rogan, "Aşiret Mektebi," 89–90; and Akpınar (67–69) indicate that several Hamidiye tribes had students in the school, including the Şemsikî, Cibran, Hayderan, Karapapak, and Millî tribes.

151. Rogan, "Aşiret Mektebi," 87, 90–91.

152. Ibid., 91.

153. Cited in ibid., 38.

154. Some fourteen tribal chiefs in the Bayazid region, for example, sent a letter to the sultan asking for imperial permission to enroll some of their children in the Tribal School. This letter was forwarded to the sultan via telegraph by Eyüb Pasha, the leader of the Zilan tribe, along with Hasan and Ali Beys, who were commanders of the Fifth and Sixth Hamidiye Regiments (see Akpınar, 38–39 and appendix, which includes a copy of the original letter and the imperial decree, and Karaca, *Anadolu Islahâtı*, 176).

155. Akpınar provides an account of the interesting tensions that developed over the question of enrolling Hamidiye students in the Tribal School (*Osmanlı Devletinde Aşiret Mektebi*, 38–43). Indeed the minister of education was correct in his interpretation of the clause in the Hamidiye regulations that spelled out the kind of education envisioned for the troops. They were to enroll in a special cavalry class, but there was nowhere in the document that mentioned the Tribal School. Those who supported the petition of the Kurdish tribal chiefs

were basing their assertion that the regulations provided for the enrollment of Hamidiye children in the Tribal School on a willful misinterpretation of the text. Incidentally, it would also be interesting to research whatever "affirmative action" policies existed for Arabs and Albanians.

156. Fitzmaurice to Hampson, no. 4, Van, Apr. 9, 1892 (FO 195/1766; FO 424/172).

157. See Karaca, *Anadolu Islahâtı*, esp. 182–90.

158. See also Kasaba, *Moveable Empire*, esp. chap. 4.

159. Ottoman Government, *Tensikat-ı Askeriyye Cümlesinden Olarak Hamidiye Süvari Alaylarına Da'ir Kanunnamedir*, article 19. See also the report from Zeki Pasha to the sultan (BOA Y.PRK.ASK 101/48, 28 Teşrin-i Evvel 1310 [Nov. 9, 1894]). Enloe has also pointed out that "tribes" were attractive to states seeking to recruit "martial races" as they were

perceived . . . as societies with rather confined societal boundaries in which bonds of personal allegiance and reciprocity play basic roles in locating authority and distributing power. . . . What was recognized within such communities was a mode of social organization that would enhance enlistments. . . . Individual enlistment may be worth the effort if the state is recruiting *officers*, for they have to have special individual characteristics, and not too many persons have to be enticed at any one time. But, to fill the ranks you need to bring in scores or even hundreds of men at a time. To fill the ranks, it is more efficient to operate through authority figures within a structure community who can draw upon existing bonds of obligation and credibility for the sake of bringing their communal subordinates into the army. Voters are mobilized in many societies in precisely the same fashion. All that is needed is (a) for those authority structures to stay intact so that communal élites maintain their superior status over subordinate members of the community, and (b) for outside military recruiters to make it rewarding for the communal élites to play this middleman role as suppliers of men to the ranks (*Ethnic Soldiers*, 27–28).

160. Fitzmaurice to Hampson, no. 18 (should be no. 13), Van, June 6, 1892 (FO 195/1766; FO 424/172).

161. Chermside to Ford, no. 9, Istanbul, Mar. 19, 1892 (FO 195/1759; FO 424/172). The British consul also reported that he had been informed by Zeki Pasha himself of the government's plans to enroll Arab tribes. The pasha reported that he had already received promises to produce regiments by the Shammar, 'Anayza, and Tay Arabs (of which only the Tay ended up forming a regiment) and that the following year enrollment was to proceed in the Fifth (Syria), Sixth (Baghdad), and Seventh (Yemen) Army Corps, which comprised most of the Arab lands (see Fitzmaurice to Hampson, no. 15, Van, June 11, 1892 [FO 195/1766; FO 424/172]). Documents from the Ottoman archives indicate that tribes in the Aleppo region (in the Fifth Army Corps) declared their loyalty and enrolled as well (BOA, Y.MTV 136, 21 Teşrin-i Sani 1310 [Dec. 3, 1894]), but little was heard from them after this point.

162. Chermside to Currie (Ambassador), Istanbul, June 4, 1894, no. 32 (FO 195/1837). See also BOA YEE.139/13.5 (11 Şubat 1308 [Feb. 23, 1893]) and YA.Res.2/79 (12 Şaban 1310 [Mar. 1, 1893]), in Süphandağ, *Büyük Osmanlı*

Entrikası Hamidiye Alayları, 97–101. I take this author's transliterations with a grain of salt, as I have compared some of the documents I happened to have on hand with his transliterations of them. He has taken certain liberties with the documents, "modernizing" a few of the Ottoman Turkish words and syntax.

163. Hampson to Blunt, no. 38, May 31, 1898 (FO 78/4936). Indeed the earliest plans for recruitment also included Bosnian nomadic tribes under the Fifth and Sixth Army Corps (BOA, Y.MTV 67/1, 23 Ağustos, 1307 [Sept. 4, 1891]).

164. Ponsonby to O'Conor, Confidential draft no. 15, Istanbul, Nov. 23, 1898 (FO 195/2016).

165. The sultan even planned at one point early in the enrollment initiatives to try to enlist Kurds from the Iranian side of the border, recognizing that the borders did not accurately reflect tribal divisions. The Iranian government was, needless to say, not fond of the idea, and the Russians supported an active campaign to dissuade tribesmen from joining the Hamidiye (Ahmad, *Kurdistan During the First World War*, 57). Ottomans also made attempts to enlist members of the Persian regular cavalry as mercenaries (Hampson to White, Erzurum, Political no. 56, June 6, 1891 [FO 195/1729]). The Iranians were watching the Hamidiye closely, however, especially to see if it was successful, then it might serve as a model for organizing similar regiments on their side of the border (see Graves to Ford, Political no. 35, Erzurum, June 10, 1892 [FO 195/1766; FO 424/172]).

166. Not all tribal peoples were Muslim, although most were. An exception in southeastern Anatolia could be found in the tribal Nestorians who lived in the Hakkari mountains. In fact, the former Armenian revolutionary, Rouben, mentions that a very small part of the Armenian population, particularly of the Sasun mountains, were constituted in some tribelike way of life, and some of them were part of other tribes (Rouben, *Armenian Freedom Fighters*, 67–68).

167. See Deringil, *Well-Protected Domains*.

168. See Ateş, "Empires at the Margin."

169. Sultan Abdülhami[d], "Dahilî iskân [1893]," in *Siyasî Hatıratım*, 73. It should also be pointed out that there did seem to be efforts, a good decade and a half after the creation of the Hamidiye, to institute some sort of system of checks and balances on the Hamidiye (and other) Kurds. In 1904, a new force of *Seyyare* gendarmes were formed from Circassian immigrants from the Bulanık district and from other parts of the Bitlis province. The British consul reporting on the formation believed that it was the intention of the government to use the Cirassian immigrants "as a check on the turbulence of the Kurds" (Heathcote to O'Conor, no. 11, Bitlis, Mar. 19, 1904 [FO 424/206]). The notion of a "Turkish Anatolia" was, as David Kushner has illustrated (*Rise of Turkish Nationalism*, esp. 50–55), becoming more prevalent during the Hamidian period. Research is needed on the dynamics introduced by large numbers of Circassians into Anatolia in the nineteenth century.

170. It is important to note that Dersim as a region was larger than the *sancak* of Dersim. Alevis constituted some 30 percent of the *sancak* of Harput-Mezre, 31 percent of the Malatya *sancak* and 43 percent of the *sancak* of Dersim-Ho-

zat, the three *sancak*s that made up the province of Harput (Ma'muret'ül-'Aziz) (see Cuinet, *La Turquie de l'Asie*, vol. 2).

171. For more extensive discussion of the debates and efforts surrounding Yezidi and Alevi recruitment see Klein, "Ein kritischer Blick."

172. This idea surfaces repeatedly in Fırat, for one, along with Ergül (*II. Abdülhamid'in Doğu Politikası ve Hamidiye Alayları*, 95). It may be true that the sultan was suspicious of the Alevis, but this does not change the fact that Zeki Pasha attempted to incorporate them into the Hamidiye anyway, perhaps in order to build bonds of loyalty along the same lines as he was doing with the other tribes.

173. See Deringil, *Well-Protected Domains*, 70, on Şakir Pasha's views on recruiting Yezidis.

CHAPTER TWO

1. Abdurrahman Bedir Khan, "Kürdler ve Ermeniler [Kurds and Armenians]," *Kurdistan*, no. 26 (1 Kânûn-i Evvel 1316 [Dec. 14, 1900]), in Bozarslan, *Kurdistan* reprint, vol. 2.

2. Ceziret-ibn-'Umar was originally attached to the Diyarbekir province's Mardin *sancak*, but was attached to Mosul around the turn of the nineteenth century. It was reattached to Diyarbekir a few decades later.

3. Izady presents a variant of this narrative in *Kurds: A Concise Handbook*.

4. The *Sharafname* mentions twenty *mîr*s, but twenty-five are mentioned in Parry, "Reigns of Bayazid II and Selim I," 71. See Tezcan, "Development of the Use of 'Kurdistan,'" 544.

5. The "later historian" is Parry, "Reigns of Bayazid II and Selim I," 72.

6. Van Bruinessen, "Ottoman Conquest of Diyarbekir," in Van Bruinessen and Boeschoten, *Evliya Çelebi in Diyarbekir*, 16–17.

7. The devastation wreaked by the Ottoman-Safavid wars on these people was mourned, for example, by Ehmedê Xanî, who versified the famous Kurdish epic, *Mem û Zîn*, in 1694. While the story is a Kurdish version of a love story between two individuals from rival clans whose union is obstructed—a recurrent theme in the literature of the entire Middle East—the story is said by many to represent, through Mem and Zîn, the protagonists, the two parts of Kurdistan divided between the Ottoman and Iranian empires and the failure of the Kurdish people to unite under a ruler of their own (for this interpretation see, for example, Hassanpour, *Nationalism and Language*, 83–90).

8. Tezcan, "Development of the Use of 'Kurdistan,'" 546.

9. Ibid.

10. Ibid.

11. See van Bruinessen, "Ottoman Conquest of Diyarbekir," 17–22.

12. Tezcan, "Development of the Use of 'Kurdistan,'" 547.

13. See *Evliya Çelebi in Diyarbekir*, with van Bruinessen's introduction to the work, and Tezcan, "Development of the Use of 'Kurdistan,'" 547–49.

14. Evliya Çelebi's *Seyahatname* in van Bruinessen and Boeschoten, *Evliya*

Çelebi in Diyarbekir, esp. 121–27. See also van Bruinessen, *Agha, Shaikh and State,* 157–61.

15. Tezcan, "Development of the Use of 'Kurdistan,'" 148–49. See also van Bruinessen, "Ottoman Conquest of Diyarbekir," 17, for instances in which hereditary grants were either revoked or reinstated by the sultan.

16. See van Bruinessen and Boeschoten, 17–28 and 121–128. Kunt also mentions the names of those who ruled the districts of the provinces of Diyarbekir and Kurdistan in 1527 (*Sultan's Servants,* 107–8). Some of these were official and others were de facto. van Bruinessen mentions that there were some practically independent emirates, such as the Baban and Soran, which existed as such into the nineteenth century, that were not officially recognized as *Ekrad Beyliği* or *Kürd hükümeti* (van Bruinessen, *Agha, Shaikh and State,* 159–60).

17. Border crossing could have dangerous consequences for an already underpopulated region. The Ottomans wanted to prevent the emigration of its inhabitants of these regions not just in the sixteenth, but also in the nineteenth and twentieth centuries. They needed to ensure that cultivation continued and that the tribes with their enormous numbers of flocks would remain part of the Ottoman economic system.

18. Abdurrahman Bedir Khan, "Welat-Weten [Homeland-Motherland]," *Kurdistan,* no. 9 (3 Kânûn-i Evvel 1314 [Dec. 15, 1898]), in Bozarslan, *Kurdistan* reprint, vol. 1.

19. The year 1250 (1835) is mentioned by Abdurrahman Bedir Khan as the year in which Bedir Khan Beg became the "ruler of Kurdistan" (*hakîmê Kurdistan*). See Abdurrahman Bedir Khan, "Bedir Xan Beg," *Kurdistan,* no. 13, 29 Zîlqe'de 1316 [Apr. 2, 1899]), 3 (in Bozarslan, *Kurdistan* reprint, vol. 1).

20. "Sister emirates" are van Bruinessen's words (*Agha, Shaikh and State,* 177). See ibid., 177–80.

21. See ibid., 178–79, after Safrastian.

22. See the map provided in ibid., 178.

23. Ahmed Lütfi, *Tarih-i Lütfi,* 474–75.

24. Van Bruinessen, *Agha, Shaikh and State,* 179.

25. Süleyman Nazif recalls seeing a coin inscribed "Emir-i Bohtan Bedirhan" from 1258 (1842 or 1843) when he was a child ("Nasturiler," *Son Telgraf* (23 Rebi-ü'levvel 1343/22 Teşrin-i Evvel 1340 [Oct. 22, 1924]). in Malmîsanij, *Cizira Botanlı Bedirhaniler,* app. 8, 261–65.

26. Ahmed Lütfi, *Tarih-i Lütfi,* 143.

27. Shields, *Mosul Before Iraq,* 57. This was not necessarily an anti-Christian pogrom, but rather a battle over local authority after alliances in the emirate of Çulamerik shifted, the shift being accompanied by a schism within the Nestorian community.

28. Ahmed Lütfi, *Bedirhan Bey,* 18.

29. The text of the speech attributed to Bedir Khan Beg upon his arrival to Istanbul is reproduced in Ahmed Lütfi, *Tarih-i Lütfi,* 506–7.

30. Davison, *Reform in the Ottoman Empire,* 55.

31. Ibid.

32. Shaw, "Nineteenth-Century Ottoman Tax Reforms and Revenue System."

33. See Findley, *Bureaucratic Reform in the Ottoman Empire*, 5–6.

34. Davison, *Reform in the Ottoman Empire*, 136–71; Ortyalı, *Tanzimattan Sonra Mahallî İdareler*.

35. Another region that deserves mention here is Cilicia, which has been studied in a fascinating article by Gould ("Lords or Bandits? The Derebeys of Cilicia").

36. Van Bruinessen, "Kurds, States, and Tribes," 169. See also chap. 2 of his *Agha, Shaikh and State*.

37. Bayazîdî, *'Edet ve Rusûmetname-i Ekradîyye*, 102.

38. [Unsigned], Report on Vilayet of Bitlis, Jan. 30, 1885 (FO 195/1521).

39. Asad's work has been important for debunking the myths of "nomadic society" or "nomadic mode of production" as "theoretically unviable concepts" ("Equality in Nomadic Social Systems?"). Haj has also provided an important essay on this theme in her book, *The Making of Iraq, 1900–1963*, 13–18. Other important critiques include Tapper, "Anthropologists, Historians, and Tribespeople"; Caton, "Anthropological Theories of Tribe"; and Beck, "Tribes and the State."

40. Shields has emphasized the flaws in the prevailing view of nomads, held until recently, that has assumed "a constant struggle between settled and nomadic populations," in her "Sheep, Nomads, and Merchants," 774–76.

41. Indeed this is a central assertion of van Bruinessen's work, *Agha, Shaikh and State*, in which he remarks that in some ways, tribes may "even be seen as *creations of the state*" (134).

42. See van Bruinessen, "Kurds, States, and Tribes," and also Tapper, "Anthropologists, Historians, and Tribespeople," on this point (esp. 65–68).

43. Bozarslan, "Tribus, confréries et intellectuels," 64.

44. Hamit Bozarslan, personal communication, Aug. 2002.

45. Some tribes were given the status of *nahiye* (local district), and their chiefs were appointed *müdür*s of those (sometimes mobile) *nahiye*s (Ortaylı, 93–94).

46. Longrigg, *Iraq, 1900 to 1950*, 25. Although Longrigg's work only deals with a small section of the region that is covered in this study, his observations appear to be valid for sections farther north.

47. Ibid.

48. Some of these were "tools" of the local notables, who, during the nineteenth century began to acquire new powers with their roles in administrative councils and the like (see Mardin, "Center-Periphery Relations," 175–80; and Duguid, "Politics of Unity," 142–45).

49. Indeed this had been an issue with which Ottoman rulers had to contend for a longer period than that under review (see Shaw, *Between Old and New*, 80–85, 98–109).

50. Hourani has suggested that the different manners and extents to which Tanzimat reforms were carried out in different parts of the empire led to a situation in which in some cases the reforms actually strengthened the local notables

from whom the government, in theory, was trying to wrest control ("Ottoman Reform and the Politics of Notables," 62).

51. Two other parts of the empire that were brought under tighter control during this period were Libya (see Anderson, *State and Social Transformation*; and Ahmida, *Making of Modern Libya*), and Transjordan (see Rogan, *Frontiers of the State*).

52. Places such as Yemen and Arabia were also areas where the state attempted to penetrate, but, like Kurdistan, were regions in which the central Ottoman government was not able to fulfill many of its objectives with regards to imposing direct rule, and where, like Kurdistan, it continued to rely on the support of certain local notables or sheikhs. On Yemen, see Dresch, *Tribes, Government, and History in Yemen*; and Farah, *Sultan's Yemen*; and on Arabia, see Ochsenwald, *Religion, Society, and the State in Arabia*.

53. See Bozarslan, "Tribus, confréries et intellectuels," 64.

54. See Ortaylı, 93–94. According to Özoğlu, the province of Kurdistan, which was created after 1847, was renamed Diyarbekir in 1867 (*Kurdish Notables and the Ottoman State*, 61–62).

55. Van Bruinessen, *Agha, Shaikh and State*, 193.

56. Sheikhs were the spiritual guides of mystical orders (*tariqats*), and were sometimes able to build huge followings and enjoyed quite a lucrative business for their mediation and other skills. Some were highly venerated. Such a profitable thing it was to be a sheikh in nineteenth-century Kurdistan that there were many who sought to be one. A British consular officer reported in 1885 that there was a revival in religious sentiment in Siirt, which was accompanied by "a strong desire on the part of several [men] . . . to assume the title of Sheikh." He observed an increase in beards and green turbans worn by those seeking sheikhdom (see [Anon.], Report on Vilayet of Bitlis, Jan. 30, 1885 [FO 195/1521]).

57. See W. Jwaideh, "Kurdish Nationalist Movement," 213–15; van Bruinessen, *Agha, Shaikh and State*, esp. 228–34; and also van Bruinessen, "Religion in Kurdistan," esp. 24–33. McDowall also provides a good summary in his *Modern History of the Kurds*, 52.

58. See Bozarslan, "Tribus, confréries et intellectuels," 64–65.

59. See Tapper's critique of this view, "Anthropologists, Historians, and Tribespeople," 61.

60. Ibid., 51. See also Ferguson and Whitehead, "Violent Edge of Empire," in Ferguson and Whitehead, eds., *War in the Tribal Zone*.

61. Van Bruinessen, *Agha, Shaikh and State*.

62. I am referring here to *mîr* in the sense of "emir"; however, it should also be remembered that tribal leaders could also be called *mîr*.

63. Van Bruinessen, *Agha, Shaikh and State*, 178–79.

64. Devey, Acting Consul for Kurdistan, to White, Ambassador, Confidential draft no. 1, Erzurum, Jan. 14, 1885 (*sic*: 1886) (FO 195/1552).

65. The term *koçer*, or shepherd, could be used as an insult among tribes in the vicinity of Mosul, where "to be a nomad is considered noble; while in the mountains the word *kochar*, or shepherd, is synonymous with 'savage,' 'ignorant' or 'brutish'" (Sykes, "Kurdish Tribes of the Ottoman Empire," 455). Thus,

Abdurrahman Bedir Khan's portrayal of Misto Agha as a "shepherd" may just have been a demeaning term used to indicate that he was of low status and undeserving of the tribe's leadership. It should also be noted that Mark Sykes himself engaged in the most rampant of stereotyping of what he considered to be different classes of Kurds and paid particular attention to physical attributes of different tribes in his classification, for example, classifying the women of one tribe as "bold and manly" (Herki tribe, 458) and the men of another (Tirikan) as "tall and well built, fairly industrious, but not very hospitable" (463). His physical characterizations seemed to overlap with Kurdish prejudices in some ways, and were certainly part of the European ideas of his time on race, class, and physiognomy. For example, of the Shemsiki tribe, Sykes wrote: "The tribesmen are very ugly as a rule, and the chiefs refined and handsome" (462).

66. Devey to White, Confidential draft no. 1, Erzurum, Jan. 14, 1885 (*sic*: 1886) (FO 195/1552). Parentheses in original. Sarah Shields has also emphasized the importance of being named paramount chief in her larger discussion of the importance of nomads to the local economy in nineteenth-century Mosul, and the interdependence of the settled and nomadic populations on one another in commercial matters ("Sheep, Nomads, and Merchants," esp. 780).

67. Acting Vice-Consul Boyadjian to Acting Consul Hampson, Confidential, Diyarbekir, Feb. 24, 1891 (FO 424/169). See also an unsigned document on information on "Moustapha Pacha" dated May–June, 1895, (MAE Nantes, E/97).

68. Devey to White, Confidential draft no. 1, Erzurum, Jan. 14, 1885 (*sic*: 1886) (FO 195/1552).

69. Boyajian to Wratislaw, Political no. 4, Confidential, Diyarbekir, Jan. 24, 1888 (FO 195/1617). Parentheses in original.

70. In the words of Sykes, "Kurdish Tribes in the Ottoman Empire," 460.

71. An attempt to catalog all the tribes in Kurdistan is beyond the scope of this study. Mark Sykes's article provides notes on hundreds of tribes ("Kurdish Tribes in the Ottoman Empire"). See also van Bruinessen for more information on how tribes lived (*Agha, Shaikh and State*, esp. chap. 2). Bayazîdî is also an interesting source to use for details on the customs and ways of life of tribal Kurds (*'Edet ve Rusûmetname-i Ekradîyye*).

72. According to Sykes, "Kurdish Tribes of the Ottoman Empire," 460; and Devey to White, Confidential draft no. 1, Erzurum, Jan. 14, 1885 (*sic*: 1886) (FO 195/1552).

73. Devey to White, Confidential draft no. 1, Erzurum, Jan. 14, 1885 (sic: 1886) (FO 195/1552).

74. The British consul at Van observed, for example, that Armenians from Şatak, accompanied by a Muslim member of the Administrative Council, would go to the Mîran camps in the nearby mountains to purchase wool (Devey to Graves, no. 9, Van, Aug. 2, 1893 [FO 195/1804]).

75. Devey to White, Confidential draft no. 1, Erzurum, Jan. 14, 1885 (*sic*: 1886) (FO 195/1552).

76. The tax exemptions were complicated and constantly a source of negotiation and confusion (BOA Y.PRK.ASK 91/97 [10 Haziran 1309 (June 22, 1893)]).

77. See van Bruinessen, *Agha, Shaikh and State*, esp. 53–59.

78. Mustafa Pasha headed regiment numbers 48 and 49. He may have been supreme commander of the two regiments, but it seems that his son, Abdulkerim, was also commander of one of the regiments and was given the rank lieutenant-colonel (see Laffont to Cambon, Diyarbekir, Feb. 6, 1898 [MAE Nantes, E/111]. Not all Hamidiye commanders were recognized by the term *pasha*, only a select few, indeed those I have chosen to highlight in this study—Mustafa Pasha (Mîran), İbrahim Pasha (Millî), and Hüseyin Pasha (Hayderan).

79. Shields, *Mosul Before Iraq*, chap. 5.

80. Ibid., 175.

81. Ibid., 173.

82. In some places, officials tried various means to simply prevent raids on sheep and other animals. The governor of Mosul, for example, tried to raise funds for mules for mule-mounted troops to patrol the region against animal theft by local tribes (Rassam to Mockler, Mosul, Sept. 22, 1896 [FO 424/189, FO 195/1941]).

83. Mustafa Pasha was noted to receive the assistance of a regiment of regular cavalry during his annual migration toward Çulamerik, while soldiers were sent to help İbrahim Pasha against his Shammar foes (see W. J. Anderson, "Report, Diarbekir Vilayet, March quarter 1902, Apr. 2, 1902, PRO FO 195/2125).

84. See Waugh to Currie, no. 2, Diyarbekir, Apr. 6, 1898 (FO 424/196; FO 195/2025); Andrus to Boyajian, Confidential, Cizre, Nov. 17, 1893 [FO 424/178, FO 195/1846]); and Boyajian to Graves, Confidential draft no. 34, Diyarbekir, Dec. 19, 1893 (FO 195/1846).

85. Maunsell to O'Conor, no. 43, Van, Oct. 30, 1899 (FO 424/199; FO 195/2063).

86. Maunsell to O'Conor, no. 43, Van, Oct. 30, 1899 (FO 424/199, FO 195/2063). In investigating a dispute between the Mîran and Tay tribes one Ottoman inspector observed that Hamidiye members had begun taking their disputes to army, rather than civil officials because they believed that they would receive more favorable treatment (BOA Y.PRK.ASK. 134/1 [28 Ağustos, 1313 (Sept. 9, 1897)].

87. The British agent in Diyarbekir reported that "if fighting takes place between a Hamidieh and a non-Hamidieh tribe, and the Hamidieh tribe suffers, it can obtain redress through the Government, whereas a non-Hamidieh tribe has no redress. In short the Hamidieh enjoy Government protection" (W. J. Anderson, "Report, Diarbekir Vilayet, March quarter 1902, Apr. 2, 1902, PRO FO 195/2125).

88. Jones to de Bunsen, Diyarbekir, May 8, 1900, Private communication (FO 195/2082).

89. Mugherditchian to Young, Diyarbekir, Nov. 27, 1907 (FO 195/2251). Let's again take the sheep trade as an example to illustrate the extended ramifications this general situation had. While it is difficult to establish exactly how this worked, as available records of contracts and transactions documenting the custody and sale of sheep are limited and difficult to access, the following can nonetheless be surmised: the livelihoods of the merchants who speculated

in sheep or gave the tribes the custody of their sheep were intimately connected with the interests of the tribes themselves. Thus, it is unlikely that merchants would entrust their sheep to tribes who could no longer guarantee the safety and well-being of the animals. Increasingly, those tribes that had the resources to ensure access to rich pastures and to protect their sheep from rustlers were tribes that had the support of the government, and this meant enrollment in the Hamidiye. Hence, this is an example of a way in which Hamidiye tribes were able to expand their resources, power, and connections at the expense of their weaker neighbors.

90. While Christians were generally less protected than Muslims in these provinces, first, because they tended to be settled, unarmed, nontribal peasants (although there were exceptions to this, notably the tribal Nestorians of Hakkari), and second because they had fewer protectors, they were not the only victims, and they were not completely without protection. Some local governors tried very hard to maintain a rule of law and uphold security in their districts, but even where local officials were unable or unwilling to protect Christian peasants, those who were attached to a particular *agha* knew they could enjoy protection. See the anecdote recounted in Report on Vilayet of Bitlis, Jan. 30, 1885 (FO 195/1521).

91. Boyajian to Graves, no. 24, Harput, July 18, 1892 (FO 424/172; FO 195/1766).

92. Freeman to O'Conor, no. 23, Ma'muret'ül-'Aziz (Harput), Sept. 13, 1901 (FO 424/202; FO 195/2104).

93. Vice-Consul Jones to de Bunsen, no. 38, Harput, Oct. 3, 1900 (FO 424/200; FO 195/2082).

94. One report details the various weapons—and great numbers of them—held by Hamidiye chiefs and mentions the various ways in which they were able to obtain these weapons. "Nominally," the informant wrote, "they are not allowed to have them, but in fact they possess considerable numbers, which are obtained in various ways." Mustafa Pasha was noted to have about two thousand breech-loading rifles, mostly Berdans, smuggled in through Russia and Iran. İbrahim Pasha was said to have about fifteen hundred rifles, mostly Martinis. Some of those were government loaners meant for instruction while the remainder were obtained through a raid on the government magazine. Other weapons were obtained through smugglers or from soldiers who had deserted with their weapons, or by robbing guards and soldiers of their arms (see W. J. Anderson, "Report, Diarbekir Vilayet, March quarter 1902, Apr. 2, 1902, PRO FO 195/2125).

95. Chermside to White, Confidential draft no. 34, Istanbul, Aug. 21, 1891 (FO 195/1718).

96. Yaşın, *Bütün Yönleriyle Cizre*, 25. The account may be rather sensational, but it is cited to show at least the legendary aspect Mustafa Pasha came to have in Cizre. Mustafa Pasha seems to have only formed two regiments of his own, but may have overseen at least one regiment formed by the Tay tribe.

97. He was one of the few Hamidiye commanders who was actually made a pasha right from the start (see Chermside to White, Confidential draft no. 34, Istanbul, Aug. 21, 1891 [FO 195/1718]).

98. Boyajian to Hampson, no. 16, Diyarbekir, May 10, 1892 (FO 195/1766; FO 424/172).

99. Yaşın, *Bütün Yönleriyle Cizre*, 25–26. The barracks were complete with special quarters for the pasha himself. Yaşın writes that Mustafa Pasha chose many high-ranking officers from among his own and other tribes as well as the settled population, including Fettah Agha (*binbaşı*), Hacı Zuraf (*yüzbaşı*), Şeyhmus-ı Kerevan of the Tayan tribe (*yüzbaşı*), and Tahir Agha (Hamidiye military *kaymakam* [lieutenant-colonel]. Yaşın further writes that he had a number of scholars attached to his family and tribe.

100. Boyajian to Graves, Confidential draft no. 34, Diyarbekir, Dec. 19, 1893 (FO 424/178; FO 195/1846).

101. Late in 1893 Mr. Andrus spoke of a "recent division in the tribe of Kochers [commonly used term for the Mîran]," which had "not been healed." In the same paragraph he speaks of the violence between Mustafa Pasha and Muhammad Aghayê Sor; hence, it may be very tentatively concluded that this is the split he was referring to (see Mr. Andrus [or A. W. Andrews] to Boyajian, Confidential, Cizre, Nov. 17, 1893 [FO 424/178; FO 195/1846]).

102. Acting Vice-Consul Boyajian to Currie, Diyarbekir, May 18, 1895 (FO 424/182; FO 195/1887).

103. Andrus to Boyajian, Confidential, Cizre, Nov. 17, 1893 (FO 424/178; FO 195/1846). Of course it should certainly be mentioned that the villagers were squeezed not only by Mustafa Pasha but by the government and other *agha*s of region as well. Andrus also includes a list of government exactions, mentioning corrupt tax collection practices, double collection of taxes from some villages, and the taking of food and supplies by gendarmes and other traveling officials. Appended to this is also a partial list of exactions for one village (Hasana, a mostly Protestant village of some fifty houses) alone, which is a massive list of all the forced labor, animals, cash, and harvest taken by the various Şirnak aghas for the years 1891–93. Incidentally, Muhammad Agha (Muhammad Aghayê Sor) was one of the *agha*s who oppressed these villagers. The list is compared against a list from a decade earlier showing a doubling in the worth of exacted goods and labor. See also "Brief Epitome of Statement received from a Correspondent at Mosul respecting Asia Minor: Partial List of Exactions upon the Village of Mosoria (Kaïmakamlik of Jeziret) by the Government and by Mustapha Pasha, Kocher, in 1893 (Communicated by Evangelical Alliance, March 29, 1895)" (FO 424/181).

104. Rassam to Mockler, Translation, Mosul, Feb. 21, 1895 (FO 424/182).

105. Acting Vice-Consul Boyajian to Currie, Diyarbekir, May 18, 1895 (FO 424/182; FO 195/1887). Similar allegations were put forth by a French consul (Unsigned report on "Mustapha Pacha" dated May–June, 1895 [MAE Nantes, E/97]).

106. Acting Vice-Consul Boyajian to Currie, Diyarbekir, May 18, 1895 (FO 424/182; FO 195/1887). Similar complaints abound for the years to follow.

107. Acting Vice-Consul Boyajian to Currie, Diyarbekir, May 18, 1895 (FO 424/182; FO 195/1887).

108. Many sources describe Mustafa Pasha's raft racket. See also the French

vice-consul [unsigned] to Constans, no. 9. Diyarbekir, Mar. 12, 1900 (MAE Nantes, Diarbékir, 1900–1914).

109. Jones to de Bunsen, Diyarbekir, May 8, 1900, Private (FO 195/2082).

110. Rohrbach, *Hatt-ı Saltanat Bağdad Demiryolu*, quoted in Tepeyran, *Hatıralar*, 319. Tepeyran quotes the original Rohrbach text almost precisely, but modernizes a few words (for the original section on Mustafa Pasha, see Rohrbach, *Hatt-ı Saltanat Bağdad Demiryolu*, 61–63). Rohrbach concluded that under the conditions of lawlessness surrounding the freedom of the Hamidiye tribes to do whatever they pleased, construction of a railway in the region would be sheer insanity (62; also copied in Tepeyran, *Hatıralar*, 320).

111. Jones to O'Conor, no. 9, Diyarbekir, Feb. 27, 1900 (FO 424/200; FO 195/2082). The Tayan tribe was also a Hamidiye tribe, which seems to have concluded a sort of alliance with Mustafa Pasha, and between the two Hamidiye commanders, seems to have taken the whole region hostage. According to the British consul, the Tayan chief at Nusaybin, "having practically constituted himself a ruler, is exacting toll from the merchants and raising constructions in the city with the evident design of holding Nisibin as Mustafa Pasha holds Jezireh" (Jones to de Bunsen, no. 40, Harput, Oct. 10, 1900 [FO 424/200; FO 195/2082]).

112. See also BOA Y.PRK.ASK. 134/1 (Ağustos, 1313 [Sept. 9, 1897]), for more on the Mîran-Tay dispute.

113. Jones to O'Conor, no. 16, Diyarbekir, May 8, 1900 (FO 424/200; FO 195/2082).

114. Laffont to Ambassador, no. 15, Diyarbekir, July 2, 1900 (MAE Nantes, E/116).

115. Vice-Consul Jones to de Bunsen, no. 38, Harput, Oct. 3, 1900 (FO 424/200; FO 195/2082).

116. Rassam to Acting-Consul Melvill, Translation, Mosul, Dec. 4, 1900 (FO 424/202). I'm not sure who Haci Agha was. This statement is corroborated by the testimony provided in a former Ottoman governor's memoirs. Ebubekir Hâzim Tepeyran, who served as *vali* of Mosul during this period, reserved good space in his memoirs to a discussion of the evils of the Hamidiye system, devoting particular attention to the deeds of Mustafa Pasha, İbrahim Pasha (Millî) and the Ertoşî tribe, and how the central government repeatedly turned a blind eye to their unsavory activities. During the time Tepeyran was in Mosul, Mustafa Pasha had attacked a neighboring Arab tribe, killing several tribespeople and carrying off numerous animals. He was contacted via telegram (by whom is unclear) and ordered to return the stolen animals, but these orders were not approved by his patron, Zeki Pasha, who said, "Mustafa Pasha is a loyal servant of the exalted sultanate. He would never be involved in such activities." Tepeyran also discusses how Zeki Pasha cleaned up Mustafa Pasha's image to his higher patron and protected him from sanctions (Tepeyran, *Hatıralar*, 317–18).

117. Hanioğlu, *Young Turks in Opposition*, esp. pp. 23–28.

118. The preceding information is from the British military attaché's biographical sketch of Zeki Pasha (Chermside report, Jan. 17, 1893 [FO 195/1794]).

119. Devey to White, no. 6, Confidential, Erzurum, Feb. 14, 1887 (FO 195/1584).

120. Wratislaw to White, no. 22, Erzurum, June 27, 1888 (FO 195/1617).

121. Graves to Nicolson, no. 24, Confidential, Erzurum, July 12, 1893 (FO 195/1804).

122. As observed by a French consul (Roqueferrier to Cambon, no. 5, Confidential, Apr. 8, 1896 [MAE Nantes, E/113]).

123. Officials were frequently transferred, often only keeping their post for weeks, months, and in rare cases, more than two years.

124. Sultan Abdülhami[d], *Siyasî Hatıratım*, 75–76. This section of his memoir was written in 1894.

125. Tepeyran, *Hatıralar*, 316.

126. Graves to Ford, no. 48, Confidential, Erzurum, Aug. 12, 1892 (FO 424/172; FO 195/1766).

127. Telegram from Graves [to Currie], Erzurum, June 18, 1897 (FO 195/1985). Shemseddin Bey, the *vali* of Van, was the son-in-law of Rauf Pasha, the *vali* of Erzurum. Numerous pieces of correspondence detail the ways in which Zeki Pasha attempted to thwart his attempts to promote just government and security in Van (see, for example, Elliot to Currie, no. 42, Confidential, Van, Aug. 18, 1897 [FO 195/1985]; telegram from Elliot [to Currie], Van, Aug. 19, 1897 [FO 195/1985]; and Currie to the Marquess of Salisbury, no. 551, Istanbul, Aug. 30, 1897 [FO 195/1985]).

128. Maunsell to O'Conor, no. 27, Van, June 20, 1899 (FO 424/199).

129. Graves to Nicolson, no. 24, Confidential, Erzurum, July 12, 1893 (FO 195/1804).

130. Graves to Currie, Private, Erzurum, Jan. 9, 1897 (FO 195/1985).

131. See Verheij's important and nuanced contribution to this subject: "'Les frères de terre et d'eau.'"

132. These conflicting reports exist even in the body of consular correspondence (see, for example: Currie to the Earl of Kimberley, no. 268, Istanbul, Apr. 30, 1895 (FO 424/182); Hallward to Cumberbatch, no. 83, Van, Nov. 26, 1895 (FO 424/184; FO 195/1893); Elliot to Currie, no. 11, Van, Feb. 28, 1898 (FO 424/195; FO 195/2021); and Elliot to Currie, no. 18, Tabriz, May 5, 1898 [FO 424/196; FO 195/2021].

133. The same can be said of the pasha's patron, the sultan, who, if he did not order the massacres, certainly allowed them to happen.

134. Karaca, *Anadolu Islahâtı*.

135. Roqueferrier to Cambon, no. 5, Confidential, Apr. 8, 1896 (MAE Nantes, E/113).

136. Kodaman, "Hamidiye Hafif Süvari," 452–58; Ergül, *II. Abdülhamid'in Doğu Politikası ve Hamidiye Alayları*, 67–72, 74–76; and Karaca, *Anadolu Islahâtı*, 89, 94, 169–70, 177–82, and 217–22.

137. According to Karaca (*Anadolu Islahâtı*, 182), Şakir Pasha's reports drew the ire of some, who suggested to the sultan that he was actually against the Hamidiye project. Although Şakir Pasha drew the sultan's attention to his role in the conception and execution of the Hamidiye scheme and emphasized

the fact that he continued to remain committed to it, his detractors were, to some extent, successful, in darkening his name to the sultan.

138. Graves to Currie, Private, Erzurum, Mar. 27, 1897 (FO 195/1985).

139. Vice-Consul Elliot to Currie, no. 46, Van, Sept. 1, 1897 (FO 424/192; FO 195/1985).

140. Graves to Currie, no. 46, Erzurum, Dec. 4, 1897 (FO 424/192, FO 195/1985).

141. Vice-Consul Maunsell to Currie, Confidential draft no. 1, Sivas, Dec. 7, 1897 (FO 424/192; FO 195/1985).

142. Elliot to Currie, no. 1, Van, Jan. 10, 1898 (FO 424/195; FO 195/2021).

143. Elliot to Currie, no. 3, Van, Feb. 2, 1898 (FO 424/195; FO 195/2021).

144. O'Conor to the Marquess of Salisbury, no. 164, Confidential, Istanbul, Apr. 6, 1899 (FO 424/198).

145. See also Abu Manneh, "Sultan Abdulhamid II and Shaikh Abulhuda al-Sayyadi"; and Duguid, "Politics of Unity," on this point.

146. See, for example, BOA Y.PRK.ASK. 81/16: 1 (7 Nisan 1308 [Apr. 19, 1892]).

147. Graves to Currie, no. 40, Erzurum, Nov. 1, 1897 (FO 424/192; FO 195/1985). See also Roqueferrier to Boulinière, Chargé d'Affaires, no. 9, Erzurum, Oct. 30, 1897 (MAE Nantes, E/115).

148. Roqueferrier to Boulinière, Chargé d'Affaires, no. 9, Erzurum, Oct. 30, 1897 (MAE Nantes, E/115).

149. BOA Y.PRK. ASK. 91/97 (8 Haziran 1309 [June 20, 1893]).

150. Freeman to O'Conor, no. 24, Ma'muret'ül-'Aziz, Sept. 26, 1901 (FO 424/202; FO 195/2104).

151. Tyrrell to O'Conor, no. 27, Van, July 4, 1905 (FO 195/2196). Other tribes were ordered to go to Yemen, but seemed to maneuver out of it (Maunsell to O'Conor, no. 42, July 11, 1905 [FO 195/2200]).

152. Tyrrell to O'Conor, no. 3, Van, Jan. 31, 1903 (FO 195/1947). Hüseyin Pasha was only a *miralay* (colonel).

153. Heard to Barclay, no. 22, Diyarbekir, June 4, 1908 (FO 195/2283). In addition to being a project that had strategic and economic importance, the railway, which was to support pilgrims to Mecca, carried great symbolic import for Sultan Abdülhamid II, who wished to elevate the position of Islam in state and society.

154. Srabian to Boppe, no. 111, Erzurum, Oct. 8, 1905 (MAE Nantes, E/118).

155. Graves to Currie, Private, Erzurum, Feb. 23, 1897 [FO 195/1985]). Apparently, their behavior in the capital was so poor that one of their (nontribal) commanders resigned (Cillière to Cambon, no. 2, Trabzon, Jan. 8, 1897 [MAE Nantes, E/113]).

156. Hamit Bozarslan suggests that in addition to other reasons for establishing the Hamidiye, the central government (the Porte here) wanted to centralize the authority of the various brigands and put it in the hands of someone close to the government, such as Zeki Pasha ("Histoire des relations kurdo-arméniennes," 160).

157. Captain Maunsell to Currie, no. 24, Sivas, Feb. 18, 1898 (FO 424/195;

FO 195/2025). The prejudices borne by many European observers with regards to their Ottoman subjects should not be forgotten. Captain Maunsell's statements about Zeki Pasha must be framed in the captain's belief in something he called "an Oriental point of view." He reminded his reader that he was aware of the "disastrous consequences of Zekki's influence," but reminded him that he must consider the question not only from a Western vantage point but "also from an Oriental standpoint, if the motives and modes of thought of this certainly remarkable man are to be properly determined. Zekki Pasha," he continued, "is not a Christian or a humanitarian, but a Mahommedan and an Oriental." Therefore, the captain wrote, "from the former point of view his acts have been in the last degree deplorable. [But] from an Oriental point of view he has only followed the tradition and teachings of history."

158. Several sources point to Russian influences among the Kurds (see Ahmad, *Kurdistan During the First World War*, 57; and Reynolds, "Inchoate Nation Abroad" (my thanks to Mike Reynolds for providing me with a copy of his article), along with earlier observers: Lake, *Narrative of the Defence of Kars, Historical and Military*, 40, cited in Reid, *Crisis of the Ottoman Empire*, 159.

159. Tyrrell to Lowther, no. 29, Istanbul, Apr. 20, 1912 (FO 424/231; FO 195/2405).

160. Crow to Currie, Monastery of Khintig Gadat, Sept. 5, 1897 (FO 424/192; FO 195/1981).

161. Crow to Currie, Private, Bitlis, Dec. 5, 1897 (FO 195/1981). However, this British consul's French colleague attributed these "these acts of venality so prejudicial to the reputation of the Marshal" not to Zeki Pasha himself but "to certain officers of the General Staff who are charged with serving the Hamidiye regiments" (Roqueferrier to Cambon, Confidential draft no. 1, Erzurum, Jan. 16, 1897 (MAE Nantes, E/115).

162. Srabian to Constans, no. 117, Erzurum, Sept. 18, 1906 (MAE Nantes, E/118).

163. The Kurdish emirates in many ways were mirrors, on a smaller scale, of the Ottoman court to which they paid at least nominal tribute (see van Bruinessen, "Kurds, States, and Tribes," 167).

164. A point made by Hamit Bozarslan (personal communication, Aug. 2002).

165. Maunsell to de Bunsen, no. 40 (*sic*: should be 41), extracts, Undated [Sept. 16, 1900] (FO 424/200; FO 195/2082).

166. Consul Heard reported, for example, that the sheikhs of Bitlis were holding secret meetings in 1907, reportedly largely with the mission of demonstrating against the liberty accorded to the Hamidiye and to call for the removal of Zeki Pasha (Heard to O'Conor, no. 5, Bitlis, Sept. 3, 1907 [FO 424/213]). It should be noted that due to the notoriously severe censorship that existed under Sultan Abdülhamid II, these complaints were certainly not voiced in any official publications, and could only be found in clandestine journals, such as *Kurdistan*.

167. See the testimony of an Armenian villager, cited in one of the many accounts provided by missionaries in the region, which serves as an example

that illustrates this point: when one Kevork Vartanina from a village in Eleşgirt complained to Rahim Pasha that Celalî men had stolen from him and killed four members of his family, Rahim Pasha replied, "The Hamidieh Kurds are the Sultan's warriors. To do thus is right. You Armenians are liars." He was imprisoned and not released until he paid a fine in gold (in Pierce, *Story of Turkey*, 390–91).

168. Tyrrell to O'Conor, no. 21, Van, July 1, 1903 (FO 195/2147). It is ironic that the leader of the Ertoşî tribe submitted this sentiment, for his tribe had benefited vastly from the Hamidiye system (see Tepeyran, *Hatıralar*, 315–17; and BOA Y.MTV. 190/43: 1 [6 Mayıs 1315 (May 18, 1899)]).

169. Lamb to O'Conor, Confidential draft no. 2, Erzurum, Apr. 15, 1901 (FO 424/202; FO 195/2104); and Lamb to O'Conor, no. 24, Erzurum, Dec. 31, 1901 [FO 424/203; FO 195/2104]). İbrahim Pasha of the Millî tribe was also able to use his standing to absorb the weaker Karakeçi tribe into his regiment (see also Smith, "John Hugh Smith's Diary," 287).

170. Heard to O'Conor, no. 19, Erzurum, Nov. 23, 1907 (FO 424/213).

171. In Sykes, *Caliph's Last Heritage*, 406.

172. Jones to O'Conor, no. 32, Harput, Oct. 18, 1899 (FO 424/199; FO 195/2063).

173. Sadettin Paşa, *Sadettin Paşa'nın Anıları*, 30.

174. Minutes of the Ottoman Chamber of Deputies, enclosed in *Takvim-i Vekayi*, no. 158 (9 Mart 1325 [Mar. 22, 1909]).

175. Sadettin Pasha noted in his memoirs on many occasions how poorly clothed the soldiers were, and how in the dead of winter some of them did not even have pants! (*Sadettin Paşa'nın Anıları*).

176. Maunsell to O'Conor, no. 21, Van, Apr. 30, 1899 (FO 424/198; FO 195/2063). This official interviewed numerous officers on the topic and added in separate report, "In Diadin, and at some other of the Russian frontier posts, many of the officers were 'jeunes Turcs' exiled from some more favorable place, and very bitter against the way the Hamidieh were pampered and readily accorded rank which it took them many years of faithful service to attain" (Maunsell to O'Conor, no. 31, Van, July 24, 1900 [FO 424/200; FO 195/2082]).

177. Chermside to Currie, Istanbul, Apr. 8, 1895 (FO 424/182). See also Sykes, *Caliph's Last Heritage*, 420–21) and Lynch, *Armenia*, 2: 422.

178. *Sadettin Paşa'nın Anıları*, 108.

179. Ibid., 124.

180. Crow to Currie, Extract, Bitlis, Oct. 4, 1897 (FO 424/192; FO 195/1981).

181. See, for example, "Kürdlere," *Kurdistan* 25 (18 Eylül 1316 [Oct. 1, 1900]); and "Kürdler ve Ermeniler," *Kurdistan* 26 (1 Kânûn-i Evvel, 1316 [Dec. 14, 1900]), in *Kurdistan*, ed. Bozarslan, vol. 2.

182. [Abdurrahman Bedir Khan], "Alayên Siwarên Hemîdî/Hamidiye Süvari Alayları [The Hamidiye Cavalry Regiments]," *Kurdistan* 28 (1 Eylül 1317 [Sept. 14, 1901]), in Bozarslan, *Kurdistan* reprints, vol. 2.

183. Abdullah Cevdet was, incidentally, one of the four founding members of the CUP. For his activities, see Hanioğlu, *Doktor Abdullah Cevdet ve Dönemi*.

184. Bir Kürd, "Untitled?" *Droşak* (January 1900), cited in Sasuni, *Kürt*

Ulusal Hareketleri, 223–24. "Bir Kürd" was one of Abdullah Cevdet's pennames.

185. Hamit Bozarslan has also drawn attention to the efforts of Kurdish and Armenian intellectuals to promote positive relations among members of the two groups, and he also cites the hostility of Abdurrahman Bedir Khan to the Hamidiye ("Histoire des Relations Kurdo-Arméniennes," 161).

186. Consul Longworth to Currie, Trabzon, Oct. 6, 1894 (CAB 37/37/31). The *vali* of Trabzon reportedly received instructions to have Abdurrezzak Bey assassinated after this. He lived until the end of World War I, so this order was not carried out, or was not successful if it was, in fact, attempted.

187. Evidence for the latter point is stated in numerous documents for other years, before and after 1894 as well.

188. Andrus to Boyajian, Confidential, Cizre, Nov. 17, 1893 (FO 424/178; FO 195/1846). It seems that this Mehmed Bey, who is actually mentioned by Boyajian as being Muhammad Bey is actually the same Mehmed Bey spoken of seven years later by Consul Freeman (cited below).

189. Freeman to O'Conor, no. 23, Ma'muret'ül-'Aziz, Sept. 13, 1901 (FO 424/202; FO 195/2104).

190. Freeman to O'Conor, no. 24, Ma'muret'ül-'Aziz, Sept. 26, 1901 (FO 424/202; FO 195/2104).

191. Lamb to O'Conor, no. 3, Erzurum, Feb. 8, 1902 (FO 195/2125).

192. Lamb to O'Conor, no. 6, Erzurum, Mar. 28, 1902 (FO 195/2125). Although Mehmed Bey was denounced to the authorities by Mustafa Pasha as being a son of Bedir Khan Beg, who had returned from Europe to incite the Kurds to revolt, he was actually a grandson of Bedir Khan Beg's brother, Salih Beg, according to this report.

193. Although interestingly, the Bedir Khans and Aghayê Sor were not always friendly. During the attempt by Osman and Huseyin Bedir Khan to carry out a rebellion and revive their family's emirate in 1878, they attacked Aghayê Sor, and his followers formed part of the coalition against the two Bedir Khans (see Trotter to the Marquis of Salisbury, Political no. 14, Diyarbekir, Dec. 28, 1878 [FO 195/1211]). This is a good example of how alliances shifted according to circumstances.

194. Maunsell to de Bunsen, no. 40 (*sic*: should be 41?), extracts, Undated [Sept. 16, 1900] (FO 424/200; FO 195/2082).

195. See Trotter to the Marquis of Salisbury, Political no. 14, Diyarbekir, Dec. 28, 1878 (FO 195/1211).

196. Extract from *The Times* (Sept. 1894), (FO 424/178; FO 195/1854). This piece simply mentions: "An influential Kurdish chief of Bedir Khan family has been invited by Russians to return to his mountain fastnesses and recover his authority as hereditary head of the clans in Kurdistan, on the understanding that he will enjoy Russian protection and assistance." See also Currie to Earl of Kimberley, no. 14, Istanbul, Jan. 7, 1895 (FO 424/181).

197. See Klein, "Claiming the Nation," for a discussion of nationalism and the Kurdish-Ottoman press, with particular attention to the Bedir Khans' role in both.

198. Lynch, *Armenia*, 2: 219.

199. It appears that Sultan Abdülhamid II attempted to forge personal bonds of loyalty with many diverse Muslim groups across the empire. The Kurdish chiefs were only one such group, and the Hamidiye was the institution through which he reached out to Kurdish chiefs. But he had other means of reaching out to different groups. See Abu Manneh, "Sultan Abdulhamid II and Shaikh Abulhuda al-Sayyadi"; and Tahsin Pasha, *Abdülhamit Yıldız Hatıraları*, 31.

200. Graves to Currie, no. 5, Erzurum, Feb. 12, 1897 (FO 195/1985).

201. The consuls might have been confused about the identity of which Zeki Pasha was to be assassinated. There was a Mehmed Zeki Pasha, also a close confidante of the sultan, who was the minister of military schools, whom Hanioğlu (*Young Turks in Opposition*, 104) notes as being a target of an assassination plot.

202. Elliot to Currie, no. 42, Confidential, Van, Aug. 18, 1897 (FO 195/1985). Murad Bey was the leader of the CUP between 1896 and 1897.

203. See the French consul's accounts (Benini to Constans, no. 20, Mosul, Sept. 19, 1902 [MAE Nantes, E/118]) and the British consul (Anderson to O'Conor, no. 20, Kharput, Oct. 9, 1902 [FO 195/2125]). Also killed were several other important members of the Mîran tribe, including one of Mustafa Pasha's sons, whom their assassins feared would take the place of his father if left alive.

204. If true, this would be added evidence that the Hamidiye had sanction like the former emirates did in that command could be passed down from father to son.

205. Indeed, as the British regional representative reported in 1907,

The general impression I gathered at Jeziré during my few days' stay there was that Abdul Kerim is the absolute master in that region. The Kaïmakam, the Hamidié Bimbashi, the Chaldean Bishop, all are his creatures, and obey him blindly. In my interviews with them I was greatly struck by their inability to do anything but lie, which they did to an extent remarkable even for this country, and I afterwards found out that the Vali had no idea what was happening in Jeziré, as they either arranged their reports to suit Abdul Kerim or else did not report at all. . . . Abdul Kerim's position appears to be unassailable. Complaints against him must pass through the Mushir's hands before action is taken, and the latter has evidently been instructed to treat him with the greatest indulgence. The Vali of Diarbekir informed me that on one occasion, when troops were sent to surround him, they were recalled by order of the Mushir (Heard to O'Conor, no. 13, Harput, July 17, 1907 [FO 424/213]).

CHAPTER THREE

1. Lowther to Grey, no. 467, Aug. 11, 1908 (FO 424/216). See also Lowther to Grey, no. 516, Aug. 26, 1908 (FO 424/216).

2. The British ambassador reported that when the news came, although most were overjoyed, the "numerous ranks of robbers and murderers" experienced great anxiety with regards to what might happen to them as a result of "the mysterious change," and opted to remain quiet for the time being. The Kurdish

beys and *agha*s were "much annoyed," as they feared it would put an end to their oppression of the "defenceless Armenians and the subject Kurdish tribes" (Lowther to Grey, no. 533, Sept. 1, 1908 [FO 424/216]). This can be compared with the situation in Albania, which had a similar social structure and members of the population who, like the Kurdish tribes, saw the sultan as their protector and did not look forward to his downfall, as they believed it would entail a loss of privileges for them (Skendi, *Albanian National Awakening*, 341–44).

3. Migdal, *State in Society*, 20.

4. Srabian to Constans, no. 73, Erzurum, Aug. 29, 1908 (MAE Nantes, E/131).

5. He was replaced in command over the Fourth Army Corps by Lieutenant-General Ahmed Pasha (not to be confused with the Ahmed Pasha who was Zeki Pasha's relative, who had commanded the Hamidiye regiments for some time in the Malazgird region (Shipley to Lowther [Amb], Confidential no. 47, Erzurum, Aug. 21, 1908 (FO 195/2284); and Srabian to Boppe, no. 66, Erzurum, Aug. 19, 1908 (MAE Nantes, E/131). The latter consul was under the apparently mistaken impression that Ahmed Pasha was the brother-in-law of Zeki Pasha.

6. Srabian to Constans, no. 117, Erzurum, Sept. 18, 1906 (MAE Nantes, E/118).

7. Hanioğlu, *Preparation for a Revolution*, 115.

8. Of course, in the larger scheme of things, Zeki Pasha was part of the wider purge of military and civilian officials that took place after the new regime came to power.

9. Shipley to Lowther, Confidential no. 47, Erzurum, Aug. 21, 1908 (FO 195/2284).

10. His replacement, Abuk Ahmed Pasha, confided to the French consul the concerns facing him as he entered his new post. The consul reported that "yesterday, when taking his leave, Ahmed Pacha did not conceal his concerns over his situation. On the one hand, he will be in charge of solving the thorny and exceedingly delicate question of the Kurdish Hamidièh cavalry regiments. 'Zeki Pacha, the creator and protector of these regiments, is departing at a critical moment. The Sultan remains a mere observer. The entire responsibility of executing these severe measures that will soon be necessary, with regards to these Kurdish regiments, will fall completely upon me alone,' he told me" (Srabian to Boppe, no. 64, Erzurum, Aug. 16, 1908 [MAE Nantes, E/131]).

11. Lowther to Grey, no. 590, Sept. 20, 1908 (FO 424/216).

12. General Report upon the Vilayet of Aleppo [by Consul Barnham, Aleppo, May 13, 1901] (FO 424/202).

13. See also Jongerden, "Urban Nationalists and Rural Ottomanists."

14. Jones to O'Conor. no. 1. Diyarbekir, Jan. 22, 1901 (FO 424/202; FO 195/2104).

15. According to Mark Sykes writing in 1908, the Millî proper only had thirty families, while the Karakeçi had some seventeen hundred and the Kîkî twelve hundred. Of course, he was writing around the time of the destruction of the Millî "empire," and numbers may have dwindled somewhat due to this

event. Nonetheless, observers seem to agree that the Millî's strength rested in its following, not in the numbers of the tribe proper (see Sykes, "Kurdish Tribes of the Ottoman Empire," 469–71; the unpublished report also appears in FO 424/213).

16. I have been unable to determine Osman Agha's tribal affiliation. He is mentioned several times in consular correspondence, but is only referred to as "one of the leading notables of the district [Siverek]" (Jones to O'Conor, no. 11, Diyarbekir, Mar. 13, 1900 [FO 195/2082]).

17. Jones to de Bunsen, no. 46, Diyarbekir, Dec. 31, 1900 (FO 195/2082).

18. The Ottoman traveler Ali Bey estimated the tribe's population to be some thirty thousand during the time of his travels between 1300 and 1304 (1880–1884). He also provides a description of life among the Shammar tribe, particularly customs of hospitality (Ali Bey, *Seyahat Jurnalı*, 24–28).

19. See, for example, Jones to O'Conor, no. 5, Diyarbekir, Mar. 12, 1901 (FO 424/202; FO 195/1204); telegram from Jones [to O'Conor], Apr. 6, 1901 (FO 195/2104); Jones to O'Conor, no. 7, Diyarbekir, Apr. 9, 1901 (FO 424/202; FO 195/1204); Jones to O'Conor, no. 8, Diyarbekir, Apr. 16, 1901 (FO 424/202; FO 195/1204); Jones to O'Conor. no. 10. Diyarbekir, Apr. 30, 1901 (FO 424/202; FO 195/2104); Jones to O'Conor, no. 11, Diyarbekir, May 7, 1901 (FO 195/2104); Lamb to O'Conor, no. 6, Erzurum, May 26, 1901 (FO 195/2104); Jones to O'Conor, no. 12, Diyarbekir, May 14, 1901 (FO 424/202; FO 195/1204). This last document mentions that some regular troops refused to join in the coalition of Hamidiye and regular troops against the Shammar, as they greatly resented the Hamidiye. Later, the Shammar chief once again tried to get in good graces with the sultan when he sent him a telegraph "that he desired to make His Majesty a present of all the property stolen from him by Ibrahim Pasha's followers" (Freeman to O'Conor, no. 24, Ma'muret'ül-'Aziz (Harput), Sept. 26, 1901 [FO 424/202, FO 195/2104]).

20. This account is largely confirmed by Ebubekir Hâzim Tepeyran, the *vali* of Mosul at the time of these events, in his memoirs. Indeed, Tepeyran devotes good space to describing the feuds of the Millî tribe with their non-Hamidiye neighbors, namely the Shammar, and how İbrahim Pasha was able to draw upon Zeki Pasha's support in order to come out ahead in these quarrels (Tepeyran, *Hatıralar*, 321–27, 333–36). See also Rohrbach, *Hatt-ı Saltanat*, 59–61; and Anderson to O'Conor, no. 10, Diyarbekir, May 4, 1903 (FO 424/205).

21. General Report upon the Vilayet of Aleppo [by Consul Barnham, Aleppo, May 13, 1901] (FO 424/202).

22. For example, the British consul reported that "Ibrahim Pasha, owing to his difficulties with the Shammar Arabs, has been obliged to abandon his usual pasture ground to the South of Viranshehr and is encroaching on the Karaketchi's ground" (Anderson to O'Conor, no. 32, Diyarbekir, Dec. 30, 1901 [FO 195/2104]).

23. Anderson to O'Conor, quarterly report, no. 14, Harput, July 2, 1902 (FO 195/2125).

24. It also makes the movements against him by the Diyarbekir notables in 1905 and 1907, mentioned below, more comprehensible to the reader.

25. Young to O'Conor, no. 7, Diyarbekir, May 2, 1904 (FO 195/2172).

26. See Young to Townley, no. 30, Diyarbekir, Dec. 15, 1904 (FO 195/2173); and Young to Townley, no. 7, Diyarbekir, Mar. 5, 1905 (FO 195/2173). See also the colorful anecdote provided by a missionary in Kurdistan that illustrates a number of themes in this chapter, particularly the favor İbrahim Pasha had curried with his imperial patron, often at the expense of local officials: Campbell, *In the Shadow of the Crescent*, 195–97.

27. Young to Townley, no. 7, Diyarbekir, Mar. 5, 1905 (FO 195/2196).

28. Wilkie Young, Vilayet of Diarbekir, Current Affairs, July 25, 1904 (FO 195/2173).

29. Young to Townley, no. 7, Diyarbekir, Mar. 5, 1905 (FO 195/2196).

30. "A Report on Ibrahim Pasha, and the present state of Western Mesopotamia," [by Mark Sykes], enclosed with Maunsell to O'Conor, no. 36, Istanbul, June 12, 1905 (FO 424/208).

31. Sykes, "Kurdish Tribes of the Ottoman Empire," 470. See this report also for a list of tribes said to be attached to the Millî under İbrahim Pasha. Sykes's full report on İbrahim Pasha from 1905 is reproduced in appendix B of Klein, "Power in the Periphery."

32. Shipley to O'Conor, no. 32, Diyarbekir, Aug. 30, 1905 (FO 195/2196).

33. It seems, however, that there was some confusion on the part of consuls as to which numbers they actually were (Avryanov has the Sixty-third and Sixty-fourth Regiments as Millî, but the British and French consuls have them as the Karapapak. Kodaman, using Ottoman sources, also puts the Forty-fourth Regiment as being Millî.

34. Avryanov, *Osmanlı-Rus ve İran Savaşlarında Kürtler*, 38–40, 47–48, 53–54 of his appendixes.

35. Telegram from Shipley, Diyarbekir, Aug. 2, 1905 (FO 195/2196). See also Jongerden, "Urban Nationalists and Rural Ottomanists."

36. Shipley to O'Conor, no. 27, Diyarbekir, Aug. 12, 1905 (FO 195/2196); telegram from Shipley to O'Conor, Diyarbekir, Aug. 8, 1905 (FO 195/2196). Shipley continued to point to various reports against İbrahim Pasha as "fabrication" on the part of the local notables (see, for example, Shipley to O'Conor, no. 34, Diyarbekir, Sept. 18, 1905 [FO 195/2196]).

37. Shipley to O'Conor, no. 37, Diyarbekir, Oct. 16, 1905 (FO 195/2196). The commission was composed of two Aleppo notables and a secretary.

38. O'Conor to Grey, no. 720, Pera, Nov. 26, 1907 (FO 424/213). Again, the French consul reported, the notables were forcing Christians and others at the marketplace to sign their petition against İbrahim Pasha (telegram from Güys, Diyarbekir, Nov. 17, 1907 [MAE Nantes, E/131]; telegram from Güys, Diyarbekir, Nov. 21, 1907 [MAE Nantes, E/131]).

39. Telegram from Memduh Pasha, Minister of the Interior, copy of original in FO 195/2251. Hanioğlu also provides an account of the antigovernment protests in Diyarbekir from 1905 to 1907, which began as a reaction against the lawless activities of İbrahim Pasha (*Preparation for a Revolution*, 106–7).

40. Mugherditchian to Young, Diyarbekir, Nov. 27, 1907 (FO 195/2251).

41. Heard to O'Conor, no. 1, Diyarbekir, Jan. 21, 1908 (FO 195/2283). In another communication, this consul remarks that in the conflicting testimony

over the matter, İbrahim Pasha's friends maintained that his enemies (including Cemil Effendi, a Diyarbekir notable who was *kaymakam* of Derik; Arif Effendi, the mayor of Diyarbekir; and Nehim Agha of the Metina tribe (in the *kaza* of Derik)) were the ones who instigated a series of raids on İbrahim Pasha's villages. İbrahim Pasha also telegraphed the capital and Zeki Pasha in complaint against these allegations, but the notables denied complicity. The consul concluded his message noting that three independent authorities confirmed that İbrahim Pasha also offered to return stolen sheep if these notables would do the same (Heard to O'Conor. no. 5. Diyarbekir, Feb. 10, 1908 [FO 195/2283]).

42. Heard to Barclay, no. 11, Diyarbekir, Apr. 15, 1908 (FO 195/2283). The French consul reported that a telegram from the Ministry of War to the commander of the Tenth Division arrived on March 31 and read: "Stop all pursuit of Ibrahim Pacha Milly and release the officers at Aleppo: An imperial decree has accorded amnesty to Ibrahim Pacha and also for the notables of Diyarbekir. . . . Major reforms will be carried out in the province" (telegram from Aleppo [Roqueferrier?], Apr. 2, 1908 [MAE Nantes, E/131]).

43. Telegram from Güys, Diyarbekir, June 5, 1908 (MAE Nantes, E/131). Fethullah Hüsni of the Hasanan tribe was also awarded a medal for his monetary contribution to the Hamidiye Hijaz railroad (*Takvim-i Vekayi*, no. 98 (8 Kânûn-i Sâni 1324 [Jan. 21, 1909]).

44. Heard to Barclay, no. 22, Diyarbekir, June 4, 1908 (FO 195/2283); Roqueferrier, Aleppo, July 3, 1908 [MAE Nantes, E/131]). The latter consul reported that Ibrahim Pasha Millî and around eight hundred Hamidiye cavalrymen armed with martinis arrived the previous day at Urfa coming from Siverek, where they would be for two or three days before departing by rail for the Hijaz. The consul continued, stating that on the occasion of his passage, local authorities received the strictest orders, and the *vali* was to have ready enough military provisions and three thousand Turkish liras, which he had yet to find. A later report in the same file added that he had arrived in Aleppo by July 10 and departed for Damascus on the July 16 (Roqueferrier, Aleppo, July 16, 1908 [MAE Nantes, E/131]). This may have been the first time İbrahim Pasha's men actually had to report for the services they offered, as on previous occasions, like his counterpart Mustafa Pasha, İbrahim Pasha had shirked his duties to fight in the Balkan Wars or to join the expedition against the Yemeni rebels (Ahmad, *Kurdistan During the First World War*, 57–58).

45. Heard to O'Conor, no. 13, Harput, July 17, 1907 (FO 424/213; FO 195/2251). Another irony is worthy mentioning: Kodaman has suggested that the groups of Hamidiye tribes in the south—including those in the Diyarbekir province—had been created, in part, to keep a check on the British. If this is the case, just as many frontier tribes actually assisted the Armenians they were supposed to counter, and here we see İbrahim Pasha attempting to garner favor with the party he was ostensibly supposed to keep in check.

46. Heard to Barclay, no. 22, Diyarbekir, June 4, 1908 (FO 195/2283). For the extent of İbrahim Pasha's domains see appendix C of Klein, "Power in the Periphery."

47. Lowther to Grey, no. 533, Sept. 1, 1908 (FO 424/216). Orders seem to

have been issued at the end of August. Lowther believed that the league of notables in Diyarbekir had incited the government to deal with İbrahim Pasha.

48. Guys to Constans, no. 57[?] Diyarbekir, Sept. 7, 1908 (MAE Nantes, E/131).

49. Heard to Lowther, no. 50, Diyarbekir, Oct. 13, 1908 (FO 195/2284). This document provides a lengthy account of the campaign against İbrahim Pasha and the Millî tribe.

50. Lowther to Grey, no. 624, Sept. 28, 1908 (FO 424/217).

51. Heard to Lowther, no. 50, Diyarbekir, Oct. 13, 1908 (FO 195/2284) and Güys to Ambassador, no. 21, Diyarbekir, Oct. 12, 1908 (MAE Nantes, E/131).

52. Telegram from Heard, Diyarbekir, Oct. 10, 1908 (FO 195/2284), and Heard to Lowther, Oct. 15, 1908 (FO 195/2284).

53. The orders were at first disobeyed by the *vali*, who was under the influence of the Diyarbekir notables, and was hostile to İbrahim Pasha's family (telegram from Heard, Diyarbekir, Nov. 10, 1908 [FO 195/2284]). It is unclear how many of Abdülhamid Bey's brothers were actually released. One telegram notes the release of İbrahim Pasha's sons on Nov. 12 (telegram from Heard, Diyarbekir, Nov. 13, 1908 [FO 195/2284]), while another remarks on Abdülhamid Bey's pleas, over a week later, for his brothers' release (telegram from Heard, Diyarbekir, Nov. 23, 1908 [FO 195/2284]).

54. Telegram from Heard, Diyarbekir, Nov. 20, 1908 (FO 195/2284); telegram from Heard, Diyarbekir, Nov. 2[?], 1908 (FO 195/2284).

55. Dickson to Lowther, Beirut, Jan. 21, 1909 (FO 195/2317).

56. A letter from Haci Adela (Hanim), the late İbrahim Pasha's third wife, was sent to Abdülhamid in prison reporting the attacks (Rawlins to Lowther, no. 6, Diyarbekir, Mar. 3, 1909 [FO 195/2317]; see also Rawlins to Lowther, no. 12, Diyarbekir, Apr. 7, 1909 [FO 195/2317]). A notice in the *Takvim-i Vekayi*, no. 162 (13 Mart 1325 [Mar. 26, 1909]), confirms this account, noting that most of the sheep belonging to the Millî were destroyed in these events, with a certain portion being raided by "the famous brigand" İdris of the Karakeçi tribe.

57. "Extract from a despatch of American Consul at Kharput, Turkey, to American Ambassador at Constantinople, Aug. 3, 1908 (Communicated to Lowther by the American Ambassador at Constantinople)," in Lowther to Grey, no. 505, Istanbul, Aug. 22, 1908.

58. Abdülkerim Bey, who became chief of the Mîran tribe upon the death of his father, Mustafa Pasha, was one who was imprisoned in late December 1908 or early January 1909 (Dickson to Lowther, Beirut, Jan. 15, 1909 [FO 195/2317]), although he was soon released and formed a new Hamidiye regiment with the reorganization of the militia. A notice in the *Takvim-i Vekayi*, no. 272 (2 Temmuz 1325 [July 15, 1909]), also mentions the arrest of other important Mîran heads including a Hamidiye regiment commander, Kasim bin Hasan, his brother Ferman, and Dimo bin Sîno, and the confiscation of some of their weapons. The notice emphasized that the Mîran tribe had been carrying out raids, arson, and murders for years in Cizre and its environs.

59. A number of notices appear in the first six months of *Takvim-i Vekayi*

that show the arrest of various tribal chiefs for various misdeeds, including Hamidiye chiefs. For example, one notice mentioned a fight between a Hamidiye member and his brother against two other brothers (apparently from a different family), in which three of them were killed. The notice emphasized that the necessary legal action was taken (apparently against the sole survivor of the affray) and also pointed out that this Hamidiye member had been sentenced repeatedly for many murders, but had remained free until then (no. 47, 11 Teşrin-i Sânî 1324 [Nov. 24, 1908]). Other notices, such as the one appearing in *Takvim-i Vekayi*, no. 99 (9 Kanun-i Sani 1324 [Jan. 22, 1909]), show that a number of tribal "brigands" in the Bitlis province were also captured or otherwise made to turn themselves in to the government and that their arms had been successfully confiscated. Many charges against them were, however, dropped.

60. Dickson to Lowther, no. 32, Van, Nov. 3, 1908 (FO 195/2284).

61. Dickson to Lowther, no. 31, Van, Nov. 3, 1908 (FO 195/2284). Of course they had plenty of their own rifles by this point. A piece in *Takvim-i Vekayi*, no. 91 (1 Kanun-i Sani 1324 [Jan. 14, 1909]), affirmed that cases between civilians and member of the Hamidiye regiments would be heard now in the civil courts and that the necessary information for implementing this change had been given to the army and the Ministry of War.

62. Armenian figures associated with the new regime were given similar tasks.

63. Lowther to Grey, no. 498, Aug. 18, 1908 (FO 424/216).

64. Morgan to Lowther, no. 17, Van, Oct. 27, 1909 (FO 195/2318).

65. Morgan to Lowther, no. 17, Van, Oct. 27, 1909 (FO 195/2318).

66. Morgan to Lowther, no. 18, Van, Nov. 17, 1909 (FO 195/2318). Parentheses in original. The document was signed by thirty-three Kurdish chiefs and twelve Armenian notables, including the acting Armenian bishop; nonetheless, there still seemed to be little enthusiasm for the event in general Armenian circles. The *vali*, Bekir Sami Bey, had been working to this end for some time. Apparently he had also held a dinner the day after his arrival in Van to which he invited "Turkish and Armenian notables," including the head of the Dashnaktsutiun, and called on the two groups to fraternize (Morgan to Lowther, no. 10, Van, June 21, 1909 [FO 195/2318]).

67. *Takvim-i Vekayi*, no. 305 (3 Ağustos, 1325 [Aug. 16, 1909]). Shortly afterward a number of Dersim chiefs sent a joint telegram to the minister of the interior in which they wished to clarify that they were not brigands as had been alleged, and that they were loyal and "by nature" Ottomans (*Takvim-i Vekayi*, no. 308 (8 Ağustos, 1325 [Aug. 21, 1909]). Presumably these chiefs had been among those who attended the "reeducation" camp.

68. Sırma, *Belgelerle II. Abdülhamid Dönemi*, 210.

69. The preceding government had engaged in a similar endeavor, particularly in 1895–96, when they sent agents to the Kurdish "tribal zone" to convince them that the reforms urged by the Europeans would benefit them more than they would the Armenians, since Kurds were more populous. Agents such as Sadettin Pasha have memoirs that are invaluable as this pasha, for one, recounts in them the lectures he gave to locals—particularly to Hamidiye chieftains. They

reveal that he also counseled them to behave well toward Armenians, although it is clear that it was not so much because it was the right thing to do but because doing otherwise would incur the attention and wrath of European powers (see *Sadettin Paşa'nın Anıları*).

70. Morgan to Lowther, no. 21, Van, Dec. 15, 1909 (FO 195/2318).

71. Morgan to Lowther, no. 6, Van, Feb. 28, 1910 (FO 195/2347).

72. Morgan to Lowther, no. 6, Van, Feb. 28, 1910 (FO 195/2347).

73. Tyrrell to Lowther, no. 54, Istanbul, Sept. 13, 1910 (FO 195/2346).

74. Tyrrell also believed the German War Office was displaying an interest in the question of the "Kurdish cavalry" (Tyrrell to Lowther, no. 54, Istanbul, Sept. 13, 1910 [FO 195/2346]).

75. Heading the commission to survey the northern section of the Hamidiye in the spring of 1910 was Binbaşı Trabzonlu Hacı Hamdi Bey, and Fahrettin (Altay) the southern (Altay, *10 Yıl Savaş ve Sonrası (1912–1922)*, 55). It is unclear whether or not they were part of the first commission to survey, or part of the commission to reorganize. Altay reported that they were attempting to gauge numbers, determine who had died, and how many animals the tribe had. As such, they were able to determine the tribes' true strength and to reorganize them accordingly.

76. Safrastian to McGregor, Bitlis, Apr. 28, 1910 (FO 195/2347).

77. McGregor to Lowther, no. 44, Erzurum, July 12, 1910 (FO 195/2347).

78. McGregor to Lowther, no. 44, Erzurum, July 12, 1910 (FO 195/2347).

79. Altay, who was part of the commission to reorganize the regiments, recounts the story behind the name change. After the information on the Hamidiye regiments had been submitted to the capital, the minister of war, Mahmut Şevket Pasha, asked for Altay's opinion: "The name Hamidiye can no longer be given to these regiments. Are you not thinking about a new name?" Altay responded, "Among them the only Arab tribe is the small Tay clan. Among those who consider themselves to be Kurds, some are originally Turks. It would be appropriate to give them a Turkish name. For example, something like Oğuz Alayları [Regiments]." Laughing, Mahmut Şevket Pasha responded, "That's nice, but if it wre mumbled, it will sound like *uyuz alayları* [mangy regiments]. Let's say the best would be Tribal Cavalry Regiments" (Altay, *10 Yıl Savaş ve Sonrası (1912–1922)*, 57; italics added). Apparently, it had been suggested as early as 1895 to drop the name *Hamidiye* from the title of the regiments during the course of the meetings of Ferik Muzafir Pasha, Ferik Vandergalty Liwa Brockdorff, and two or three others (headed by Müşir Ahmed Şakir Pasha), who comprised the commission to reorganize the Hamidiye (Chermside to Currie, Istanbul, Apr. 8, 1895 [FO 424/182]).

80. Telegram from Matthews to Lowther, Harput, Aug. 27, 1910 (FO 195/2347); Matthews to Lowther, no. 38, Harput, Aug. 27, 1910 (FO 195/2347); McGregor to Lowther, no. 62, Erzurum, Sept. 2, 1910 (FO 195/2347).

81. Matthews to Marling, Diyarbekir, Dec. 13, 1910 (FO 195/2347). This step was accompanied by the recommendations that first, the regiments should receive three months of training a year, and second, that recruits should only be between twenty and thirty years of age.

82. *Aşiret Hafif Süvari Alayları Nizamnamesi.* The regulations are reproduced in appendix E of Klein, "Power in the Periphery."

83. Although it should be noted that expeditionary forces were sent to suppress Albanian and Druze insurrections, during which the opportunity was reportedly taken by the Ottoman army to seize men for conscription (Tyrrell to
Marling, no. 7, Istanbul, Jan. 16, 1911 [FO 195/2386]).

84. Ergül, *II. Abdülhamid'in Doğu Politikası ve Hamidiye Alayları*, 81 (after
Günay).

85. Of course many of these points had also been decreed at various times
under the previous regime; however, the question here would be whether or not
they would actually be enforced.

86. Sadettin Pasha notes in his memoirs that some of the Kurdish chiefs
with whom he met spoke no Turkish, and he required an interpreter (*Sadettin
Paşa'nın Anıları*, 139, 142).

87. It should also be mentioned that although the assimilating drive of the
Young Turk government was clear and has been well established in scholarship
to date, not all signals they sent were so strikingly clear. For example, in 1912
the British consul at Mosul mentioned a project put together by the military at
Mosul to have better chances at conscripting Kurds. The new scheme stipulated
that frontier soldiers should know the Kurdish and Persian languages. The government seemed to recognize, in the consul's words, that "it is quite likely that
many who would refuse to be 'conscripted by the Turks' will have no objection
to serving of their own free will more or less in their own country" (Hony to
Lowther, no. 4, Feb. 14, 1912 [FO 195/2398]).

88. Tyrrell to Lowther, no. 8, Istanbul, Jan. 17, 1910 (FO 195/2346).

89. McGregor to Lowther, no. 5, Erzurum, Jan. 17, 1912 (FO 195/2398).
Much more realistic numbers were mentioned this time around. The British
consul claimed that fewer than seventy-five men in total had arrived at Erzurum
to participate in this project.

90. Yaşın, *Bütün Yönleriyle Cizre*, 26–27.

91. Monahan to Lowther, no. 46, Erzurum, July 23, 1912 (FO 195/2405).

92. Altay, *10 Yıl Savaş ve Sonrası (1912–1922)*, 61.

93. Mentioned by name in various consular reports have been the Cibranli,
Haydaranli, Mîran, Millî, Kîkî, Daqorî, and Holajî (only the last tribe seems
to be a new addition, although it is in Sykes's list of Milan tribes [see above]).

94. Although Mugerditchian believed that it was just a pretext by the government to distribute arms to the Kurds, while the local Christians were prohibited
from carrying arms (Mugerditchian to Monahan and Fontana, no. 27, Diyarbekir, Sept. 30, 1912 [FO 195/2405]).

95. Talay is one who has mentioned the role of the Hamidiye in the Balkan
Wars. Talay's mission is to show how militarily useful the Hamidiye were to
the Ottomans in the prelude to the Balkan Wars. According to this author, the
tribal regiments played an important role in Trablusgarb and even frightened
the Italians into not approaching the region for some time. He also asserts that
in response, the Italians attempted to form parallel regiments from among the
local population (*Eserleri ve Hizmetleriyle Sultan Abdülhamid*, 86).

96. See Ergül, *II. Abdülhamid'in Doğu Politikası ve Hamidiye Alayları*, 82.

97. Report by Colonel Hawker, Oct. 31, 1913 (FO 195/2450). However, the same report also noted that the planned drills never took place; the tribes were once again armed with government rifles and ammunition, but did not have to report for training.

98. Report submitted to the Ministry of War by Sabık Aşiret Müfettişi Mirliva Emin (9 Nisan, 1330 [Apr. 22, 1914]), reproduced in Balcıoğlu, "Hamidiye AlaylarındanAşiret Alaylarına Geçerken Harbiye Nezareti'ne Sunulan İki Rapor," 49–50.

99. Report submitted to the Ministry of War by Aşiret Müfettişi Kaymakam Yusuf İzzet (9 Nisan, 1330 [Apr. 22, 1914]), reproduced in Balcıoğlu, 50–51.

100. Smith to Mallet, no. 19, Van, July 18, 1914 (FO 195/2458).

101. Plans to incorporate Kurds into the subofficers' school at Erzincan is evidence of this point. They were also supposed to be habituated to the new order of things in other ways as well. For example, in September 1910 nearly three hundred new Christian recruits from the Balkans were sent to Van to acquaint the soldiers and tribesmen there with the European element of the new army, and to "reconcile" them to the company of Christians in their ranks (Molyneux-Seel to Lowther, no. 19, Van, Sept. 7, 1910 [FO 195/2347]).

102. Monahan to Lowther, no. 49, Erzurum, July 29, 1912 (FO 195/2405), after a letter from Knapp, a missionary at Mardin.

103. Monahan to Marling, no. 60, Erzurum, Sept. 23, 1913 (FO 195/2450).

104. See, for example, "Joint Report by Messrs. Shipley and Minorsky, British and Russian Delegates, on the State of Affairs on the Turco-Persian Frontier, June 8–September 16, 1911" (FO 195/2398).

105. For a nuanced look at the equally complex responses of the empire's Arab population to these changes see Kayalı, *Arabs and Young Turks*.

106. It is certainly true, however, that like *Kurdistan*, contributors to this journal also had a distinct vision of "the Kurds" as a distinct entity among the Ottoman peoples.

107. Süleymaniyeli Fethi, Untitled ["Tribal Military Service"], *KTTG* 1 (Dec. 5, 1908), 5–6; and "Aşayir Askerliği, Mâba'd [Tribal Military Service, continued]," *KTTG* 2 (29 Teşrin-i Sânî 1324 [Dec. 12, 1908]), 13–14. The series was supposed to be continued, as indicated at the end of the second piece in the series, but there was no further addition to the series in subsequent issues. Therefore, the topic was interrupted midsentence in *KTTG* 2. This writer's opinion was embraced by others. Süleymaniyeli Seyfullah, for example, seconded his fellow countryman's views (see Süleymaniyeli Seyfullah, "Siyasîyât, Mâba'd [Political Topics, continued]," *KTTG* 2 (29 Teşrin-i Sânî 1324 [Dec. 12, 1908]), 10 (transliteration in Bozarslan, *KTTG*).

108. Said-i Kurdî "Kürdler Neye Muhtac," *KTTG* 2 (29 Teşrin-i Sânî, 1324 [Dec. 12, 1908]), 13 [journal paginated in a series, starting with no. 1], in Bozarslan, *KTTG* reprints. Said-i Kurdî repeated these thoughts in his address to the Ottoman deputies (see Molla Said-i Kurdî, "Bediüzzaman Said-i Kurdî'nin Meb'usana Hitabı, Mâba'd [Bediüzzaman Said-i Kurdî's Address to Deputies]" *KTTG* 4 (13 Kânûn-i Evvel 1324 [Dec. 26, 1908]), 31 (Bozarslan, *KTTG*).

109. Rahmetli Şeyh Ubeydullah Effendi'nin Oğlu, Abdulqadir, "Cem'iyetimizin Reis-i Fezail'enisi Seyyid Abdulqadir Ubeydullah Effendi'nin Nümûne-i Fikr ü İrfanı," *KTTG* 1 (22 Teşrin-i Sânî, 1324 [Dec. 5, 1908]) (Bozarslan, *KTTG* reprints). Article dated Nov. 20, 1908.

110. Karakeçi Aşireti Reisi Halil [Halil, the chief of the Karakeçi tribe], letter dated Dec. 5, 1908, in *KTTG* 2 (29 Teşrin-i Sânî, 1324 [Dec. 12, 1908]), 18 (Bozarslan *KTTG*, 104–5).

111. Letter signed Umum Haydaran Aşireti Reisi Hamidiye Mirlivası Hüseyin [chief of the Haydaran tribe, Hamidiye Major-General Hüseyin], in *KTTG* 8 (19 Kânûn-i Sânî 1342 [Jan. 23, 1909]), 69 (Bozarslan reprints of *KTTG*).

112. Letter signed Harûnan Aşireti Reisi Ahmed Fakih and Reşkotan Aşireti Reisi Haci Mehmed Mustafa, dated Dec. 31, 1908 in *KTTG* 8 (19 Kânûn-i Sânî 1342 [Jan. 23, 1909]), (Bozarslan *KTTG*). Following this letter, the editors of *KTTG* explained how the Reşkotan tribe had always been a headache to the government, which had tried endlessly to capture and punish its leaders. They found it thus even more incredible that this chief would embrace the new regime, and they then thanked him for his letter.

113. Letter signed Midyat kazanın Hevêrkî Rüesasından Aziz Halil Haco, Nusaybin Rüesasından Kelebrulu Ahmed, Nusaybin Eznavir Nahiyesi Rüesasından Hasan Sivûk, and Diğeri Ahmed el-Yusuf, dated Jan. 6, 1909, in *KTTG* 8 (19 Kânûn-i Sânî 1342 [Jan. 23, 1909]) (Bozarslan *KTTG*).

114. Telegram submitted to the Ministry of the Interior, signed Şeyh Mahmud, Şeyh Yusuf, and 'Omer, leader of the Babus tribe in Garzan and Yusuf of Maden, one of the leaders of the Şirvan tribes, *Takvim-i Vekayi*, no. 51, (12 Teşrin-i Sânî [Nov. 25, 1908]). A very similar telegram was also sent to the Ministry of the Interior by heads of the Bişîrî, Sinikan, 'Osman, and Maşeref tribal heads, in which the latter proclaimed their joy at hearing the speech in Turkish and Kurdish given by Süleyman Faik Bey, and vowed to put aside their differences with the Reşkotan tribe, and then took an oath sacrifice their lives for the constitution and the fatherland (*Takvim-i Vekayi*, no. 98 (8 Kanun-i Sani 1324 [Jan. 21, 1909]), 7. This subgovernor seemed to be particularly active in promoting the new government in a language that appealed to the people of his district, and it is possible that he encouraged them to submit their thoughts to the capital perhaps so that he could get credit for all of the new "conversions."

115. *Takvim-i Vekayi*, no. 83 (20 Kânûn-i Evvel, 1324 [2 Jan. 1909]). See also the letters sent by the Arab Çilikli tribe of Midyat, 'Ali Remo and Musa Ağazade Emin, *Takvim-i Vekayi*, no. 86 (27 Kânûn-i Evvel, 1324 [Jan. 9, 1909]); the telegram from the Zilan tribal head, 'Omer; the Babus chief, Mehmed Saîd, and the Diyat tribal head, Nimr; and Mela Şekir and Bervarî Saîd, *Takvim-i Vekayi*, no. 87 (28 Kânûn-i Evvel 1324 [Jan. 10, 1909]); and the telegram from the Hêvat, Sihanli, and Pîlekî tribes to the grand vizier, in which the writers wish to assure the government that since the reinstatement of the constitution they had been peaceful, and would continue to uphold the constitution. They blamed their previous misdeeds on "ignorance," of which the previous regime took advantage (*Takvim-i Vekayi*, no. 111 (21 Kanun-i Sani, 1324 [Feb. 3, 1909]).

116. Scott, *Domination and the Arts of Resistance*, 3.

117. Ibid., 3–4.

118. It seems to have been the second meeting.

119. "Les Kurdes," *Stamboul* (Sept. 1908) (MAE Nantes, Kurdes/E 131); italics added.

120. This was probably the first organizational meeting held. Article by Colonel Süleyman for *Stamboul* of Sept. 1908 (MAE Nantes, Kurdes/E 131). Translation from French.

121. Heard to Lowther, Beirut, Jan. 3, 1909 (FO 195/2317). Based on a report submitted by Mugerditchian on Dec. 22, 1908.

122. Again these clubs can be compared to those that were established in Albania at the same time, where, according to Skendi, "Not all of the programs of the clubs were alike; their special features corresponded to the particular needs of the place in which they had been established" (*Albanian National Awakening*, 347). See also 346–65.

123. Parts of this section have been developed further in Klein, "Kurdish Nationalists and Non-Nationalist Kurdists."

124. Heard to Lowther, Beirut, Jan. 3, 1909 (FO 195/2317). Based on Mugerditchian's report of Dec. 22, 1908. And the local Kurds exploited this situation further through their manipulation of local officials, or at least those who were inclined toward manipulation. For example, it was reported in *Takvim-i Vekayi*, no. 41 (4 Teşrin-i Sânî, 1324 [Nov. 17, 1908]) that Haci Mehmed of the Reşkotan tribe had spread a rumor that he, in concert with the Sheikh of Zilan, would instigate a massacre against the Armenians. For this action he was arrested, but when the authorities came to arrest the Sheikh of Zilan, he told them that the meeting of Kurdish chiefs he held was not held for any other reason than to give the Kurdish *agha*s who had gathered there advice about the articles of the constitution and the benefits that would be gained by freedom and equality, and that he had done this in accordance with instructions given by the Kurdish Committee of Union and Progress.

125. A subsequent report indicates that members of the Diyarbekir club argued, when denounced by certain CUP circles as being unfriendly to Christians, that they had a perfect right to organize under the constitution and were just trying to protect the rights of the Kurds. They then invited the Christians of the town to join with them "against a bad government and all evil doers both now and in the future," to show that they were not anti-Christian (see Dickson to Lowther, Beirut, Jan. 15, 1909 [FO 195/2317]). However, they did not stop demonstrating in favor of Islamic law. In Bitlis, for example, the members of the Kurdish club, which was comprised of all the influential local Kurds, compelled the local Young Turk officers under threats of death to sign a telegram addressed to the cabinet of Tevfik Pasha demanding the full application of the sharia (Islamic law) (see Safrastian to Shipley, Bitlis, June 8, 1909 [FO 195/2317]).

126. Dickson to Lowther, Beirut, Feb. 13, 1909 (FO 195/2317), based on Mugerditchian's report of Feb. 2, 1909. Some Christians may even have been associated with the KTTC, as is evidenced in a piece in *Takvim-i Vekayi*, in which the subgovernor of Harput says that Christians had joined the central branch of the KTTC (although *which* central branch is unclear), although his point was

actually to lament the fact that in spite of this, no Muslims were enrolled in any Armenian organizations (*Takvim-i Vekayi*, no. 104 (14 Kanun-i Sani, 1324 [Jan. 27, 1909]).

127. Rawlins to Lowther, no. 29, Harput, June 23, 1909 (FO 195/2317). The subgovernor of Harput, however, claimed that upon an investigation into the matter it was found that the rumor was false (*Takvim-i Vekayi*, no. 104 (14 Kanun-i Sani 1324 [Jan. 27, 1909]).

128. Matthews to Lowther, no. 6, Confidential, Diyarbekir, Mar. 7, 1910 (FO 195/2347).

129. Matthews to Lowther, no. 22, Diyarbekir, June 25, 1910 (FO 195/2347).

130. McGregor to Lowther, no. 45, Confidential, Erzurum, July 16, 1910 (FO 195/2347). It remained unclear who the individual was actually working for. It should also be noted that on the *vali*'s later tour of his province, he found the various Kurdish chiefs all vying with one another to display to him their goodwill (McGregor to Lowther, no. 59, Erzurum, Aug. 29, 1910 [FO 195/2347]).

131. Rawlins to Lowther, no. 42, Harput, Aug. 27, 1909 (FO 195/2318). The part about the Millî tribe was asserted by the *mutassarıf* of Siverek, but his report may actually have been filed upon the instigation of enemies of the late İbrahim Pasha. Several Yezidi tribal leaders contacted the British dragoman as well as a missionary at Mardin, Mr. Andrus, with the desire to embrace Christianity. The British consul deemed the move political, and he believed that they were either trying to escape persecution or to now have the advantages they believed Christians now enjoyed.

132. Safrastian to McGregor, no. 2, Bitlis, Jan. 20, 1911 (FO 195/2375).

133. This dissatisfaction can again be compared with similar feelings of discontent among Albanians, some of whom (especially the Kosovars), had not been displeased with Sultan Abdülhamid II's rule, and who had grown accustomed to certain privileges, which were now threatened. Skendi devotes a chapter of his work to detailing the clash between these disaffected Albanians and the new regime in his work, *Albanian National Awakening*, esp. 391–404.

134. Scott, *Domination and the Arts of Resistance*, xiii.

135. Mugerditchian to McGregor and Fontana, no. 10, Diyarbekir, May 7, 1912 (FO 195/2405). And the following year, the Armenian bishop at Muş reported to the British consul that Kurds were instructed and assisted by the officials to seize Armenian lands and scatter their inhabitants, and that the court cases involving land and other property were all favorable to the Kurdish tribal chiefs (Armenian Bishop of Muş to Consul Monahan, Muş, Feb. 15, 1913 [FO 195/2450]).

136. Monahan to Lowther, no. 76, Erzurum, Oct. 28, 1912 (FO 195/2405). The Chaldean bishop of Cizre reported to the British consul that "a flag was handed with great pomp to the Kurdish chief Abdul Kerim Bey Mirani as a leader of Tribal Light Cavalry while he was passing by the town of Jezireh with his nomad tribe in their annual migration."

137. Hayderanî Hüseyin Pasha was another Hamidiye chief whom the government was courting. His position on the Russian frontier was of key impor-

tance to the government (see Monahan to Marling, no. 61, Erzurum, Sept. 29, 1913 [FO 195/2450]).

138. They also tried to open a technical school in Cizre (Safrastian to McGregor, no. 10, Bitlis, Apr. 29, 1911 [FO 195/2375]).

139. Safrastian to McGregor, no. 10, Bitlis, Apr. 29, 1911 (FO 195/2375).

140. McGregor to Lowther, no. 46, Confidential, Erzurum, June 28, 1911 (FO 195/2375). A later report mentioned Hasan Bey and Mustafa Bey instead of Hüseyin Pasha.

141. Safrastian to McGregor, no. 20, Bitlis, July 17, 1911 (FO 195/2375).

142. Safrastian to McGregor, no. 20, Bitlis, July 17, 1911 (FO 195/2375). Safrastian was reporting on Father Bonté's observations. Interesting comparisons can be made with the situation in Albania, where revolts against the government took place from 1910 to 1912. The Kosovar revolutionaries in Albania were after administrative autonomy and educational and linguistic freedoms, and had an increasingly nationalist program (see Skendi, *Albanian National Awakening*, esp. 405–37). Due to the many similarities that existed not only in the demands and discourse produced by Kurdish and Albanian intellectuals and other notables, the Ottoman government was naturally worried that Kurdistan would go the way of Albania, in successfully demanding administrative autonomy.

143. For accounts of this affair see, for example, extract of a letter from Père de Boissieu, to P. Roussel, Head of the Dominican Fathers at Van, Siirt, Apr. 17, 1912 (MAE Nantes, E/45); Addaï Scher, Chaldean Bishop of Siirt to the French Consul, Siirt, Apr. 27, 1912 (MAE Nantes, E/45); extract of a letter addressed by the Père de Boissieu, in charge of the mission of the Dominican Fathers at Siirt, to Père Roussel Supérieur des Dominicains, Van, Siirt, May 4, 1912 (MAE Nantes, E/45); Zarzecki to Bompard, no. 20, Van, May 16, 1912 (MAE Nantes, E/45); and Monahan to Lowther, no. 30, Erzurum, May 22, 1912 (FO 195/2405).

144. Smith to Mallet, no. 1, Van, Jan. 10, 1914 (FO 195/2456; FO 424/251).

145. Michael Reynolds presented an interesting paper on Abdurrezzak's Russian connections: "Ottoman Diplomat, Russophile, and Kurdish Patriot: Abdurrezzak Bedirhan and the Seams of Empire, 1910–1918."

146. Smith to Mallet, no. 3, Van, Feb. 14, 1914 (FO 195/2458).

147. Bozarslan emphasizes the fact that the fear of losing their traditional authority combined with the threat of losing the lands they had usurped from the Armenians during the massacres of 1895 pushed many Kurds toward a nationalist revolt ("Tribus, confréries et intellectuels," 65).

148. Ahmad suggests that due to the hostility with which many Hamidiye tribes regarded the new regime, the central government had to establish good relations among many other tribes in order to assure that they had a reliable fighting force for the impending wars of the period (*Kurdistan During the First World War*, 58).

149. See Klein, "Turkish Responses to Kurdish Identity Politics."

CHAPTER FOUR

1. Letter signed Umum Haydaran Aşireti Reisi Hamidiye Mirlivası Hüseyin [chief of the Haydaran tribe, Hamidiye Major-General Hüseyin] in *KTTG* 8 (19 Kânûn-i Sânî 1342 [Jan. 23, 1909]) (Bozarslan, reprints of *KTTG*).

2. Some historians have also rightly acknowledged "fears of Armenian ascendancy" as playing a prominent role in early Kurdish nationalism (namely, W. Jwaideh, "Kurdish Nationalist Movement," 212).

3. Van Bruinessen, *Agha, Shaikh and State*, 53–54.

4. Haj, *Making of Iraq*, 12.

5. Again, see ibid.

6. Haj, "Problems of Tribalism," 55.

7. Ibid., for this on Iraq. Indeed, Sultan Abdülhamid II recognized the growing importance attached to land ownership, and became the first sultan to massively extend his *sanniya* (crown) holdings in the region. After the CUP came to power in 1908, these lands were immediately transferred to the state (see A. Jwaideh, "*Saniyya* Lands of Sultan Abdul Hamid II," 326–36.

8. Haj, "Problems of Tribalism," 54–55; and A. Jwaideh, "Midhat Pasha and the Land System of Lower Iraq," 108.

9. The British consul at Diyarbekir writes that his province did not see the Land Code applied officially until 1872, and in reality until 1878. He adds that at the time of writing (1910) it had still not been applied in some parts (Matthews to Lowther, no. 50, Diyarbekir, Oct. 19, 1910 [FO 424/225]).

10. A. Jwaideh shows that although the central government in the second half of the nineteenth century embarked on a more rigorous program of bringing its tribal areas under direct control, it did not have a consistent policy for dealing with the tribes in different regions. Indeed, the relations between the tribes and the government were not the same everywhere, and as Jwaideh shows, the conditions of land-tenure in the various tribal regions helped in large part to determine the relations between the government and the tribes ("Midhat Pasha and the Land System of Lower Iraq," 112–13).

11. Haj, "Problems of Tribalism," 55; A. Jwaideh, "Midhat Pasha and the Land System of Lower Iraq," 118–20; and Gould, "Lords or Bandits? The Derebeys of Cilicia."

12. See Orhonlu, *Osmanlı İmparatorluğu'nda*; and Kasaba, *Moveable Empire*.

13. Haj, "Problems of Tribalism," 55. In many areas these settlement strategies produced results. Longrigg has observed that by the later part of the nineteenth century, the tribes of the middle Euphrates showed a trend of settlement (*Iraq, 1900–1950*, 25).

14. Ibid., 37.

15. Haj, *Making of Iraq*, 12. See also Farouk-Sluglett and Sluglett, "Transformation of Land Tenure and Rural Social Structure," 496.

16. According to Sykes, the Hayderan tribe was the largest Kurdish tribe in existence from Muş to Urumia (in Iran), numbering some twenty thousand families ("Kurdish Tribes of the Ottoman Empire," 478).

17. Roqueferrier to Cambon, no. 6, Confidential, Apr. 13, 1896 (MAE Nantes, AA, E/113). Note the distinct irony of the title of his post.

18. Hampson to White, Political no. 3, Erzurum, Jan. 16, 1891 (FO 424/169; FO 78/4342; and FO 195/1728).

19. Graves to Nicolson, no. 9, Erzurum, Feb. 14, 1894 (FO 424/178; FO 195/1846).

20. Hampson to White, Political no. 3, Erzurum, Jan. 16, 1891 (FO 424/169; FO 78/4342; and FO 195/1728).

21. Hampson to White, Political no. 34, Erzurum, Apr. 4, 1891 (FO 424/169; FO 78/4344).

22. Graves to Nicolson, no. 9, Erzurum, Feb. 14, 1894 (FO 424/178; FO 195/1846).

23. Hampson to White, Political no. 3, Erzurum, Jan. 16, 1891 (FO 424/169; FO 78/4342; and FO 195/1728).

24. Roqueferrier to Cambon, no. 6, Confidential, Apr. 13, 1896 (MAE Nantes, E/113).

25. Tyrrell to O'Conor, no. 43, Van, Dec. 24, 1903 (FO 424/206); parentheses in original.

26. Graves to Currie, no. 41, Erzurum, June 8, 1894 (FO 195/1846).

27. See Fitzmaurice to Hampson, no. 8, Van, May 6, 1892 (FO 424/172; FO 195/1766) and Graves to Currie, no. 41 Erzurum, June 8, 1894 (FO 195/1846).

28. The consul continued, stating his observation—an observation so commonly made about Hamidiye chiefs—that "since [Hüseyin Pasha] has received the rank of Lieutenant-Colonel in the Hamidiye regiments, he no longer fears any sort of civil official," and is protected and pampered by Zeki Pasha, and free to commit crimes with impunity (Roqueferrier to Cambon, no. 6, Confidential, Apr. 13, 1896 (MAE Nantes, AA, E/113).

29. Graves to Currie, no. 59, Erzurum, Sept. 1, 1894 (FO 424/178; FO 195/1846).

30. See Chermside to Currie, no. 43, Istanbul, Nov. 28, 1895 (FO 195/1880). The French consul also reported: "It would take too long to report all of his misdeeds, but suffice it to say that deserving of special mention are his exploits at Patnos and Tchilikan [Çilikan] during the massacres which bloodied the sanjak of Bayazid" (Roqueferrier to Cambon, no. 6, Confidential, Apr. 13, 1896 (MAE Nantes, AA, E/113).

31. Roqueferrier, Erzurum, Dec. 16, 1895 (MAE Nantes, E/113).

32. Roqueferrier to Cambon, Confidential draft no. 1, Erzurum, Jan. 16, 1897 (MAE Nantes, E/115) According to another source, Emin Pasha may not actually have been a Hamidiye officer either, but he nonetheless pretended he was. In 1900 the British military consul at Van reported that Emin Pasha had wanted to raise a regiment in his name, but his offer was not accepted. When he was arrested along with his two associates, his badges of rank, which he had apparently worn perhaps for a decade and had employed to his advantage, were removed by the authorities upon his incarceration (Maunsell to O'Conor, no. 5, Van, Jan. 3 [*sic*: Feb. 3], 1900 [FO 195/2082]). If this is the case, it is unclear, then, how he achieved the rank of pasha, or if he even did.

33. Major Williams to Currie, no. 43, Van, Dec. 15, 1896 (FO 424/191; FO 195/1944); Consul Graves to Currie, no. 2, Erzurum, Jan. 7, 1897 (FO 424/191; FO 195/1985).

34. Roqueferrier to Cambon, Confidential draft no. 1, Erzurum, Jan. 16, 1897 (MAE Nantes, E/115).

35. Extract from a report by the Russian Vice-Consul at Van, dated Apr. 10 (22), 1897 (FO 424/191). The Russian consul reported that Hüseyin Pasha and his brother Sultan Bey had saved more than thirty villages from the pillage wreaked by their brother-in-law, Emin Pasha, the main instigator of the disorders in the *kaza* of Erciş.

36. Consul Graves to Currie, no. 23, Confidential, Erzurum, May 28, 1897 (FO 424/191; FO 195/1985).

37. Graves [to Currie], Erzurum, Aug. 28, 1897 (FO 195/1985).

38. Graves to de Bunsen, no. 15, Erzurum, June 27, 1898 (FO 195/2021); de Bunsen to the Marquess of Salisbury, no. 395, Pera, July 7, 1898 (FO 424/197).

39. Bayazîdî, '*Edet ve Rusûmetname-i Ekradîyye*, 143.

40. Ibid., 95–94 (note: page numbers in the Kurdish section of this text are in reverse order).

41. See, for example, Cumberbatch to Herbert, Erzurum, Nov. 21, 1895 (FO 424/184; FO 195/1893).

42. For example, in 1879, Musa Agha of the Hayderan tribe was reported to be plundering and burning Kurdish villages around Bayazid (Trotter to Layard, no. 90, Erzurum, Sept. 19, 1879 ([FO 195/1237]).

43. Hampson to Fane, no. 72, Erzurum, Aug. 1, 1891 (FO 424/169; FO 195/1729).

44. Hampson to White, Erzurum, Jan. 16, 1891 (FO 424/169, FO 78/4342, FO 195/1728).

45. Hampson to White, Erzurum, Jan. 16, 1891 (FO 424/169; FO 78/4342; FO 195/1728).

46. See Safrastian to Shipley, Bitlis, June 22, 1908 (FO 195/2283); "Translation of Memorandum of atrocities committed by barbarous Kurds in the 250 villages comprising the sancak of Mush by Krikoris, Archbishop of Mush, July 28, 1879" (FO 195/1237); Everett to Trotter, Political no. 17, Confidential, Erzurum, Aug. 19, 1882 (FO 195/1420); and Report on Vilayet of Bitlis, Jan. 30, 1885 (FO 195/1521). However, tribal Kurds were not the only parties who robbed or looted Christian churches. There are numerous examples of government troops engaging in these activities as well. While many such incidents occurred in the course of expeditions against Armenian revolutionaries, many others occurred quite beyond these expeditions. See, for example, Memorandum of Occurrences at Van and Vicinity, from a letter, dated Van, June 25, 1893 (FO 424/175).

47. Devey to Lloyd, no. 45, Van, Oct. 31, 1890 (FO 195/1688). Hüseyin Pasha would use churches for building materials for many years (see, for example, the letter from the Armenian Murakhas of Adelcivaz respecting the state of suffering of Armenians of that *kaza* under Hüseyin Pasha, enclosed with Tyrrell to O'Conor, no. 48. Van, Oct. 11, 1904 [FO 424/206]).

48. As in the case when some Kurds from Modkan stole carpets from the mosque at the government *konak* (Safrastian to Shipley, Bitlis, June 22, 1908 [FO 195/2283]).

49. Roqueferrier to Cambon, no. 6, Confidential, Apr. 13, 1896 (MAE Nantes, E/113). Of course Hüseyin Pasha was not the only Hamidiye chieftain to disregard the sacred nature of such property. Mustafa Pasha Mîran pulled down a monastery in Cizre and used the materials to construct a rather fine bazaar. He also "remodeled" a Cizre mosque into his Hamidiye barracks. This was apparently only one of fifteen such mosques Mustafa Pasha destroyed for their building materials (Vice-Consul Tyrrell to O'Conor, no. 23, Van, Oct. 7, 1902 [FO 424/203, FO 195/2125]).

50. Maunsell to O'Conor, no. 36, Van, Sept. 10, 1899 (FO 424/199; FO 195/2063).

51. Maunsell to O'Conor, no. 36, Van, Sept. 10, 1899 (FO 424/199; FO 195/2063).

52. Hallward to Graves, no. 22, Van, Aug. 27, 1894 (FO 424/178; FO 195/1846).

53. Hampson to Cumberbatch, Muş, Oct. 9, 1895 (FO 424/184; FO 195/1893), writes that "a serious evil is the granting by the Government of the tithes of Christian villages . . . to Hamidié officers in lieu of pay."

54. Freeman to O'Conor, no. 3, Bitlis, Feb. 28, 1903 (FO 195/2147).

55. "Visit to the Cazas of Akhlat, Boulanyk, and Malasgird, August, 1897," enclosure in Crow to Currie, no. 27, Bitlis, Oct. 10, 1897 (FO 424/192; FO 195/1981).

56. Srabian to Constans, no. 47, Erzurum, June 6, 1905 (MAE Nantes, E/119).

57. Anderson to O'Conor, no. 28, Diyarbekir, Oct. 22, 1901 (FO 424/202; FO 195/2104).

58. Srabian to Constans, no. 114, Erzurum, Sept. 11, 1906 (MAE Nantes, E/119).

59. Vice-Consul Geary to O'Conor, Bitlis, Sept. 18, 1906 (FO 424/210).

60. Memorandum by Col. Chermside, Strictly confidential, Istanbul, June 3, 1890 (FO 195/1698; FO 78/4294).

61. Vice-Consul Shipley to O'Conor (no. 31), Diyarbekir, Aug. 28, 1906 (FO 424/210; FO 195/2222).

62. Telegram from Trotter, June [?], 1880 (FO 195/1316).

63. Maunsell to O'Conor, no. 8, Van, Feb. 20, 1899 (FO 424/198; FO 195/2063).

64. Maunsell to O'Conor, no. 10, Van, Mar. 13, 1899 (FO 424/198; FO 195/2063). Hüseyin Pasha continued to hoard wheat for years. In 1905 the British consul at Van reported that the largest holder of wheat in Van was Hüseyin Pasha of Patnos, against whom the local government was powerless without orders from the capital (Tyrrell to O'Conor, no. 10, Van, Mar. 20, 1905 [FO 424/208]).

65. Maunsell to O'Conor, no. 19, May 2, 1900 (FO 195/2082).

66. Dickson to O'Conor, no. 24, Van, Dec. 31, 1907 (FO 195/2251).

67. See, for example, Heard to O'Conor, no. 12, Bitlis, Oct. 7, 1907 (FO 195/2251); Heard to O'Conor, no. 15, Bitlis, Oct. 22, 1907 (FO 195/2251); and Heard to O'Conor, no. 2, Diyarbekir, Jan. 28, 1908 (FO 195/2283).

68. "Report by Sir Mark Sykes on Northern Jazirah or Northern Mesopotamia," enclosed with O'Conor to Grey, no. 431 Confidential, Pera, June 24, 1906 (FO 424/210).

69. Indeed, Bayazîdî, one of the few Kurdish sources we have from the nineteenth century, mentions property theft by *hekîm*s and *axa*s. He was narrating his piece, *'Edet ve Rusûmetname-i Ekradîyye*, around the mid- to late nineteenth century. According to Bayazîdî, however, some Kurds turned some of their property over to *waqf*s so that it would not be appropriated by these strongmen (114).

70. An interesting point presented by van Bruinessen (personal communication, spring 2001) is that in some cases the Kurdish chiefs were attempting to restore their hereditary "rights" over the land and its peasants, which in some parts may have been challenged as peasants registered their land, thus bypassing the *agha*s.

71. Fontana to Herbert, no. 40, Harput, Aug. 17, 1896 (FO 195/1944).

72. Williams to Currie, no. 10, Van, Mar. 12, 1897 (FO 424/191; FO 195/1985).

73. Safrastian to McGregor, Bitlis, July 25, 1910 (FO 424/224); parentheses in original, brackets added.

74. Fontana to Currie, no. 30, Harput, June 15, 1897; and Fontana to Currie, no. 40, Harput, Aug. 31, 1897 (FO 424/192; FO 195/1981).

75. Translation of letter from the Catholicos of Akhtamar to the Armenian Patriarch at Istanbul, enclosed with Hallward to Graves, no. 48[?], Van, June 16, 1895 (FO 424/192). Writing a decade after the massacres, the French consul recalled the impact of the massacres on Armenian holdings in Van:

> Before the massacres of 1896, Van's Armenians were prosperous and had almost all the wealth in their hands. There was good security, development of agriculture and industry and commerce. Peasants owned many flocks and cultivated their lands and relations between Armenians and Turks and Kurds was good, even fraternal. But the massacres of 1896 changed everything. The Armenians were dispossessed, most of their homes were burned, and wealth changed hands to the hands of the Kurds. During this time the Armenian population, especially of the countryside, was unable to recover (enclosure in P. Calvière Acting Vice-Consul at Van, to Constans, no. 9, Van, Apr. 2, 1906, quarterly report [MAE Nantes, E/119]).

The government, however, officially refuted the Armenian patriarch's claims. In the *Sabah* of Nov. 4/16, 1895, it was written that nothing that the Haydaranî Hamidiyes had done had been contrary to the will of the sultan, and that the patriarch's claims were untrue (extract from the Sabah of Nov. 20, 1895 [FO 424/184]).

76. Herbert to Marquess of Salisbury, no. 583, Istanbul, Nov. 2, 1895 (FO 424/184); Hallward to Cumberbatch, no. 79, Van, Nov. 6, 1895 (FO 424/184; FO 195/1983).

77. Monahan to Currie, no. 61, Bitlis, Nov. 24, 1896 (FO 424/189; FO 195/1944).

78. Crow to Currie, no. 35, Bitlis, Dec. 28, 1897 (FO 195/1981).

79. Letter from the Armenian Murakhas of Adilcevaz, enclosed with Tyrrell to O'Conor, no. 48, Van, Oct. 11, 1904 (FO 424/206).

80. Monahan [to de Bunsen], no. 15, Bitlis, Aug. 14, 1898 (FO 195/2021).

81. Crow to Currie, no. 35, Bitlis, Dec. 28, 1897 (FO 195/1981); Crow to Currie. no. 36. Bitlis, Dec. 28, 1897 (FO 424/195).

82. Matthews to Lowther, no. 50, Diyarbekir, Oct. 19, 1910 (FO 195/2347). See also the anecdote provided by Sadik Shahid Bey in his *Islam, Turkey, and Armenia* (96–97), as it is particularly interesting for the light it sheds on one of the myriad means employed to acquire the land of Armenian peasants.

83. Satow to de Bunsen, no. 3, Van, Jan. 3, 1901 (FO 195/2104).

84. Maunsell to O'Conor, no. 19, May 2, 1900 (FO 195/2082).

85. Srabian to Constans, no. 76, Erzurum, June 7, 1906 (MAE Nantes, E/119).

86. Satow to O'Conor, no. 13, Van, June 10, 1901 (FO 424/202; FO 195/2104).

87. Report communicated by M. Hagopian respecting ill-treatment of Armenian prisoners at Van (translation), Van, July 17, 1906 (FO 424/210).

88. Notes on journey from Van to Erzingan, by Molyneux-Seel, no. 5, Van, Feb. 6, 1911 (FO 424/226; FO 195/2375).

89. Crow to Currie, [Private], Bitlis, Feb. 13, 1898 (FO 424/195; FO 195/2021).

90. Safrastian to McGregor, Bitlis, July 25, 1910 (FO 424/224). See appendix G of Klein, "Power in the Periphery," for the details on this kind of usurpation, and for the full text of the report that outlines the numerous ways in which lands were taken over.

91. Monahan to de Bunsen, Private, In Camp, Gumgum, Varto kaza, Aug. 31, 1898 (FO 195/2021).

92. Safrastian to McGregor, Bitlis, July 25, 1910 (FO 424/224).

93. O'Conor to Grey, no. 206, Istanbul, Apr. 5, 1907 (FO 424/212).

94. Safrastian to Shipley, Bitlis, Feb. 16, 1907 (FO 195/2250).

95. Heard to O'Conor, no. 15, Bitlis, Oct. 22, 1907 (FO 195/2251).

96. Safrastian to McGregor, Bitlis, July 25, 1910 (FO 424/224). Quataert has written about the Agricultural Bank, which was part of Sultan Abdülhamid II's larger effort to promote agricultural reform programs. Quataert also notes the problems that arose either due to confusion over the lending process or to the "deliberate fraud or manipulation of the bank by local notables or dishonest bank officials," a problem that does not seem to have been confined to the regions under review in the present study ("Dilemma of Development," esp. 214–15).

97. Tyrrell to O'Conor, no. 27, Urmia, Iran, Nov. 16, 1902 (FO 195/2125).

98. Tyrrell to O'Conor, no. 41, Van, Oct. 11, 1905 (FO 195/2196).

99. Telegram from Shipley, Cizre, Mar. 28, 1906 (FO 195/2222).

100. Srabian to Constans, no. 5, Erzurum, Nov. 21, 1904 (MAE Nantes, E/119).

101. Safrastian to to Shipley, Bitlis, June 22, 1908 (FO 195/2283).

102. Acting Vice-Consul Decedrat [?] to Bapst, no. 59, Apr. 25, 1904 (MAE Nantes, E/118).

103. As Captain Dickson noted, the Hamidiye, led by their officers, "make raids on the villages, ill-treat the people, take their cattle and sheep and crops, often killing an odd Armenian as well. These Kurds give as excuse for these raids—if excuse is needed—that the villagers are revolutionaries, or are harbouring revolutionaries, the latter excuse being often true, though quite against the wish of the Armenians" ("Report on the Armenian Position in the Van Vilayet," enclosed with Dickson to Barclay, no. 4, Van, Sept. 24, 1906 [FO 424/210]).

104. At the same time, it should also be considered that Kurdish peasants who were dispossessed of their lands had nobody to advocate on their behalf, while the Armenians found strong voices in Europe.

105. Minas Ter Minassian (aka Rouben), a former Armenian revolutionary, also details the process whereby Turks and Kurds (and Muslim immigrants from the Caucasus) took over Armenian lands, often in complicity with agents of the Agricultural Bank, in a process he believed was designed to cleanse the region of Armenians by uprooting them and replacing them with Muslims (*Mémoires d'un Partisan Arménien*, 59–64; 109–10). He further suggested that Şakir Pasha communicated to "the Turks that the only means for them to take possession of the land was through economic domination" (61). However, Rouben also points out that Armenians and Kurds at one point joined together to revolt against the immigrants who had seized their lands (115–16).

106. See, for example, Srabian to Constans, no. 94, Erzurum, July 26, 1906 (MAE Nantes, E/119).

107. Safrastian to Shipley, Bitlis, May 11, 1907 (FO 424/212; FO 195/2250). According to a later report on the methods used to deprive peasants of their lands, the British agent noted in 1910 that "Armenian lands and in certain cases whole villages have been distributed amongst Moslem immigrants under the old Government. The cases of Yonjalu, Abri, Hannasheikh, etc., villages in Bulanik, of Vartenis, Dormerd, etc., in Mush, remain unsolved hitherto" (Safrastian to McGregor, Bitlis, July 25, 1910 [FO 424/224]).

108. [Signature illegible] to Cambon, no. 86, Beirut, Sept. 10, 1898 (MAE Nantes, E/116).

109. Tyrrell to O'Conor, no. 16, Van, May 12, 1903 (FO 195/2147).

110. Tyrrell to O'Conor, no. 16, Van, May 12, 1903 (FO 195/2147).

111. Grenard to Constans, no. 45, Erzurum, Aug. 18, 1903 (MAE Nantes, E/118).

112. Robin to Constans, no. 29, Van, May 29, 1904 (MAE Nantes, E/119).

113. Enclosure in P. Calvière, Acting Vice-Consul at Van, to Constans, no. 9, Van, Apr. 2, 1906, quarterly report (MAE Nantes, E/120).

114. Safrastian to Shipley, Bitlis, June 6, 1908 (FO 195/2283). Terzibaşoğlu has described how local tribes in the Ayvalık region had been drafted to suppress

the revolt of the Greeks in Anatolia at the same time as the 1821 independence revolt, and how the arrival of Muslim refugees from the Balkans contributed to the displacement of the local population; later (in the 1860s) some of these tribes were settled in the region, Terzibaşoğlu believes, perhaps as a kind of reward for their services to the Ottomans ("Landlords, Refugees, and Nomads," 55, 67). Davison has made a similar point in his *Reform in the Ottoman Empire*, in which he has described the process whereby the Ottoman government, which needed to settle the mass of Tatar and Circassian immigrants, sent a number of them to the Tuna province, where it was hoped they could serve as border guards against Serbia and along the Danube, and likely also as a force to counter Bulgarian separatist activity. In order to do this, however, the local government needed to provide the immigrants with the land and provisions with which to settle, a move that caused the resentment of the local population (151–52).

115. A notice in the *Takvim-i Vekayi* (no. 88) of February 10, 1909 (29 Kânûn-i Evvel 1324) shows that many such claims had been recently submitted in the İzmid district as well.

116. Tyrrell to O'Conor, no. 44, Van, Sept. 28, 1904 (FO 424/206). The memoirs of the former Armenian revolutionary, Minas Ter Minassian, aka Rouben, also attest to this fact.

117. Dickson to Lowther, no. 31, Van, Nov. 3, 1908 (FO 195/2284).

118. Lowther to Grey, Istanbul, Dec. 21, 1908 (FO 424/218). See also Özok-Gündoğan's interesting work on the land-dispute petitions drafted by Armenian and Kurdish villagers in the Diyarbekir province ("'Peripheral' Approach to the 1908 Revolution").

119. Dickson to Lowther, no. 32, Van, Nov. 3, 1908 (FO 195/2284).

120. Dickson to Lowther, no. 29, Van, Sept. 30, 1908 (FO CAB37/95/137).

121. Dickson to Lowther, no. 32, Van, Nov. 3, 1908 (FO 195/2284).

122. Dickson to Lowther, no. 29, Van, Sept. 30, 1908 (FO CAB37/95/137).

123. Dickson to Lowther, no. 29, Van, Sept. 30, 1908 (FO CAB37/95/137).

124. A perusal of the run of *Takvim-i Vekayi* for the years following the reinstatement of the constitution shows that during this time, especially during the first year that the CUP was in power, efforts to restore land to their previous owners were made, and they were publicized in the official Ottoman journal to prove that the new regime was serious about its efforts in this endeavor.

125. *Anadolu'nun muhal-ı muhtelifesinde emlak ve arazi-yi mağsube hakkında ermeni patrikhanesince teşkil eden komisyon-ı mahsus tarafından tenzim olunan raporların muddet tercumesi* (1327/1909), Belediye Kitapları no. 4571. This report offers a detailed picture of the Armenian lands and other properties usurped over the preceding decades. My thanks to Bedross Der Matossian and Nilay Özok-Gündoğan for providing me with copies of this document.

126. Shipley to Lowther, no. 31, Erzurum, Oct. 25, 1909 (FO 195/2318).

127. Srabian to Bompard, no. 32, Erzurum, Apr. 6, 1910 (MAE Nantes, E/120).

128. Lowther to Grey, no. 541, Pera[?], Aug. 3, 1910 (FO 424/224). Apparently, the Ministry of the Interior was unwilling to order the return of the lands

the patriarch had listed without confirming them through their own investigation (see Srabian to Bompard, no. 35, Erzurum, Apr. 21, 1910 [MAE Nantes, AA E/120]).

129. Safrastian to Shipley, Bitlis, Sept. 9, 1909 (FO 424/221; FO 195/2318).

130. In November 1908, for example, a notice appeared in the 34th issue of *Takvim-i Vekayi* (27 Teşrin-i Evvel 1324 [Nov. 9, 1908]) that two individuals named Allahverdi and Hidayet from the village of Ekrak in the Bulanık district, whose land had been taken over and who had been expelled from their village by the Cibran (Hamidiye) chief Lieutenant Haydar Agha, had been resettled in their village with their lands restored to them, and that the matter had been sent to the courts.

131. Morgan to Lowther, no. 18, Van, Nov. 17, 1909 (FO 195/2318).

132. Dickson to Lowther, no. 29, Van, Sept. 30, 1908 (PRO CAB 37/95/137).

133. For colorful descriptions of Hüseyin Pasha's machinations to offer his services in hopes of rewards and his efforts to not, in fact, have to perform said services see Tyrrell to O'Conor, no. 3, Van, Jan. 31, 1903 (FO 195/2147); Srabian to Boppe, no. 72, Erzurum, July 18, 1905 (MAE Nantes, E/119); Tyrrell to O'Conor, no. 34, Van, July 28, 1905 (FO 195/2196); Srabian to Boppe, no. 89, Erzurum, Sept. 1, 1905 (MAE Nantes, E/119); Shipley to O'Conor, no. 27, Erzurum, Aug. 7, 1905 (FO 195/2196); Shipley to O'Conor, no. 28, Erzurum, Aug. 15, 1905 (FO 195/2196); Tyrrell to O'Conor, no. 34, Van, July 28, 1905 (FO 195/2196); Srabian to Boppe, no. 111, Erzurum, Oct. 8, 1905 (MAE Nantes, E/119).

134. Dickson to Lowther, no. 35, Van, Nov. 29, 1908 (FO 195/2284).

135. The British consul reported in September, 1908 that the upcoming election in Van appeared to be a contest more between the two Armenian parties, the Armenakan and Dashnaktsutiun parties, than between Armenian and Muslim candidates (Dickson to Lowther, no. 29, Van, Sept. 30, 1908 [PRO CAB 37/95/137]).

136. Dickson to Lowther, no. 29, Van, Sept. 30, 1908 (PRO CAB 37/95/137).

137. Dickson to Lowther, no. 29, Van, Sept. 30, 1908 (PRO CAB 37/95/137).

138. Dickson to Lowther, no. 35, Van, Nov. 29, 1908 (FO 195/2284).

139. Dickson to Lowther, no. 31, Van, Nov. 3, 1908 (FO 195/2284).

140. Dickson to Lowther, no. 35, Van, Nov. 29, 1908 (FO 195/2284). This is corroborated by an interview by Consul Heard with a poor Hamidiye tribesman, who suggested that even among the Hamidiye there were serious divisions in wealth (Heard to O'Conor, no. 19, Erzurum, Nov. 23, 1907 (FO 424/213).

141. Marling to Grey, no. 942, Pera, Dec. 1, 1909 (FO 424/221).

142. Safrastian to McGregor, Bitlis, Apr. 17, 1910 (FO 195/2347).

143. Lowther to Grey, no. 69, Istanbul, Feb. 7, 1910 (FO 424/222).

144. Lowther to Grey, no. 69, Istanbul, Feb. 7, 1910 (FO 424/222). A notice in the *Takvim-i Vekayi*, no. 325 (26 Ağustos, 1325 [Sept. 8, 1909]), confirms the government's intent at the time on forcing the Hayderan tribe to submit. According to the notice, all of the tribes in Dersim had come to tender their submission except for the Hayderan tribe (the part of which was in Dersim),

which offered only "stubbornness and disobedience." A military expedition was suggested in order to bring the Hayderan tribe to heel.

145. Lowther to Grey, no. 69, Istanbul, Feb. 7, 1910 (FO 424/222).

146. Rapport sur la situation politique du vilayet de Van pendant le 2ième trimester, June 30, 1910 (MAE Nantes, E/45).

147. Rapport sur la situation politique du vilayet de Van pendant le 2ième trimester, June 30, 1910 (MAE Nantes, E/45).

148. Rapport sur la situation politique du vilayet de Van pendant le 2ième trimestre, June 30, 1910 (MAE Nantes, E/45), and Safrastian to McGregor, Bitlis, Apr. 22, 1910 (FO 424/223). The former Armenian revolutionary, "Rouben," notes in his memoirs that even before the reinstatement of the constitution, Armenian revolutionaries forged relationships with the Kurdish peasantry in some areas, using the "agrarian question," which was not yet a "question," and other oppressive acts by the Kurdish *agha*s against the peasantry as grounds for uniting (125–27).

149. McGregor to Lowther, no. 41, Confidential, Erzurum, June 21, 1910 (FO 424/224; FO 195/2347).

150. Tyrrell to Lowther, no. 29, Istanbul, Apr. 20, 1912 (FO 424/231; FO 195/2405). This conversation arose in the context of discussion Hüseyin Pasha's recent (re)appointment as honorary commander of the Sixteenth Tribal Light Cavalry Regiment.

151. Srabian to Bompard, no. 35, Erzurum, Apr. 21, 1910 (MAE Nantes, E/120).

152. Safrastian to McGregor, Bitlis, July 25, 1910 (FO 424/224).

153. See Lowther to Grey, no. 495, Therapia, July 18, 1910 (FO 424/224); and Srabian to Bompard, no. 42, May 18, 1910 (MAE Nantes, E/120).

154. Safrastian to McGregor, Bitlis, July 25, 1910 (FO 424/224).

155. Srabian to Boppe, no. 56, July 23, 1910 (MAE Nantes, E/120).

156. Safrastian to McGregor, Bitlis, July 18, 1910 (FO 424/224).

157. Safrastian to McGregor, Bitlis, July 25, 1910 (FO 424/224); parentheses in original.

158. Matthews to Lowther, no. 50, Diyarbekir, Oct. 19, 1910 (FO 424/225).

159. Matthews to Lowther, no. 41, Harput, Sept. 5, 1910 (FO 195/2347). The translation of *ya derdimize derman, ya katlimize ferman* should be "either a remedy for our problem or an order for our execution."

160. Morgan to Lowther, no. 10, Van, Apr. 25, 1910 (FO 424/223 [may also be in FO 195/2347]).

161. Safrastian to McGregor, Bitlis, Nov. 19, 1910 (FO 424/225; also in FO 195/2347?).

162. Safrastian to McGregor, Bitlis, Nov. 19, 1910 (FO 424/225; also in FO 195/2347?).

163. Morgan to Lowther, no. 7, Van, Apr. 3, 1910 (FO 424/223; FO 195/2347).

164. This was a decision made, for example, by the provincial council of Diyarbekir in the Spring of 1910 (Matthews to Lowther, no. 12, Diyarbekir, Apr. 11, 1910 [FO 195/2347]). The law for settling tribes in the Diyarbekir province

is reproduced in *Salname-i Servet-i funûn,* supplemental section for 1911–12, 71. Mark Sykes, the British traveler who wrote extensively on the Kurds, pointed to this policy, noting in particular its detrimental effects on the tribes themselves who had been settled. He mentioned the Zirikan (Hamidiye) tribe as an example of one that had been caught in this policy, which he believed was to control the tribes and assimilate them into the peasant class (in body and spirit). According to Sykes, just two decades before the Zirikan had been "wealthy, independent shepherds," but now that they had been (at least partially) settled, they were unable to attend to their flocks as fully as before, and their revenue diminished (*Caliph's Last Heritage,* 403–5).

165. See, for example, Safrastian to McGregor, no. 16, Bitlis, June 18, 1911 (FO 424/228; FO 195/2375); McGregor to Marling, no. 53, Confidential, Erzurum, July 7, 1911 (FO 424/228; FO 195/2375); and *Travels and Politics in Armenia* (London, 1914), cited in Walker, *Armenia,* 193.

166. Lowther to Grey, no. 596, Therapia, Aug. 23, 1910 (FO 424/224).

167. Vice-Consul Molyneux Seel to Lowther, no. 20, Van, Oct. 9, 1911 (FO 424/229, FO 195/2375).

168. See, for example, Molyneux Seel to Lowther, no. 20, Van, Oct. 9, 1911 (FO 424/229; FO 195/2375). A similar point is made by Terzibaşoğlu in his study of land struggles around Ayvalık during the same period. Terzibaşoğlu has described the effects of the population growth in the nineteenth century, part of which was connected to the influx in immigrants from the Caucasus and the Balkans, and how this dramatically altered the land-labor ratio. Terzibaşoğlu has found, similarly to what I have argued here, that "this effect of this change on the distribution of existing land and on intercommunal relations was fundamental," although "tensions [also] arose between the local Muslim population and the newly arriving Muslim Circassians and Cretans" ("Landlords, Refugees, and Nomads," 69).

169. See McGregor to Lowther, no. 25, Confidential, Erzurum, May 1, 1910 (FO 424/223; FO 195/2347).

170. Smith to Mallet, no. 3, Van, Feb. 14, 1914 (FO 195/2458).

171. Extract from the "Tanin" of July 5, 1910; translation (FO 424/224).

172. The article of the *Tanin* on July 5 and 6 has been reproduced in its entirety in appendix F of Klein, "Power in the Periphery."

173. McGregor to Lowther, no. 41, Confidential, Erzurum, June 21, 1910 (FO 424/224; FO 195/2347).

174. McGregor to Lowther, no. 64, Confidential, Erzurum, Aug. 21, 1911 (FO 424/228; FO 195/2375).

175. Mugerditchian to McGregor and Fontana, no. 10, Diyarbekir, May 7, 1912 (FO 195/2405).

176. Kurdish intellectuals, however, urged their compatriots to resolve the land question, particularly in the interests of peace between the Kurdish and Armenian communities. One writer submitted his thoughts on the matter in an issue of *Rojî Kurd,* a Kurdish journal, in which he suggested that unless Kurds and Armenians settled the land question, "shake each other's hands," and come to an agreement on the matter, no real cooperation would be possible in the

future. He added that claimants should press for the resolution of their cases in the courts and that the courts themselves should be made to apply neutral laws not designed to serve any particular group's interests, hinting that the resolution of the land question should not be determined in the favor of those who held power (Hüseyin Şükrî, "Arazi Meselesi," *Rojî Kurd* 4 (30 Ağustos, 1329 [Sept. 12, 1913], 5–7).

177. Pandey, *Routine Violence*, 43.

178. Ibid., 52.

179. See ibid., 34, on this point.

180. Mann, *Dark Side of Democracy*, 21.

CHAPTER FIVE

1. Dündar, *İttihat ve Terakki'nin Müslümanları*, 142–43 (after Evsile).

2. Olson, *Emergence of Kurdish Nationalism*, 11.

3. Yaşın, *Bütün Yönleriyle Cizre*, 27; and Altay, *10 Yıl Savaş ve Sonrası (1912–1922)*, 61.

4. Ergül, *II. Abdülhamid'in Doğu Politikası ve Hamidiye Alayları*, 85 (after Arfa). For more information on the role of the Hamidiye in the First World War, now sometimes called *İhtiyat Süvari Alayları* (Reserve Cavalry Regiments), see Ergül, *II. Abdülhamid'in Doğu Politikası ve Hamidiye Alayları*, 82–87; Lazarev, *Emperyalizm ve Kürt Sorunu*, 17; Talay, *Eserleri ve Hizmetleriyle Sultan Abdülhamid*, 84; Gültepe, "Hamidiye Alayları," 50 (incidentally, Gültepe—as a nationalist writer—does not mention that the Hamidiye were Kurdish, and instead refers to them as "Turkmen" tribes); Günay, "Hamidiye Hafif Süvari Alayları ve Erzurum," 43.

5. Dersimi, *Dersim'e ve Kürt Milli Mücadelesine Dair Hatıratım*, 49.

6. See Bozarslan, "Histoire des relations kurdo-arméniennes," 165; and Ahmad, *Kurdistan During the First World War*, esp. chap. 5.

7. McDowall, *Modern History of the Kurds*, 104–5.

8. Dersimi, *Dersim'e ve Kürt Milli Mücadelesine Dair Hatıratım*, 50.

9. Sadettin Pasha repeatedly tried to dispel this rumor when he met with Kurdish chiefs in the Van region in 1896 (see *Sadettin Paşa'nın Anıları*). It was understandable, however, that many Kurds believed it after they got wind of the reform plan put forth by France, England, and Russia. This plan spoke of the six provinces as the Armenian provinces and proposed unifying them as one super *Armenian* province to be under special administration (see the reform agenda reproduced in Dersimi, *Dersim'e ve Kürt Milli Mücadelesine Dair Hatıratım*, 58–66).

10. Cited in Ahmad, *Kurdistan During the First World War*, 159.

11. McDowall, *Modern History of the Kurds*, 104. According to Dündar, loyal tribes were settled near their homelands while suspect tribes were relocated to regions lying westward (143). This policy may also have played a role in the grab for land and who benefited from it. It was also useful to settle these tribes as well as the many refugees on some of these lands (Dündar, *İttihat ve Terakki'nin Müslümanları*, 183–84). Suny (*Looking Toward Ararat*, 28–29)

provides a brief but sound summary of what lay behind the Armenian genocide—although, for the purposes of the present study it should be mentioned that he, too, does not consider the various factors, including economic ones, that drove many Kurds to join in the massacres of their Armenian compatriots. According to Suny, the Hamidiye were simply employed by the Ottoman state and against the Armenians.

12. Klein, "Claiming the Nation."

13. Klein, "Kurdish Nationalists and Non-Nationalist Kurdists."

14. Tunçay, *Türkiye Cumhuriyeti'nde Tek-Parti Yönetimi'nin Kurulması*, 112, n. 5; Kâzım Karabekir, *Kürt Meselesi*. Some regiments may also have been used to suppress internal rebellions, including the Kurdish Koçgiri rebellion of Dersim, which took place during the war of independence. Esengin mentions the Sixth Cavalry Regiment of Sivas in this context (*Millî Mücadelede İç Ayaklanmalar*, 183–85). It is not completely clear, however, that this regiment was affiliated with the remnants of the Hamidiye organization.

15. As McDowall has suggested, with the declaration of the six vilayets as an inseparable part of the empire and the stated need to preserve the integrity of the empire along with the sultanate and caliphate that was declared at the Erzurum Congress in July 1919, "How could any Kurd reject the preservation of Anatolia's integrity against the Christian threat or, for that matter, the preservation of the sultanate and caliphate, those elements that bound together Muslims of different ethnic origin?" (*Modern History of the Kurds*, 127).

16. Olson, *Emergence of Kurdish Nationalism*, 37.

17. Ibid., 27–34; and van Bruinessen, *Agha, Shaikh and State*, 280–88.

18. Karabekir, *Kürt Meselesi*.

19. See McDowall, *Modern History of the Kurds*, 191–92; van Bruinessen, *Agha, Shaikh and State*, 282–83; and Bozarslan, "Tribus, confréries et intellectuels," 65–70.

20. Van Bruinessen, *Agha, Shaikh and State*; Olson, *Emergence of Kurdish Nationalism*; Cemal, *Şeyh Sait İsyanı*; W. Jwaideh, "Kurdish Nationalist Movement"; Kazemi, "Peasant Uprisings"; and McDowall, *Modern History of the Kurds*.

21. Cemal, *Şeyh Sait İsyanı*, 66.

22. Alakom, *Hoybûn Örgyütü ve Ağrı Ayaklanması*.

23. İhsan Nouri Pasha, *La revolte de l'Agri Dagh*, 74–75. It is also apropos to mention at this point that İhsan Nuri viewed Kör Hüseyin as an "opportunist," as evidenced by his betrayal of his comrades-in-arms during the Ararat revolt, when he ordered their passage across the border to be blocked. İhsan Nuri believed this to be evidence that he had then decided to work for the Turks (117–21).

24. Vanly, introduction to İhsan Nouri Pasha, *La revolte de l'Agri Dagh*, 40–41.

25. Olson, *Emergence of Kurdish Nationalism*, 12.

26. Ibid.

27. Smith to Mallet, no. 3. Van, Feb. 14, 1914 (FO 195/2458).

28. *Türk Yılı* (1928), 86. See also Tunçay, *Türkiye Cumhuriyeti'nde Tek-Par-*

ti, 112, n. 5; Cemal, *Şeyh Sait İsyanı*, 31; Altay, *10 Yıl Savaş ve Sonrası (1912–1922)*, 61; and Mumcu, cited in Ergül, *II. Abdülhamid'in Doğu Politikası ve Hamidiye Alayları*, 91.

29. Şimşek, "Ayrılıkçılığa karşı 113 Yıl sonra yeniden [Hamidiye Alayları]." Şimşek does not specify his source for this claim.

30. T. C. Köy Kanunu, section 8.

31. Kıvılcımlı's review of the Turkish press in 1930 shows that militia units were created among locals in the "east," again headed by the *agha* class (*İhtiyat Kuvvet: Milliyet*, 149).

32. It is not within the scope of this chapter to discuss the history of the PKK. Interested readers may consult İmset, *The PKK*; McDowall, *Modern History of the Kurds*, chap. 20; and Marcus, *Blood and Belief*.

33. As reported by the BBC, "Policing by Villagers in Turkey" (BBC *Summary of World Broadcasts*, Oct. 6, 1984); italics added.

34. BBC, "Appointment of Temporary Village Guards" (BBC Summary of World Broadcasts, Mar. 29, 1985). Other modern precedents also existed outside of Turkey; recall the village guards used in Vietnam, for example.

35. McDowall, *Modern History of the Kurds*, 354–57.

36. One author even wrote a book making the connection: Aytar, *Hamidiye Alaylarından Köy Koruculuğuna*.

37. There are exceptions to this statement; that offered by McDowall, for example, although brief, is certainly sound (*Modern History of the Kurds*, 421–23).

38. See Klein, "Turkish Responses to Kurdish Identity Politics."

39. Scott, *Domination and the Arts of Resistance*, 2.

40. Pandey, *Routine Violence*, 130.

41. Ibid., 84.

42. In Pandey's words (ibid., 146). Pandey describes the process during and after Partition in India and Pakistan, but his insights are helpful to the study at hand.

43. Ibid., 171.

44. Scott, *Seeing Like a State*, 82.

45. Pandey, *Routine Violence*, 132.

46. Mann, *Dark Side of Democracy*, 7.

47. Akçam, *From Empire to Republic*, 44.

48. Ibid., esp. chaps. 2–4.

49. Mann, *Dark Side of Democracy*, 20.

50. Kasaba, for one, outlines some of these practices in his *Moveable Empire*.

51. If one looks beyond the surface in the Darfur conflict, one finds the conflict to have started out less as an ethnic conflict and more as one over concrete material resources even if it became ethnicized in the process. Here, too, the state harnessed an on-the-ground conflict for its own purposes with results similar to those I have described for the case of late-Ottoman Kurdistan in this book. See, for one, de Waal, "Tragedy in Darfur."

52. Mann, *Dark Side of Democracy*, ix.

Bibliography

ARCHIVAL SOURCES

Archives du Ministère des Affaires Étrangères (Nantes)

Constantinople/E. Turquie-Situation intérieure.
Constantinople/E. Affaires Consulaires.
Série D. Correspondance Consulaire.
Série E: Dossiers Thematiques. Affaires Arméniennes.

Archives du Ministère des Affaires Étrangères (Paris)

Correspondence Commerciale, Turquie.
Correspondence Politique et Commerciale, nouvelle série.
Série E. Correspondence Politique et Commerciale, Levant.

Archives du Ministère de la Défense (Château de Vincennes)

Comité de Guerre.
Conseil Superieur de Guerre.
EMA 2e Bureau.
Fonds Clemenceau.

Başbakanlık Osmanlı Arşivi (Başbakanlık Ottoman Archives, Prime Ministry Archives; Istanbul)

Yıldız Esas Evrak, Analitik Envanteri (Y.EE).
Yıldız Mütenevvi (Y.MTV).
Yıldız Perakende Askerî Maruzat (Y.PRK.ASK).

Public Record Office (London)

Records of the Air Ministry and Ministry of Defence.
Records of the Cabinet.
Records of the Foreign Office.

KURDISH/OTTOMAN JOURNALS AND NEWSPAPERS

Kürd Teavün ve Terakki Gazetesi (Kurdish Journal of Mutual Aid and Progress). 1908–9. Reprinted with introduction, transliterations, and translations into Modern Turkish and Kurdish by M. Emîn Bozarslan. Uppsala: Weşanxana Deng, 1998.

Kurdistan (Istanbul). 1898–1902. Reprinted with introduction, transliterations, and translations into modern Turkish in *Kurdistan*, ed. M. Emîn Bozarslan. 2 vols. Uppsala: Weşanxana Deng, 1991.

Kurdistan. Nos. 17–18, 1898–1902. Reprinted with introduction and transliterations by Malmîsanij, in *Abdurrahman Bedirhan ve İlk Kürt Gazetesi Kurdistan Sayı: 17 ve 18.* Spånga, Sweden: n.p. [Sara Distribution, Stockholm], 1992.

Kurdistan. 1919.

Rojî Kurd (Istanbul). 1913.

Takvim-i Vekayi (Istanbul). Nos. 1–771, 1908–10.

PUBLISHED OTTOMAN SOURCES

Ahmed Lütfi. *Bedirhan Bey.* Istanbul: Kürd Azm-i Kavi Cemiyeti, [1908].

———. *Tarih-i Lütfi.* Vol. 8. Dersaadet [Istanbul]: Sabah Matbaası, 1328/1912.

Anadolu'nun muhal-ı muhtelifesinde emlak ve arazi-yi mağsube hakkında ermeni patrikhanesince teşkil eden komisyon-ı mahsus tarafından tenzim olunan raporların muddet tercumesi. Istanbul: Doğramaciyan Matbaası, 1327/1909.

Osmanlı Arşivi Yıldız Tasnifi: Ermeni Meselesi (Ottoman Archives Yıldız Collection: The Armenian Question). 3 vols. Istanbul: Historical Research Foundation, 1989.

Ottoman Government. *Aşiret Hafif Süvari Alayları Nizamnamesi.* Istanbul: Matbaa-i Askeriyye, 1326/1910.

———. *Aşiret Hafif Süvari Alayları Nizamnamesi Suretidir.* Reprinted in *Takvim-i Vekayi,* nos. 685–89. Istanbul, 1326/1910.

———. *Tensikat-ı Askeriyye Cümlesinden Olarak Hamidiye Süvari Alaylarına Da'ir Kanunnamedir.* Istanbul: Matbaa-i Osmaniye, 1308/1890.

Salnâme-i Servet-i Funun. Istanbul, 1911–12.

Salnâme-i Vilayet-i Bitlis. Bitlis, 1310/1892.

Salnâme-i Vilayet-i Diyarbekir. Diyarbekir, 1316/1898; 1319/1901.

Şemseddin Sâmî. *Kâmûs al-'alam.* Vol. 5. Istanbul: Mihran Matbaası, 1314/1896.

Süphandağ, Kemal. *Büyük Osmanlı Entrikası Hamidiye Alayları.* Istanbul: Komal, 2006.

FIRSTHAND ACCOUNTS AND MEMOIRS

Abdülhamit II, Sultan. *Siyasî Hatıratım.* Introduced by Ali Vehbi Bey. 1974. Repr., Istanbul: Dergah Yayınları, 1987.

Ali Bey. *Seyahat Jurnalı: İstanbul' dan Bağdad'a ve Hindistan'a min sene 1300 ilâ sene 1304.* Istanbul: A. Asaduriyan Matbaası, 1314/1896–97.

Altay, Fahrettin. *10 Yıl Savaş ve Sonrası (1912–1922).* Istanbul: İnsel Yayınları, 1970.

Andrus, Mr. "Persecution of the Yezidees." *Missionary Herald,* vol. 89, Apr. 1893.

Avriyanof. *XIX. Yüzyılda Rusya'nın İran İle Savaşlarında Kürtler/Türkiye, İran ve Rusya Kürtleri'nin Günümüz Politik Durumu.* Translated from Russian. Tblisi, 1900. Ed. Mehmet Bayrak, 1994. Repr., Ankara: n.p., 1926.

Avyarov [Avriyanof]. *Osmanlı-Rus ve İran Savaşlarında Kürtler, 1801–1900.* Translated from the Ottoman Turkish by Muhammed (Hoko) Varlı (Xanî). Ankara: Sipan Yayıncılık, 1995.

Bayazîdî, Mahmud. *'Edet ve Rusûmetname-i Ekradîyye.* Edited and translated into Russian (with Kurdish original) by M. B. Rudenko. Moscow: Izd-vo vostochnoi lit-ry, 1963.

Campbell, J. Alston. *In the Shadow of the Crescent.* London: Marshall Brothers, 1906.

Creagh, James. *Armenians, Koords, and Turks.* London: Samuel Tinsley, 1880.

Dersimi, M. Nuri. *Dersim'e ve Kürt Milli Mücadelesine Dair Hatıratım.* Prepared by Mehmet Bayrak. Ankara: Öz-Ge Yayınları, 1992.

———. *Kürdistan Tarihinde Dersim.* Aleppo: Ani Matbaası, 1952.

Evliya Çelebi. *Seyahatname.* In *Evliya Çelebi in Diyarbekir: The Relevant Section of the Seyahatname Edited with Translation, Commentary and Introduction,* edited by Martin van Bruinessen and Hendrik Boeschoten. Leiden: E. J. Brill, 1998.

Fırat, M. Şerif. *Doğu İlleri ve Varto Tarihi.* Ankara: Millî Eğitim Basımevi, 1961.

Greene, Frederick Davis. *Armenian Massacres and Turkish Tyranny.* Philadelphia: International Publishing, 1896.

Harris, Walter B. *From Batum to Baghdad via Tiflis, Tabriz, and Persian Kurdistan.* Edinburgh: William Blackwood and Sons, 1896.

Hayderani, Hasan Sıddık. "Aşiret Mektebi ve Aşiret Alayları." *Yakın Tarihimiz* 2, no. 14 (May 1962): 147–48.

İhsan Nouri Pasha. *La revolte de l'Agri Dagh "Ararat," 1927–1930.* Introduced by Ismet Chérif Vanly. Geneva: Éditions Kurdes, 1986.

Karabekir, Kâzım. *Kürt Meselesi.* Repr., Istanbul: Emre Yayınları, 1994.

Löbells jahresberichte über das neer und kriegswesen, vol. 13. Berlin, 1886.

Lynch, H. F. B. *Armenia: Travels and Studies.* 2 vols. London: Longmans, Green, 1901.

M[ehmed] 'Arif, *Başımıza Gelenler.* Cairo: Maarif Maatbası, 1321/1903.

[Mayevski]. *Van ve Bitlis Vilayetleri Askerî İstatistiği.* Translated from Russian into Ottoman Turkish by Mehmed Sadık. Istanbul: Matbaa-i Askeriyye, 1330/1914.

Pierce, Rev. James Wilson. *Story of Turkey and the Armenians.* Baltimore: R. H. Woodward, 1896.

Rohrbach, Paul. *Hatt-ı Saltanat Bağdat Demiryolu.* Istanbul: Elhaf Matbaası, 1331/1915.

Rouben [Minas Ter-Minassian/Rouben Der Minasian]. *Armenian Freedom Fighters: The Memoirs of Rouben Der Minasian.* Translated and edited by James G. Mandalian. Boston: Hairenik Press, 1963.

——. *Mémoires d'un partisan arménien: Fragments.* Translated from the Armenian by Waïk Ter-Minassian. Provençe: Éditions de l'aube, 1990.

Sadettin Paşa. *Sadettin Paşa'nın Anıları: Ermeni-Kürt Olayları (Van, 1896).* Prepared by Sami Önal. Istanbul: Remzi Kitabevi, 2003.

Sadik Shahid Bey. *Islam, Turkey, and Armenia and How They Happened.* St. Louis: C. B. Woodward, 1898.

Sasuni, Garo. *Kürt Ulusal Hareketleri ve Ermeni-Kürt İlişkileri, 15. yy'dan Günümüze.* Stockholm: Orfeus, 1986.

Smith, John Hughes. "John Hugh Smith's Diary of a Journey from Aleppo to Urfa by way of Deir Zor and the Khabur." In *Dar-ul-Islam: A Record of a Journey Through Ten of the Asiatic Provinces of Turkey.* Edited by Mark Sykes. London: Bickers and Son, 1904.

Sykes, Mark. *The Caliph's Last Heritage.* London: Macmillan, 1915.

——. "The Kurdish Tribes of the Ottoman Empire." *Journal of the Royal Anthropological Institute of Great Britain and Ireland* 38 (1908). Also published in PRO, FO 424/213.

T. C. Köy Kanunu (Turkish Republic Village Law). Section 8. Online at: www.hukuki.net/kanun/442.13.text.asp (accessed Jan. 14, 2011).

Tahsin Pasha. *Abdülhamit Yıldız Hatıraları.* Istanbul: Muallim Ahmet Halit Kitaphanesi, 1931.

Tepeyran, Ebubekir Hâzim. *Hatıralar 1. Canlı Tarihler,* vol. 1. Istanbul: Türkiye Yayınevi, 1944.

Türk Yılı. Istanbul: Yeni Matbaa, Türk Ocakları, 1928.

Wigram, W. A., and Edgar T. A. Wigram. *The Cradle of Mankind: Life in Eastern Kurdistan.* London: Adam and Charles Black, 1914.

William, Stephen, Rev. ["An Old Indian"]. *Historical Sketch of Armenia and the Armenians in Ancient and Modern Times with Special Reference to the Present Crisis.* London: Elliot Stock, 1896.

SECONDARY SOURCES

Abou-El-Haj, Rifa'at 'Ali. *Formation of the Modern State, the Ottoman Empire Sixteenth to Eighteenth Centuries.* Albany: State University of New York Press, 1991.

Abu Manneh, B. "Sultan Abdulhamid II and Shaikh Abulhuda Al-Sayyadi." *Middle Eastern Studies* 15, no. 2 (1979): 131–53.

Adelman, Jeremy, and Stephen Aron. "From Borderlands to Borders: Empires, Nation-States, and the Peoples in Between in North American History." *American Historical Review* 104, no. 3 (June 1999): 814–41.

Ahmad, Kamal Madhar. *Kurdistan During the First World War.* Translated by Ali Maher Ibrahim. London: Saqi Books, 1994.

Ahmida, Ali Abdullatif. *The Making of Modern Libya: State Formation, Colonization, and Resistance, 1830–1932.* Albany: State University of New York Press, 1994.

Akçam, Taner. *From Empire to Republic: Turkish Nationalism and the Armenian Genocide.* London: Zed Books, 2004.

Akpınar, Alişan. *Osmanlı Devletinde Aşiret Mektebi.* Istanbul: Göçebe Yayınları, 1997.

Aksakal, Mustafa. *The Ottoman Road to War in 1914: The Ottoman Empire and the First World War.* New York: Cambridge University Press, 2008.

Anadol, Cemal. *Tarihin Işığında Ermeni Dosyası.* Istanbul: Turan Kitabevi, 1982.

Alakom, Rohat. *Hoybûn Örgütü ve Ağrı Ayaklanması.* Istanbul: Avesta, 1998.

Anderson, Lisa. *The State and Social Transformation in Tunisia and Libya, 1830–1980.* Princeton, N.J.: Princeton University Press, 1986.

Asad, Talal. "Equality in Nomadic Social Systems?" *Critique of Anthropology* 11, no. 3 (Spring 1978): 57–65.

Ateş, Sabri. "Empires at the Margin: Towards a History of the Ottoman-Iranian Borderland and the Borderland Peoples, 1843–1881." Ph.D. diss. New York University, 2006.

Aytar, Osman. *Hamidiye Alaylarından Köy Koruculuğuna.* Istanbul: Medya Güneş Yayınları, 1992.

Balcıoğlu, Mustafa. "Hamidiye Alaylarından Aşiret Alaylarına Geçerken Harbiye Nezareti'ne Sunulan İki Rapor." *Toplumsal Tarih* (Apr. 1994): 48–51.

Ballentine, Karen, and Jake Sherman, eds. *The Political Economy of Armed Conflict: Beyond Greed and Grievance.* Boulder, Colo.: Lynne Rienner, 2003.

Balta, Evren. "Military Success, State Capacity, and Internal War-Making in Russia and Turkey." Ph.D. diss. City University of New York Graduate School, 2007.

Beck, Lois. "Tribes and the State in Nineteenth- and Twentieth-Century Iran." In *Tribes and State Formation in the Middle East,* edited by Philip S. Khoury and Joseph Kostiner, 185–225. Berkeley: University of California Press, 1990.

Berdal, Mats, and David M. Malone, eds. *Greed and Grievance: Economic Agendas in Civil Wars.* Boulder, Colo.: Lynne Rienner, 2000.

Bozarslan, Hamit. "Histoire des relations kurdo-arméniennes." In *Le Kurdistan et L'Europe: Regards sur l'histoire kurde (19e–20e siècles),* edited by Hans-Lukas Kieser, 329–40. Zurich: Chronos, 1997.

———. "Tribus, confréries et intellectuels: Convergence des réponses kurdes au régime Kémaliste." In *Modernisation autoritaire en Turquie et en Iran,* edited by Semih Vaner, 61–80. Paris: Éditions L'Harmattan, 1991.

Bragge, Lawrence, and Ulrike Claas, and Paul Roscoe. "On the Edge of Empire: Military Brokers in the Sepik 'Tribal Zone.'" *American Ethnologist* 33, no. 1 (2006): 100–113.

Brown, Michael F., and Eduardo Fernandez. "Tribe and State in a Frontier Mosaic: The Asháninka of Eastern Peru." In *War in the Tribal Zone: Expanding States and Indigenous Warfare,* edited by R. Brian Ferguson and Neil L. Whitehead, 175–97. 1992. Repr., Santa Fe: School of American Research Press, 1999.

Bruinessen, Martin van. *Agha, Shaikh and State: The Social and Political Structures of Kurdistan.* London: Zed Press, 1992.

————. "Kurds, States, and Tribes." In *Tribes and Power: Nationalism and Ethnicity in the Middle East,* edited by Faleh Jabar and Hosham Dawod, 165–83. London: Saqi Books, 2002.

————. "Religion in Kurdistan." In *Mullas, Sufis, and Heretics: The Role of Religion in Kurdish Society; Collected Articles,* 13–36. Istanbul: Isis Press, 2000.

Bruinessen, Martin van, and Hendrik Boeschoten, eds. and trans. *Evliya Çelebi in Diyarbekir: The Relevant Section of the Seyahatname Edited with Translation, Commentary, and Introduction.* Leiden: E. J. Brill, 1988.

Çakaloğlu, Cengiz. "Yemen Halkından Yerel Askerî Teşkilat Kurma Denemeleri." *Askerî Tarih Araştırmaları Dergisi* 7, no. 14 (Aug., 2009): 1–18.

Caton, Steven C. "Anthropological Theories of Tribe and State Formation in the Middle East: Ideology and the Semiotics of Power." In *Tribes and State Formation in the Middle East,* edited by Philip S. Khoury and Joseph Kostiner, 74–108. Berkeley: University of California Press, 1990.

Cemal, Behçet. *Şeyh Sait İsyanı.* Istanbul: Sel Yayınları, 1955.

Chatterjee, Partha. "The Nationalist Resolution of the Women's Question." In *Recasting Women: Essays in Indian Colonial History,* edited by Kumkum Sangari and Sudesh Vaid, 233–53. New Brunswick, N.J.: Rutgers University Press, 1990.

Cuinet, Vital. *La Turquie de l'Asie.* 2 vols. Paris: Ernest Leroux, 1891.

Dasnabedian, Hratch. *Histoire de la Fédération révolutionnaire arménienne, Dachnaktsoutioun, 1890–1924.* Translated by Haroutiun Kurkjian. Milan: Oemme Edizioni, 1988.

Davison, Roderic. *Reform in the Ottoman Empire, 1856–1876.* New York: Gordian Press, 1973.

Deringil, Selim. "The Ottoman Twilight Zone of the Middle East." In *Reluctant Neighbor: Turkey's Role in the Middle East,* edited by Henri J. Barkey, 13–22. Washington, D.C.: United States Institute of Peace Press, 1996.

————. *The Well-Protected Domains: Ideology and the Legitimation of Power in the Ottoman Empire, 1876–1909.* London: I. B. Tauris, 1998.

Derisziger, N. F., and R. A. Preston. "Polyethnicity and Armed Forces: An Introduction." In *Ethnic Armies: Polyethnic Armed Forces from the Time of the Habsburgs to the Age of the Superpowers,* edited by N. F. Dreisziger, 1–20. Waterloo, Ont.: Wilfrid Laurier University Press, 1990.

Douglas, Mary. *How Institutions Think.* Syracuse, N.Y.: Syracuse University Press, 1986.

Douwes, Dick. "Reorganizing Violence: Traditional Recruitment Patterns and Resistance Against Conscription in Ottoman Syria." In *Arming the State: Military Conscription in the Middle East and Central Asia, 1775–1925,* edited by Erik J. Zürcher, 111–27. London: I. B. Tauris, 1999.

Dresch, Paul. *Tribes, Government, and History in Yemen.* Oxford: Clarendon Press, 1989.

Duguid, Stephen. "The Politics of Unity: Hamidian Policy in Eastern Anatolia." *Middle Eastern Studies* 9, no. 2 (1973): 139–55.

Dündar, Fuat. *İttihat ve Terakki'nin Müslümanları İskân Politikası, 1913–1918.* Istanbul: İletişim Yayınları, 2001.

Enloe, Cynthia H. *Ethnic Soldiers: State Security in a Divided Society*. New York: Penguin Books, 1980.

Ergül, Cevdet. *II. Abdülhamid'in Doğu Politikası ve Hamidiye Alayları*. İzmir: Çağlayan Yayınları, 1997.

Esengin, Kenan. *Millî Mücadelede İç Ayaklanmalar*. Istanbul: Ağrı Yayınları, 1975.

Farah, Caesar E. *The Sultan's Yemen: Nineteenth-Century Challenges to Ottoman Rule*. London: I. B. Tauris, 2002.

Farouk-Sluglett, Marion, and Peter Sluglett "The Transformation of Land Tenure and Rural Social Structure in Central and Southern Iraq, *c*. 1870–1958." *International Journal of Middle Eastern Studies* 15, no. 4 (Nov. 1983): 491–505.

Ferguson, R. Brian, and Neil L. Whitehead, eds. *War in the Tribal Zone: Expanding States and Indigenous Warfare*. 1992. Repr., Santa Fe: School of American Research Press, 1999.

Findley, Carter. *Bureaucratic Reform in the Ottoman Empire: The Sublime Porte, 1789–1922*. Princeton, N.J.: Princeton University Press, 1980.

Foucault, Michel. "Governmentality." In *The Foucault Effect: Studies in Governmentality*, edited by Graham Burchell, Colin Gordon, and Peter Miller, 87–104. Chicago: University of Chicago Press, 1991.

Fuccaro, Nelida. *The Other Kurds: Yazidis in Colonial Iraq*. London: I. B. Tauris, 1999.

Gazigiray, A. Alper. *Osmanlılardan Günümüze kadar Vesikalarla Ermeni Terörü'nün Kaynakları*. Istanbul: Gözen Kitabevi, 1982.

Giddens, Anthony. *The Nation-State and Violence: Volume Two of a Contemporary Critique of Historical Materialism*. Berkeley: University of California Press, 1985.

Gingeras, Ryan. *Sorrowful Shores: Violence, Ethnicity, and the End of the Ottoman Empire, 1912–1923*. Oxford: Oxford University Press, 2009.

Gould, Andrew. "Lords or Bandits? The Derebeys of Cilicia." *International Journal of Middle East Studies* 7, no. 4 (Oct. 1976): 485–506.

Guest, John. *Survival Among the Kurds: A History of the Yezidis*. London: Kegan Paul International, 1992.

Guha, Ranajit. "The Prose of Counter-Insurgency." In *Selected Subaltern Studies*, edited by Ranajit Guha and Gayatri Chakravorty Spivak, 45–86. New York: Oxford University Press, 1988.

Gültepe, Necati. "Hamidiye Alayları." *Hayat Tarih Mecmuası* 12 (July 1976): 47-50.

Günay, S. Selçuk. "Hamidiye Hafif Süvari Alayları ve Erzurum." *Türk Dünyası Tarih Dergisi*, no. 17 (May 1988): 40–43.

Gürün, Kamuran. *The Armenian File: The Myth of Innocence Exposed*. New York: St. Martin's Press, 1985.

Haj, Samira. *The Making of Iraq, 1900–1963: Capital, Power, and Ideology*. Albany: State University of New York Press, 1997.

———. "The Problems of Tribalism: The Case of Nineteenth-Century Iraqi History." *Social History* 16, no. 1 (January 1991): 45–58.

Hanioğlu, M. Şükrü. *Doktor Abdullah Cevdet ve Dönemi.* Istanbul: Üçdal, 1981.

———. *Preparation for a Revolution: The Young Turks, 1902–1908.* New York: Oxford University Press, 2001.

———. *The Young Turks in Opposition.* Oxford: Oxford University Press, 1995.

Hassanpour, Amir. *Nationalism and Language in Kurdistan, 1918–1985.* San Francisco: Mellen Research University Press, 1992.

Holm, Tom. "The Militarization of Native America: Historical Process and Cultural Perception." *Social Science Journal* 34, no. 4 (1997): 461–74.

Hourani, Albert. "Ottoman Reform and the Politics of Notables." In *Beginnings of Modernization in the Middle East: The Nineteenth Century,* edited by William Polk and Richard L. Chambers, 41–68. Chicago: University of Chicago Press, 1966.

Hovannisian, Richard G. *Armenia on the Road to Independence.* Berkeley: University of California Press, 1967.

İmset, İsmet. *The PKK, 1973–1992.* Ankara: Turkish Daily News Publications, 1992.

Itzkowitz, Norman. *Ottoman Empire and Islamic Tradition.* 1972. Repr., Chicago: University of Chicago Press, 1980.

Izady, Mehrdad R. *The Kurds: A Concise Handbook.* Washington, D.C.: Crane Russak, 1992.

Jongerden, Joost. "Urban Nationalists and Rural Ottomanists, Political Struggle in Diyarbekir at the turn of the 20th century." Paper presented at the Middle East Studies Association (MESA) Annual Meeting, Boston, November 2009.

Jwaideh, Albertine. "Midhat Pasha and the Land System of Lower Iraq." In *St. Antony's Papers Number 16: Middle Eastern Affairs,* no. 3, edited by Albert Hourani, 106–36. London: Chatto and Windus, 1963.

———. "The *Saniyya* Lands of Sultan Abdul Hamid II in Iraq." In *Arabic and Islamic Studies in Honor of Hamilton A. R. Gibb,* edited by George Makdisi, 326–36. Cambridge, Mass.: Harvard University Press, 1965.

Jwaideh, Wadie. "The Kurdish Nationalist Movement: Its Origins and Development." Ph.D. diss. Syracuse University, 1960.

Karaca, Ali. *Anadolu Islahâtı ve Ahmet Şâkir Paşa, 1838–1899.* Istanbul: Eren Yayıncılık, 1993.

Karpat, Kemal H., and Robert Zens, eds. *Ottoman Bordlerlands: Issues, Personalities, and Political Changes.* Madison: University of Wisconsin Press, 2004.

Kasaba, Reşat. *A Moveable Empire: Ottoman Nomads, Migrants, and Refugees.* Seattle: University of Washington Press, 2009.

Kayalı, Hasan. *Arabs and Young Turks: Ottomanism, Arabism, and Islamism in the Ottoman Empire, 1908–1918.* Berkeley: University of California Press, 1997.

Kazemi, Farhad. "Peasant Uprisings in Twentieth-Century Iran, Iraq, and Turkey." In *Peasants and Politics in the Modern Middle East,* edited by Farhad Kazemi and John Waterbury, 101–24. Miami: Florida International University Press, 1991.

Kévorkian, Raymond H. Introduction to "La formation des régiments de cavalrie kurde Hamidié d'apres les documents diplomatiques italiens," by Maurizio Russo. *Revue d'Histoire Arménienne Contemporaine* 1 (1995): 31–32.

Kévorkian, Raymond H., and Paul B. Paboudjian. *Les arméniens dans l'Empire ottoman à la veille du génocide.* Paris: Les Éditions d'Art et d'Histoire, 1992.

Khoury, Dina Rizk. *State and Provincial Society in the Ottoman Empire: Mosul, 1540–1834.* Cambridge: Cambridge University Press, 1997.

Kıvılcımlı, Hikmet. *İhtiyat Kuvvet: Milliyet (Şark).* Istanbul: Yol Yayınları, 1979.

Klein, Janet. "Çevreyi İdare Etmek: Osmanlı Devleti ve Hamidiye Alayları." In *Tarihsel Perspektiften Türkiye'de Güvenlik Siyaseti, Ordu ve Devlet*, edited by Evren Baltan and İsmet Akça, 105–24. Istanbul: Bilgi, 2010.

———. "Claiming the Nation: The Origins and Nature of Kurdish Nationalist Discourse; A Study of the Kurdish Press in the Ottoman Empire." M.A. thesis, Princeton University, 1996.

———. "Conflict and Collaboration: Rethinking Kurdish-Armenian Relations in the Hamidian Period, 1876–1909." *International Journal of Turkish Studies* 13, no. 1–2 (2007): 153–66.

———. "Ein kritischer Blick auf den sunnitischen Faktor bei der Aufstellung kurdischer Stammesregimenter unter Abdülhamid II" (Whose Hamidiye? Another Look at the Sunni Factor in the Creation of Kurdish Tribal Regiments by Sultan Abdülhamid II and His Associates). *Kurdische Studien* 2, no. 1 (June 2002): 131–53.

———. "Kurdish Nationalists and Non-Nationalist Kurdists: Rethinking Minority Nationalism and the Dissolution of the Ottoman Empire, 1908–1909." *Nations and Nationalism* 13, no. 1 (Jan. 2007): 135–53.

———. "The Kurdish Voice in the Modern Era: Kurdistan, The First Kurdish Newspaper." Unpublished paper, Department of Near Eastern Studies, Princeton University, 1994.

———. "Noble Savages or Savage Notables? Tribes, the State, Race, and Civilizing Missions in the Ottoman Empire and the United States, 1890–1914." Presented at the American Historical Association Conference, Philadelphia, January 2006. (Paper read by Ryan Gingeras due to car accident en route to conference.)

———. "Power in the Periphery: The Hamidiye Light Cavalry and the Struggle over Ottoman Kurdistan, 1890–1914." Ph.D. thesis, Princeton University, 2002.

———. "Tribal Militias from the Wild West to the Wild East: U.S.-Ottoman Frontier Projects in the Late-Nineteenth and Early Twentieth Centuries." Paper presented on the panel titled "Rethinking the Ottoman Military, 1876–1922," Middle East Studies Association Annual Conference, Montreal, Nov. 2007.

———. "Turkish Responses to Kurdish Identity Politics: Recent Developments in Historical Perspective." In *The Kurdish Policy Imperative*, edited by Gareth Stansfield and Robert Lowe, 79–96. London: Chatham House/Royal Institute of International Affairs, 2010.

Kocabaşoğlu, Uygur. *Anadolu'daki Amerika: 19. Yüzyılda Osmanlı İmparatorluğu'ndaki Amerikan Misyoner Okulları.* Istanbul: Arba Yayınları, 1989.

Kodaman, Bayram. "Hamidiye Hafif Süvari Alayları (II. Abdülhamid ve Doğu-Anadolu Aşiretleri)." *İstanbul Üniversitesi Edebiyat Fakültesi Tarih Dergisi* 32 (1979): 427–80.

———. *Sultan II: Abdülhamid Devri Doğu Anadolu Politikası.* Türk Kültürünü Araştırma Enstitüsü Yayınları (Publication of the Turkish Cultural Research Institute). Ankara: Ankara Üniversitesi Basımevi, 1987.

Kühn, Thomas. "An Imperial Borderland as Colony: Knowledge Production and the Elaboration of Difference in Ottoman Yemen, 1872–1914." *MIT Electronic Journal of Middle Eastern Studies* 3 (Spring 2003): 5–17.

Kunt, I. Metin. *The Sultan's Servants: The Transformation of Ottoman Provincial Government, 1550–1650.* New York: Columbia University Press, 1983.

Kurat, Yuluğ Tekin. "1877–78 Osmanlı-Rus Harbinin Sebepleri." *Belleten* 26, no. 103 (July 1962): 526–42.

Kushner, David. *The Rise of Turkish Nationalism, 1876–1908.* London: Frank Cass, 1977.

Kutlay, Naci. *İttihat Terakki ve Kürtler.* Ankara: Beybûn, 1992.

Lazarev, M. S. *Emperyalizm ve Kürt Sorunu, 1917–1923.* Translated into Turkish from Russian by Mehmet Demir. Ankara: Özge, 1989.

Longrigg, Stephen Hemsley. *Iraq, 1900 to 1950: A Political, Social, and Economic History.* London: Oxford University Press, 1953.

Longworth, Philip. *The Cossacks: Five Centuries of Turbulent Life on the Russian Steppes.* New York: Holt, Rinehart and Winston, 1969.

Makdisi, Ussama. *The Culture of Sectarianism: Community, History, and Violence in Nineteenth-Century Ottoman Lebanon.* Berkeley: University of California Press, 2000.

Malmîsanij. *Abdurrahman Bedirhan ve İlk Kürt Gazetesi Kurdistan Sayı: 17 ve 18.* Spånga, Sweden: n.p. [Sara Distribution, Stockholm], 1992.

———.*Cızira Botanlı Bedirhaniler ve Bedirhani Ailesi Derneği'nin Tutanakları.* 1994. Repr., Istanbul: Avesta, 2000.

Mann, Michael. *The Dark Side of Democracy: Explaining Ethnic Cleansing.* Cambridge: Cambridge University Press, 2005.

Marcus, Aliza. *Blood and Belief: The PKK and the Kurdish Fight for Independence.* New York: New York University Press, 2007.

Mardin, Şerif. "Center-Periphery Relations: A Key to Turkish Politics?" In *Post-Traditional Societies*, edited by S. N. Eisenstadt. New York: W. W. Norton, 1974.

McCarthy, Justin. *Death and Exile: The Ethnic Cleansing of Ottoman Muslims, 1821–1922.* Princeton, N.J.: Darwin Press, 1995.

McDowall, David. *A Modern History of the Kurds.* London: I. B. Tauris, 1996.

McNeal, Robert H. *Tsar and Cossack, 1855–1914.* New York: St. Martin's Press, 1987.

Migdal, Joel S. *State in Society: Studying How States and Societies Transform and Constitute One Another.* Cambridge: Cambridge University Press, 2001.

Minorsky, Victor. "Kurds." *First Encyclopedia of Islam* 4. Edited by M. Th. Houtsma et al. New York: E. J. Brill, 1987.

Moreau, Odile. "Bosnian Resistance to Conscription in the Nineteenth Century." In *Arming the State: Military Conscription in the Middle East and Central Asia, 1775–1925*, edited by Erik J. Zürcher, 129–38. London: I. B. Tauris, 1999.

Nalbandian, Louise. *The Armenian Revolutionary Movement: The Development of Armenian Political Parties Through the Nineteenth Century*. Berkeley: University of California Press, 1963.

Nicolai, Martin L. "A Different Kind of Courage: The French Military and the Canadian Irregular Soldier During the Seven Years' War." *Canadian Historical Review* 70, no. 1 (1989): 53–75.

Ochsenwald, William. *Religion, Society, and the State in Arabia: The Hijaz Under Ottoman Control, 1840–1908*. Columbus: Ohio State University Press, 1984.

Olson, Robert. *The Emergence of Kurdish Nationalism, 1880–1925*. Austin: University of Texas Press, 1989.

Orhonlu, Cengiz. *Osmanlı İmparatorluğu'nda Aşiretlerin İskânı*. Istanbul: Eren Yayıncılık, 1987.

Ortaylı, İlber. *Tanzimattan Sonra Mahallî İdareler, 1840–1878*. Ankara: Sevinç Matbaası, 1974.

Özbek, Nadir. "Policing the Countryside: Gendarmes of the Late 19th-Century Ottoman Empire." *International Journal of Middle East Studies* 40, no. 1 (2008): 47–67.

Özok-Gündoğan, Nilay. "A 'Peripheral' Approach to the 1908 Revolution in the Ottoman Empire: Land Disputes in Peasant Petitions in Post-Revolutionary Diyarbekir." In *Diyar-ı Bekir: Political, Religious, and Economic Changes and Developments Between 1850 and 1910*, edited by Joost Jongerden and Jelle Verheij. Leiden: E. J. Brill, 2011, forthcoming.

Pandey, Gyanendra. *Routine Violence: Nations, Fragments, Histories*. Stanford, Calif.: Stanford University Press, 2006.

Parry, V. J. "The Reigns of Bayazid II and Selim I, 1481–1520." In *A History of the Ottoman Empire to 1730*, edited by M. A. Cook, 54–78. Cambridge: Cambridge University Press, 1976.

Philliou, Christine. "Communities on the Verge: Unraveling the Phanariot Ascendancy in Ottoman Governance." *Comparative Studies in Society and History* 51, no. 1 (2009): 151–81.

Quataert, Donald. "Dilemma of Development: The Agricultural Bank and Agricultural Reform in Ottoman Turkey, 1888–1908." *International Journal of Middle Eastern Studies* 6, no. 2 (1975): 210–27.

Reid, James J. *Crisis of the Ottoman Empire: Prelude to Collapse, 1839–1878*. Stuttgart: Steiner, 2000.

Reynolds, Michael. "Inchoate Nation Abroad: Tsarist Russia, Nation Building, and the Kurds of Anatolia." Paper presented at the Association for the Studies of Nationalities Seventh Annual Convention, Columbia University, New York, Apr. 2002.

———. "Ottoman Diplomat, Russophile, and Kurdish Patriot: Abdurrezzak Bedirhan and the Seams of Empire, 1910–1918." Paper presented at the annual
Middle East Studies Association Meeting, Boston, Nov. 2009.

Rogan, Eugene L. "Aşiret Mektebi: Abdülhamid II's School for Tribes, 1892–
1907." *International Journal of Middle Eastern Studies* 28, no. 1 (1996):
83–107.

———. *Frontiers of the State in the Late Ottoman Empire: Transjordan, 1850–
1921.* Cambridge: Cambridge University Press, 1999

Russo, Maurizio. "La formation des régiments de cavalrie kurde Hamidié
d'apres les documents diplomatiques italiens." *Revue d'Histoire Arménienne
Contemporaine* 1 (1995): 31–44.

Scott, James C. *Domination and the Arts of Resistance: Hidden Transcripts.*
New Haven, Conn.: Yale University Press, 1990.

———. *Seeing Like a State: How Certain Schemes to Improve the Human Condition Have Failed.* New Haven, Conn.: Yale University Press, 1998.

Shaw, Stanford J. *Between Old and New: The Ottoman Empire Under Selim
III, 1789–1807.* Cambridge, Mass.: Harvard University Press, 1971.

———. "The Nineteenth-Century Ottoman Tax Reforms and Revenue System."
International Journal of Middle Eastern Studies 6, no. 4 (1975): 421–59.

Shields, Sarah D. *Mosul Before Iraq: Like Bees Making Five-Sided Cells.* Albany: State University of New York Press, 2000.

———. "Sheep, Nomads, and Merchants in Nineteenth-Century Mosul: Creating Transformations in an Ottoman Society." *Journal of Social History* 25,
no. 4 (Summer 1992): 773–89.

Sırma, İhsan Süreyya. *II. Abdülhamid'in İslâm Birliği Siyaseti.* Istanbul: Beyan
Yayınları, 1994.

———. *Belgelerle II. Abdülhamid Dönemi.* Istanbul: Beyan Yayınları, 1998.

Skendi, Stavro. *The Albanian National Awakening, 1878–1912.* Princeton,
N.J.: Princeton University Press, 1967.

Stone, Frank Andrews. *Academies for Anatolia: A Study of the Rationale, Program, and Impact of the Educational Institutions Sponsored by the American Board in Turkey, 1830–1980.* Lanham, Md.: University Press of America, 1984.

Suny, Ronald Grigor. *Looking Toward Ararat: Armenia in Modern History.*
Bloomington: Indiana University Press, 1993.

Şimşek, Erdal. "Ayrılıkçılığa karşı 113 Yıl sonar yeniden [Hamidiye Alayları]."
Yeni Şafak Web site, www.yenisafak.com/diziler/hamidiye/index.html (accessed November 14, 2010).

Talay, Aydın. *Eserleri ve Hizmetleriyle Sultan Abdülhamid.* Istanbul: Risale,
1991.

Tanzimat. Istanbul: Milli Eğitim Bakanlığı, 1940.

Tapper, Richard. "Anthropologists, Historians, and Tribespeople on Tribe and
State Formation in the Middle East." In *Tribes and State Formation in the
Middle East*, edited by Philip S. Khoury and Joseph Kostiner, 48–73. Berke-
ley: University of California Press, 1990.

Tepedelenlioğlu, Nizamettin Nazif. *Hürriyet'in İlanı ve II. Abdülhamit.* Istanbul: Ufuk Yayınları, 1999.

Ter Minassian, Anaide. *Nationalism and Socialism in the Armenian Revolutionary Movement, 1887–1912.* Translated by A. M. Berrett. Cambridge, Mass.: Zoryan Institute, 1984.

———. "The Role of the Armenian Community in the Foundation and Development of the Socialist Movement in the Ottoman Empire and Turkey, 1876–1923." In *Socialism and Nationalism in the Ottoman Empire, 1876–1923,* edited by Mete Tunçay and Erik J. Zürcher, 109–56. London: British Academic Press, 1994.

Terzibaşoğlu, Yücel. "Landlords, Refugees, and Nomads: Struggles for Land Around Late-Nineteenth-Century Ayvalık." *New Perspectives on Turkey,* no. 24 (Spring 2001): 51–82.

Tezcan, Baki. "The Development of the Use of 'Kurdistan' as a Geographical Description and the Incorporation of this Region into the Ottoman Empire in the 16th Century." In *The Great Ottoman-Turkish Civilization,* 4 vols., edited by Kemal Çiçek, 3: 540–53. Ankara: Yeni Türkiye, 2000.

Troutt Powell, Eve M. *A Different Shade of Colonialism: Egypt, Great Britain, and the Mastery of the Sudan.* Berkeley: The University of California Press, 2003.

Tunçay, Mete. *Türkiye Cumhuriyeti'nde Tek-Parti Yönetimi'nin Kurulması, 1923–1931.* Ankara: Yurt Yayıncılık, 1981.

Türkiye Cumhuriyeti. Dahiliye Vekâleti Jandarma Umum Kumandanlığı, *Dersim.* Report no. 55058. Published as *Dersim / T. C. Dahiliye Vekâleti, Jandarma Umum Kumandanlığı.* Istanbul: Analiz Basım Yayın Tasarım Uygulama Ltd. Şirketi, 1998.

Ure, John. *The Cossacks.* London: Constable and Company, 1999.

Vanly, Ismet Chérif. *Survey of the National Question of Turkish Kurdistan with Historical Background.* N.p.: Hevra, 1971.

Verheij, Jelle. "'Les frères de terre et d'eau': Sur le rôle des Kurdes dans les massacres arméniens de 1894–1896." In *Les annales de l'autre Islam* 5, edited by Martin van Bruinessen, 225–76. Paris: ERISM, 1998.

de Waal, Alex. "Tragedy in Darfur." *Boston Review,* Oct.–Nov. 2004.

Walker, Christopher J. *Armenia: The Survival of a Nation.* Rev. 2nd ed. London: Routledge, 1990.

White, [W.] Bruce. "The American Indian as Soldier, 1890–1919." *Canadian Review of American Studies* 7, no. 1 (Spring 1976): 15–25.

Yaşın, Abdullah. *Bütün Yönleriyle Cizre.* Cizre, Turkey: Dicle Kitabevi, 1983.

Yosmaoğlu, İpek. "Counting Bodies, Shaping Souls: The '1903 Census' and Ottoman Identity in Macedonia." *International Journal of Middle East Studies* 38, no. 1 (2006): 55–77.

Young, Warren L. *Minorities and the Military: A Cross-National Study in World Perspective.* Westport, Conn.: Greenwood Press, 1982.

Zürcher, Erik Jan. "The Ottoman Conscription System in Theory and Practice, 1844–1918." In *Arming the State: Military Conscription in the Middle East and Central Asia, 1775–1925,* edited by Erik J. Zürcher, 79–94. London: I. B. Tauris, 1999.

Index

Abdülhamid II, Sultan, 51, 113;
Albanians and, 36, 222n2, 233n133;
and Armenians, 22, 191n8, 192n22,
216n33; ascent to throne (1876), 21;
and Baghdad Railway, 217n153;
Bedir Khans vs., 90, 91–93;
censorship, 218n166; centralization,
22–23, 59; and Cossacks, 42–43,
77, 201nn119,122; and Hamidiye,
1–5, 8, 23, 27–49, 52, 59, 70–71,
77, 81, 83–85, 92, 94, 99–100, 102,
199n92, 221n199; and Islam, 8,
217n153; land purchases, 61, 235n7;
loyalty to, 75, 113, 176–77, 221n199;
overthrow (1909), 5, 93, 105, 107;
public transcript, 36–37; tax reforms,
59; tribal orthodoxy policies, 46–51;
vs. Ubeydullah, 42, 190n5; Zeki
Pasha's closeness with, 3, 27, 75–85,
97
Abdullah Cevdet, 89, 105
Abdulqadir, Seyyid, 105, 116–17, 121,
155
Abou-El-Haj, Rifa'at 'Ali, 15
Adelman, Jeremy, 11
Aghayê Sor: and Bedir Khans, 90,
220n193; vs. Mustafa Pasha, 68–69,
71, 73, 89, 90, 93
"agrarian question," 171, 233n135,
239n79, 241nn105,107; CUP
and, 128–69, 242–43nn124,128;
Hamidiye and, 19, 128–69; Kurdish

alliances with Armenians, 157, 168,
171, 244n148; Kurdish intellectuals
and, 245–46n176. See also land-
grabbing
Agricultural Bank, 146–47, 150,
240n96, 241n105
agricultural settlement: pastoral
nomadism changed to, 43, 130–35,
149–50, 165–66, 235n13, 244–
45n164. See also peasants
Ağrı Dağ (Ararat) revolt, 175, 177, 178,
247n23
Ahmet Izzet Pasha, 125
Akçam, Taner, 182
Albanians: and Abdülhamid II, 36,
222n2, 233n133; army recruitment,
49–50; revolts, 229n83, 234n142;
schools for, 47, 205n155
Alevis: Dersim, 50, 145, 206n170;
Hamidiye recruitment plans, 50–51,
207n172; transformed into tenants,
145
Americans: American-Indian boarding
schools, 47–48, 204n149; Armenians
and, 25; "savage"/"noble savage"
concept, 43
Anadolu Ordu Müşiriyeti, Kurdistan
attached to, 62
'Anayza tribe, 134
Arabs: army recruitment, 49–50,
205n161; schools for, 47–48, 49,
205n155; settlement, 135

The authorized representative in the EU for product safety and compliance is:
Mare Nostrum Group
B.V Doelen 72
4831 GR Breda
The Netherlands

www.ingramcontent.com/pod-product-compliance
Lightning Source LLC
Chambersburg PA
CBHW020658270326
41928CB00005B/176